In memory of

Constance

Mark

Cinzia

Margaret

Larry

Jens

Florence

Diane

Tillie

Victor

This book is for you, Papa.

Working-Class Girls Don't Become Artists

Working-Class Girls Don't Become Artists

Looking at Art and Class

JANET ZANDY

UNIVERSITY OF
ILLINOIS PRESS
Urbana, Chicago, and Springfield

1 2 3 4 5 C P 5 4 3 2 1
♾ This book is printed on acid-free paper.

Cataloging data available from the Library of Congress

LCCN 2026932211
ISBN 978-0-252-04973-6 (cloth : alk.)
ISBN 978-0-252-08939-8 (paper : alk.)
ISBN 978-0-252-04889-0 (ebook)

The manufacturer's authorized representative in the EU for product safety is Mare Nostrum Group B.V., Mauritskade 21D, 1091 GC Amsterdam, The Netherlands. Email: gpsr@mare-nostrum.co.uk

Contents

Preface

Workin' on a world I may never see
thinking of the ones who came before
—Iris DeMent

It was after John Kennedy's assassination and before the American war in Vietnam heated up, external events shadowing my family and school worlds. I was a scholarship college student living at home. Occasionally, I crossed small frontiers of family and culture. I would walk up the steep hill from my family's small duplex house on Kingsland Avenue in Lyndhurst, New Jersey, to take the 32 DeCamp bus into Manhattan.[1] The bus bumbled past the undeveloped meadowlands, etched with debris and waste, paused briefly in Secaucus, which still carried the odor of its former pig farms, skirted Union City, and finally entered the Lincoln Tunnel, a womb into Manhattan. I always watched for the marker delineating New Jersey from New York and gave a silent cheer. From the Port Authority Bus Terminal, I would walk to Forty-Second Street, averting my eyes from the porn movie ads, up to Fifth Ave, where I usually stopped at St. Patrick's Cathedral, and then headed for MOMA (the Museum of Modern Art) on Fifty-Third. From there I went straight to Picasso's *Guernica.*[2]

Since there were no trips to museums in my working-class high school, my first awareness of *Guernica* remains a mystery. It is likely I was a college student when its power called me. My eyes saw its broken world—horse, bull, women, babies, knives, teeth, flaring nostrils, open mouths, dangling hooves, reaching hands. Out of the stillness of art on a museum wall emerged movement, the urgency of escape. I heard its familiar message—terrible things are done to innocent people.

Paintings can lead to self-taught history. Making a painting or any art form, as the artists in this collection recognize, can recover history.[3] How art history can lead to broader historical knowledge is an underrecognized element of art studies.

Much later, after college, after family losses, I learned about Guernica/Gernika, the Basque market town bombed on April 26, 1937, and the international Abraham Lincoln brigades, the volunteers who fought fascism in Spain. Who will paint Ukraine's Guernica? Before I protested against the American war in Vietnam and saw its impact on my hometown generation of patriotic boys, I glimpsed war from this painting. War was part of my unspoken childhood background—my father, his brothers, and my mother's older brothers served in the military during World War II; the younger two brothers just missed being sent to Korea. Their military service was never talked about—at least not in front of the children.

As counterpoint to *Guernica* there was the Cloisters. It was probably a Sunday and a rare day of rest for my father, who worked three time shifts in his chemical factory job. He likely took out one of his folded maps to make the drive in our secondhand car to Fort Tryon Park so we could walk through the Met's Cloisters. Stillness and beauty and devotion and peace. Again, I brought no knowledge to the experience. I was aware of the Middle Ages as historical period, but not of the complicated history of museums and their artifacts, or the emergence of modernism. What struck me was the collective sensibility and artistry that produced the gothic arches, tapestries, and religious statuary. My remembered visit to the Cloisters during the early 1960s includes no café, no audio guide, no gift shop, no purchase, just peaceful beauty.

I loved to draw but was too shy and too fearful that I was not good enough to take art classes in high school or college. I took sewing instead. Always, though, I longed for art—to see it and to make it. Does this undernourished longing linger in other working-class lives?

"My mother would have liked to go to art school, but on Bankbottom nobody had heard of such a thing," writes Hilary Mantel, whose mother "was put into the mill at fourteen" and whose grandmother became a mill worker when she was twelve. "The work was hard and took a painful toll on immature muscle and bone." Mantel, attuned to what's thwarted and what's expressed, remembers her mother as a Midland Cinderella, "who danced and sang through her evenings in amateur shows and pantomines."[4]

I remember both—the talents limited, reduced, thwarted, as well as the channels of creative expression. My parents had to leave school after ninth grade to support their families. They worked and worked, faced chronic illness and untimely deaths, yet still had capacity for beauty and joy. My mother baked and blessed her cakes; my father constructed bookcases and planted roses and tomatoes. Simple things. Art school, though, would not have occurred to them.

I am the first woman in my family to go to college and accumulate degrees. My undergraduate education at a state teachers' college was financed by a company scholarship from Trubeck Labs, the pre-OSHA chemical plant where my father worked and where, I believe, his life was shortened to forty-nine years. My father's father, Philip Ballotta, was born in southern Italy, and somehow, around the age fifteen or sixteen, migrated to Hoboken, New Jersey, where he married Jennie and had seven children. He worked at the Bright Star Battery Company in Clifton, New Jersey. On the way home from work one day, he and Nathan Leff, a carpenter born in Russia, were killed in a car crash on Route 3, described in a newspaper account as "Death Highway." It is the same highway I would travel by the DeCamp bus from northern Jersey to Manhattan in order to stare at the paintings in the Museum of Modern Art, especially Picasso's *Guernica*.

My mother's mother, Anna Ennis Parisi, arrived in America at the age of thirteen or fourteen. She left the shelter of her orthodox rabbi father and traveled by herself to Ellis Island. She must have been very observant of signs and signals since she was also illiterate. I surmise from bits of information that she was sent to America as a servant of sorts for wealthier relatives. My mother recalled Anna's stories about how as a child, she hid in the carcass of a cow when the soldiers would come. I put the word *pogrom* to those stories. In New Jersey, Anna met her husband, Albert, an Italian Catholic, and was made pregnant by him (did she even know what was happening to her?). She married Albert and so her family in Europe (who originally came from Russia and migrated to Germany or perhaps Luxembourg) cast her out and sat *shiva*. Albert and Anna produced fourteen children, ten living to adulthood. I remember my aunts and uncles as affectionate, teasing, and joking. They never—at least not to my child's ears—talked about jobs or money. The family was poor, although my aunts insisted that they were not, and said, "we had love." Most of the men died of heart disease, suddenly, as did the women, only less suddenly.

Birth-class circumstances, I understand now, shape my thinking about art and artists—and theory. I write *theoretically* about art by situating myself as coming out of the working class. From my narrow perch in Rochester, New York, I see that my planetary background was influenced by class in ways far different from those art historians and museum curators who come from an art world lineage and Ivy League educations. I realize now, at a far distance from the young art-hungry girl/woman who took the bus into Manhattan, how class shadows the production and control of art.

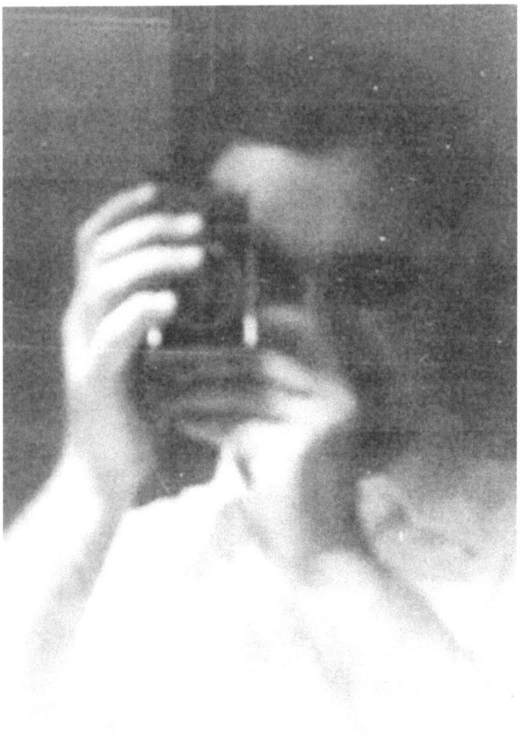

Author's father, Charles Ballotta (1915–1965), with his camera.

If I had to choose one model of how to be a learning human being it would be my father, Charles. My father was a sharp dresser and an avid photographer. I still have his army pictures of demolished buildings in Germany around 1945, the year I was born. I still have his camera and its roll of undeveloped film. Although I never saw bitterness or resentment, I know that his life could have flowered in other ways. Circumstances forced him to end his formal education and take the name of a deceased older brother, "Johnny," so he could get his working papers. Taking advantage of the GI Bill was not possible for him since he worked three time shifts and probably got no encouragement to do so. But he read. He taught himself mathematics. He completed everyone's tax forms. He was engaged with the wider world. And he encouraged his two daughters to learn and get the elusive "sheepskin" that wasn't his. I never talked to him about the trip to the Cloisters. Maybe he needed, without saying so, the peace and beauty of artistic space. I know he had the capacity to value both.

In *Class Lines: Craftsmen*, two workers, having finished a day's labor, emerge. They appear tired, hollowed-eyed in their work clothes. Hovering above them is an ornate chair, perhaps an expensive reproduction of an antique. I imagine they used their skills to carve, refine and polish that chair. The chair is out of their reach, physically and financially. As is true for many workers, laborers, and artisans, they build what they could not afford to own. This is a description of an artist proof etching by Charles Roth. In the mid 1980s, we rented it monthly from Rochester's Memorial Art Gallery until we accumulated enough months and money to purchase it outright. I recall it cost $250, including the frame. I look at it every day. I don't pretend to know those two workers, nor would I want to own that chair, but I do know that it speaks to me fully about class lines.

Seeing art has been crucial to my humanity, as it may be to everyone's. How class circumstances enhance or interfere with access to art—which means access to history, form, beauty—is still under-recognized. The working-class writer Tillie Olsen once called class and its relationship to literature "the

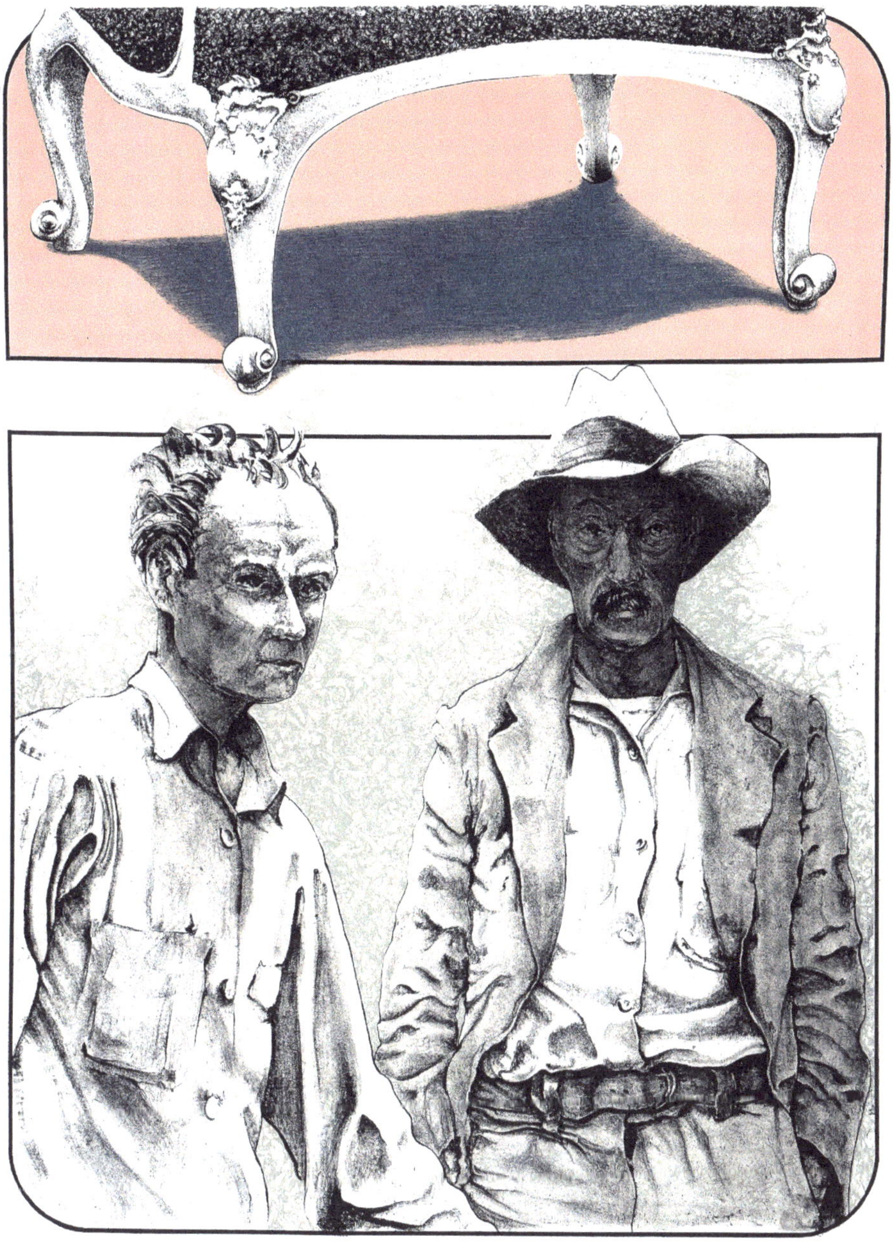

Class Lines: Craftsmen, etching, Charles E. Roth, 1984.

great unexamined." This book asks the same question about the unexamined, in this case, the unexamined tendrils of people's labor, struggles, hopes, and occasional uncommodified joy as related to the creation of visual arts.

As I edge toward my eightieth year, I wish to witness for those who did not have my entry points. I write this book for my parents, who created spaces for study and who, in their own way, shaped objects beautifully.

Introduction

Looking at Art and Class

I am disillusioned with all the hate that is in the world
—Käthe Kollwitz

. . . because realism is the common language of everybody and everybody thus has an entry into my work. Once they are inside the work, once they have a sort of link, then I can take them by the hand and lead them up the slopes of aesthetics, but the thing is to get them in.
—Raymond Mason

Democracy, in silence, biding its time, ponders its own ideals
—Walt Whitman, *Democratic Vistas*

Entry

In 1897 a plumber working near New York's Metropolitan Museum of Art had "some nooning to himself" and, wearing his work overalls, was "determined to have a look at the Museum." The Met's doorkeepers refused to admit him. Some labor-sympathizing journals raised concerns, but the *New York Times* was clear in its editorial that "a plumber fresh from a job of work is no more eligible in a place where he is likely to come into contact with other people or with works of art than a painter in the same condition. For him to attempt to visit the Museum in such a guise and without removing the traces of his toil argues either mere carelessness or lack of self-respect."[1]

New York's Metropolitan Museum of Art opened to the public at its current location on March 30, 1880. It is now an international tourist attraction. There are restrictions on what you can bring into the museum, but not on dirty and dusty work clothes (as far as I know). You just need the price of admission. Workers are inside (security guards, ticket takers, restroom cleaners, food servers) and outside (food truck vendors, cabbies, grounds-keepers) the museum walls. How many spend their noon break looking at art? Would today's plumbers and painters with jobs in the neighborhood of Fifth Ave and Eighty-Second Street be interested in entering the mighty Met? Did that plumber in 1897 ever decide to change his clothes and take another look inside?

Truman Chambers, who worked as a security guard at the Toledo Museum of Art, calls for a "mechanism by which the frontline staff (security guards, visitor service workers, custodians, etc.) can shape the content of the museum." He recognizes how "curators are often socially disconnected from the communities which the museum nominally serves."[2]

In Madrid's Prado Museum, guard and art mover Manolo Osuna was an unlikely star of an Instagram video series when he was given ten minutes to talk about an artwork. He chose a portrait of a "ragged Greek philosopher with a toothless grin and grimy fingernails" by the Spanish Baroque painter Jusepe de Ribera. Mr. Osuna said, "He's like a peasant . . . Ribera's characters are people from the street." And "he felt a special bond to the smiling man because of his hands, worn by years of labor."[3]

Ken Grossinger looks at museums, memorials, and ways curatorial decisions can impact local communities. He describes the work of the Legacy Museum and the National Memorial for Peace and Justice in Montgomery, Alabama, in connecting the historic past with current community actions, as well as creating spaces for imagining a more just future. These institutions raise the question "what can be done?" One answer, as Grossinger recognizes, is the decision by Tom Finkelpearl, then director of Queens (New York) Museum of Art, to hire and involve a community organizer in developing a programming plan, "a paradigm shift from one of inviting audiences to view exhibitions determined by art world experts to one of facilitating partnerships between museums and the local community."[4]

Enlarging entry points calls for shifts in power relationships, but also in recognizing a wider, perhaps metaphysical, role that museums have in society. Bronx-born poet and artist Annie Lanzillotto asks, "How do we move forward as a society, as . . . humans?" She recalls how she and her mother sat under a stained-glass window in the American Wing of the Metropolitan Museum of Art.

We sat in Gallery 700 because there were benches there, there was air there. So for people who are healing, you need a place to sit. You need a place to breathe. And you need a place to be still. So we're sitting in Gallery 700, there's beautiful statues all around, there's Diana in bronze, naked with her bow and arrow. There's open skylights and there's Tiffany windows. [My mother] *was so taken by the stained glass. . . . The name of the window was "Autumn Landscape" (1923–24). The way the glass is bent into color and layered, it's a miracle . . . When I asked my mother how she survived domestic violence and how she maintained her resilience and sparkle, she shocked me with her answer. She said to me, "colors." And now thinking back at her, mesmerized by this Tiffany autumn landscape, this waterfall with the folded blue colors and the greens and the foliage, the gold, the light. She allowed that into herself, into her soul. She invited it in.*

Annie Lanzillotto grew up a working-class kid who gave herself permission to be an artist. *The word artist seemed out of reach, but art and doing things with beauty and care and making was infused in everything we did. . . . So, there's art in everything. Every meal was beautiful.*[5]

Gallery director Michael Findlay advises seeing art without listening to audio commentary or reading wall texts, prophylactic measures that mask looking-at-art insecurities. Instead, he encourages slow and careful looking.[6] But doesn't that take time and space not available to the working classes? The plumber, after all, only had his noon-hour break. Lanzillotto would agree with Findlay but would add a class-conscious museum-utopia twist: *Do poor kids need a chance to be alone in front of works of art? Yes. Make it happen. Make a new system of ushering, create opportunities for stillness for working people. When it's quiet, no big crowds, no one's rushing you—that's privilege. And now look at a work of art. You know, your whole soul opens up.*

Looking at Class, Looking at Art

While race, ethnicity, sexuality, and gender have rightly drawn overdue attention in discourses about art, **class** (as economics, access, affirmation) is less obvious, harder to measure, and more complicated as identity, especially in the United States. What does it mean to write art history from a working-class perspective? Or, to look at it another way, how many curators, museum directors, board members and trustees come from the working classes? Are there implicit and unacknowledged class assumptions in the circuitry of patronage, grants, curatorial judgments, gallery ownership, distribution and canonical determination? What unspoken and perhaps deeply ingrained biases against labor are harbored in the exhibit selection process, textual wall commentary, and tone of art criticism? Are the uniformed guards the only consistent working-class presence inside museums? The problem is much larger than a scarcity of worker representations in artworks themselves.

There are plenty of sowers, peasants, laborers, and servants in numerous paintings—generally intended for bourgeois audiences.[7] Rather, what is missing or hidden are the power relationships beneath the surface representations and the power relationships that make art accessible or inaccessible. Is there class bias etched into the insistence on categorization? Why, for example, is Ralph Fasanella labeled an "outsider" instead of a history painter? Is it difficult for the art establishment to see the dignity and intelligence of workers?

In "Let's talk about Class and Art," UK-born theorist Mike Watson observes, "I have found that it is generally only the working class who think we need to talk about class; the middle and upper classes treat the subject as little other than a bearable annoyance, a fact of birth, or of history, but nothing can be done about it." Recognizing working-class solidarity as an alternative to feeling class shame, he adds, "here we see the vast gulf between the spontaneous and uncalculated giving, sharing and celebrating of the working class and the calculated patronage of the powerful." Watson urges, "talk about class division in the art world as art helps to provide us with the symbolic tools for conveying who we are, and right now those symbolic tools are in the hands of the elite."[8]

Art is integral to human existence, not something to be plucked by those with the most power. John Dewey saw art as a "continuity of esthetic experience with normal processes of living." Dewey reminds us that "[m]ost European museums are . . . memorials of the rise of nationalism and imperialism," and how "[t]he growth of capitalism has been a powerful influence in the development of the museum as the proper home for works of art, and in the promotion of the idea that they are apart from the common life."[9] In *Potential History: Unlearning Imperialism,* Ariella Aïsha Azoulay argues that "Art should be understood as a world-building set of activities irreducible to the creation of discrete objects. Through these activities, people's place in a shared world and their right to this place are carved."[10]

Human beings are as drawn to visual expression as they are drawn to storytelling. When that longing for beauty is thwarted or denied, ridiculed or demeaned, humans suffer. Class location, identity, situation, lineage, opportunities, associations—not to mention reliable or unreliable income—are inherent to making art and to writing about art. Coming from the working classes, with their multiple and intersecting racial and ethnic identities, does not shut the door to art, but access and opportunity are certainly narrower. And writing about art from a working-class perspective is rarely affirmed or even recognized—unless it disrupts academic norms. In writing this book, I know I am a trespasser.

I wish to invite the metaphoric and actual plumber into a commons of art practices linked to democracy and community. This book is an intervention, or *detour* as John Dewey understood, from the familiar but largely class-unconscious path of categorization, expertise, ownership, preciosity, and exclusion. It presents an orchestration of multiple art making practices, all grounded in respect for diverse working-class people, their histories, and lived material circumstances. It traces the potency and physicality of *making*—shaping, scoring, printing, assembling, marking, weaving—all human actions of connection. It proffers seeing, viewing, even touching, as an antidote to exclusion, pain and anger. Assembled in a time of plague, death, anger, and violence (which is to say, any time), it is premised on the belief that art and art making are essential to the practice of democracy.

Commons and Commoning Art

There's a hole in every wall, and thus
a commons behind every enclosure.[11]
—Peter Linebaugh

This project rescues the word *common* from its class-oppressive meaning of vulgar, its many commercial appropriations (dining commons, mall commons), and its degradation to commodity. In an American culture of individualism, competition, and corporate ownership, the British history of commons and commoning may seem misplaced. But Americans do understand sharing, potlucks, and neighborliness. The link that is less visible is between commonality and class consciousness. Even more obscure as discourse, but not unheard of as practice, is the relationship between art making and commoning—meaning accessibility, not enclosure; mutuality, not isolation. To bring class as lived experience to the surface of art writing, consider the archival research of historian Peter Linebaugh.

Linebaugh takes us inside the practice of access to unenclosed pastureland. Drawing on evidence in texts—the *Magna Carta and the Charter of the Forest*—and literally grounded in the land itself, in trees and "peasants planting orchard trees in the wild,"[12] Linebaugh demonstrates how commons is both geography (unenclosed woods, and, later, plaza, *Zócalo, Maidan*, square, park, sidewalk)[13] and something more than a static thing. It is also a verb, *commoning,* fueled with agency and meaning: "The allure of commoning arises from the mutualism of shared resources. Everything is used, nothing is wasted. Reciprocity, sense of self, willingness to argue, long memory, collective celebration, and mutual aid are traits of the commoner."[14] (These traits describe my working-class childhood, especially if you throw in family secrets, gambling, and food.) In his "Principles of the Commons," Linebaugh claims commoning as "primary to human life," beginning in the family.[15] How class-inflected are these characteristic ways of being? This is not to argue some class essentialism, but rather to recognize the *necessity* of working-class solidarity as a survival strategy.

Artists I know work alone but rely on and participate in a community of other artists. A sensibility of commonality produces good work. (How did you get that effect? What pigment did you use there?)[16] We hear the noise of art markets but not the organizational murmurs of art collectives and their shared spaces, ideas, resources, and support. Take, for example, The Commons in Provincetown, Massachusetts, a physical and collaborative space for artists who live in a community with a long history of nurturing artists. Better known, the *Taller de Gráfica Popular* was a socially conscious printmaking collective founded in Mexico City in 1937 that was crucial to the artistic development of Elizabeth Catlett, one of its members, and that greatly influenced Milton Rogovin's photographic practices.

I have a particular affinity for this word *common.*[17] *Common, communal, community* mean something larger than shared physical space. The ethos of community—sets of relationships, affinities, and concerns—is integral to racial and ethnic identities. That is the stuff of generational survival. But that adhesive societal element has to be sustained within a structure of hyper individualism, capital expansion, unequal resources, and privatization. That is the stuff of struggle.

Despite differences of time, genre, and identity, the artists assembled in this book are all concerned with the accessibility of their art. The commons, as a construct, is proffered as an alternative to thinking about art as *enclosed* in markets, money, and ownership. Commoning is widespread in practice as well as place: consider murals, anthologies, and choruses. See the documentary *Choral Singing in America*. Notice how one candle lights another.[18]

This book is a space, a commons, where artists from different backgrounds and times can be seen in relationship to each other and to their historical, political, and cultural contexts. It is an alternative to reading art history as separate from a viewer's material existence. It sees art dialogically and dialectically, not as individual masterpieces. It shapes a coherence (to borrow the language and method of Antonio Gramsci) "through multiple branchings out."[19] Alignment, affiliation, and relationships are not only elements of class struggle, but are also theoretically informed ways to perceive class-conscious art practices.

The Commons, literally and metaphorically, is an alternative to the ideology of Walls—geographic walls, political walls, institutional and academic walls. Some artists, like muralist Mark Rogovin, reclaim walls and transform them into commons. All the artists included here—and there are many others—show us through the alchemy of their visual tools how to challenge and transform walls of separation into commons of inclusion.

Rationale, Structure, Method

I write out of my own aesthetic/life intersections, inserting personal commentary as connective tissue. I write for those who may not read art books but who, in multiple individual ways, love and perhaps even long for art. What these artists have in common is a grounding in communities, not just their own singularity. Their work recognizes the real violence done to people when their lived realities have no cultural reflection or outlet for expression (as Gramsci understood). What guided the selection of these particular artists—who do not necessarily come out of the working class—was not *identity* (filiation), but rather *affiliation*[20]—especially their sense of the aesthetics of human relationships as evidenced in their art practices, but also in their contacts with working people. Whenever possible, artists' own voices are foregrounded, particularly what shaped and formed their artistic consciousness and practices. Art is personal for the creator, to be sure, but also for the viewer, hungry for visual meaning.

This book is rooted in "Mapping Working-Class Art," an essay I wrote for the *Routledge International Handbook of Working-Class Studies*.[21] In preparing to write that essay, I searched for artists who included workers as subjects in their art and who were politically affiliated with class struggle. My metaphoric map became too small for all the artists, practices, and concerns inherent to the relationship of working-class people and art. I needed a larger analytical infrastructure and so shifted metaphors from the map to the commons. The outcome is this book of hybrid composition—scholarly, experiential, descriptive, experimental, and personal. My focus is not on *singularity*—the great artist (or author) approach, but rather on *relationality*—parts to whole, one artist to another—and *intersectionality*—individual artists whose lives are impacted by historical and political shifts, oppressions, struggles, and their own witnessing eyes.

Why are we drawn to look at certain art? How do we understand the unspoken rumblings of appreciation, awe, and awareness that some artworks evoke in us? I curated these particular artists because of the ways their art burrows under the surface to evoke working-class lives. I paired them with an eye on the parallels in their work, allowing for unexpected and unintentional similarities. These artists are multigenerational, multicultural, and, for some, multi-genre: painters, printmakers, photographers, weavers, and sculptors who practice democracy in the way they make art. Through the pairings constructed in this book they also speak to each other—albeit not directly or knowingly. That dialogue is presented in the juxtapositions I assemble:

Käthe Kollwitz (German, 1867–1945) and Elizabeth Catlett (African American and Mexican, 1915–2012) in *Drawing, Printing, and Sculpting the Labor of Mothers*

Ruth Asawa (Japanese American, 1926–2013) and Marilyn Anderson (American, 1937) in *Looping and Weaving*
Milton Rogovin (American, 1909–2011) and Jens S. Jensen (Swedish, 1946–2015) in *Photography and the Art of Returning*
Mark Rogovin (American, 1946–2019) *in Activism as Artistry*
Ralph Fasanella (Italian American, 1914–1997) and Raymond Mason (British/Scottish/French, 1922–2010) in *History and Beauty, Crowds and Multitudes*

These artists—perhaps every artist—wrestle with what Raymond Mason calls the essential problem: "the meeting point of aesthetics and life."[22] Life, though, could mean struggle, trouble, tragedy, as well as vibrance and community. Meeting points are embedded in the artistic work and practice itself, as well as the literal, geographic, and material meeting points that produce the work—Milton Rogovin's neighborhoods, Marilyn Anderson's Guatemalan villages, Ruth Asawa's communally organized public fountains and sculptures.

The idea of juxtaposing artists comes from looking at museum walls and noticing the potential shifts that happen when an artwork by one artist is seen in relationship to another artist. Notice, for example, the similarities and differences of women's labor as embodied in the work of Elizabeth Catlett and Käthe Kollwitz. View Raymond Mason's sculptural density in relation to Ralph Fasanella's festas, marches, and demonstrations. Discern how all the artists in this book reach for what James Agee called "human actuality."[23] That is the expanded visual space that interests me. My intent is to cultivate dialogue, invite dialectic without closure, and encourage readers, especially students, to place their own discovered artists (even AI?) side by side. This book seeks engagement, not a dusty bookshelf.

I have written about Ralph Fasanella and Milton Rogovin before, taught books by and about Rogovin, and value his family's presence in my life. Marilyn Anderson's work is inextricably connected to the labor and arts community in my home city of Rochester, New York. I arranged visits with Jens S. Jensen in Gothenburg, Sweden, after being struck by the similarities between his photography and Rogovin's. Unbeknown to each other, Jensen and Rogovin practiced a photography of return, photographing the same people and the same place (in geographically different locations!) over a period of forty years. This is not nostalgia, but a rarely spoken kind of aesthetics—that of human relationships.

There is one outlier to the pairings structure—Mark Rogovin, son of Milton. Mark wanted me to read Rebecca Zorach's interview with him, sent with his usual flourish of exclamation marks. He surmised that I would find a way to use his words and experiences not only to advance his father's work or his own activism (not to mention, his own superb art work, which he rarely exhibited), but also to show how the interview demonstrates and documents collective ways of creative and political expression. I did not know then that Mark had an incurable disease that would soon take him.

What holds these artists together is not only their intent of "picturing the invisible" (to borrow Milton Rogovin's language), but also their political understanding of art's potential to resist, decolonize, and liberate.

I draw on theory as a tool to enlarge understanding, not as a frame to determine meaning. The circuitry of this book, its intersecting and shaping elements, emerges out of my study of working-class literatures, interpretations of working-class cultures (guided by Raymond Williams and Antonio Gramsci, among others), through my efforts to abstract meaning from my lived working-class life, and out of respect for the process of making art. I understand art making better now that I have my own studio.

Theorist Ariella Aïsha Azoulay engages a process of "unlearning," that is, questioning presumptions such as the neutrality of archives. She identifies exploitative and imperialist practices at the root of art institutions. Her "potential history" views art making as a restoration of a common world, "a form of being with others, both living and dead, across time, against the separation of the past from the present, colonized peoples from their worlds and possessions, and history from politics." She identifies a rift "between scholars interested in labor and those interested in art."[24] I question the labor/art dichotomy by noting the many labor historians who are deeply interested in human expressive cultures (Raymond Williams, E. P. Thompson, Herbert Gutman, Alice Kessler-Harris, and Jacqueline Jones, to name a few). But I see what she reveals about *art* as institutionalized, as taxonomies, as systems, *and* as violations, violence, and theft. I also see myself as forging bonds between labor and art.

Azoulay takes the word "shutter," a camera's component, and employs it as metaphor or synecdoche "for the operation of imperial enterprise altogether." It is apt: on windows, literally blocking out the light, with cameras "capturing" what is seen through a lens. Open. Close. Hold. Control. But what if the relationship between artists and subjects is not about control, domination, or ownership? What if we understood art *as a means to answer sorrow?* What if we saw *outsider* art as *insider* art? The artists in this book are inside by virtue of their relationships with their subjects (Kollwitz, Rogovin) or they emerge from inside the same space (Fasanella). This is another way of understanding identity.

Instead of Azoulay's critique of the imperialist *shutter,* I choose the *hinge.* Consider the physical work of the hinge. It allows opening and closing, slowly or quickly. It is flexible. It is a joint, a means of connection. It is fluid, not final. It is intended for use. And for return. The artists in this book construct hinges between themselves and the subjects of their art making, whether through photography, sculpture, painting, printmaking, drawing, or weaving. The art that is made is itself a hinge. These artists are not exploiters, dominators, thieves, or imperialists. What they hold in common is inside the connective tissue of this book.

Art and life intersect. This book is a sampling of those intersections: for the artists, a process of witnessing, answering, and creating; for the viewer, unexpected awakenings and evoked memories. These artists possess a secular spirituality that sustains their work and elicits something larger in their audiences than merely an encounter with the material of artworks.

Class and Language

Cultural historian Raymond Williams is also a language architect who exposes word foundations, parts, and measured meanings. He writes from his own linguistic ground of being, "a small rural community right on the Welsh-English border,"[25] and tells of an experience when he was at Cambridge University as a scholarship student. His Shakespeare professor claimed that nobody understands the meaning of *neighbor* in the twentieth century, as compared to Shakespeare's time. Summoning his working-class voice, Williams responded, "I know perfectly well what 'neighbor,' in that full sense, means," referring to a "recognition of certain kinds of mutual responsibility."[26]

With his great capacity to turn over words and look prismatically at them, Williams addresses the problem inside the term community, especially for those who leave working-class home places and enter more privileged class spaces. "For there is, of course, a habit of mutual obligation which easily becomes the ground on which exploitation is possible. If you have a sense that you have this kind of native duty to others it can expose you very cruelly within a system of the conscious exploitation of labor."[27] Also, Williams is self-reflective about language. He elaborates on what he calls his "saddest discovery," when he found in himself "a form of imperialism" when and where "parts of your mind are taken over by a system of ideas, a system of feelings, which really do emanate from the power centre."[28]

This is the dilemma of finding the right language to write about class and culture from a working-class perspective to a mixed-class, likely more middle and upper, audience. I have not perfected that language, but I am conscious of its complexity.

I also wish to clarify any confusion about whiteness and class. To speak about class is not to diminish or ignore the power of white skin privilege. The working classes are multiracial and multiethnic and multi-geographic. But the intersections of race, ethnicity, and class can be conveniently obscured, as the history of pitting one laboring class against another attests. The American artists in this book recognize how class and race intersect, photographing (Rogovin) and painting (Fasanella) and printing (Catlett) those intersections. In 1990 I had a conversation with Manning Marable when he visited the

Rochester Institute of Technology.[29] I asked him how best to understand the differences between ethnic (considered white) working class and Black working class. He said, as I remember, "imagine you are forced to hold a rope in your hand. If you are ethnic/white, the rope marks your skin, if you are black it cuts into your flesh." I have not forgotten that difference.

Navigating Methods and Language

Some of the terms, concerns, keywords, and references that infuse my thinking about class and culture include the following:

Formation: How to become an artist? The German words *Bild, Bildung, Bildungsroman, and Künstlerroman* inform how we understand artistic development as well as *human* development, evolution, education, cultivation, and process. (This is not the language of business—outcomes and profits. One has to be alert to that intrusive language, what philosopher Mark Fisher calls "business ontology.")[30] This is the language of consciousness, of how to be a *learning* human being. The art historian Peter Selz writes, "Humanity is not something with which man is born. It has to be learned and fought for, and often the artist becomes the individual in whom the struggle to maintain or achieve true humanity manifests itself."[31] John Dewey observed that "[i]t is no linguistic accident that 'building,' 'construction,' 'work,' designate both a process and finished product[;] . . . without the meaning of the verb that of the noun remains blank."[32] This is not to say that great artists are great human beings, but it is to notice how the artists assembled here did not separate self-reflective, politically aware consciousness from their developing artistry.

Voice: Listen for the intermingling of artistic and human development in these voices. By foregrounding artists' own voices, I create spaces for their own explanations, process, self-doubt, obligations, allegiances, memories, and craft. I hope my academic voice is not too intrusive. I honor multi-vocality.

Beauty: *A thing is beautiful when it is strong in its kind. What beautiful designs a fruit vendor makes with his piles of oranges and apples. He takes much trouble and I am sure has great pleasure in arranging them so that you can see them at their best.* So observed Robert Henri in his classic, *The Art Spirit.*[33] See beauty in Raymond Mason's affection for Parisian markets and Ralph Fasanella's pleasure in a carefully prepared and arranged plate of food. See beauty, as Dalila Scruggs does, as a "lifeline in the struggle for justice" in Elizabeth Catlett's artistry[34]

Repair: Can art heal wounds? During the nineteenth-century American Civil War, some soldiers carried tintypes of their loved ones in their breast pockets. Other tintypes, perhaps taken by federal photographers, documented soldiers' battle wounds. The techniques of art making can address emotional needs as well as pragmatic purposes. The frequently photographed poet Walt Whitman combined the literal and the lyrical in his 1865 Civil War poem, "The Wound Dresser." Whitman attended soldiers' wounds, witnessed suffering, and offered solace to one wrecked human body after another.[35] What is the relationship between mental health and access to art? Art can assist healing. Or prevent more harm, as cartoonist Lynda Barry seriously/humorously observed: *Art is a public-health concern because it keeps you from killing yourself and others.*[36]

The Work of Art (Making)

As anyone who has picked up a pencil or brush and faced a blank paper or canvas knows, making art (once you batten down your own self-doubt and insecurities) is work. It is certainly more than a way to pass the time. It answers a call within human nature, like the impulse toward storytelling, mentioned earlier, a call to express. Children draw; they draw all the time until they reach a point in their schooling where self-consciousness or self-criticism beats expression. Ruth Asawa described drawing as "her greatest pleasure and the most difficult." A free "Drawing Guide" was available at the Whitney Museum of American Art's exhibit of Ruth Asawa drawings ("Ruth Asawa Through Line," September 16, 2023–January 15, 2024). Written in English and Spanish, it offers these suggestions for drawing: "Learning to See; Rhythms and Waves; Growth Patterns; Curiosity and Control." More than guidelines, these are also metaphysical nudges, in the Ruth Asawa spirit, on how to look at the world around you, artistically.

John Berger describes the mystery and lure of drawing:

> *Every artist discovers that drawing—when it is an urgent activity—is a two-way process. To draw is not only to measure and put down, it is also to receive. . . . The encounter of these two energies, their dialogue, does not have the form of question and answer. It is a ferocious and inarticulated dialogue. To sustain it requires faith. It is like a burrowing in the dark, a burrowing under the apparent. The great images occur when the two tunnels meet and join perfectly. Sometimes when the dialogue is swift, almost instantaneous, it is like something thrown and caught. I offer no explanation for this experience. I simply believe very few artists will deny it. It's a professional secret.*[37]

Here's Berger in his signature style of writing simultaneously about a specific artist (in this case a Russian sculptor whose work he glimpsed only through photographs), and declaring something larger: "Criticism is always a form of intervention: intervention between the work of art and its public. . . . I have come to see that the arranging of artists in a hierarchy of merit is an idle and essentially dilettante process. What matters are the needs which art answers."[38]

It is in recognition of those needs that I have composed this book, this intervention.

BEAUTY

Käthe Kollwitz
saw
beauty
in laboring bodies
in Königsberg longshoremen
in women bending
in mothers' protective strength
in the *la Carmagnole* song and dance
in the march
of Silesian weavers.

Elizabeth Catlett
saw
beauty
in the weight of a child against a mother's chest
in literacy
in struggle
in African masks
in communal art making.

Hugh Wolfe,
furnace tender
in *Life in the Iron Mills*
thirsted for beauty.
Out of waxen korl
he shaped and sculpted
"strangely beautiful" figures.
Out of his furnace,
quenching his thirst,
he carved.

Unexpected beauty
Unclaimed art

Longing

Drawing, Printing, and Sculpting the Labor of Mothers

I use my own body in working. When I am bathing or dressing, I see and feel how my body looks and moves. I never do sculpture from a nude model . . . Mostly, I watch women.

—Elizabeth Catlett

No man with a starched face
asked of Effie
how many shirts it took
to make a washer woman

—Wilma Elizabeth McDaniel, "Shirts"

Museums can provide solace; art can heal wounds. The Queens Museum in New York City offers art therapy programs to improve participants' mental health. In "Therapeutic Creative Expression," the *New York Times* recognized the work of this museum and other efforts to link art and mental health during times of crisis. To illustrate this linkage, the *Times* reproduced *The Laundress* (1863), a painting by Honoré Daumier.[1] Why choose this particular painting? The painter creates a quiet mood. It is nearing the end of the day. We see a woman and child reach the top of stairs, climbing up from the Seine River below. The child has something in her hand, maybe a shovel; the woman, the mother, holds the child with one hand and secures a large bundle of laundry with the other hand. The *Times* caption informs the reader that the Metropolitan Museum of Art "has a list of paintings that might offer some calm, like this one of domestic tranquility." It is a beautiful painting of contrasting light and shadow, but it is **not** domestic tranquility. Rather, it is domestic **labor**. Imagine carrying a bundle of wet laundry up from the river to the street above while holding the hand of a child. Looking down from his studio window Daumier observed washerwomen coming up from the *bateaux-lavoirs*, public laundry boats anchored in the Seine.[2] To reference this painting in the context of tranquility is to resist, perhaps unconsciously, the actuality of labor. Wet laundry is heavy.

Recognizing labor from birth to death as an inseparable part of impoverished women's lives is integral to the art of Käthe Kollwitz and Elizabeth Catlett. They perceived and understood *weight*—the weight of physical work on a human body, the weight of sheltering children, the weight of struggle against poverty, war, and racial oppression, and the weight of wet laundry. In drawings, carvings, and prints, Käthe Kollwitz and Elizabeth Catlett embody the lives of workers, especially women. A central figure in Kollwitz's *March of the Weavers* (1893–1898) is a gaunt woman carrying a sleeping child on her back. Elizabeth Catlett's *The Negro Woman* linocut series (1946–47, retitled *The Black Woman* in the 1960s) depicts women laborers scrubbing, hoeing, and cleaning "other folks' homes." Their art speaks the body language of labor, but also—in the gestures of arms and hands—how oppression is resisted—the thrusting body pointing toward freedom in Catlett's linocuts of Harriet Tubman (1946–47) and *Harriet Tubman* (1953–54) and *Harriet* (1975), and the fierce upward arm of Kollwitz's *Never Again War* poster (1924). They shaped maternal labor, love, and loss into art. They answered war, racial oppression, and injustice with a transnational vision of the efficacy of art to heal and transform.

Käthe Kollwitz

Structures of Feeling

July 8, 1867, Königsberg, East Prussia–
April 22, 1945, Moritzburg, Germany

*Poverty and hunger are shameful and humiliating—
no one has respect for you if you are poor or hungry.*
—Agnes Smedley, *Daughter of Earth*

*The working-class woman shows me, through her appearance
and being, much more than the ladies who are totally limited
by conventional behavior. The working-class woman shows me
her hands, her feet and her hair. She lets me see the shape and
form of her body through her clothes. She presents herself and
the expression of her feelings openly, without disguises.*
—Kathe Kollwitz

the revolutionary look
that says I am in the world
to change the world
—Muriel Rukeyser

One meaning of the expression "take in" is "to give shelter to." Once, on a rare visit to Paris in 1904, Käthe Kollwitz encountered one of her former Munich art studies classmates. Frau Gretor was impoverished, struggling to support her son, Georg. Moved by her friend's dire circumstances, Kollwitz offered to take in the boy. The mother, trusting her friend, agreed, and young Georg went to Berlin to live with the Kollwitz family. In her later written reflections, Käthe recalls how her children and family would present entertaining theatrical performances, and mentions Georg Gretor as the son of an old friend who *lent Georg to us for a lengthy stay—he was the same age as our Hans.*[1] A perceptive generosity, especially toward women in need, shape Kollwitz's human relationships as much as the lines and shadows of her graphic arts.

When she was seventeen, Käthe Schmidt became engaged to Karl Kollwitz, a boyhood friend of her brother Konrad. Käthe's father, Carl Schmidt (1825–1898), was not enthusiastic about an early marriage, concerned about how marriage and motherhood might be obstacles to his daughter Käthe's promising artistic future. In a 1941 written reflection, Kollwitz traced her own ambivalence: *I so liked the free life in Munich that I began to wonder whether I had not made a mistake in binding myself by so early an engagement.*[2] Yet, despite her father's reservations and her own, Käthe, seven years after her engagement, married Karl Kollwitz and settled in a north Berlin tenement at 25 Weissenburgerstrasse No. 58, where Karl was a *Kassenarzt*, a doctor to local working-class and impoverished people, practicing a form of socialized medicine.[3] There they established living space, Karl's medical office, and Käthe's art studio.

This environment shaped Käthe's consciousness as much as her formal art education and cosmopolitan travels. Hans Kollwitz, her firstborn son, recalls how his mother "would see anyone who wanted to call on her, although these visits often sapped her strength. People would bring their griefs and problems to her and usually left feeling relieved. But then *she* would have one more burden to bear."[4] The willingness to *take in* the condition and circumstances of others, even more, to affect material change, is usually not named as an attribute of a great artist. Käthe Kollwitz, given her mastery of the graphic arts and sculpture, was, indeed, a great artist, but also one whose artistry was inseparable from her awareness of human struggle.

Käthe Kollwitz's gift to the history of art is a foregrounding of workers, especially working-class women, that is still rare and unsurpassed. Not ornamental or intended for amusement, her workers have verisimilitude: backs bent, rounded, and burdened; hands enlarged and labor-scarred; elongated arms clutching tools and embracing children. Kollwitz's technical skills are inseparable from her humanistic strength. Her figures are not flat; they contain possibility despite grievous loss. A kernel of agency and resistance could uncoil.[5] That's the Kollwitz light within the darkness of her drawings and print cycles.

Born into an educated, cultured, and progressive German family, Kollwitz's affinity for workers and their lived experiences was rooted in affiliation not filiation.[6] Kollwitz took up the complex challenge of shaping art based on the histories, stories, and living conditions of those the powerful deemed least important and, certainly, least beautiful. Her drawings, lithographs, woodcuts, and etchings—of women and children, of death thieving the lives of starving babies, of grieving parents and widows, of collective rebellion and struggle—build "structures of feeling." Raymond Williams's neglected insight is rarely applied to visual analyses, and the word "feeling" seems to scare some critics. However, it fits Kollwitz. Williams insisted on the word "feeling," a word that includes ideology and worldview but is not constrained by political categories—as neither was Kollwitz.

Williams elaborates "structures of feeling" as (still in process) "characteristic elements of impulse, restraint, and tone; specifically affective elements of consciousness and relationships: not feeling against thought, but thought as felt and feeling as thought: practical consciousness of a present kind, in a living and interrelated community."[7] Look at any Kollwitz drawing or print and you will see a visual conception of structures of feeling.[8] She visualized the body language of gesture and embrace and the relational language of families and comrades. She worked art through her own grief and periods of depression. Until the end of her life, facing the immensity of war and loss, she continued to make art in solidarity with common people. She contained others. And, without bourgeois sentiment or condescension, she found beauty in the bodies of workers.[9]

Her drawings, lithographs, and etchings reveal a grounded interior deeper than professed political ideology. She witnessed the damage done to families by exploitative work.

> *I should like to say something about my reputation for being a "socialist" artist. . . . Unquestionably my work at this time, as a result of the attitudes of my father and brother and of the whole literature of the period, was in the direction of socialism. But my real motive for choosing my subjects almost exclusively from the life of the workers was that only such subjects gave me in a simple and unqualified way what I felt to be beautiful. For me the Koenigsberg longshoremen had beauty; the Polish jimkes on their grain ships had beauty; the broad freedom of movement in the gestures of the common people had beauty. Middle-class people had no appeal for me at all. Bourgeois life as a whole seemed to me pedantic. The proletariat, on the other hand, had a grandness of manner, a breadth to their lives. Much later on, when I became acquainted with the difficulties and tragedies underlying proletarian life, when I met the women who came to my husband for help and so, incidentally, came to me, I was gripped by*

the full force of the proletarian's fate. Unsolved problems such as prostitution and unemployment grieved and tormented me, and contributed to my feeling that I must keep on with my studies of the lower classes. And portraying them again and again opened a safety-valve for me; it made life bearable.[10]

Kollwitz and the American working-class writer Agnes Smedley were friends. Smedley visited her in Berlin in 1925, and Kollwitz visited Smedley when she was hospitalized in 1928, drawing a sketch of her lying in a hospital bed.[11] They were both keenly attuned to the lives of impoverished women and advocated for them. This relationship is worth noting as a caution to reading Kollwitz's perception of beauty as romanticizing or, worse, reifying workers. Kollwitz understood, as Smedley wrote in *Daughter of Earth,* that a "desire for beauty . . . walk[s] hand in hand with unloveliness and all that negates life."[12] Smedley's biographers underscore this distinction, noting, "Smedley's militant and creative use of personal rage evoke the same disturbing emotions as do the images of the poor we find in the etchings by her friend Käthe Kollwitz. Like Kollwitz and Emma Goldman, she did not romanticize the poor or the working class, and she never glorified their way of life."[13]

As Kollwitz trained as an artist, as she read literature, history, and theory (such as Zola's *Germinal*, August Bebel's *Woman and Socialism,* and Arne Garborg's *From a Man's World*), and as she absorbed the historical and contemporary never-ending assaults on workers, Kollwitz found subjects to match her artistic gifts. She became an artist-witness. Advocacy through her art was her job, and her own safety valve.

To "take in" Kollwitz, to see the power and virtuosity of her signature line and form, to recognize why her prints and posters were embraced by common people, to understand how her anti-authoritarian art threatened Kaiser and Fuhrer, it is more useful to think metaphorically rather than categorically. She built a human and artistic life without compartmentalizing her public creations from her private ethos. The German concept of *Bildung*—of educating, shaping, developing, harmonizing, picturing—may seem counterintuitive to the deeply ingrained American goal orientation of terminal degrees, winners, and losers. Understood as more than bourgeois advancement, *Bildung* is a better linguistic tool (than representation, identity, and, certainly, success) to approach Kollwitz—the daughter of a builder—as an artist and as a human being. The German *Bild* and the notion of picturing the self, not as self-enhancement but as self-development and self-understanding, also informs our appreciation of why Kollwitz drew so many self-portraits (more than one hundred according to the Käthe Kollwitz Museum in Köln), which she considered a "visual form of soliloquy." These two portraits (see following pages), created when she was about twenty-one years and then around fifty-seven years, testify to her consistent self-probing and self-questioning in relation to the wider world.

I have been through a revolution, and I am convinced that I am no revolutionist. My childhood dream of dying on the barricades will hardly be fulfilled, because I should hardly mount a barricade now that I know what they are in reality. . . . I thought I was a revolutionary and was only an evolutionary.[14] Or, maybe, she was a nascent pacifist.

Käthe was the fifth child born to Katharina and Karl Schmidt. Her mother suffered the loss of three other children. Recalling the death of her little brother Benjamin from meningitis, Käthe worried as a child that she might be responsible since she was then enamored with Greek gods, not Christian saviors. She saw in her mother a stoicism that she recognized in other women as well, *although she never surrendered to the deep sorrow of those early days of her marriage, it must have been her years of suffering which gave her forever after the remote air of a madonna.*[15] Her father was trained as a lawyer but, given his political and religious views as a member of the Social Democratic Workers Party, he abandoned a law career and became a mason and successful builder. Her mother's father, Julius Rupp, formed and lead his own church. The scholarly Rupp was imprisoned for two years for his religious views and founded a breakaway religious community, Friends of Light or the Free Congregation, grounded in the mores of early Christian communities. Later, her father, Karl, became a leader of the same congregation. Kollwitz was spiritually attuned, not conventionally religious, possessing an intellectuality equally open to contemporary, politically accented literature as to Bible readings.

In many ways Käthe was a fortunate girl. Her family's religious affiliations gave her ethos without domination. As a young girl, she had freedom to roam—what her translators call "loafing," echoing Walt Whitman. *All this apparently aimless loafing undoubtedly contributed to my artistic growth,* she later reflected.[16] She attended a small private school rather than a public one. *My parents followed the principle of giving us the opportunity to develop ourselves without their pushing our noses into things.*[17] She had access to literature (Goethe was particularly important to her) and music, and, as she developed her artistic gifts, recognition and material support from her father. *From my childhood on my father had expressly wished me to be trained . . . as an artist.*[18] Undoubtedly, she faced institutional gender restrictions and limitations (the Academy of Arts in Königsberg did not allow female students at the time), but she did not have to waste youthful energy, especially as a female, rebelling against authoritarian controls. She had the *generous confidence* of her parents.[19] Her strong will and sense of self also shaped her determined independence from her father's control of her artistic path.

Her father's view of her as a painter did not hinder his efforts to seek out the best teachers available for his daughter's artistic training. She began at age thirteen with engraving and etching lessons with Rudolph Mauer,

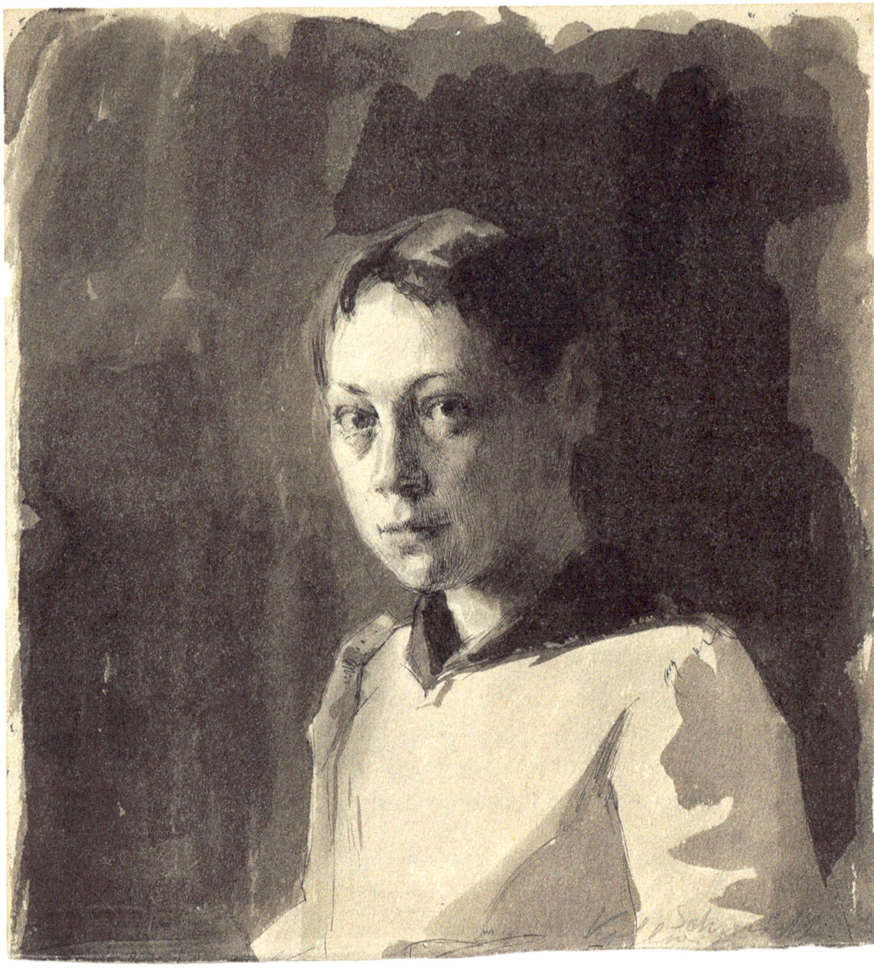

Käthe Kollwitz (1867–1945), Self-portrait, c. 1888, pen, brush and sepia on drawing paper, 260 × 248 mm, NT unknown. On permanent loan from the estate of Marianne Fiedler, Käthe Kollwitz Museum Köln, www.kollwitz.de, courtesy of Christian Nitz at the Käthe Kollwitz Musuem, Köln.

followed by private painting lessons with Emile Neide. At seventeen she joined her older brother Konrad in Berlin, where he was a university student and where she attended an art school for girls. There she studied with Karl Stauffer-Bern, who encouraged her drawing rather than painting. Her father still saw her as a painter and persuaded her to paint a genre painting, *Before the Ball*, which was framed, exhibited, and sold. She was relieved not to follow up with another similarly thematic painting since she considered such subjects *the worse trash*.[20] When she first arrived in Berlin in 1885, her brother Konrad took her to Friedrichshain Cemetery, where she viewed the rows of square stone graves of the more than two hundred workers killed on March 18, 1848.[21] This is an early instance of how her political

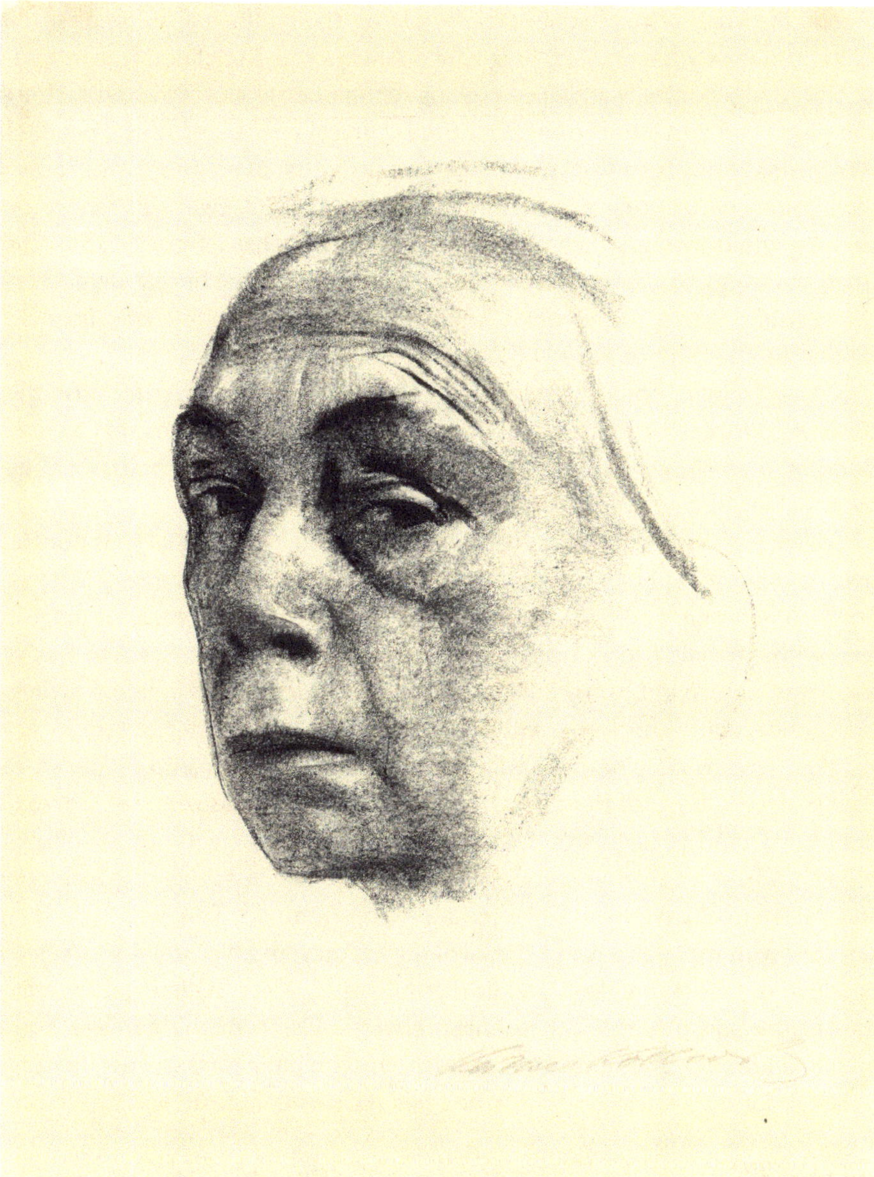

Käthe Kollwitz (1867–1945), Self-portrait, 1924, crayon lithograph (transfer), 290 × 225 mm, Kn 209 b. Käthe Kollwitz Museum Köln, Inv. Nr. 70300/87020, www.kollwitz.de.

consciousness and awareness of public working-class history inspired her private art making.

In 1889, wanting to delay a too-early marriage, her father agreed to send her to Munich to study at the Women's School of Art, an extension of the Munich Academy of Art. In Munich she experienced formal art training with painter Ludwig Herterich, who *knew how to train my eyes,*[22] and enjoyed a lively artistic life with other female artists, joining their informal "Composition Club" and newly formed "Etching Club." Always the disciplined learner/artist, Kathe methodically acquired etching techniques from respected etchers and engravers and labored through the technical challenges of the process. Her inclination was toward the expressive potential of graphic forms rather than color and painting, especially after reading Max Klinger's brochure on painting and drawing, which posited that "[d]rawing has a freer relationship [than painting] to the representational world."[23] Also, painting demanded more studio space and involved higher costs for canvas and oils, financial resources she did not have.

Käthe Kollwitz could draw. And a drawing, as writer/artist John Berger observed, "forces us to stop and enter its time." Berger makes this distinction between drawing and painting: "Drawings reveal the process of their own making, their own looking, more clearly."[24]

Kollwitz observed and absorbed. She recognized her bisexuality as normative: *As a matter of fact I believe that bisexuality is almost a necessary factor in artistic production.*[25] She was an avid hiker and walker—once sojourning on foot with a female friend, tracing the coastal route from Florence to Rome. She loved nature but rarely incorporated the natural world in her drawings.

To understand the pivots in Kollwitz's artistic trajectory, contemporary readers have to imagine or maybe re-imagine the relationship of literature to visual arts. One of her first strong drawings was inspired by German poet Ferdinand Freiligrath's poem "The Emigrants." Also, while training in Munich, she produced an evocative drawing, a tavern scene of conspiracy and resistance, based on Emile Zola's novel *Germinal*. This was a pattern she followed throughout her life, evoking literary and historical sources to produce drawings, etchings, and lithographs that, while depicting a specificity of time and place, also presented a larger vision of the damage done to human beings by the owning, political, and military classes. Her literary/political consciousness also informed her narrative impulse and inclination toward visual series.

In 1893 Kollwitz attended a premier of Gerhart Hauptmann's play *The Weavers (Die Weber)* at the Freie Bühne theater. Despite being banned by the Berlin police as subversive, the Independent Stage Company of Berlin staged the play. Kollwitz had a ticket for that morning's performance and was deeply moved by both the specificity of the Silesian linen weavers' conditions and by workers' historical oppression and, importantly, their critical turn toward awareness/consciousness and resistance/struggle, which led more often than not to defeat—but not always. *That performance was a milestone in my work. I dropped the series on* Germinal *and set to work on* The Weavers.[26]

Kollwitz's *A Weavers' Revolt* (*Ein Weberaufstand*), or *The Weavers Cycle*: *Poverty* (empty loom and unemployment), *Death* (of a weaver's child dead from hunger, triggering the revolt), *Conspiracy* (avenging the dead child), *March*

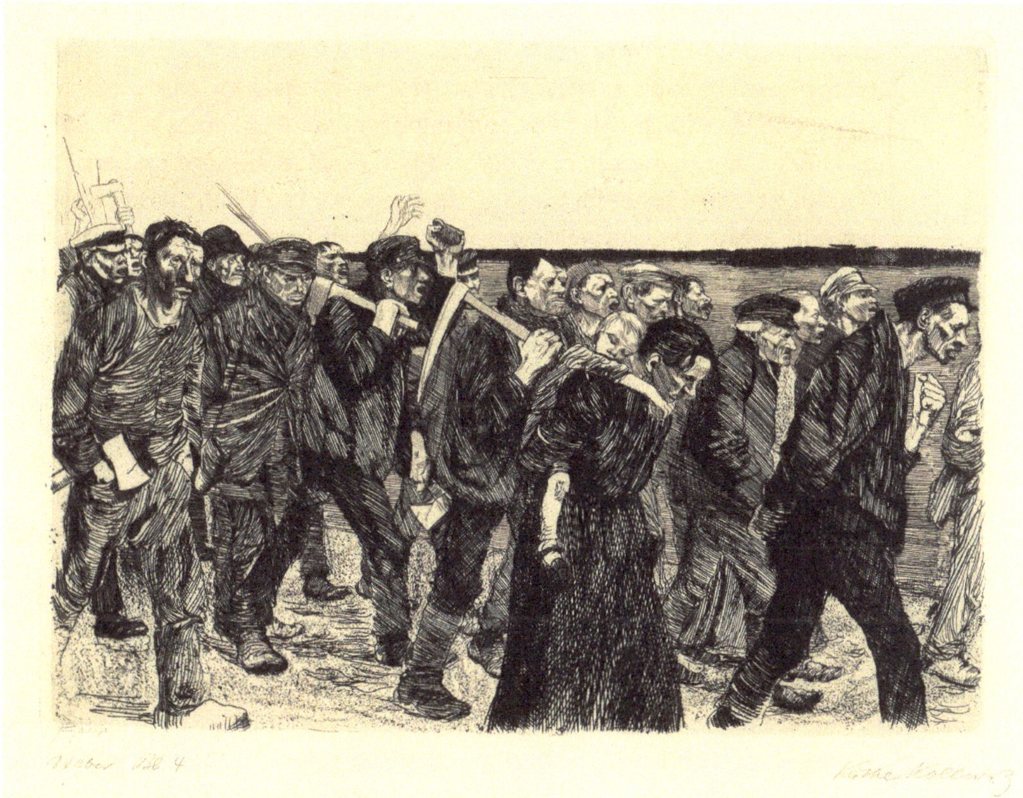

Käthe Kollwitz (1867–1945), *March of the Weavers*, sheet 4 of the cycle "A Weavers' Revolt," 1893–1897, line etching and sandpaper, 216 × 295 mm, Kn 36 II a. Käthe Kollwitz Museum Köln, Inv. Nr. 70300/84002, www.kollwitz.de.

of the Weavers (to the factory owner's house), *Riot or Attack* (on the boss's mansion), and *The End* (deaths of resisting workers) developed (1893–1897) as three lithographs and three folios of etchings.

The word *cycle* has multiple meanings here—the construct of her artistic production, the circuitry of cultural forms, and the cycle of poverty and crushed rebellion.[27] The Prussian Silesian weavers were caught in a spiral of declining subsistence wages triggered by new technologies, enlarged populations, and foreign competition. Starving, they fought back, roughly attacking machinery and their exploiters' mansions. Their rebellion was suppressed by Prussian troops and workers were killed. Not a unique story. But this eruption in 1844 signaled a shift in workers' consciousness. Karl Marx, who published *The Communist Manifesto* with Friedrich Engels in 1848, recognized this shift, as did the playwright Hauptmann. And Kollwitz caught the spirit of this uprising and subsequent suppression. Her cycle is much more than pre-photography illustration; rather, it is a deep visual articulation of human consciousness awakened or darkened by suffering. She acquired a dialogic, rather than representational, relationship to literary sources and historical events. In her graphic series and other cycles, Kollwitz *positioned* herself in alliance with Silesian weavers or resisting peasants or rural laborers carrying their makeshift tools as weapons, or parents grieving for children killed by starvation, disease, or war. For contemporary viewers, the specific political and historical circumstances underlying her visual renderings are informative but not essential to understanding the work. It's the cycle that matters and how the art moves us as human beings. After all, there is no easy **capturing** of oppression. (I resist the arrogant word "capture" in relation to photographs, and I resist it here as well. The best artistic work acknowledges the viewers' ignorance yet willingness to see and know, not the dominance of capture.)

In 1896, while working on *A Weavers' Revolt,* Käthe's second son, Peter, was born. Soon after completing the series, her father died. Shown at the *Great Berlin Art Exhibition* in 1898, *A Weavers' Revolt* was acclaimed and won Kollwitz national recognition and the Gold Medal. Proposed by artist Adolf Menzel, the award to Kollwitz was initially rejected by Kaiser Wilhelm II but later awarded by the King of Saxony.[28] Kollwitz was astonished to find herself, at the age of thirty-two, *counted as among the foremost artists of the country.*[29]

My life between thirty and forty was very happy in every respect.[30] Her children were growing up. Karl's medical practice was sufficient for their needs. She had opportunities to travel, visiting Paris twice, including Rodin's studio. But she did not settle into bourgeois domestic tranquility, ignoring the rest of the world. She made many drawings and studies of working-class women in her Berlin neighborhood. She grasped the strength of humble women and saw the potential for the heroic in them. She sought a visual voice for women as resistance fighters and leaders. Charles Dickens's *A Tale of Two Cities* shaped her understanding of women's role in the French Revolution and inspired her etching and aquatint *La Carmagnole* (1901), the ferocious dance of the Revolution. She loved the *grace of movement* of dance,[31] perhaps even more as it is politicized in *La Carmagnole*. Whether or not she read Engels's history, *The Peasant War in Germany* (1870), of the sixteenth-century uprising in Germany (1522–25), she was aware of the peasant leader "Black Anna," (*die schwarze Anna, Schwarze Hofmännin)* after reading Wilhelm Zimmermann's book on the Peasants War (1841–1843). Her 1902–03 etching *Charge [Losbruch, Outbreak*] foregrounds a woman of indeterminate age but not young, whose face is turned toward the crowd as the viewer sees only her back, her upraised arms, her large clenched fists, and her shoe-less feet, as she pitches forward, speaking a visual body language of resistance—ENOUGH—urging peasants to fight back with whatever feeble weapons they possess. This 1525 heroine becomes in Kollwitz's hands and imagination a breakthrough female figure, not victim or muse, but leader. (We see another female resistance leader in Elizabeth Catlett's *Harriet Tubman.*) Kollwitz's *Charge* won the

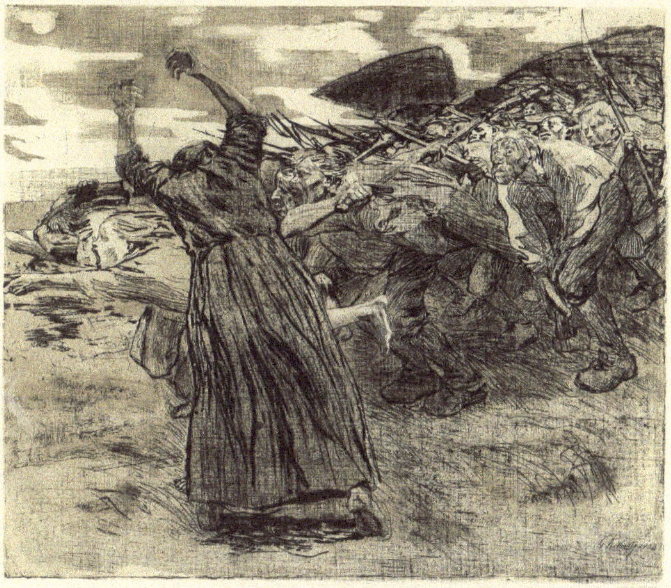

Käthe Kollwitz (1867–1945), *Charge*, sheet 5 of the cycle "Peasants War" 1902/1903, line etching, drypoint, reservage and soft ground with imprint of two fabrics and Ziegler's transfer paper, 515 × 592 mm, Kn 70 VIII b. Käthe Kollwitz Museum Köln, Inv. Nr. 70300/01012, www.kollwitz.de.

acclaim of the German Association for Historical Art and the commission to complete a series on the Peasants' War.

Just as Kollwitz defies easy art and political categorization, her experimental printing techniques are distinct, hybrid, slightly unorthodox. Seven images comprise *Peasants War* (1901–1908) [*Bauernkrieg*, German Peasants' War], a cycle in which she pushed to link technique to content: *The Ploughman, Raped, Sharpening the Scythe, Arming in a Vault, Charge, Battle Field, The Prisoners*. On the strength of this work, she was awarded the 1907 *Villa Romana Prize*—a cost-free residency in Florence. She accepted but experienced an away-from-home ambivalence in the saturation of Italian art and the luxury of a villa; however, the milder Italian climate did encourage her son Peter's recovery from tuberculosis. During this time her stature (probably a word she wouldn't use) as a graphic artist heightened, and she was hired to create a series of drawings for the progressive magazine *Simplicissimus*. It was work she enjoyed: she was given free rein to draw her chosen subjects as well as earning much needed supplementary income for the family. She appreciated the opportunity to present *the many quiet and loud tragedies of city life.*[32]

How to represent, artistically, common people? This is a question attuned particularly to photography but is just as essential to the graphic arts as shaped by Käthe Kollwitz. She and her doctor husband Karl Kollwitz were not literally of the uneducated working classes, but lived and worked among those who daily struggled to feed their children, secure housing, and survive work injuries and unemployment. **Struggle** is the key word here. This is the ground from which the seeds of Käthe's art grew and flourished. Rather than dwell on which classification—expressionist, naturalist, realist—to clap onto Kollwitz's work, it is better, but more difficult, to take in the relationship between working people's lives and artistic expression. *All my work hides within it life itself. . . .*[33] Think of that relationship as reciprocal rather than exploitive or merely representational. The work would not exist without the source—the human subject matter. Kollwitz etched and drew this connection, which she acknowledged could be severed or could devolve into "preciosity." Always self-critical about technique, she wanted to produce art that was not shallow in the eyes of the average viewer. She created posters, woodcuts, etchings, and lithographs, not for the privacy of the privileged or the ownership of galleries or museums, but to be seen and distributed to those barely allowed into the art cathedrals of the owning class. She created a Kollwitz commons.

Prior to the devastation of World War I, the prescient Käthe, conscious of the cost of Germany's industrial and urban growth to the working poor, developed several etchings on the theme of death. She also awakened her long interest in sculpture, having attended a sculpture class at the *Academie Julian* during her 1904 visit to Paris. At the end of her life, she remarked, *If I could live once more, I would work exclusively as a sculptor.*[34] As she developed as an artist, acquiring the spatial conditions of a sculpture studio depended on both family and financial concerns and so was often out of reach for her. It wasn't until 1919, during the Weimar Republic, that she had access to a large studio suitable for sculpture when she was elected to the Prussian Academy of Arts as full professor.

Sculpture, rather than the micro technique requisite of etching, answered the monumental call of war's outrage and grief. During the calamity of Germany's nationalistic fervor in 1914 and the eruption of war, Käthe and her family were caught up in the rhetoric of duty to fatherland. Her older son, Hans, joined the army, her husband cared for the sick, and Käthe volunteered as a cook and cafeteria helper.[35] Despite his parents' apprehension, eighteen-year-old Peter enlisted as a rifleman. They expected the war to end swiftly. Peter "fell" in action on October 22, 1914. And then, during a second war to protect/advance the fatherland, her grandson Peter was killed in Russia on October 12, 1942. She had to navigate the space between her love for her

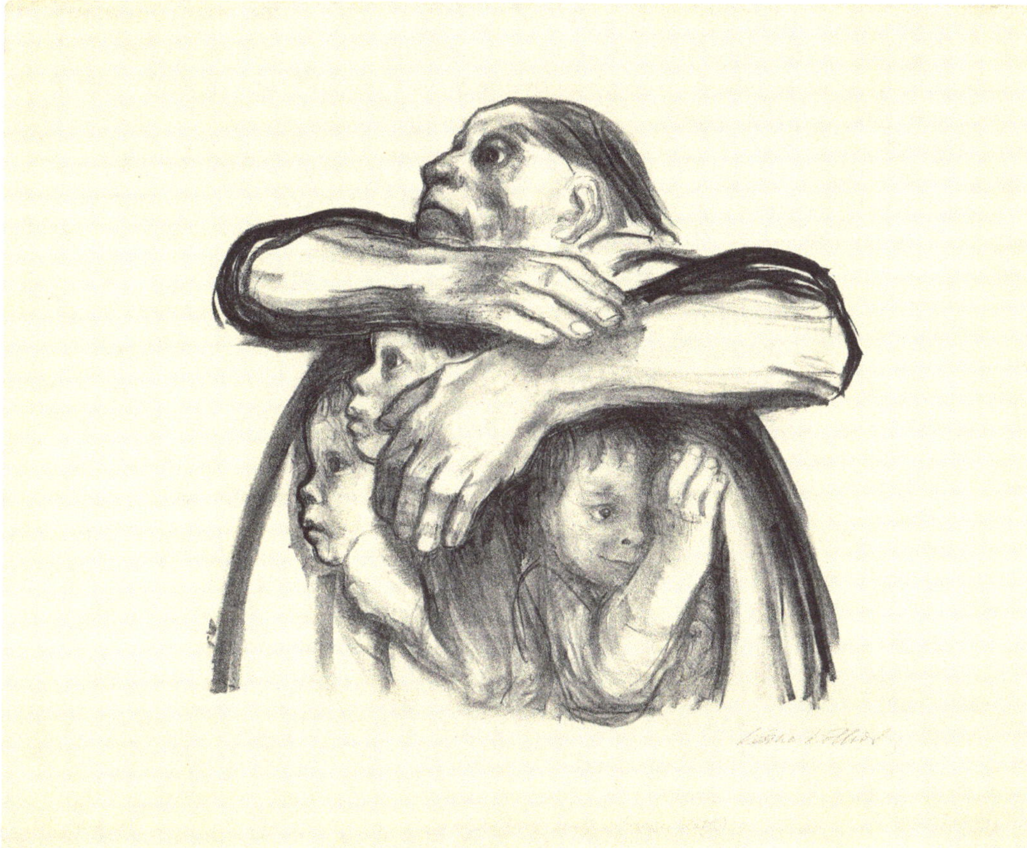

Käthe Kollwitz (1867–1945), "*Seed for sowing should not be milled,*" 1941, crayon lithograph, 370 × 395 mm, Kn 274. Käthe Kollwitz Museum Köln, Inv. Nr. 70200/87024, www.kollwitz.de.

son and grandson and their ideals of sacrifice—as German soldiers—with her own growing commitment to pacifism—and her duty as an artist. She worried that her generation had betrayed Peter (son and grandson) and millions of other younger people.

After her son Peter's death, she found the creative force within her to continue her artistry. She was inspired by Goethe's "seed corn for the planting must not be ground" (or *Seed for sowing shall not be milled*, depending on the translation) to create *Saatfrüchte sollen nicht vermahlen werden*, a 1941 lithograph; she cited this quote from Goethe in a letter protesting the continuation of World War I. It is an apt analogy of the creative seed planted within her to continue as a cultivator/artist and, more so, it is a political statement. Printed in 1942 as resistance to the Nazis' attempt to recruit children into the army, it is, fittingly, her final graphic—demanding an end to the sacrifice of our children.[36]

That seed bore the fruit of a memorial for Peter and his fellow fallen soldiers—and, as it developed—a recognition of their parents' grief. It took her eighteen years to place that monumental and reconceived memorial—the grieving father and mother—in the Roggeveld military cemetery in Belgium (relocated to Vladslo in 1956). What may be overlooked in viewing the sorrowful parents is that Kollwitz moved from a sculptural homage to an individual—her son Peter—to a collective imaginary of all the lost dead children and their grieving parents—now betrayed.

Inclined toward perfectionism, Kollwitz sought new techniques and new subject matter and found both in the German woodcut tradition. Out of this technical shift came the *Liebknecht Memorial* woodcut. Karl Liebknecht and Rosa Luxemburg, leaders of the German Communist Party and the Spartacus League, were assassinated in 1919 in Berlin. Kollwitz's woodcut groups fourteen workers surrounding Liebknecht's coffined body, including a mother holding a child above the head of a mourning worker, who holds his worn hat in one hand and with the other touches the bier. Kollwitz profiles Liebknecht's head and carefully delineates with the fluidity of her woodcutting skill the surrounding workers' facial language of disappointing loss and grief. She included a rare inscription: *Die Lebenden den Toten. Erinnerung an den 15. Januar 1919* (The Living to the Dead. In Memory of January 15, 1919). Her crowded grouping stood in for the thousands who mourned Liebknecht's death and the collapsing of a workers' revolution. Hundreds of prints of that woodcut sold for a few marks, money intended for artists and workers. (This public mourning is reminiscent of Ralph Fasanella's 1954 painting *Death of a Leader*, a tribute and memorial to the sudden death of Congressman Vito Marcantonio.)[37] During this period she also developed a series of woodcuts on the theme of war. *The War Cycle* (1921–22) pierced the militaristic and nationalistic view of war with seven woodcuts from the perspective of parents, volunteers, widows, and ordinary, powerless people. Working hands that can no longer feed and protect dominate these taut images.

Committed to the rousing and instrumental potential of art, Kollwitz responded to postwar poverty, inflation, and profiteering with a series of posters, fourteen in all. Wrestling with her own cyclical depressions, Kollwitz continued to use her tools and talent as a worker artist to visually articulate *the never-ending sufferings heaped mountain-high. This is my task, but it is not an easy one to fulfill.*[38] Combining text with a youth of indeterminate gender whose right arm and hand thrust upward and whose open mouth declares, *Nie Wieder Krieg!* [Never Again War!] (1924), Kollwitz produced an anti-war image that transcends time and geography.

Kollwitz's art making—especially during her prolific poster production in the 1920s and her self-portraits and sculpture—expresses a compression of

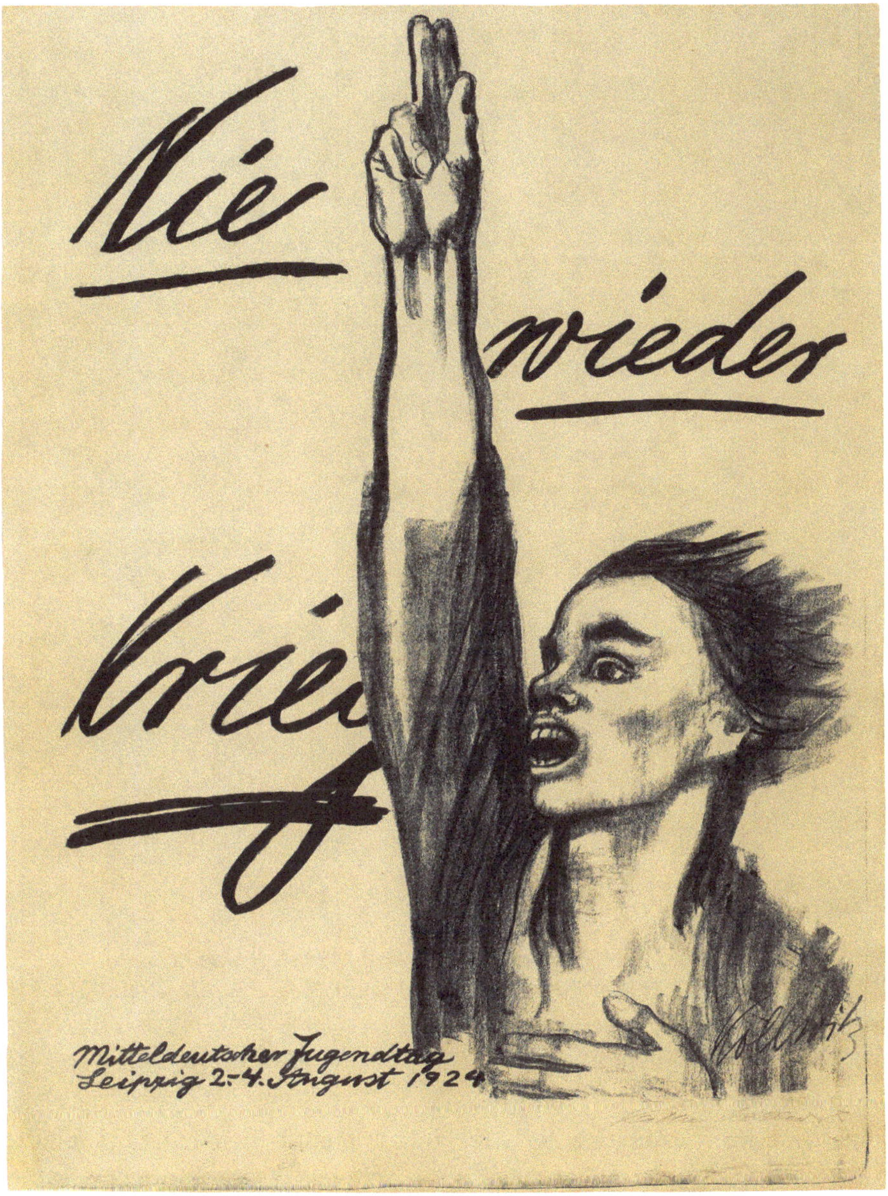

Käthe Kollwitz (1867–1945), "*Never Again War*," poster, 1924, crayon and brush lithograph, (transfer), c. 940 × 685 mm, Kn 205 III b. Käthe Kollwitz Museum Köln, Inv. Nr. 70300/88018, www.kollwitz.de.

complex feelings and experiences (Williams's "structures of feeling") within a visual distillation of form and line. This body of work endures because the artist's epistemology, her way of knowing and working, is immense. She shifted art history from male visual domination to *the woman watching who feels everything*.[39]

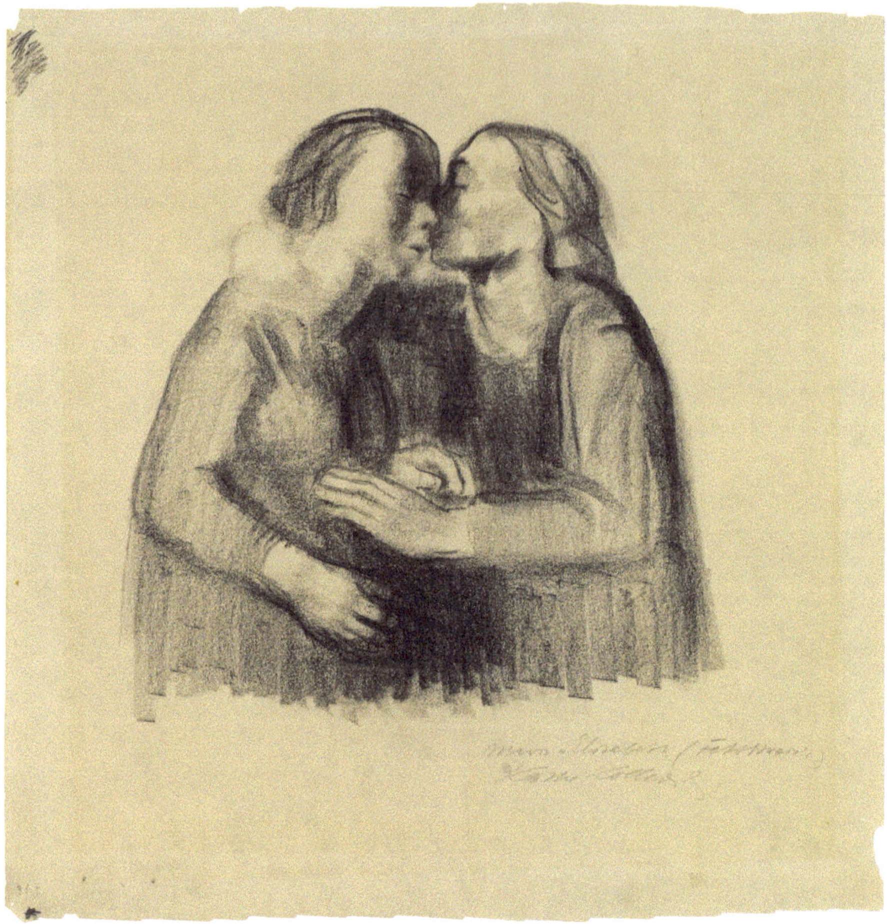

Käthe Kollwitz (1867–1945), *Maria and Elizabeth,* 1924?, grease crayon, 540 × 465 mm, NT 1134. Käthe Kollwitz Museum, Köln, Inv. Nr. 70200/01015, www.kollwitz.de.

Buoyed from exhibiting her work in communist Russia in 1927 for the revolution's ten-year anniversary, Kollwitz created a rare (for her) religious art reference—an encounter between two pregnant women—Mary, who will mother Jesus, and Elizabeth, who will mother John the Baptist (*Maria and Elisabeth,* 1924?). This tender drawing expresses a compassionate relationship of one woman towards another as they both are on the cusp of labor and the sacrifice of motherhood.

Kollwitz practiced an aesthetic of relationships and potentiality, evident in the less known lithograph *Brothers* (*Fraternity/Verbrüderung* 1924), where she depicts an older man and a younger man facing each other, arms commingled. These images of two women and two men were presciently oppositional to the emerging Nazi regime's glorification of motherhood and male allegiance to the fatherland, not to each other as workers.

In 1928 she was promoted to a full-time position at the Prussian Academy of Art, a breakthrough for a woman artist, where she taught master classes in the graphic arts. During this period, a coalition of women's organizations successfully supported the Social Democratic Party in blocking the Nazi Party (The National Socialist German Workers Party). But as Germany plunged into economic depression and chaos, the Nazi Party gained strength in the next election.

On April 22, 1931, Kollwitz exhibited plaster models for *Trauernde Eltern* [Mourning Parents]—*Die Mutter* [The Mother] and *Der Vater* [The Father]—at the Prussian Academy of Arts. To grasp the serene quality of Kollwitz's mourning parents, contrast them with the perspective and size of other memorials to soldiers on the western front of World War I. She portrays love, not military or nationalistic might. She understood in her mind and body that "grief is the price we pay for love."[40]

As Nazi governmental control loomed, Kollwitz, along with her husband Karl, Heinrich Mann (brother of Thomas Mann), Albert Einstein, and other public figures, signed an appeal to socialist and communist parties on the Left to unite in opposition to the Nazi Party. She signed a second, courageous appeal for unity against the Nazis prior to the March 1933 elections. As a result of complete Nazi control and Hitler's ascendancy, she and Heinrich Mann were forced to resign from the Academy. *I want to and must be among those who have been slapped down.*[41]

By 1936 her work vanished from public display in Germany but was increasingly recognized, purchased, and exhibited in multiple galleries in the United States. Denied her Academy studio space for sculpture, Käthe turned toward her never-waning graphic skills and produced eight lithographs on the theme of death, *Tod* [Death], as well as a profound self-portrait in 1934. She finished her last self-portrait in charcoal in 1943. In July 1936 the Gestapo interrogated Käthe and Karl because of an interview that appeared in the Moscow newspaper *Isvestija*. The Kollwitz family was shocked by Kristallnacht (November 9–10, 1938). Her sister, Lise Stern, who was married to (then diseased) George Stern, a German Jew, was vulnerable too, as their daughter Katta, a professional dancer, was forbidden by the Nazis to dance with her international troupe.

Käthe, aware of an oppressive silence since she was labeled "degenerate,"[42] turned to sculpting reliefs, first for the artist Ernst Barlach, her friend and mentor, then for the Levy family, who had not yet escaped Germany, and then one intended as a headstone for the family grave in the central cemetery in Berlin, a relief entitled, *Resting in the Peace of His Hands* (from Goethe). On July 19, 1940, Karl Kollwitz died. By 1943 Allied bombings forced her out of Berlin. On November 23, 1943, her Berlin tenement home was destroyed. Many photographs, letters, and drawings were lost. Offered refuge by the younger artist Margarete Boning until that country location was unsafe, she was then "taken in" (as she had done for Georg Gretor so many years earlier) by a collector of her work, Prince Ernst Heinrich of Saxony, and moved to two rooms in his estate in Moritzburg. There, on April 22, 1945, in the company of her granddaughter, Jutta, Hans's daughter, she died.

From her beginnings as an art student to her ending as a renowned figure fleeing Allied bombing over Germany in 1945, Käthe Kollwitz was in the world and her art was not separate from it. Considering her many somber self-portraits, drawings of impoverished proletarians, and her own struggle with the fog of depression, it is important to remember her capacity for joy—*for joy is really equivalent to strength*, she wrote in her diary.[43] She was a precursor of writers like Tillie Olsen, who also expressed a great empathetic imagination and an expansive embrace of laughter and music. Muriel Rukeyser wrote in her 1971 poem, "Epilogue: Kaethe Kollwitz," "my lifetime listens to yours."[44] Or as one writer put it, "All Roads Lead Back to Käthe Kollwitz."[45]

How to "listen" to the artistic voice of Käthe Kollwitz? She infused sound into muted suffering. She drew, sculpted, and etched the human body, especially the female body, as shelter. (See her *Aerial Bomb*, 1924/1925, brush and black ink drawing.)[46] And when circumstances—war and poverty—obliterate that shelter, when one's child is snatched away by death, she portrayed what cannot easily be seen—the missing, absent, and lost. She pushed past the parched desert of grief to claim the reciprocal, restorative power of art.

The contemporary Chinese artist Ai Weiwei connects human struggle with art making: "I think art is about human difficulties . . . I would say art itself is subversive. And it should be done in [a way that] destroys the old structure. Spiritually, it has to be violent. Not physically violent, don't get them mixed . . . An artist should be someone who has a clear vision and has a clear responsibility. And should have some skill to make the expression effectively, to be heard."[47]

Käthe Kollwitz's words, *to take life as it is and, unbroken by life—without complaining and overmuch weeping—to do one's work powerfully. Not to deny oneself, the personality one happens to be, but to embody it* [48] have sustained me, and no doubt others, in carrying the death of my own son.

Elizabeth Catlett

Long Memory

April 15, 1915, Washington, DC–
April 2, 2012, Cuernavaca, Mexico

Teach us, Forever Dead, there is no Dream but Deed, there is no Deed but Memory
—*The Autobiography of W. E. B. Du Bois*

Workers can also realize that art is a career and a social activity that is useful, and not the idle pastime that the bourgeois philosophers pretend it is.
—*Taller de Gráfica Popular*, The People's Print Shop

Art can't be the exclusive domain of the elect. It has to belong to everyone.
—Elizabeth Catlett

An Elizabeth Catlett sculpture, *Woman Fixing Her Hair,* is contained inside a vitrine in Rochester, New York's Memorial Art Gallery. The figure sits on a blunt stool. She is at rest, hands on her head. Even through the vitrine we can see the power in the figure's lower body, the strength of her legs and feet. We see the dip of her skirt covering her open legs, a sculptural Catlett signature. We do not see the statute's implicit labor. We do not see

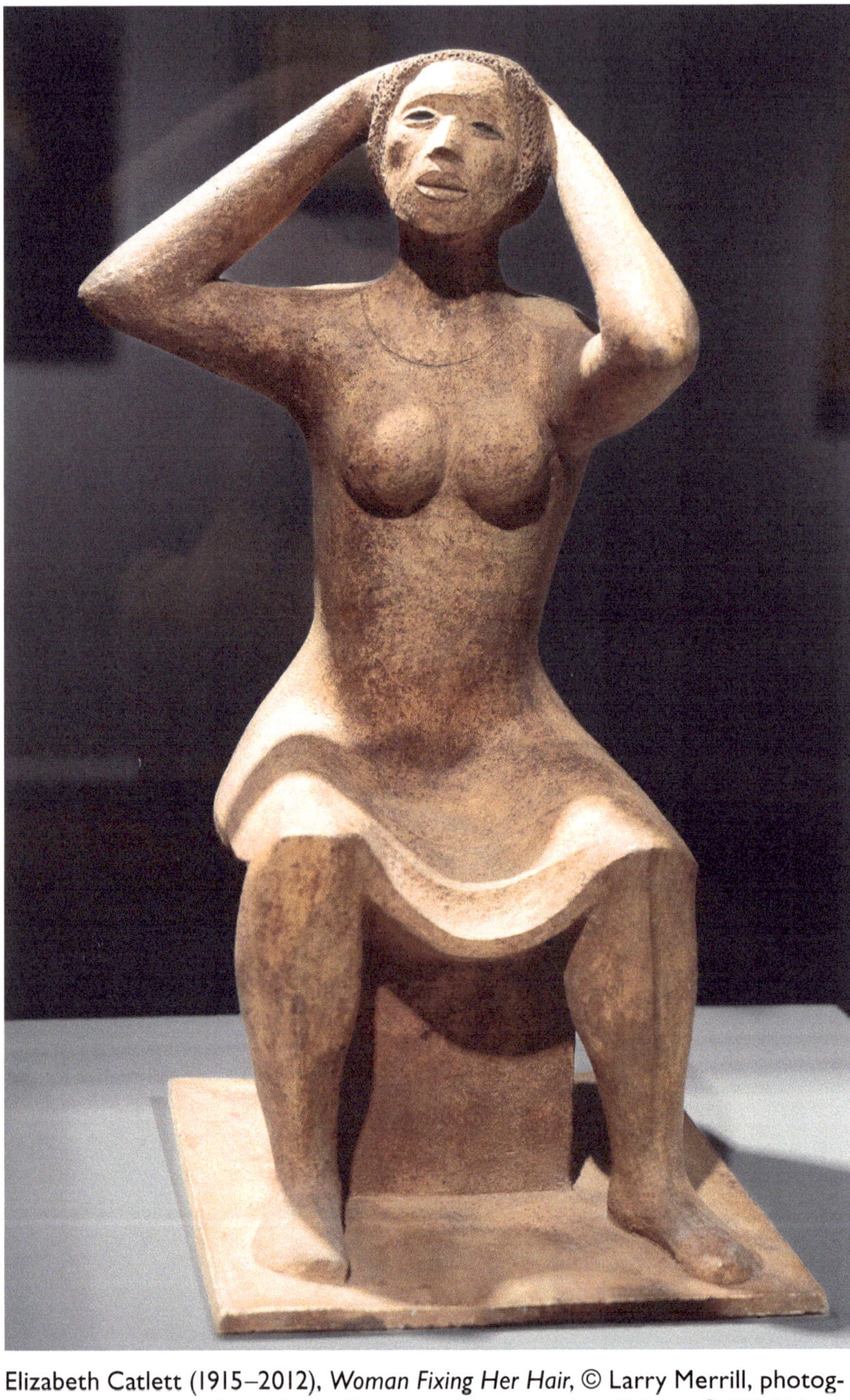

Elizabeth Catlett (1915–2012), *Woman Fixing Her Hair*, © Larry Merrill, photographer, permission, Sarah Jesse, Director, Memorial Art Gallery. © 2024 Mora-Catlett Family/Licensed by VAGA at Artists Rights Society (ARS) NY.

the work the imagined figure did *before* she sat down or the work she is *expected* to do. We cannot discern Catlett's sculptural knowledge of interiority in relation to exteriority, or how she shaped a figure from awareness of her own body. We see the protected weight of the statute but not the unsaid weight of history. After all, it is just a terracotta figure.[1]

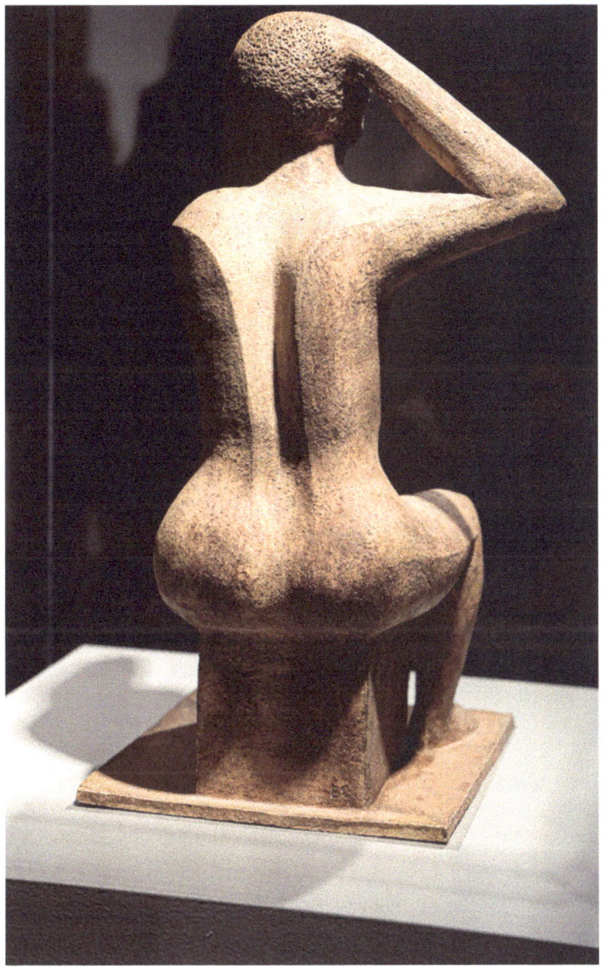

Elizabeth Catlett (1915–2012), *Woman Fixing Her Hair*, © Larry Merrill, photographer, permission, Sarah Jesse, Director, Memorial Art Gallery. © 2024 Mora-Catlett Family/Licensed by VAGA at Artists Rights Society (ARS) NY.

The identifying label in 2021 states that Catlett "was deeply committed to the causes of social justice" and that after Catlett completed her formal education, she moved to Mexico where she "chose to stay." The museum's rewritten and shorter label in 2024 identifies Catlett as "Mexican, born United States," as did the earlier version, and also connects her work to indigenous sculptural traditions. Words carry deeper contextual meanings. The word "chose" used in the earlier label assumes a degree of autonomy that Catlett had only in a very complicated and limited way. It does not encompass the shaping circumstances—political, economic, and racial—that Catlett faced in Jim Crow and Cold War–era America. However, "chose" does fit Catlett's awareness of the public art movement in Mexico (post 1910 revolution) and its potential for socially conscious art.

The Whitney Museum in New York exhibits a Catlett sculpture, *Head* (1947), unenclosed. The accompanying label identifies Washington, DC, as her place of birth (maybe a better identifier than nationality) and states, "Elizabeth Catlett believed that making artworks about ordinary people was a political gesture." This is closer to Catlett's political context. Museum labels, perfect or imperfect, are, necessarily, short. The more complex issue (and challenge for museums) is how they *invite* the viewer to learn more,

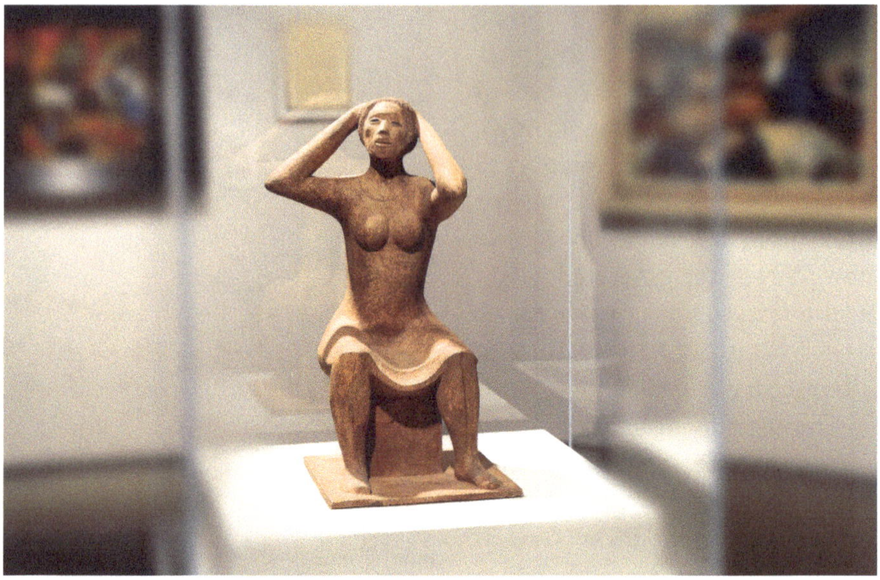

Elizabeth Catlett (1915–2012), *Woman Fixing Her Hair,* © Larry Merrill, photographer, permission, Sarah Jesse, Director, Memorial Art Gallery. ©2024 Mora-Catlett Family/Licensed by VAGA at Artists Rights Society (ARS) NY.

to explore the artwork's hidden meanings as well as the artist's creative process *after* looking carefully at the work itself.

Alice Elizabeth Catlett was born in Freedmen's Hospital in Washington, DC, in 1915, the granddaughter of enslaved people. Her father, John Catlett, was a professor of mathematics at Tuskegee Institute, as well as a musician and woodcarver, who died shortly before her birth. She was raised by her mother, Mary Carson Catlett, a widow with three young children, a teacher and later a truant officer/social worker in DC public schools, who had to take on extra jobs to support her children. Mary Catlett recognized Elizabeth's early pleasure in drawing, bringing her pencils, crayons, and paper, and supporting her aspirations to be an artist. On the difference her educated parents made in her life, Catlett said, *I was able to study and became a sculptor—a field generally reserved for white men—only because my ex-slave grandparents could educate my mother, and she, in turn, as a widow would dedicate herself to the education of her children. So, you see, I am not of the exceptional. I am rather of the fortunate.*[2] The viewer of *Woman Fixing Her Hair* cannot see the trajectory of Catlett's life—the American strand of racial and political oppression or the Mexican strand of communal art making, nor can the viewer perceive the inseparability of her political consciousness from her artistry. So much is embedded in the *ordinary*, a statue of a woman fixing her hair.

Elizabeth Catlett was a practicing artist, inspiring teacher, and avid learner all her life. We know about her formal education at Howard University in Washington, DC, and at the State University of Iowa in Iowa City, but her earned degrees offer only a glimpse of her development as an artist. On the occasion of the opening of a Catlett exhibit at the Columbia Museum of Art in South Carolina in 2022, Wendell George Brown, professor, gallery director, and fiber artist, used the geological term "stratigraphic," indicating layers of sediments and rock formations, to discuss the evolution of Catlett's life and work. He imaginatively listens to the stories Catlett heard from her maternal grandparents about slavery and emancipation, noting how these stories were etched into Catlett's DNA.[3] Catlett reclaimed her family's history of surviving enslavement, and also caught some of the spirit of her grandmother's resistance and inherent dignity. *My grandmother had no inhibitions about talking of slavery.*[4]

Catlett decided to be an artist when she was a child. That future was nourished at Dunbar High School (named after Paul Laurence Dunbar, author of the poem "We Wear the Mask").[5] Her art teacher, Haley Douglass, was a descendant of Frederick Douglass. These are early rock formations, strata of political awareness layered within her developing artistic skills. *I remember in high school, standing in front of the Supreme Court building in Washington with a noose around my neck, protesting lynching. I don't remember what group it was, all I remember was that the police took us away.*[6]

Catlett's young resistance calls to mind Audre Lorde's (1934–1992) encounter with Jim Crow Washington, DC, when she and her family were denied service at a soda fountain. The trip was intended as a high school graduation present for Audre but became a racial revelation instead: "The waitress was white, and the counter was white, and the ice cream I never ate in Washington, DC that summer I left childhood was white, and the white heat and the white pavement and the white stone monuments of my first Washington summer made me sick to my stomach for the whole rest of the trip and it wasn't much of a graduation present after all."[7]

Catlett answered the white racism of Washington, DC, through her sculptural imagination and her skill in shaping her materials—whether black marble or mahogany or clay or orange onyx—into forms, inseparably abstract and representational, that announce the past inside the present.

There was no question that Elizabeth would go to college after high school. Her first choice was Carnegie Tech in Pittsburgh (now Carnegie Mellon). The admissions committee was impressed with her application but rescinded her acceptance: "It's too bad she's colored."[8] Instead, in 1931 she went to Howard University, whose pioneering art department was led by practicing and accomplished artists James V. Herring, James A. Porter, Loïs Mailou Jones, and James Lesesne Wells. She began as a design major but changed to painting in her third year. Howard University initiated her into a world of ideas and debates about art—on modernism and traditionalism, and on European, African, and Latin lineages. She began to see art from a transatlantic perspective that included African sculpture and textiles, as well as the communal sensibility of Mexican muralists. In her third year at Howard, she acquired some extra income with the Public Works of Art Project (PWAP), a job arranged by her teachers, but she painted few murals and did not continue in the program. Her interest was sculpture. She graduated from Howard University in 1935 and then taught art for two years in Durham, North Carolina, where she fought to obtain equal pay for Black teachers with white teachers.[9] As a high school art teacher, responsible as well for supervising art programs for eight elementary schools, she earned $59 a month, about half of what she would have made if she were white.[10] Finding it difficult to be both a public school teacher and a developing artist, she pursued a graduate art degree in what seems like an unlikely place—the State University of Iowa in Iowa City, where it was less expensive to live and study. American painter Grant Wood was one of her professors. She learned a methodical way of working and thinking from him (as Ruth Asawa did from Josef Albers) and responded to his advice about telling *her* own story, creatively.

> *I found out for the first time from the way he worked that creating a work of art has a process. . . . He made us begin with a line drawing. First, he said, "What are you going to do? It should be something that you know the most about." I decided to do a little black girl ironing; I knew a lot about ironing. Then we did a diagram, from which we reworked our line drawing. Then we did a drawing on brown wrapping paper using charcoal and chalk to get the values straight, and only then could we go into a painting, where we limited to three or four colors. And as we learned what we could do with those colors, then we could add other colors.*[11]

Catlett interpreted regionalism, a term associated with Grant Wood, as more about communities of peoples than a specific place and geography. She became the first student in Iowa's graduate program to earn a master of fine arts in sculpture. Her first exhibited sculpture, *Negro Mother and Child* (1940, location unknown, limestone, 35" height), is the beginning of a large body of work honoring Black maternity. This thesis sculpture won first prize in sculpture at the Diamond Jubilee of Negro Progress (1940, also known as the Black World's Fair, commemorating the seventy-fifth anniversary of the end of slavery) in Chicago. Catlett wrote her intentions in her thesis statement: *To create a composition of two figures, one smaller than the other, so interlaced as to be expressive of maternity, and so compact as to be suitable to stone, seemed quite a desirable problem. The implications of motherhood, especially Negro motherhood, are quite important to me, as I am a Negro as well as a woman.*[12] Catlett created this mother/child sculpture when she was around twenty-four years old, before she became a mother herself. This was the beginning of her many sculptures, whether in clay, wood, bronze, or stone, of the physical fusion between a mother and her baby child.

Catlett was keenly aware of the labor of mothering, the strength it takes to give birth and to care for a child: *Because I am a woman and know how a woman feels in body and mind, I sculpt, draw, and print women, generally black women. Many of my sculptures and prints deal with maternity because I am a mother and a grandmother. Once in a while I do men because I love my husband and sons. I share their sorrows and joys and I fear for them in the unsettled world of today.*[13] Over the decades, Catlett's political perceptions of "unsettled worlds" would sharpen her transnational feminism. In 1963 she attended the Congress of Women of the Americas in Cuba and was a member of the Unión Nacional de Mujeres Mexicanas (National Union of Mexican Women). Motherhood, as Catlett always understood, is not sentimentality.

Catlett was inclined to extract the best from whatever her location or circumstances. She advised students to learn from their teachers even if the teacher's art practice didn't match their own style. There is something to be learned from a teacher's experience, especially if they themselves are makers (as Ruth Asawa advocated). Still, there was the complexity of the political moment. Catlett never had the luxury of being untouched by external political and racist forces. Iowa was a white world. Since she could not live in the segregated dorms, she found housing off campus with the writer Margaret Walker (1915–1998), author of the prose poem "For My People."[14] This is one instance of the rich cross-currents of Black women's cultures, then and now. Catlett's relationships and friendships, especially with other Black women, deepen our understanding of cultural formations, whether in visual arts or literature or music: art making is not an isolated thing but part of a larger movement. Catlett highlights this difference:

> *We work alone but we also work with and for others, and it is expressed by two words:* one *is "solitarity," in which we create out of what is in us, from our innermost feelings, ideas, emotions, knowledge—all of this combined in other elements also; we also create from "solidarity," which is what we have in our inner most selves that comes from what we have gotten from our solidarity with other people. I always feel that collective thought is better than individual thought. There's the give-and-take and coming together and a separating that are very important in developing ideas.*[15]

In 1940 Catlett returned to teaching art. First she took a summer job at Prairie View College in Texas and then became chair of the art department at Dillard College in New Orleans (now Dillard University, a historically Black college). Samella Lewis, artist, art historian, and collector of African American art, was one of her students. Lewis recalls how Catlett encouraged her and other students to develop their own art collections by purchasing art, perhaps for $10 a week or month, *from each other*. She also recalls Catlett defying (and sometimes discarding) "sit in the back of the bus" signs in Jim Crow New Orleans.[16] Lewis said that Catlett wanted people who weren't educated to understand what she was trying to do with her art. Catlett raised this question: *How do we go about opening the door to get Black people, who have been principally involved in survival, interested in the arts?*[17] Catlett's works, whether in the graphic arts or sculpture, show how collective knowledge inhabits individual bodies and consciousness. Wendell George Brown, director of the Henry Ponder Gallery at Benedict College (Columbia, South Carolina), distinguishes between Catlett's appreciation of murals and her own inclination to "liberate" a figure in a mural and then widen that individual life to suggest its many cultural and political resonances.[18]

Catlett wanted her students to have access to the larger world of art. When a traveling Picasso exhibit, *Picasso: Forty Years of His Art*, opened at the Isaac Delgado Museum (now the New Orleans Museum of Art), Catlett, having visited this exhibit in New York and Chicago, was determined to take her students to see it, but she faced the obstacle of the museum's location in segregated City Park.

> *I was teaching art at Dillard University in New Orleans. Late that fall, when a retrospective exhibition of Picasso's paintings . . . came to New Orleans' Delgado Art Museum, I decided to take the 130 young Black men and women in my art history class to see it. But the museum was closed to us because it was in City Park, where Blacks were not permitted. Through a friend I arranged a visit . . . when the museum was closed, and we were bussed in. The students were excited and fascinated by the paintings. . . . No one had ever been in an art museum before.*[19]

Catlett resigned from Dillard after faculty were forced to teach summer school on their ten-month contracts.

In the summer of 1941, Catlett traveled to Chicago, where she studied lithography at the South Side Community Art Center and ceramics at the School of the Art Institute of Chicago. In Chicago she was involved with a community of artist activists, what became known as the Black Chicago Renaissance, and met her first husband, the artist Charles White. In 1942 she and White moved to Harlem, New York, where they joined a circle of Black writers and artists. This period was rich with experiential learning for her, especially when she began teaching in 1944 at George Washington Carver School, a Harlem community school opened to workers, where she offered classes in sculpture *and* sewing, witnessed poverty that was not part of her previous lived experience, and observed the hunger for culture of ordinary people. Her praxis threaded theoretical conversations about class and race, part of her intellectual milieu, with her deepening awareness of the actual economic and racial discrimination her worker students faced. Her class-consciousness involved learning *from* poor and working-class people, reciprocally, not just in voicing charitable concern. The daughter of teachers, Catlett understood, in the words of Paulo Freire, "the great political importance of the teaching act," as well as how memory, Freire's "many fabrics," soaked in history and culture, is carried.[20] She visualized the work of *maestras*, women teachers (a Mexican visual motif) in her 1953 lithograph *Alfabetización* with its implicit liberatory message. She advised young people to pursue education but *base what they're doing on all of us.* That sensibility guided her direction in art, her decision to portray Black women as *beautiful, dignified, strong people*, and *to take art to our people who do not go to museums, and to do this we have to get art by our people into museums.*[21]

Catlett was attuned to the dialogic process as a teacher but also as a learner, acquiring ideas and techniques from her teachers that she would interpret and use as they fit her own consciousness and skills as a developing and teaching artist. In New York's Greenwich Village, she studied briefly in 1942 with émigré sculptor Ossip Zadkine (who also taught a summer course at Black Mountain College) and through observing his practice, expanded her awareness of the potentialities of concave and convex forms as well as the abstract and representational qualities of African art. In 1943 she accompanied Charles White to Hampton Institute (now University) in Hampton, Virginia, when White won a Rosenwald grant to paint a mural, *The Contribution of the Negro to Democracy in America.* Like her experiences in Harlem's Carver Community School, this was another period of dialogic teaching and learning for her—she taught sculpture for a semester at Hampton and learned through her conversations with Hampton professor Viktor Lowenfeld about artistic development in children and about visual-haptic approaches to art education. Lowenfeld expanded Catlett's orbit of intellectuals who influenced her art making. Always conscious of the value of technique and honed skills, she studied sculpture with Francisco Zúñiga during her early years in Mexico, and some years later, woodcarving with sculptor José L. Ruiz. These are some of the stratifications and sediments of Catlett's development as an artist, an ongoing process (akin to Kollwitz's sense of *Bildung*). She was an extraordinary gleaner, not an imitator.

In 1945 she won a Julius Rosenwald Fellowship, renewed in 1946, which funded her travel to Mexico, where she proposed working on *a series of linoleum cuts, paintings, and sculpture depicting the oppression, struggles and achievements of the black woman.* These were intended as resistance not only to stereotypes and caricatures, but also to the erasure of Black women's lives, work, and historical contributions. She was committed to distributive public art practices and decided to focus on making linocut prints rather than on painting murals. In Mexico City she joined the *Taller de Gráfica Popular* (TGP), a collective workshop rooted in Mexico's long graphic arts tradition and practice, and worked alongside some thirty Mexican artists:

> *We did linoleum prints because that is a suitable medium for public art—easy and inexpensive and you can make the editions as large as you need them. We*

were involved in the problems of the Mexican people: many of the artists in the group were developed socially and politically. We worked for trade unions, student organizations, and for the government's anti-illiteracy campaign to build schools. Here were strong artists and weak artists, and each one learned from the other. Everybody offered something. When you saw the results, you saw a collective product that you had helped to form even if you were not as technically advanced as some of the other artists. It makes a difference in your desire to work and your understanding of what you're doing. And, at the same time, we did individual work too. I would say that this was a great social experience. I learned how to put art in the service of people.

The people were exposed to art because it was placed around as posters and leaflets all over town. People would come to the workshop if they had problems: if students were on strike, or if trade unions had labor disputes, or if peasants had problems about their land, they would come into the workshop and ask for something to express their concerns. The artists at the Taller would volunteer to do the work together or individually; after the preliminary sketches were made they were put up for more collective discussion.[22]

Catlett now had some time and space to develop her own ideas, long germinating. Her series *The Negro Woman* (1946–47), later retitled *The Black Woman series*, blended historical knowledge (based on available reproduced images as well as texts) with her informed empathy for contemporary Black women (vulnerable to sexual and racial assaults) to produce technically accomplished and accessible visual narratives. Consider the Mexican collective imaginary combined with Catlett's history-infused assemblage of so many parts and pieces as visual *commons* and the distribution of prints as visual *commoning*. Influenced by the *Taller*'s large portfolio of linocuts of the Mexican Revolution, *Estampas de la Revolución Mexicana*, and drawing on her own insights about the pedagogical agency as well as aesthetic power of works in a series (such as those by painter Jacob Lawrence),[23] Catlett produced a visual "poem" of fifteen linoleum cuts that presented the lives and history of enslaved, freed, working-class, and impoverished Black women in the context of racial oppression in America. A skilled and published writer, Catlett's captions work dialectically and informatively with each linoleum cut. She begins with *I am the Negro Woman* and draws/cuts a determined outward glance of a single Black woman. But Catlett's declarative "I" is not singular; it announces something larger, a tunnelling into the history of African Americans through the lives of Black women. Her "I" is a Whitmanian, historically rooted, collective containing many "we's." This multiple "I" is threaded through all the subsequent figures: *I Have Always Worked Hard in America* . . . features three women bending, crouching, kneeling, and cleaning—most likely—other people's homes.

This image might be viewed as her city depiction as contrasted to . . . *In the Fields*, where she presents a barefoot woman hoeing rows of crops, with a sharecropper's shack in the background. . . . *In Other Folks' Homes* portrays a single woman with her tool, a broom, evoking with her posture not only a familiar Grant Wood painting, but all the Black women employed as cleaners by white families, "the Black Back-Ups," as the poet sings.[24] And then there's a turn in the series toward culture and history: *I have given the world my songs.*

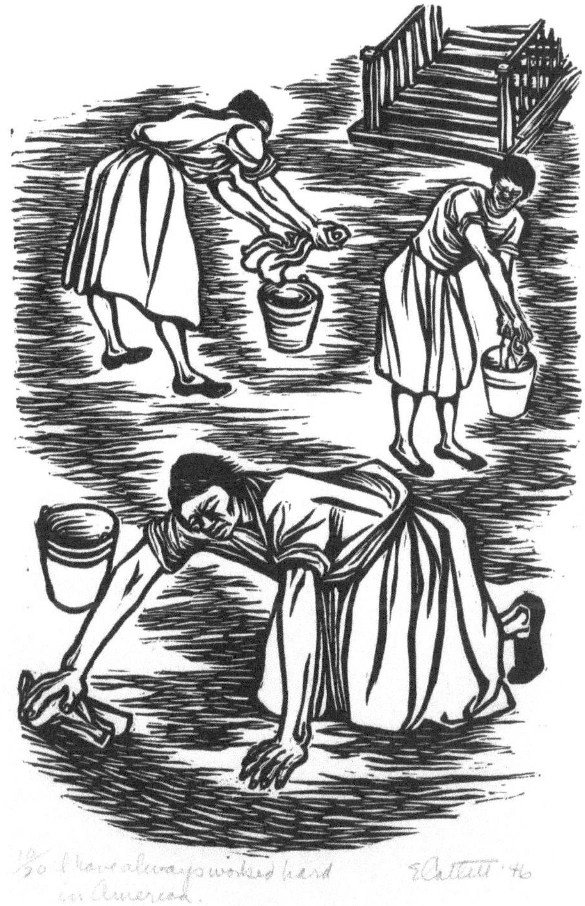

Elizabeth Catlett (1915–2012), "I Have Always Worked Hard in America," from *The Negro Woman*, 1946–47 [*The Black Woman* series]. Linocut, 8½ x 6 inches. Permanent Art Collection. Miami-Dade Public Library System. ©2024 Mora-Catlett Family/Licensed by VAGA at Artists Rights Society (ARS) NY.

In the foreground, a Black woman plays a guitar. The figure is concentrating on the music. Her knee bends slightly with the weight of the guitar—notice the dip in her skirt, reminiscent of *Woman Fixing Her Hair*. In the swirling background, Catlett cut into the linoleum a white cross in flames and a white-hooded Klansman attacking a Black man. This context of racial oppression is inseparable from the language of Black music—sorrow songs, blues, jazz, soul. Catlett, like the father she never knew, had musical inclinations and expressed a desire to become a blues singer at one time but turned toward the visual arts instead.[25] Perhaps she was familiar with European paintings like Renoir's portraits of women and guitars, as well as with how guitars are represented or abstracted in the paintings of Georges Braque and Pablo Picasso. Charles White also painted a couple, man and woman, with guitars. Or was she inspired by *The Banjo Lesson* (1893) by Henry Ossawa Tanner and his stunning depiction of teaching and learning, from the old to the young, the wealth of culture despite the poverty of ordinary life? Years later, Catlett recognized how dictatorships seek to destroy indigenous culture in her 1986 linocut *Central America Says No* and the murder of singer/song writer Victor Jara in Chile under the Pinochet regime. (This link between political violence sup-

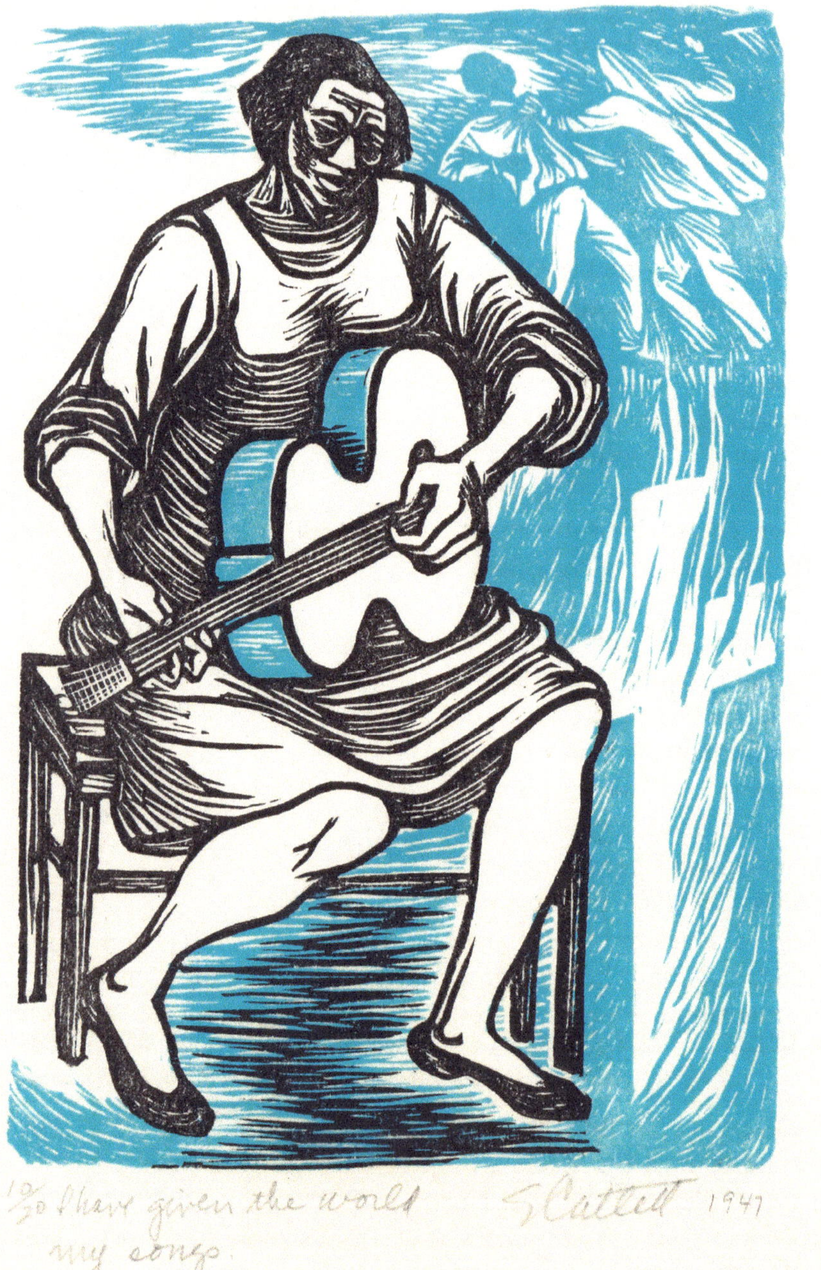

Elizabeth Catlett (1915–2012), "I have given the world my songs," or *Blues* from *The Negro Woman*, 1946–47 [*The Black Woman* series]. Color Linocut. 7½ x 5 inches. Permanent Art Collection, Miami-Dade Public Library System. ©2024 Mora-Catlett Family/Licensed by VAGA at Artists Rights Society (ARS) NY.

pressing cultural expressions is well documented in Marilyn Anderson's work on textiles in Guatemala.)

Catlett's drawings/linocuts of historical figures teach Black history, especially the contributions of women, through visual representations: Her linocut *In Phillis Wheatley I Proved Intellectual Equality in the Midst of Slavery* links illiteracy to the chains of enslavement. Born in West Africa, Phillis Wheatley (1753–1784) wrote a book of her own poetry at a time of limited literacy for Blacks and most whites. With Wheatley, Catlett locates the beginnings of a deeply textured lineage of Black women writers. The linocut *In Sojourner Truth I fought for the Rights of Women as well as Blacks* recognizes *voice—speeches*—as well as writings by evoking Sojourner Truth's 1851 "Ain't I A Woman?" women's rights speech. *In Harriet Tubman I Helped Hundreds to Freedom* Catlett depicts Tubman, one of the conductors in the Underground Railroad, showing the road out of slavery to Black families, a man with a bundle over his shoulder, a woman holding a baby. This is a reminder of a longer, continuous migration history, out of slavery, out of Jim Crow South, out of discriminatory housing and working conditions, toward freedom and elusive equality. Catlett created two more linocuts of Tubman, *Harriet Tubman* (1953–54, reproduced in Paul Robeson and Louis Burnham's Harlem newspaper, *Freedom*) and the dynamic *Harriet* in 1975. The physicality of Catlett's 1975 *Harriet* is reminiscent of Käthe Kollwitz's *Black Anna.* Catlett knew and admired Kollwitz's graphic portraits. Catlett was drawn to Tubman's liberatory human (and military?) imagination (as, perhaps, Kollwitz was to Black Anna). In November 2024, Harriet Tubman received a posthumous commission as a brigadier general in the Maryland National Guard.

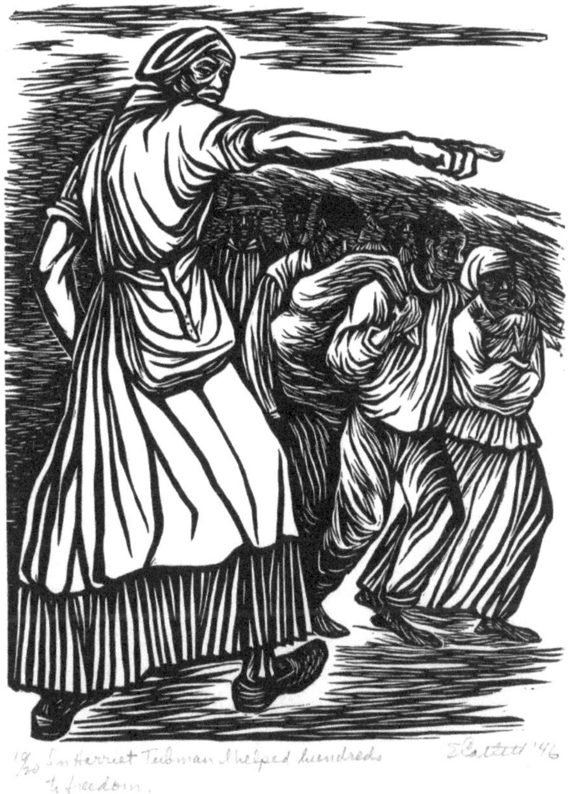

Elizabeth Catlett (1915–2012), "In Harriet Tubman I Helped Hundreds to Freedom," from *The Negro Woman*, 1946–47 [*The Black Woman* series]. Linocut, 9 × 6⅞ inches. Permanent Art Collection, Miami-Dade Public Library System ©2024 Mora-Catlett Family/Licensed by VAGA at Artists Rights Society (ARS) NY.

Catlett, the teaching artist, writes complete sentences instead of just the names of the figures. Notice the potency of the preposition *in*. These figures are *in history* and *in* the lineage of Black American struggle. And so, viewer, student, and creator are all, also, *in* history. Catlett invites historical consciousness—in everyone.

Catlett moves from historical references to illuminating Jim Crow America with her ironic treatment of *specialness*. *I Have Special Reservations* presents four Black women sitting (not by choice) in the back of a bus with the sign "Colored Only" across the body of the foregrounded figure. Catlett continues her ironic observations with . . . *Special Houses*, that is, decrepit and more expensive housing "reserved" for Blacks. These images remind contemporary viewers of the lasting effects of red-lining in cities and suburbs across this country.

(I wonder whether Catlett was familiar with the photography of Marion Palfi, a European émigré, who photographed the contradictions between American democracy as an ideal and the realities of American racial segregation [apartheid?]. Palfi, a friend of Langston Hughes, published photographs in Black newspapers and magazines of juxtaposed white and Black schools, segregated housing, and an image [which is little known, but deserves to be iconic] of a Black man and Black woman sitting in the back of a bus beneath a "This Part of the Bus for the Colored Race" sign.)

Special reservations.[26]

Like Käthe Kollwitz, Catlett acknowledged and depicted resistance and struggle. Her linocut *My Role has been Important in the Struggle to Organize the Unorganized*, presents a Black woman labor organizer raising a clenched fist as she talks to mixed-race male workers. Catlett recognized, from her socialist/communist circles in Chicago and New York and from Mexican labor rights activism, the fight for safe and equal working conditions as a multiracial struggle. Her Black woman organizer reminds us of Maida Springer Kemp and Hattie Canty, and so many other women fighters for labor. It also points to the reality of Black workers forced into blind alley menial jobs, "reserved" for them.

I Have Studied in Ever Increasing Numbers recalls Black women's determination to be educated as well as the path taken by the women in Catlett's own family, from her grandmother's enslavement to her mother's college degree. *My reward has been bars between me and the rest of the land* is timely today, as it evokes awareness of the continuous arrests and imprisonment of Black women in higher proportions than white women, and with longer sentences.[27]

. . . *And a special fear for my loved ones* depicts a Black man with a knotted rope around his neck. Is he lying on the ground or is he swirling in space? Near his body are the shoes of other men; are they too dangling in space or are they stepping on the rope as observers or as resisters? Catlett's images have stratifications, layers of meaning. In addition to recognizing the legitimate fear (past and present) Black mothers have for the safety of their children, especially in encounters with police, the viewer might also acknowledge the pleasure some whites enjoyed in witnessing lynchings.[28] *My right is a future of equality with other Americans* is a single, heavily textured and lined face peering upward, a perfect drawing of hope and possibility.[29] Consider how pioneering Catlett's narrative of Black women's history and culture was then (1946–47) and its importance now as an accessible, visual commons. From a teacher's perspective, it is a model of compressed historical lessons.

Although not a continuation of this series, Catlett produced other historically informed and race-conscious linocuts about American history. *Civil Rights Congress* (1950) depicts a boy sitting safely on a chair, surviving the threat of the lynching rope and the white sheeted Klan/death figure, because of the work of the CRC, Civil Rights Congress.[30] In *Sharecropper* (1952), a sturdy older Black woman with a straw hat and a safety pin in her sweater announces something more than survival. Her body speaks strength, knowledge, and dignity. But the title also utters another language of sharecropping injustice: tilling someone else's land for meager income. The benign word "share" belies the exploitative, punitive debt system that affected whites as well as Blacks. This may be somewhat different (I do not know the conditions of the rental) from Ruth Asawa's parents who had to rent their land because they were not allowed, as Japanese, to purchase it.

Elizabeth Catlett did not separate race oppression from class oppression from gender oppression. Her exposure to the cultural and economic circumstances of workers in Harlem's Carver school underscored her understanding of how labor intersects with race and gender. She produced a series of portraits of workers between 1942 and 1946 that included *War Worker* (1944), *Red Cross Woman (Nurse)* (1944), and *Black Worker* (1945). Not part of The *Black Woman* series is a lesser-known lithograph of a Black woman in a segregated restaurant, *Restaurant Patron (for Colored Only)* (1946). Catlett was well acquainted with segregated spaces. A Red Cross–certified swimmer, she integrated Iowa University pools.

Catlett's first solo exhibit was at the Barnett-Aden Gallery in Washington, DC, "Paintings, Sculpture, and Prints of the Negro Woman," in December 1947. Cofounded by one of Catlett's Howard University art professors, James V. Herring, the Barnett-Aden Gallery (1943–1969) was the first Black-owned commercial art gallery in the United States.

After returning to New York to divorce Charles White, she established Mexican residency in 1947 when she married Mexican artist Francisco Mora and later became the mother of their three sons (Francisco Mora Catlett, musician, Juan Mora Catlett, filmmaker, David Mora Catlett, visual artist).

Moving permanently to Mexico enabled Catlett to get some relief (at least until the collusion between the reactionary Mexican government and the

United States House Un-American Activities Committee) from America's racial and political oppressions. It also enriched her view of the possibilities, artistically and politically, of common art. *Taller De Gráfica Popular* (TGP, People's Graphic Arts Workshop) was catalytic for Catlett, perhaps as Black Mountain College was for Ruth Asawa. The TGP was concerned with the efficacy of art to advance emancipatory/political consciousness as well as literacy. Catlett acquired, through TGP, not only a refining of her graphic skills, but also a methodology for informing and critiquing art in a communal setting. During TGP weekly Friday night meetings, attended by members and others, projects were discussed and individual prints were critiqued. *Each artist would select a theme, go home, and do a drawing. Then the drawings were brought in and put up so we could see how they related to the assignment. The criticism was always constructive.* Catlett brought this critique method into her home as well where she, her husband, Francisco Mora, and children (when available) would "discuss the ways an idea or concept can be visualized formally."[31] Perhaps Milton Rogovin learned this method of critique from Catlett. Rogovin would post one of his photographs on the bulletin board above the family's kitchen table and everyone would study and critique it.

In Mexico she worked within a politically conscious community of artists and artisans with a keen sense of audience and agency. Her "I" was never a solo figure. Her life and work encompassed historical knowledge, an informed, skilled, and talented presence, and an imagined future, not necessarily about her own fame, but rather about the necessity of art, how essential it is to the formation and sustenance of community. She never wavered from identifying herself as a Black woman, born in the United States, who lived in Mexico. Citing Stuart Hall's writing on identity, Catlett's biographer Melanie Herzog posits Catlett's grounding as a Black woman as being an informed *positioning*, not an essence.[32]

Think of Catlett (maybe anyone?) in plural terms: she had *identities* in dialogue with *communities*.

The importance of community to Catlett's artistic and human development cannot be overstated. It is worth pausing over the ubiquitous word *community* to appreciate the breadth of Catlett's vision and practice. In *Keywords*, Raymond Williams traces how community is grounded etymologically (and often materially; see introduction) in the commons or common people, especially to distinguish them from those of rank or in locations of central power, as well as to parse the difference between the commons and amorphous notions of society.[33] Williams realized that the word community could be usurped by un-communal forces and so he emphasized its meaning in relation to mutuality, responsibility, affirmation, and reciprocity. These are Catlett's communal sensibilities, and they are matched by her emotional strength, intellectual imagination, and deep technical artistry.

Catlett, though, had to live through anti-communal political realities, including the Mexican government's efforts to suppress national strikes. She was freer in Mexico without having to face stubborn U.S. Jim Crow racism, but she wasn't free from Cold War political censorship and oppression. In 1955 she was summoned to the United States embassy and questioned about her political affiliations. In 1959, according to Herzog, "one evening, when she was alone with her children, a group of men came to the door, demanded that she identify herself, and took her away without explanation. She was imprisoned for several days."[34] Catlett's experience, that of being suddenly, yet not unexpectedly, *unsafe* was like the Gestapo's threatening knock on the door of Käthe and Karl Kollwitz's home in 1936, and like Milton Rogovin's summons to appear before the House Un-American Activities Committee in 1957 or the arrest of Ruth Asawa's father in 1942 while he was tending his strawberry fields. How do artists sustain their creative concentration if they are not safe? How is unsafety threaded through their work?

In 1961 Catlett presented "The Negro Artist and American Art at Mid-Century," a keynote address at the National Conference of Negro Artists (founded in 1959) in Washington, DC. Her speech linked her communal Mexican experience with her desire to make art accessible to African American communities: *let us exhibit where Negro people meet—in the churches, in the schools and universities, in the associations and clubs and trade unions* . . . And, typical of Catlett's grasp of the reciprocal and answerable elements of art making, she added, *let us seek inspiration in the Negro people—a principal and never ending source.*[35]

After the experience of being arrested and out of her awareness of her political vulnerability, Catlett decided to apply for Mexican citizenship, which was granted in 1962. She was unable to return to the United States for another ten years because she could not get a visa, having been identified as an "undesirable alien" by the U.S. State Department. Her TGP membership and graphic work sustained her during her early years in Mexico living in modest circumstances and raising, with a supportive husband, three children close in age. By the mid-1950s, she was able to return to sculpture (after her youngest was in school full time). In 1959 she had her own studio as professor of sculpture at the Escuela Nacional de Artes Plásticas, where she had her first Mexican solo exhibit. She won the Tlatilco Prize in Mexico's first national Sculpture Biennial for her large-scale *Figura* in 1962. While she emphasized acquiring technical skills as the most important element of attending art school, she also encouraged students' intellectual development, encouraging them to read about the lives of diverse artists.[36] Her life story is also about women's work as caregivers and women's work as creative beings and how to sustain them both. It is a struggle for time. Time for oneself (such as fixing one's hair), time to think, time to develop one's work.

In the 1960s Abstract Expressionism influenced the Mexican art world. Catlett, though, well aware of the political and aesthetic efforts to resist race oppression in America, was drawn to the Black Arts Movement and the shaping of a Black aesthetic. Like Kollwitz's commitment to producing posters as an element of political struggle, she produced a multilingual serigraph poster, *Freedom for Angela Davis and All Political Prisoners* (1969–70), and the linocut, serigraph, and monoprint *Malcolm X Speaks for Us* (1969) and *Homage to My Young Black Sisters* (1969). Catlett straddled geographic political worlds as a Black revolutionary anti-imperialist artist, producing *Latin America Says No* (1968) and, in 1986, *Central America Says No*. Conscious of the disappeared young people in Central America and the student protestors in Mexico City, she created *The Torture of Mothers* (1970), depicting the death of a boy in the mind of his mother. She was interested in African ancestral forms as a means to convey ideas: "*All African art interests me. I see such force, such life!*"[37] She retired from teaching in 1975 and lived and worked in Cuernavaca, Mexico with Francisco Mora.[38] Her United States citizenship was restored in 2002.

In 2024, an exhibit, *Of Her Becoming: Elizabeth Catlett's Legacy in Chicago,* included contemporary Black women printmakers at the Arts + Public Life's Arts Incubator Gallery Chicago. That same year, a major retrospective, *Elizabeth Catlett: Black Revolutionary Artist and All That It Implies,* opened at the Brooklyn Museum and traveled to Washington's National Gallery, culminating at the Art Institute of Chicago. This exhibit and its accompanying catalog present Catlett's masterful artistic work, graphic and sculptural, as *resistance* to injustice and imperialism through transnational solidarity. It offers a model for how art can be a force for the recognition, repair, and healing of colonized minds. It answers the power of the colonizers, the plantation and haciendas owners, in the past and present, with art that holds revolutionary agency.

Listen to Catlett's ideas about art making:

> *Art must be realistic for me, whether sculpture or printmaking. I have always wanted my art to service my people—to reflect us, to relate to us, to stimulate us, to make us aware of our potential. . . . Learning how to do this and passing that learning on to other people have been my goals. I have learned from many people: from the restlessness and inquisitiveness of the young, from my mother, from other people who have struggled to better themselves—from childhood right on up to now. It has taken a long time to find out that technique was the main thing to learn from art schools. It's so important—technique—how to do things well. It's the difference between offering our beautiful people art and offering them ineptitude. They deserve the very best and we have to equip ourselves to give them our very best. You can't make a statement if you don't speak the language.*
>
> *The search for learning took me to Mexico, to the Taller de Gráfica Popular, where we worked collectively, where we had strong artists and weak artists,*

and each one learned from the other. Everybody offered something—and when you saw the product, even if you were weak, you saw a collective product that you had helped form. It makes a difference in your desire to work and your understanding of what you're doing. And at the same time we did individual work. I would say it was a great social experience, because I learned how you use your art for the service of people, struggling people, to whom only realism is meaningful.

I try to keep away from galleries, they flatter you, seduce you, they buy and sell you. While the Popular Graphics Workshop lasted, it was really worthwhile. Among other things, I learned that my sculpture and my prints had to be based on people's needs. The needs of whomever I'm creating for determine what I do. Some artists say they express themselves; they just reflect their environment. We all live in a given moment in history, and what we do reflects what level we are on in that moment. Whether you are in the white man's game, which is competition, and fighting to get to what's called the top; or whether you're really with the people trying to get everybody to the top or at least see that everybody has a chance to keep on living; or whether you're in limbo, creating art for art's sake—you have to consciously determine where your level is. I decided a long time ago that mine is with the only people in the United States that can call each other "brother" and "sister," and with the Mexicans who are trying to get food and freedom for everybody—so that the way one is going to live or lose his life is not predetermined by somebody's greed. What comes out in my sculpture or prints can only reflect this level. It's not possible for me to work within what's called the Universal, or Modern Art, movement. I can't do what white people with money want at the same time I'm doing what my people need. Trying to bring these two extremes together only creates chaos.

. . .

I think we have to find a way collectively—not working alone. I think we have to find it with our people, and according to their needs. That's the art that's going to be part of us, coming out of our lives. That's the art that's going to carry over to other people throughout the world. It might not win prizes and it might not get into museums, but we ought to stop thinking that way. . . . We ought to stop thinking we have to do the art of other people. We have to create an art for liberation and for life.[39]

Elizabeth Catlett died in Cuernavaca, Mexico, on April 2, 2012.

Catlett reminds us, "let us not be narrow."[40]

Perhaps, we should add, let us think more fully about art and audiences. Let us think of the possibilities inherent in Catlett's "both": American *and* Mexican, abstract *and* representational, form *and* idea. Let us think about identity, whether fixed or fluid, in relation to affiliations of justice seekers. Let us focus on the human needs that art answers and its catalytic potential to forge a full human consciousness that rightly unsettles and disrupts any adoration of golden calves.[41]

Looping and Weaving, Artists and Workers

They do not distinguish between art and craft. "Art is doing," Asawa said. Born into farming families of differing geographies and ethnicities, Ruth Asawa and Marilyn Anderson built their own paths as artists. As children they could draw and observe and turn the prosaic into the unexpected. They both experienced abrupt changes to their family lives. Asawa's family was caught in an immense political injustice, the relocation and incarceration of Japanese and Japanese Americans during World War II. Anderson's family was forever altered by the death of her mother in childbirth and their relocation from the farm to city life. Becoming mothers and evolving into artists were not separate. During her first trips to Guatemala, Anderson sterilized her babies' bottles on a Primus stove. Asawa's six children daily witnessed their mother's hands at work, tending gardens, looping wire. The art they produced is optic and haptic, visual and tactile: for Ruth Asawa, it is in the looping of wire, the creation of masks, the building of communal sculptures, and the artistry of advancing art education; for Marilyn Anderson, it is the photographing of Guatemalan weavers and their looms, learning to weave as taught by the women she photographed, and drawing, carving, and printing the hand work of Guatemalan artisanal workers. They witnessed government domination—incarceration/concentration camps for Asawa and her family, the aftermath of military violence on Maya communities in Guatemala for Anderson. They are cultural preservers *and* innovators. Their lives and work show how the creation of beauty is shadowed by the threat of violence. They created public learning spaces. Asawa advocated for artists as teachers. Anderson matched her portraits of Guatemalan weavers with documentation of political and cultural suppression. For them art and work are intricately connected. Work is artful; art making demands work.

Ruth Asawa

Woven Geometries

January 24, 1926, Norwalk, California–
August 6, 2013, San Francisco, California

Ruth Asawa is an unusual artistic talent
—Josef Albers[1]

The idea of the women of America, (extracted from this daze, this fossil and unhealthy air which hangs around the word lady), develop'd, raised to become the robust equals, workers, and, it may be, even practical and political deciders with the men—greater than man, we may admit, through their divine maternity
—Walt Whitman, "Democratic Vistas"

I was just a farmer from Los Angeles
—Ruth Asawa

Ruth Asawa refused to be uprooted—at least not artistically or metaphysically. After the Japanese attack on Pearl Harbor on December 7, 1941, her father, Umakichi Asawa, burned Japanese family artifacts for fear of association with the attack and in self-protection against the growing intolerance and hostility toward the Japanese community on the West Coast. Umakichi

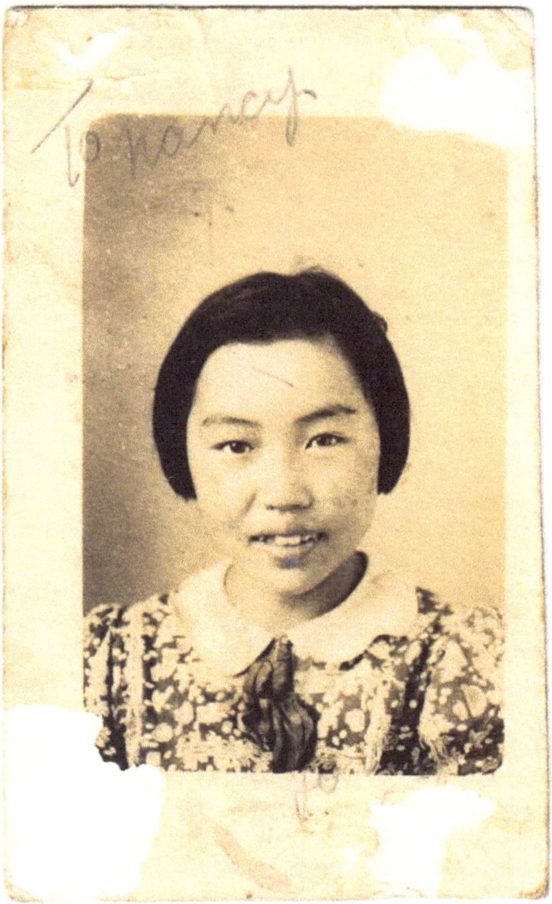

Ruth Asawa (1926–2013), 8th Grade yearbook photo, Norwalk, California, 1939. Courtesy Ruth Asawa Lanier, Inc.

had come to the United States to avoid being drafted into the Japanese army. He and his "picture bride," Haru, raised seven children—Ruth was the middle child—and operated a truck farm on eighty acres in Norwalk, California. Because of the Alien Land Law of 1913, Japanese American farmers were not allowed to own the land they tilled. "Till" aptly describes their lives of work, work, and more work, cultivating and planting, growing and gathering.

When asked how she brought art into family and community, Ruth Asawa responded by talking about work: *I think it goes back to my parents. They knew how to work. They learned how to work. And they came to this country as immigrants, and they had to work. And they taught us how to be good workers regardless of how we felt about anything. So we learned primarily to work.*"[2] Seed corn, not wasted or crushed, has metaphoric, anti-war meaning for Käthe Kollwitz.[3] For Asawa's parents it was a material necessity, as they wisely held back the seeds from their best tomatoes for next season's crop.

Asawa's parents did allow time for Ruth and her siblings to attend local schools as well as a Saturday Japanese language and cultural school, where Ruth practiced the brush strokes of calligraphy. She drew the natural world around her as well as the world she imagined; her drawing of the Statute of Liberty won a school art competition.

Consider Ruth Asawa a worker-artist. Her ethos, learned as a child, encompassed contributory labor, patience, process, and a sense of self that was inclusive, part of something larger, whether family, actual incarceration survival, communal living at Black Mountain College, or promoting teaching artists in the public schools. Her *wabi sabi* approach to art making, grounded in a reverence for the natural world and conscious of the relationality of aesthetics, was the antithesis of an individualistic, precious artist persona.[4] Her way is a life centered and grounded, not compartmentalized, where private art making and public art structures are both part of a larger human commons. Her art is delicate and tough, embracing light and shadow, balletic, reflecting the artist's love of dance and Tai Chi practice.

To say she resisted uprootedness is to understand how her maturing sense of self was not dependent on a specific geography or even on racial and ethnic identity. In a 1948 letter to her future husband, Albert Lanier, she identified herself as a "citizen of the universe,"[5] a view reminiscent of the Japanese children's classic *How Do You Live?,* which describes a Copernican way of thinking that relinquishes the self-centered, childish view of seeing one's self in the world and develops instead a realization that a single self is one molecule in a vast universe.[6] But this is a more complicated cosmology in racist America. Asawa developed a universalist, strategic approach to very real racial oppression, slurs, and discrimination. In that same comment about the universe and citizenship, she distinguishes tolerable physical pain, such as *hands scratched by wire*, and the pain of racial intolerance. She was determined not to succumb: *I no longer want to nurse such wounds. . . . You will have to look at me on a streetcar or bus when you hear someone shout, "dirty Jap." I hope we never have to experience it, but expect it, but do not fear it. I've overcome most of the fear. I've reached a point where I can no longer nurse such stupidity. This attitude has forced me to become a citizen of the universe, by which I grow infinitely smaller than if I belonged to a family, or province, or race.*[7]

On February 19, 1942, President Roosevelt signed Executive Order 9066, calling for the "relocation" of "persons considered a threat to national security" from the West Coast to sites further inland. Ruth was sixteen years old. Her fifty-nine-year-old father, while working in his strawberry fields that early California spring, was arrested by FBI agents. Those agents waited until family members pressed a clean white shirt for Umakichi's only suit for his unknown journey. It would be some time before the family learned where or why he was taken. From a Los Angeles County jail he was sent to Santa Fe, then detained for two years in Lordsburg, New Mexico. In April, not knowing where her husband was, Ruth's mother, Haru, who spoke little English, received orders to close their farm and report to be "relocated" with her children. Ruth, her mother, and siblings were among 120,000 people of Japanese descent, primarily from California, Washington, and Oregon, who were ordered to leave their West Coast homes; 70,000 were American-born citizens.[8]

There is the language of a particular moment in time, and then there is the language of historical reflection. "Relocation" is not choice; "internment" is incarceration, not freedom. They were labeled "evacuees," but they were in fact prisoners. Ruth, her mother, and siblings were first "assembled" at a makeshift camp in the Santa Anita racetrack, where they coped with the stench of horse manure and inadequate food and sanitation. Then they were "relocated" to a camp (concentration camp with guards and barbed wire)

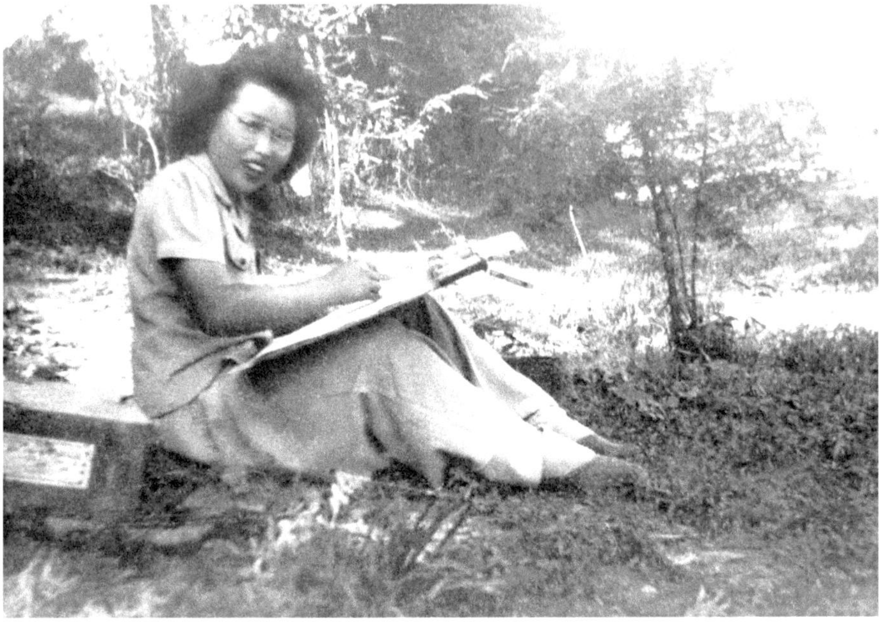

Ruth Asawa (1926–2013), Ruth Asawa drawing while incarcerated in Rohwer, Arkansas, 1943. Courtesy, Ruth Asawa Lanier, Inc.

in Rohwer, Arkansas. They were to trade the stench of horse stalls for the mosquito-rich swamps of Arkansas. They could take only what they could carry in a suitcase.

Such a seismic change to family life cannot or perhaps should not be measured by outsiders. We know that Asawa took art lessons from (also imprisoned) Disney Studios–employed Japanese American artists, that she had an encouraging art teacher, and that she was adept in weaving string for pole beans.

When questioned about this experience, she said, *I had very good advice from a teacher in camp. And she said, "Our people talk about Americans doing something terrible to the Japanese in this country. But you must forego that and make the best of what you will get." And I think that was very good advice to me because then I didn't feel that I was a victim. I didn't want to feel victimized by that [treatment]. I wanted to be on top of it. So I think that attitude was very good for me to have.*[9] For Ruth Asawa, art making was about the formation of beauty through design, form, idea, observation, and skill, not identity. Her marriage to Albert Lanier was grounded in their shared sense of artistry, not their differences. *I keep thinking that it's very dangerous to make Black Mountain as a reason to be unique, or being a mixed couple as being unique. We don't think of that part as being unique. We think we're unique because of what we do.*[10]

Ruth Asawa was an intrepid letter writer. She and her siblings conducted a letter writing campaign to federal officials urging (politely) their father's release. *I think my father . . . is worthy of being with us.*[11] Her persuasive letter-writing skills did not ensure the immediate release of her father but were called upon later in her life in her various San Francisco community projects, particularly art education in the public schools.

After graduating from Rohwer Camp high school in 1943, Asawa wanted to attend college, but first she had to sign a loyalty oath—and then determine how to find tuition money and support herself. She received a tuition-covering scholarship from the Quakers (the Quaker American Friends Service Committee provided modest scholarships to get college-age citizens out of the camps.) Still, like other working-class girls before and after, her choices were limited, even more so because she had to find a geographically interior college, not necessarily the best school, and she had to choose a practical path, training to be an art teacher rather than an artist. She enrolled in Milwaukee State Teachers College—the School of the Art Institute of Chicago was out of financial reach—and supported herself at first as a live-in house cleaner and babysitter with a Milwaukee family. Later she took a job as a checker in a tanning factory, where she worked the morning shift, dealing with the fumes of soaking animal skins, before her college classes.[12]

Ruth Asawa's choices were limited by wartime conditions and few financial resources. But her world began to open up in unexpected ways. In Milwaukee she developed a friendship with Elaine Schmitt, an artist from a family of artists, who told her about an experimental liberal arts college in North Carolina, Black Mountain College. Ruth was interested but was committed that 1945 summer to joining her older sister, Lois (Masako), on a planned bus trip to Mexico City, where Lois improved her Spanish and Ruth absorbed the crafts, colors, and murals of Mexican culture. She took classes at *Escuela de Pintura y Escultura,* where she learned to prepare plaster for fresco painting, and at the *Universidad de Mexico* with the Cuban/Mexican designer Clara Porset, who also told her about Black Mountain College and its leading teacher and Porset's friend, Josef Albers. During a subsequent visit to Mexico, Ruth taught art and English classes at a school in Toluca, Mexico, as a volunteer of the Quaker Friends Service Committee, observed a local method of looping wire egg baskets from a single wire without needles or crochet hook, and began to learn the playfulness and potential of wire looping.[13]

As she was completing her college degree at Milwaukee State Teachers College, Asawa faced another obstacle. She was not allowed to finish her teaching certificate and graduate because she was blocked from student teaching as a Japanese American, presumably because of concerns for her safety. This obstacle, essentially the deprivation of her earned college degree and the means to support herself as a teacher, forced Ruth to look in another direction. With insightful recommendations from friends and acquaintances, Ruth applied to the 1946 Black Mountain College summer session, and with the help of a small church scholarship, was able to attend. Once there, she hoped to study textile weaving with Anni Albers.

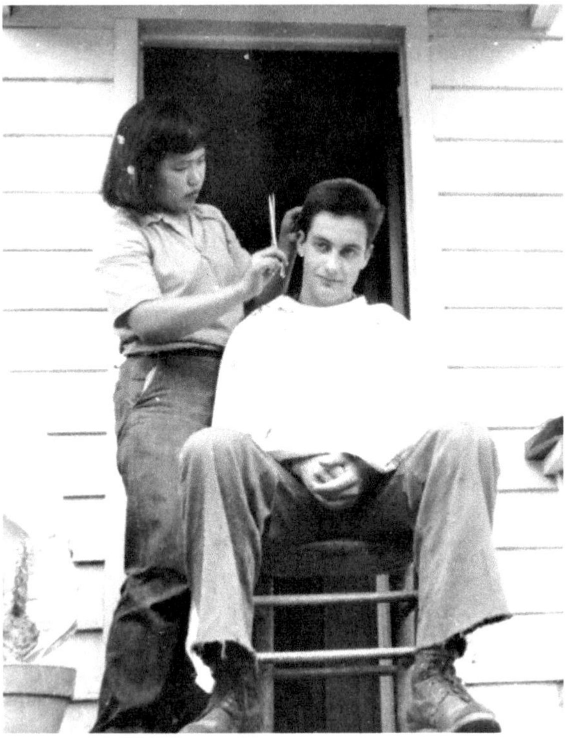

Ruth Asawa (1926–2013), Ruth Asawa cutting Jerrold Levy's hair at Black Mountain College, North Carolina, c. 1947–1949. Courtesy of Ruth Asawa Lanier, Inc.

But Anni Albers turned her down, claiming it was not possible to acquire complex weaving techniques within six summer weeks. (She didn't know Ruth.) A Jewish émigré from fascist Germany, Anni and her non-Jewish husband, Josef, a professor at Bauhaus, found refuge, a modest living, and eager students at Black Mountain College. They were what Albert Lanier called "refugee scholars," Europeans fleeing Hitler, who brought a sensibility about art and design and artistic and intellectual discipline to rural (640 acres) Black Mountain College. There Asawa turned rejection of one plan into the evolution of another. Any portrait of Ruth Asawa's life, especially her artistic trajectory, her *Künstlerroman*, must include her studies and friendships at Black Mountain College.

Asawa's work ethic served her well. She had no privileged-class hesitation about cleaning and scrubbing, or about communal living, nor did she collapse or confuse self-need for artistic expression. *That was the thing at Black Mountain that helped me because I was a good worker and they needed workers, because most people were idea people, and I could scrub floors or I could do menial work.*[14] She could also drive a tractor, turn milk into butter, and cut hair, becoming Black Mountain's skilled barber.

Asawa developed her painting and drawing skills, her artist's eye linked to the shapes and forms of the natural world and her artist's hand inseparable from her accustomed physical labor. Josef Albers and R. Buckminster Fuller recognized her fertile artistic temperament. She learned the power of the meandering line and the relationality of color from Albers, who buttressed her own respect for humble found objects whether in built or natural environments. "Bucky" Fuller's ideas reinforced her sensibility about the preservation of the planet, respect for the innate intelligence of children, and, paradoxically, perhaps, the value of failure. She also joined modern dance classes with Merce Cunningham and sang Bach in BMC's chorus. Discipline (taking a course on Geometry for Artists) and play (performing in a student production of Stravinsky's *The Rite of Spring*) were integrated in Asawa's Black Mountain experience.

Much has been written about the postwar milieu of Black Mountain College and the multidisciplinary, cosmopolitan artists who taught there, especially during summer sessions.[15] But the word "taught" may be misleading; Black Mountain was not particularly attached to customary academic bookkeeping, nor did it grant degrees. Teachers and students shared common spaces and meals as well as engaged in joint amateur theatrical productions. Some of the participatory artists included John Cage, Merce Cunningham, Robert Motherwell, Robert Creeley, Robert Rauschenberg, Susan Weil, Cy Twombly, Elaine and Willem de Kooning, Jacob Lawrence and Gwendolyn Knight, Japanese American sculptor Leo Amino, Ben Shahn, Leo Lionni, the photographers Nancy and Beaumont Newhall, Harry Callahan, Arthur Siegel, and Aaron Siskind. One of Josef Albers's strengths as a leader, his own particular style of human collaging, was his willingness to invite artists for summer sessions who didn't necessarily think about art or make it as he did. For all his Bauhausian austerity, Albers understood the link between art making and democracy, having read John Dewey's *Art as Experience,* which was translated into German in 1916.[16] Dewey visited Black Mountain College, served on its board of advisors, and donated books to the library.

The deprivation of learning about and making art harms people and thwarts democracy. That is the quiet, steady theme of this book. Art is **not** extracurricular. This philosophical root is less visible, but more important from a human development perspective, than academic art categorization or even institutions. Asawa's later advocacy for artists teaching in public schools in a hands-on manner demonstrates this lineage of Dewey-Albers-Black Mountain College-Asawa *and* the Ruth Asawa San Francisco School of the Arts. It was situational art making space that was important to Albers and Asawa.

After her childhood in a crowded two-room farm house, her incarceration in horse stalls and barracks, and her job as live-in housekeeper, I imagine Ruth Asawa experiencing a new kind of joy with her own studio and living space at Black Mountain College. (Although, dutifully, she did attempt to take some time away from her Black Mountain studies to help her parents resettle their farming life after the war, until Josef Albers and the head of the school, Theodore Dreier, recruited her to return.) At Black Mountain she began acquiring her distinctive "sculptural vocabulary," emerging from her drawings and later developed into "the open and closed" structures of her looped-and tied-wire forms.[17] And there she met and later married the aspiring architect Albert Lanier. On the surface, they couldn't have been more different. Albert, well-spoken and lean, was born in Georgia, the son of a district attorney, a distant relative of the poet Sydney Lanier, and offspring of generations of small-town Southerners. But, like Ruth, he was receptive to pioneering new forms and methods of architectural practices, leaving Georgia Tech, serving in the navy during the war, and contributing

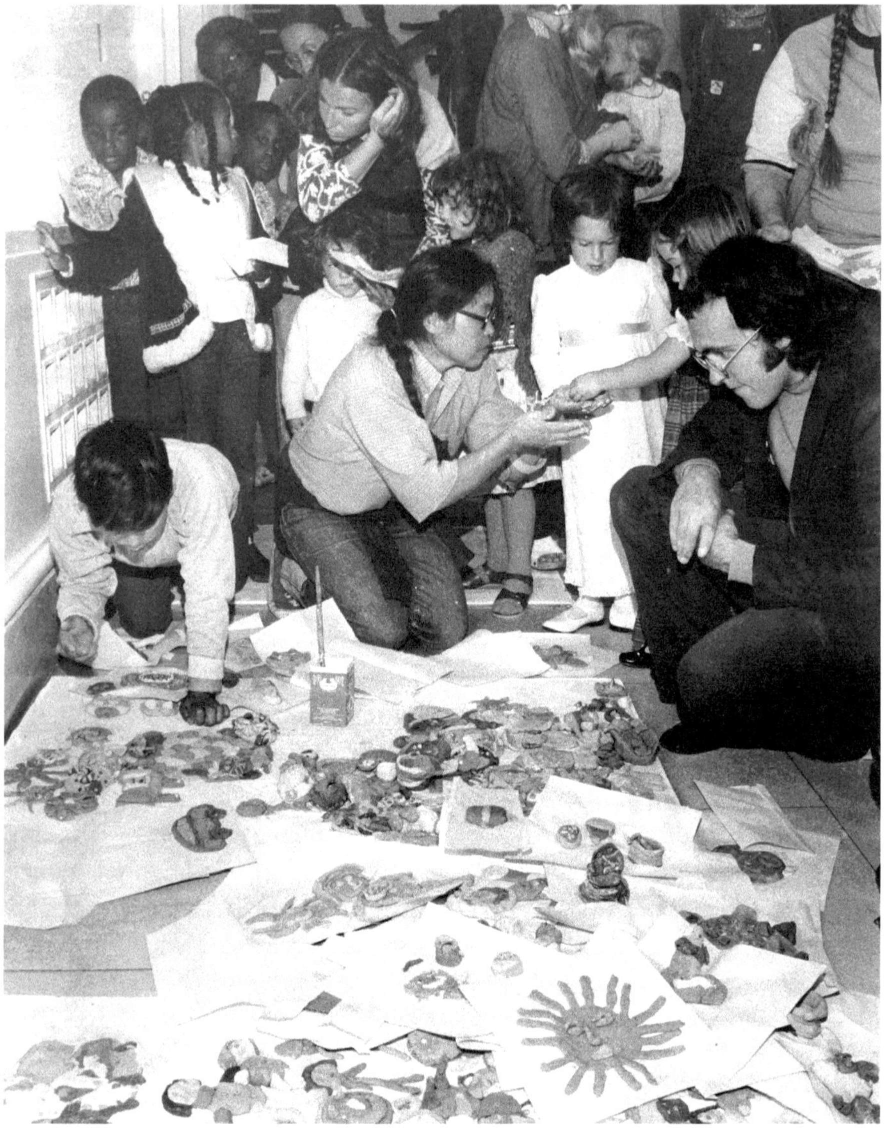

Ruth Asawa (1926–2013), Ruth Asawa teaching a Baker's Clay demonstration at the San Francisco Museum of Art (now SFMOMA), California, 1973. Courtesy Ruth Asawa Lanier, Inc.

to an architectural course of study at Black Mountain College. With fellow architecture students, Lanier designed and built what they called Minimum House, a dwelling of four hundred square feet made from local stone and wood and salvaged industrial materials. Respect for simple materials and unadorned design linked to a determined and adventurous sensibility characterized both Ruth and Albert, who were married in 1949 in San Francisco, nine months after the California Supreme Court legalized interracial marriage. Over the years, their partnership drew many friends and fellow artists, in particular, the "modernist photographer of botanicals and nudes," Imogen Cunningham, who advised Ruth to keep her last name (not her husband's).

Imogen Cunningham, with her Rolleiflex camera, took aesthetically powerful photographs of Asawa, her family, her home, and her work, especially her work. A 1957 Cunningham photograph of Asawa surrounded by four of her children (there would be six in all, two adopted as infants) is a quiet presentation of human and artistic interrelationships: there's the nude baby Adam drinking from a bottle, the cross-legged Aiko holding a dowel near her mother's spool of wire, and two crouching boys, Xavier and Hudson, one hidden by a bulbous dangling sculpture, the other reading, perhaps puzzling, hand to chin. Their mother, Ruth, sits on the floor among them, her head down and her partly obscured hands looping wire. Huge hanging sculptures surround them, translucent yet weighty, not separate but integral to the family tableau. This is not a Madonna and children depiction; it upends such art history representations. This is the inseparability of the labor of mothering and the labor of art making—as evidenced by Käthe Kollwitz, Elizabeth Catlett, and Marilyn Anderson as well. See Imogen Cunningham's iconic portrait of Ruth Asawa and children and a photo of mother Ruth juggling the needs of several of her children at once on the following pages.

How Ruth Asawa developed from a farmer from Los Angeles into a distinct artist whose artwork is in museums and public squares, whose wire sculptures are pictured on U.S. postage stamps, whose name is attached to a crater on the planet Mercury, and whose legacy endures in San Francisco public schools can be attributed to her unusual talent, as Josef Albers recognized, her work ethic, and her collective sense of self. Despite the obstacles she encountered, she respected herself. Self-respect is no small thing for a girl/woman from the working class. Self-respect should not be confused with entitlement; rather, it is the rightful desire to value one's own work and to have it seen, though its continuation would not depend on an audience or a market.

Asawa's first public recognition came in 1948 for her painting in a group show, *Tomorrow's Artists*, at the Addison Gallery in Andover, Massachusetts. Steady recognition followed: for looped wire sculpture in the San Francisco Art Association annual exhibit (1950); a cover image (by photographer Imogen Cunningham) in *arts & architecture* (1952); a solo exhibit at Design Research in Cambridge, Massachusetts (1953); a solo exhibit at Peridot Gallery in New York City (1954), reviewed in the *New York Times*; inclusion in annual exhibits at the Whitney in New York and the Art Institute of Chicago (1955); sculpture in the 3rd Biennial São Paulo, Brazil (1955); in the Whitney's annual exhibit of sculpture, watercolor, and drawings (1956); and in the annual group exhibit at the Art Institute of Chicago, where three sculptures were reproduced on the exhibit's catalog cover (1957). During this same decade she gave birth, dealing with acute morning sickness (*I'm*

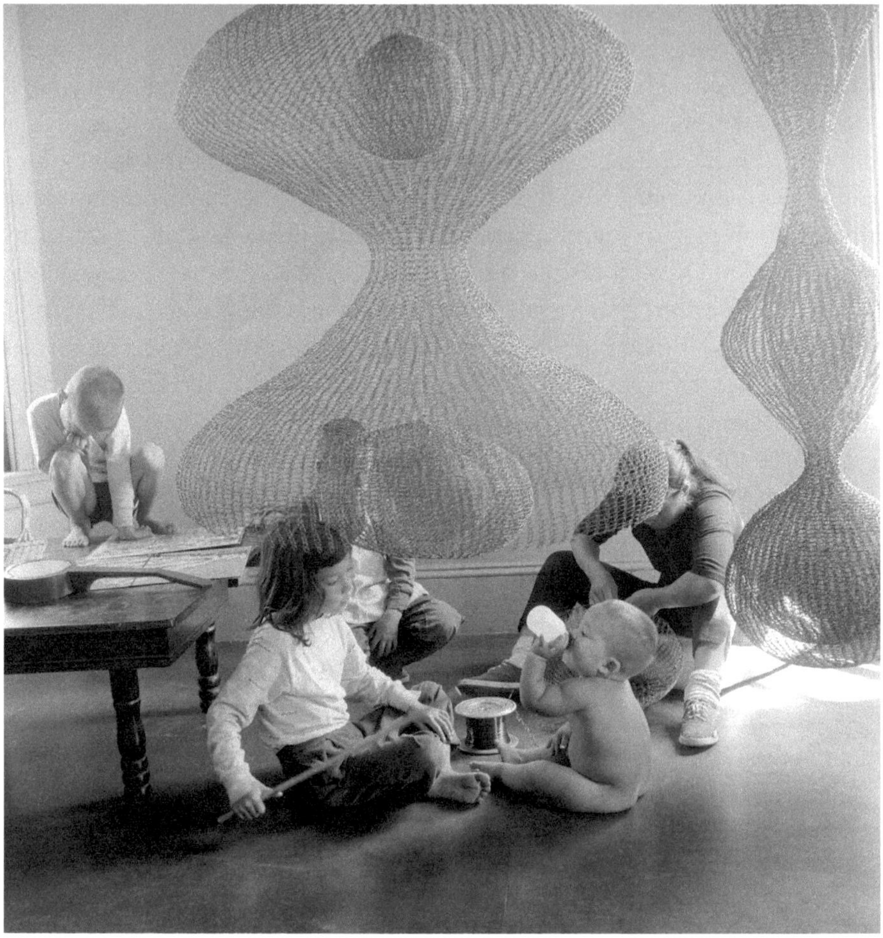

Ruth Asawa (1926–2013), *Ruth Asawa, Sculptor, and her Children, 1957*, Photo © 2026 Imogen Cunningham Trust. Artwork ©2026 Ruth Asawa Lanier, Inc./Artists Rights Society (ARS), New York, Courtesy David Zwirner.

one of those who remains sick thruout the pregnancy),[18] to Aiko (1950) and adopted infant son Xavier (1950), gave birth to Hudson, named after his paternal grandfather (1952), adopted son Adam (1956–2003), gave birth to daughter, Addie Laurie (1958), and to a sixth and final child, son Paul (1959). And that's one decade.

The 1950s were lean financial years for Ruth, Albert, and their growing family. Ruth declined opportunities to commercialize her sculpture. Albert said, "We gave up necessities so we could afford luxuries" (that is, art materials and tools). Ruth said, "He made a living as an architect and I made a livelihood as an artist." Albert added, "We refused to acknowledge that we were poor."[19]

After several moves, the family settled in the Noe Valley neighborhood of San Francisco. Lanier worked with several San Francisco architects before

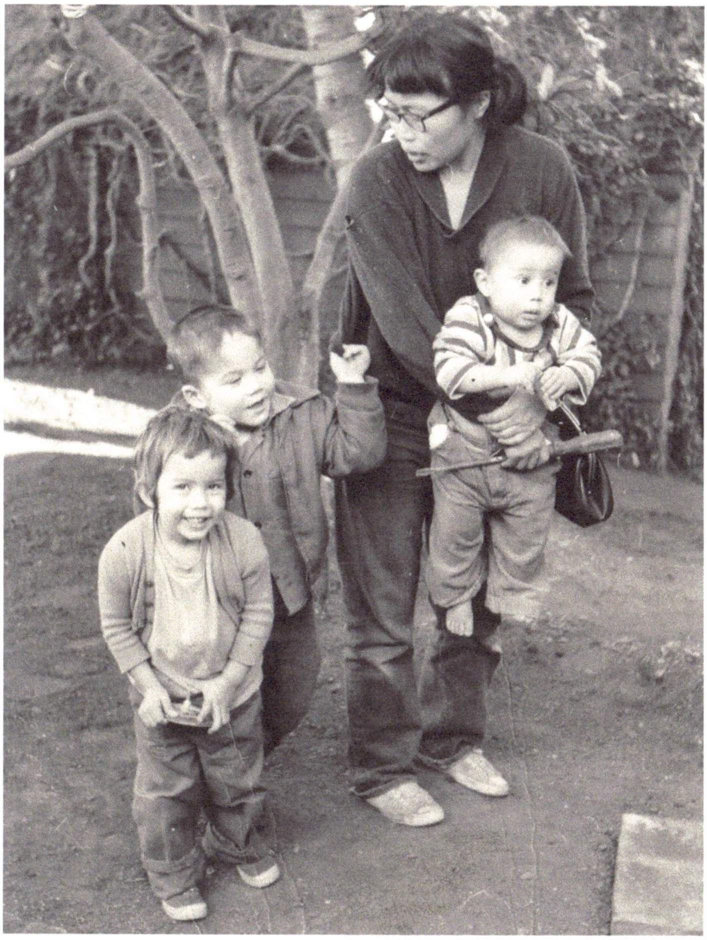

Ruth Asawa (1926–2013), *Ruth Asawa and* (L to R) *Addie, Adam and Paul Lanier* outside their home, San Francisco, California, 1961. Courtesy Ruth Asawa Lanier, Inc.

establishing his own architectural firm with Paul Sherrill. Long before it was trendy or ecologically recognized, Lanier and Sherrill advocated for preservation over demolition.

A January 1955 *Time* magazine review (titled "Eastern Yeast") of exhibits by Isamu Noguchi and the twenty-eight-year-old Ruth Asawa described Ruth as a "San Francisco housewife and mother of three."[20] Categorization can be a form of unacknowledged tyranny. The problem with the "housewife and mother" category is the embedded and unacknowledged "just" before the word housewife. That "just" is not a celebration of the real labor of feeding and nurturing children; rather, it's another version of Samuel Johnson's dancing dog observation about women preachers. In order to **see** Ruth Asawa's art—to "open eyes" in the Albers sense—it is necessary to integrate the act of looking with a conscious haptic sense, a link between the optical and the tactile, between substance and space, between inside and outside, indiscernible like a Mobius strip. There's Asawa's bulbous forms and there's the geometry and transparency of a spider's web.[21] Ruth Asawa carried Albers's teaching, with its emphasis on observation and articulation, into the fruition of her sculptures (as well as her prints, paintings, drawings, lithographs, carvings, and hundreds of life masks). Her artistic practices became her own praxis, a quiet, theoretically infused way of making art, where theory is visible *after* the practice (as Albers articulated, theory is the outcome of practice).[22] It's another paradigm, another way of knowing (and recognizing not knowing) that may be discombobulating to critics and academics.

Despite good intentions, academic art historians may unwittingly try to box Asawa into categories that not only do not quite fit, but, more importantly, miss the intentionality of the works and the process of their creation. Paul Karlstrom, for example, led an interview with Ruth and Albert with questions about modernism. She hears "modern" and tells of the value of experimentation at Black Mountain College but also the respect for form and materials. Is it important to her whether Albers should be labeled a formalist or modernist? No. It is not about academic categories. What is important is what she learned and how she learned: *Well, I think that Black Mountain gave you the right to do anything you wanted to do. And then you put a label on it afterward. I think that's the nice thing about what Black Mountain did for its students. They gave you permission to do anything you wanted to do. And if it didn't fit, they'd make a category for you.*[23]

Praxis is key—not just the idea/concept but how to move ideas into actuality. *I have always used ideas, but I want to take them and work on them to finally become something—not just the concept but the idea behind it.* [. . .] *I think the craft is important to a concept. One works in dough and then that is made into bronze. There are many steps between the concept and the project. And I think that one should experience that.*[24]

And further: *Just as I learned from my parents. If I plant a tomato seed, I will get a tomato plant out of it. Then I will get tomatoes from that. I like that. I like the steps that one gets from merely planting a seed, or planting a plant. I like what happens, because you know you get an eggplant every time you plant an eggplant seed. Or you know you're going to get a melon. I like that. I like getting a cucumber. Or what if I've got a cucumber and a mixture, a hybrid. I like that, too, because I'll get something new. . . . Well, if you take material you like and you know how far you can take it from what is traditional to do, like a piece of paper, you like to take it another step. And if it teaches you some geometry and not just for writing something, and you find that you can go from two dimensions to three dimensions, that . . . interests me. And it can be any material. It doesn't have to be wire.* And, regarding the interviewer's question about the distinctions between craft and art: *It doesn't bother me. Whether it's craft or whether it's art. That is a definition that people put on things. And what I like is that the material*

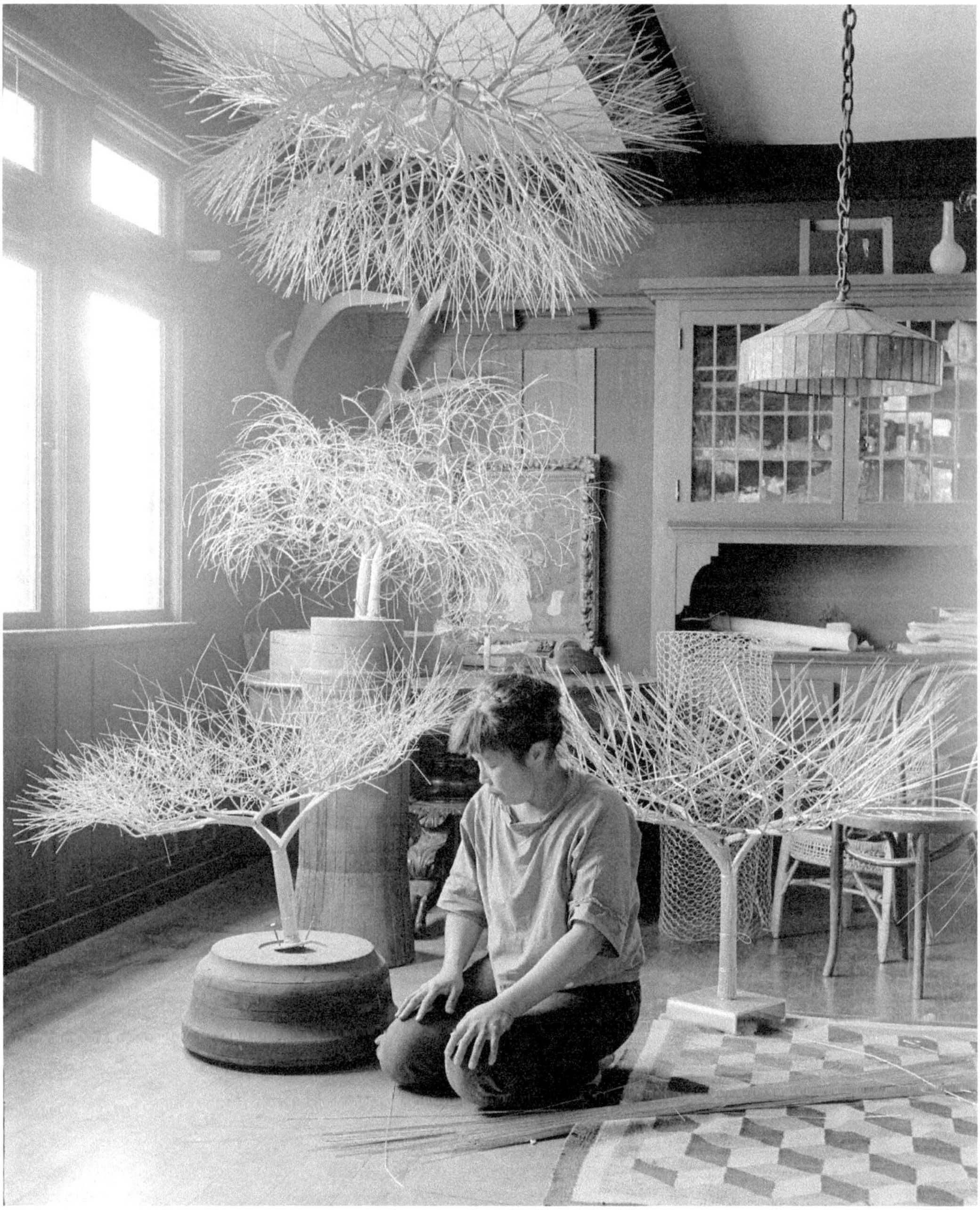

Ruth Asawa (1926–2013), *Ruth Asawa in Her Dining Room with Tied-Wire sculptures,* 1963. Photo © 2026 Imogen Cunningham Trust. Artwork ©2026 Ruth Asawa Lanier, Inc./Artists Rights Society. (ARS), New York, Courtesy David Zwirner.

is irrelevant. It's just that that [wire] happens to be material I use. And I think that is important. That you take an ordinary material like wire and you make it, you give it a new dimension. That's all.[25] This is an Asawa interpretation of Albers's concept of *matière*—material studies.

Asawa seldom titled her artwork—really, how could she? And how would words interfere with the challenge to the viewer of seeing her sculpture, inside and outside? She extended the meandering line to wire. From the summer of 1947 in Toluca, Mexico, where she observed and learned to make open wire baskets, to her single and multi-lobed sculptures—her forms within forms, conical and hyperbolic—to her tied/bundled wires, branching their "leaves," she connected iteration with experimentation. She sculpted with paper, wood, ceramics, plaster, and baker's clay. She loved drawing and wanted her many meandering and masterful line drawings to be seen in juxtaposition with her wire sculptures; indeed, sculptures emerged out of her early drawing practices. Only unexpected illnesses, first lupus, the wolf, in 1985, which returned later in her life when she also endured a series of strokes, limited her continuous art making, as did the sacrificing of precious art making time to attend countless public meetings as an advocate for the arts.

Asawa brought art out of her house/studio into the community—through public commissions and through centering art and gardening in public schools. She was savvy about contacts to raise money for the arts in schools. She showed up for causes and for children. I once asked Julie Olsen Edwards, daughter of the writer Tillie Olsen, if she knew Ruth Asawa when Julie and her sisters were growing up in the Mission District of San Francisco. She said, "Oh, everyone knew Ruth Asawa." This is another way of understanding fame and art. Ruth Asawa did not compartmentalize her life; she practiced a non-hierarchical, Whitmanesque approach to people—foundry workers, neighbors, wealthy businessmen, institutional trustees, and, of course, children. All the while she was developing and refining her artistry, taking courses when she could, accepting, with her family's support, a fellowship to study lithography at the Tamarind Workshop in Los Angeles, advancing her calligraphy practice with Zen master Hodo Tobase, and experimenting with electroplating and galvanizing her sculptures. Guggenheim award readers repeatedly turned her down, unaware of or unresponsive to the many public acknowledgments for her work as a citizen-artist. Did they have trouble **seeing** Ruth Asawa's multiple forms of art making? Her art contains contradictions—the blending of inner and outer, folded paper transformed into bronze sculptural fountains. Her public commissions were both solo achievements and models of community inclusion. In 1966 she received a commission to design *Andrea,* a fountain for Ghirardelli Square in San Francisco, which depicted nursing mermaids, turtles, and frogs and confounded the Square's designer, who wanted a tall, phallic, squirting sculpture.

Other commissions followed, including the *San Francisco Fountain*, a bronze fountain at the Hyatt Hotel near Union Square. This had a typical Asawa signature, indicative of her capacious imagination, which combined abstraction and narration: over 250 people contributed to this portrayal of places and lives in San Francisco, creating baker's clay models for the cast-bronze sculpture/fountain. Two commissions, the researched and precisely narrative *Japanese American Internment Memorial* in San Jose (1994) and the abstract rock-designed *Garden of Remembrance* in San Francisco State University (2002) honoring the many Japanese and Japanese Americans incarcerated during World War II, brought her back to a painful public and personal historical memory that she had carried all her life. About incarceration, she said, *The arts saved us.*[26]

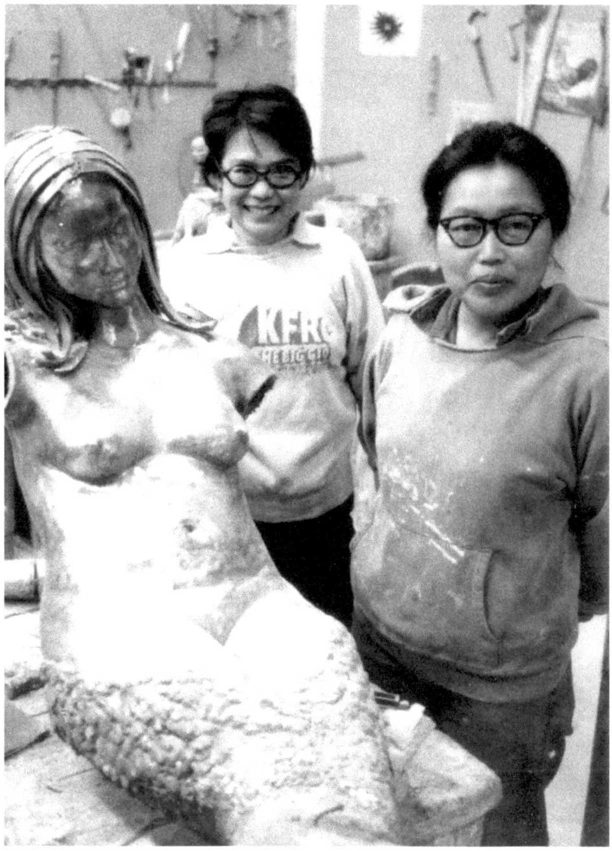

Ruth Asawa (1926–2013), Ruth Asawa (R) and her assistant Mae Lee (L) with wax version of *Andrea* for Ghirardelli Square, San Francisco, California, 1966. Artwork © 2026 Ruth Asawa Lanier, Inc. /Artists Rights Society (ARS), New York. Courtesy David Zwirner.

Ruth Asawa defies categorization or summing up. There are the concrete forms of legacy: her delicate/sturdy wire sculptures on permanent display in the Education Tower of the de Young Museum in Golden Gate Park, their shadows making art of museum walls; her name and hanging sculptures are on Forever U.S. postage stamps; her fountains and memorials open to public view and touch. There is the personal legacy of the beauty of human relationships in the lives of her children and grandchildren, and the hundreds of people whose lives were changed because of contact with Ruth. There is the intangible legacy of teaching—how many great artists are also great teachers and proponents of art education? There is, especially, the Alvarado School Arts Workshop, began by Ruth and her friend and neighbor, architectural historian Sally B. Woodbridge. They insisted that art education should be more than coloring in mimeographed images of turkeys or Easter bunnies, and that art classes should be available to all students—whatever

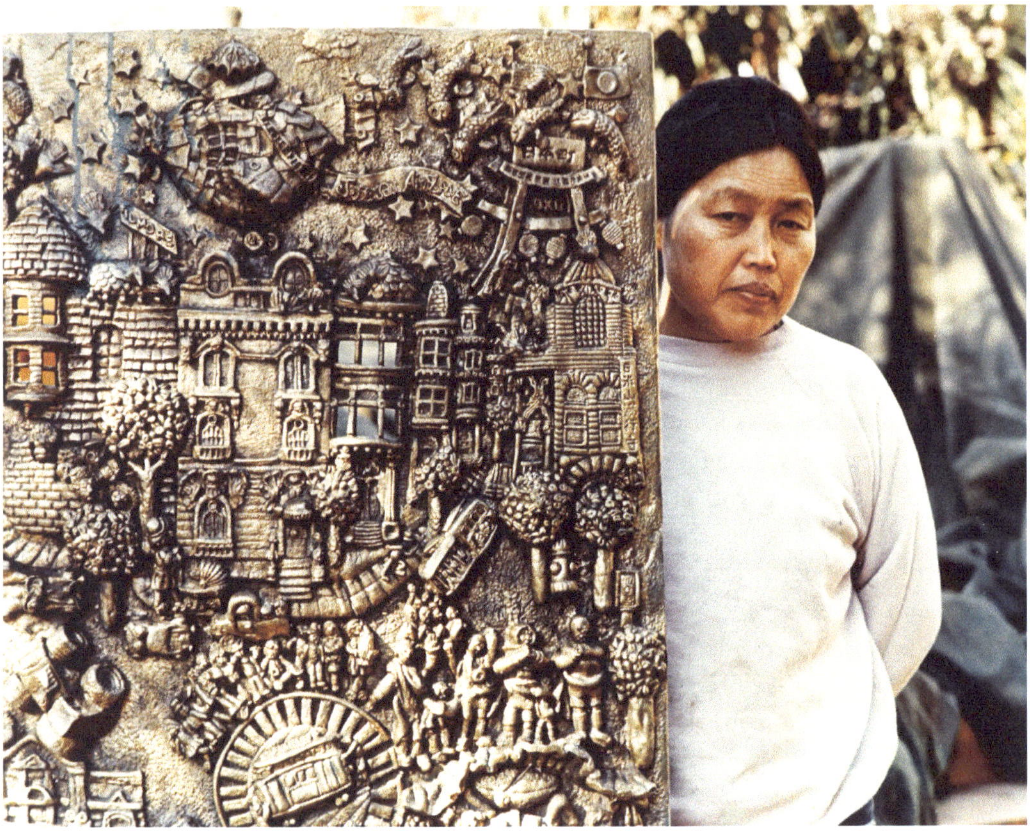

Ruth Asawa (1926–2013), Ruth Asawa with a bronze panel from the *San Francisco Fountain*, c. 1973. Artwork ©2026 Ruth Asawa Lanier, Inc./Artist Rights Society (ARS), New York, Courtesy David Zwirner.

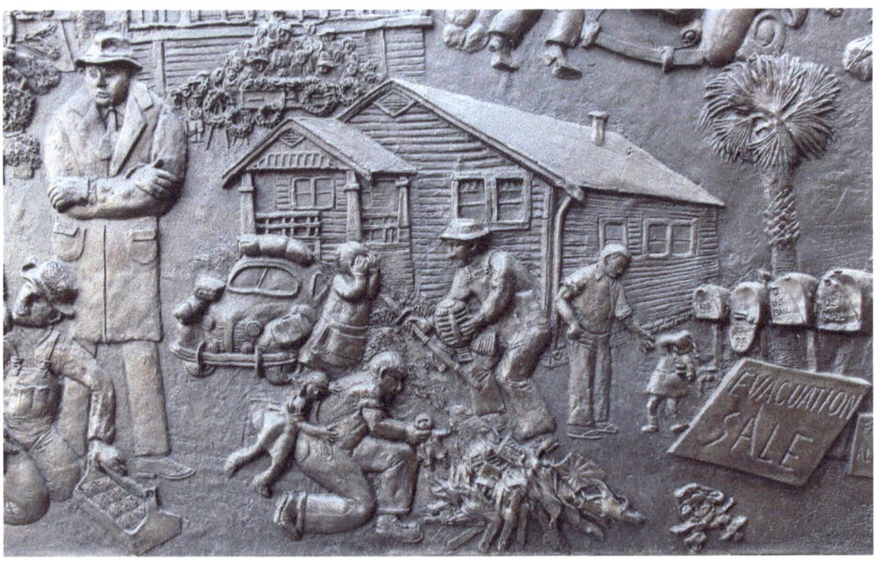

Ruth Asawa (1926–2013), Detail view of Ruth Asawa's *Japanese American Internment Memorial* with scene depicting her family burning Japanese family objects. Photo by James Jue, c. 2021. Artwork © 2026 Ruth Asawa Lanier, Inc./Artists Rights Society (ARS), New York. Courtesy David Zwirner.

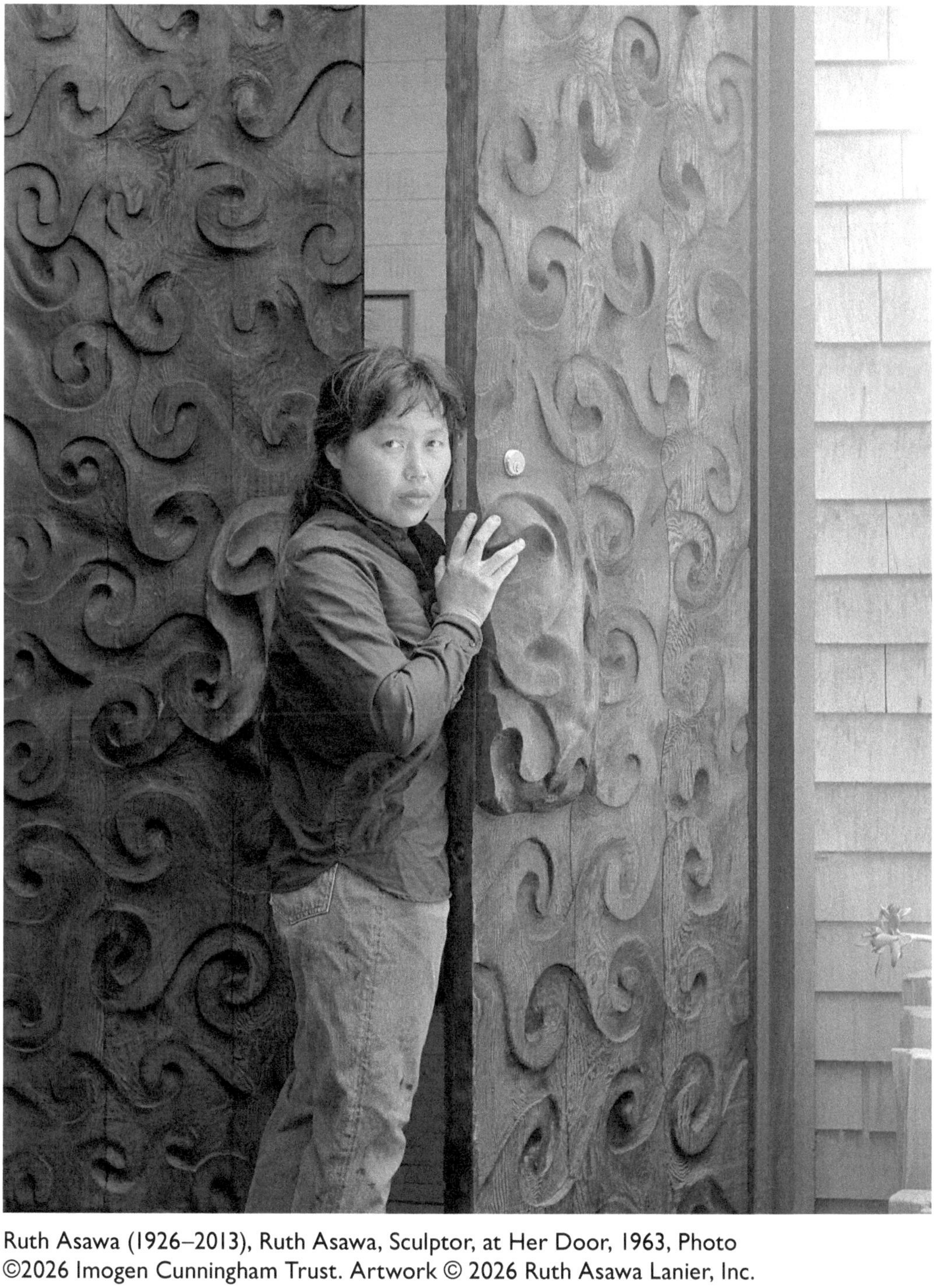

Ruth Asawa (1926–2013), Ruth Asawa, Sculptor, at Her Door, 1963, Photo ©2026 Imogen Cunningham Trust. Artwork © 2026 Ruth Asawa Lanier, Inc.

their abilities or disabilities. It demonstrated the linkages between art making and gardening: *I wish I could make every school a garden but the principal only gave me a little square.*[27] San Francisco now has its Ruth Asawa School of the Arts (although still awaiting, at the time of this writing, her preferred geographical location that ensures the flow of art makers and performers to classrooms and students). Her friend Woodbridge quotes Ruth's remarks about art and education: *I am primarily concerned with art and art education because I have devoted most of my life to the study and practice of art. I have made doing it part of my life. Art is doing. There is either doing or talking about it. Art deals directly with life. . . . The only step* [in art making] *that is truly real is the first step. The making of the object. That is the step that children should be involved with completely. This involvement helps them to learn their capabilities and limitations. It is learning by making. For this reason the most highly skilled persons should be teaching them.*[28]

Less tangible and rarely discussed in art history is her legacy of respect for labor. Piero Mussi, bronze artisan from Piacenza, Italy, and director of Art Works Foundry, said, "For Ruth, I would do anything." He remembers Ruth this way: "She was very humble. She was very friendly. . . . She gave credit to everybody who touched her work. . . . Some artists don't want to share their art. She was never afraid to give away anything."[29]

Ruth Asawa turned spools of wire into embodied objects of beauty and joy—what one critic described as "homemade cosmogonies," and what she saw as nature's "transparent geometries."[30] She practiced an aesthetic of relationships—with wire and other materials, with family and friends, with school children, with other artists, and with space, light, and shadows. A life force.

Marilyn Anderson

Weaving Connections

April 7, 1937, Mollala, Oregon

In understanding what good work means and what it does to the worker, the paradigm of the artist is most relevant. There is an element of art in good work.
—Dorothee Soelle with Shirley A. Cloyes, *To Work and To Love*

Many hand tools haven't changed for centuries: they have such balance and are so functional. The human body is like a tool.
—Jacob Lawrence, on his *Builders* paintings

To weave was to think, to feel, to know.
—Anni Albers

The art she makes is grounded in art/craft labor practices of thousands of years. Marilyn Anderson is a weaver-artist, literally, as she learned the techniques of Guatemalan backstrap weaving, but also figuratively, as a woodcut printmaker, painter, and photographer. She illuminates how art/craft work in the world *and* the worlds inside the processes of making. She confronts opacity with methods of seeing. She engages the homemade without consumerist sentimentality. She has absorbed, not merely the banality of evil, but also the ruthless, hovering, endless, and unimagined ugly surprises of human brutality. Yet she has produced stunning photographs, drawings, prints, books, and exhibits that answer cultural oblivion and political amnesia.

In a small gallery at a community college in Western New York, Marilyn Anderson had a 2019 retrospective exhibit of her body of work. Actually, it was merely a glimpse of a large oeuvre of drawings, paintings, prints, and photographs—a life's work. By any measurement, it is a significant achievement. What was not visible, partly because her work has not had the theoretical analysis and national attention it deserves, was how she upends assumptions about identity, cultural appropriation, and political engagement. In the crowded, loud discourse about art and the art world, bicoastal or transatlantic, with often facile labels, impulsive categorization, and aggressive monetization, it is no surprise that Marilyn Anderson's work and persona are not seen or heard. Her artistry contains and calls for a different kind of intellectuality, a complexity rooted in living with and learning from the unfamiliar. She is the antithesis of Ariella Aïsha Azoulay's critique of artists and institutions as art looters of other cultures.[1] Why is she not a looter? Because she is a learner and a maker. How she learned to be a weaver-artist—a *Homo faber*—a human as maker—is both a personal story *and* a public theoretical and practical model for how to build artful practices.

She was born, a twin, at home on a family farm near Mollala (the name of an Indian tribe), Oregon, on April 7, 1937. Her Swedish American father was a transplant from Minnesota. Her mother came from a German hop-growing family who migrated to Oregon in 1868. *My parents demonstrated much affection for each other and for my two brothers, older sister, and for me and my twin sister. Being a twin shaped my life in many ways. Early on, I drew constantly and she* [her twin sister] *had talent for music, playing the piano by ear. I loved music, influenced by my mother, who played the piano, and [by] my older sister. On Saturday afternoons, we listened to the Metropolitan Opera and symphony concerts with Arturo Toscanini.*

Although my mother died when I was only five, I have many memories of her. My twin and I had hand embroidered bedspreads [that she made]. *(I still have mine tucked away). And at five years old, one of my last memories of my mother, very pregnant, was of her sitting in a rocking chair with her feet elevated as she embroidered. Hidden away in a cardboard box, I found* [her] *wonderfully rendered pencil drawing of a cup and saucer from her high school days. She hung prints in our dining room of "The Gleaners" and a wonderful Dutch windmill by Rembrandt. In the summer, she canned fruits and vegetables, filling rows of glass jars on cellar shelves. She adored flowers and it is hard to count the many kinds she grew. She died in childbirth. Her death completely changed our house.*

My sisters and I took over cooking, cleaning and washing clothes. My father began to work in Portland. He still helped with farm work, but he and my brothers drifted farther away from the farm. It was difficult for my father to hold on [to the farm]. *I tried to show my love for him with gifts of my drawings. Finally, he moved us all to Portland where he ran a successful service station. My twin sister and I were very sad to leave our farm and our animals. But with the move many educational advantages came (Saturday art classes, summer German classes). My Catholic girls high school experience was stressful. But my art always gave me a strong sense of self. I needed it because most of my fellow high school students were from more middle class or upper-class families.*[2]

To recall the handwork of family and community members, to recognize the artistry inherent in *making*—a meal, an embroidered covering, a bookcase—is not about retrieving some idyllic past. Rather, it is a willingness to find artistry in what institutions and markets tend to dismiss. The commonplace inspires artists like Marilyn Anderson. *Now that I am older, I understand how much my parents and grandparents made me into the person I am. Shortly before his death, I showed my father my books about weaving. When he saw them, he recalled that as a farm boy in cold Minnesota, he did wool spinning for his mother to knit socks and sweaters. My maternal grandmother sewed and made rag rugs. While gardening with my paternal grandfather, I found an arrowhead, a relic left by a native person who once trod the land which became my grandfather's farm. Even as a child, that incident affected me deeply.*[3]

My commitment to "art" began as a child and making art has been central in my life since then. I did not know any artists and knew nothing about what being an artist meant. I only knew that I was fascinated by art I saw in books and I drew constantly. The one-room country elementary school I attended had a series of art books of world masterpieces in its small library. But perhaps most important to me was a little black and white volume of the paintings of Rosa Bonheur, the 19th century painter who was especially known for her large-scale painting, The Horse Fair [now in the Metropolitan Museum of Art]. *As I was going through a horse-crazy phase, I had begun to do many drawings of horses. Rosa Bonheur's work validated my own and was a model for me to emulate.*

Anderson studied art at Marylhurst College in Oregon (closed in 2018) and the School of the Art Institute of Chicago. *All art schools I attended have had importance to me but the School of the Art Institute of Chicago has had lifelong meaning. Instructions I received there grounded me as an artist. When I applied and was admitted on a half scholarship, leaving my father to pay the rest, I didn't fully realize that I was going to one of the finest art schools in the country. With my father's old steamer trunk full of my clothing, paint brushes and supplies, we drove to the Portland rail station and I rode two and a half days on the Great Northern to Chicago. Studying at the Chicago Art Institute was almost the happiest time of my life. On my way to classes in 1958–59, I could see a Degas, look up at the large El Greco* Virgin Mary *and contemplate Seurat's* Sur La Grande Jatte.

Anderson turned toward photography in the late 1960s when she realized that her paintings and prints could not be used for social purposes as could photography. She studied at the Rochester Institute of Technology and received a MFA in photography from the Visual Studies Workshop in Rochester. In the 1970s she photographed and wrote about the Maya textile tradition in Guatemala (*Backstrap Weaving*, 1975, and *Guatemalan Textiles Today*, 1978). Before her 2016 book, *Guardianes de las Artes/Guardians of the Arts,* she published with Jonathan Garlock[4] the extraordinary *Granddaughters of Corn* in 1988. She and Garlock devised a means of exhibiting photography and texts so that both could travel to open, uncharged, community spaces. As another example of her communal outreach, she also created multilingual educational coloring books on Guatemalan weavers and craft makers as well as other contemporary workers. In the 1980s and 1990s, she and Garlock collaborated on several documentary projects: "The Honor of Labor," "The Craft of Silk Workers of the 80s," and "Rochester: A Community of Workers." She is the recipient of numerous fellowships and grants.

Marilyn Anderson's public art story originated in Guatemala in 1964. She began photographing weavers in 1968, and returned over four summers between 1970 and 1975. She entered cultures (plural because of the diversity of Guatemalan highland weavers) not her own with respect and humility, willing to risk the vulnerability and disorientation of the nascent learner. She listened and observed. She witnessed the companionship of weavers and, in turn, became an artist/companion to weavers.[5] She learned to weave as she learned to photograph, print, and paint. She saw the inherent beauty in individual and collective productive work. She answers now frequent critiques aimed at art institutions about their cultural appropriations and neo-colonialism with a methodology that employs artistic tools as conduits. Marilyn Anderson is worldly in the best moral sense; why is her work not in museums?

The genesis of my books and photographs happened in the mid 1960s before I did any picture taking at all. It began with my learning the use of the ancient weaving apparatus, the backstrap loom. Initially, I found weaving difficult and only slowly mastered the use of the loom. That experience made me understand how demanding it was to become a proficient weaver. It required nothing less than complete attention. Weavers had to exert constant vigilance to keep the loom operable. This extended to the details of rolling it up correctly after use. The different aspects of the loom's construction—its simplicity, functionality and the ingenuity of its design—evoked a sense of historical continuity. This instrument has been used for thousands of years by thousands of Maya women. Learning to weave and doing the weaving drew me imaginatively closer to these women and their looms. When I lived in Jacaltenango, a Mayan town, weavers worked all around. When I asked, "Who knows how weaving is done?" I was told, "Everyone."

Although the backstrap loom, constructed with threads and supported by sticks, seemed initially uncomplicated, many kinds of weaving techniques were possible. I realized how loom construction could change from place to place. They had dif-

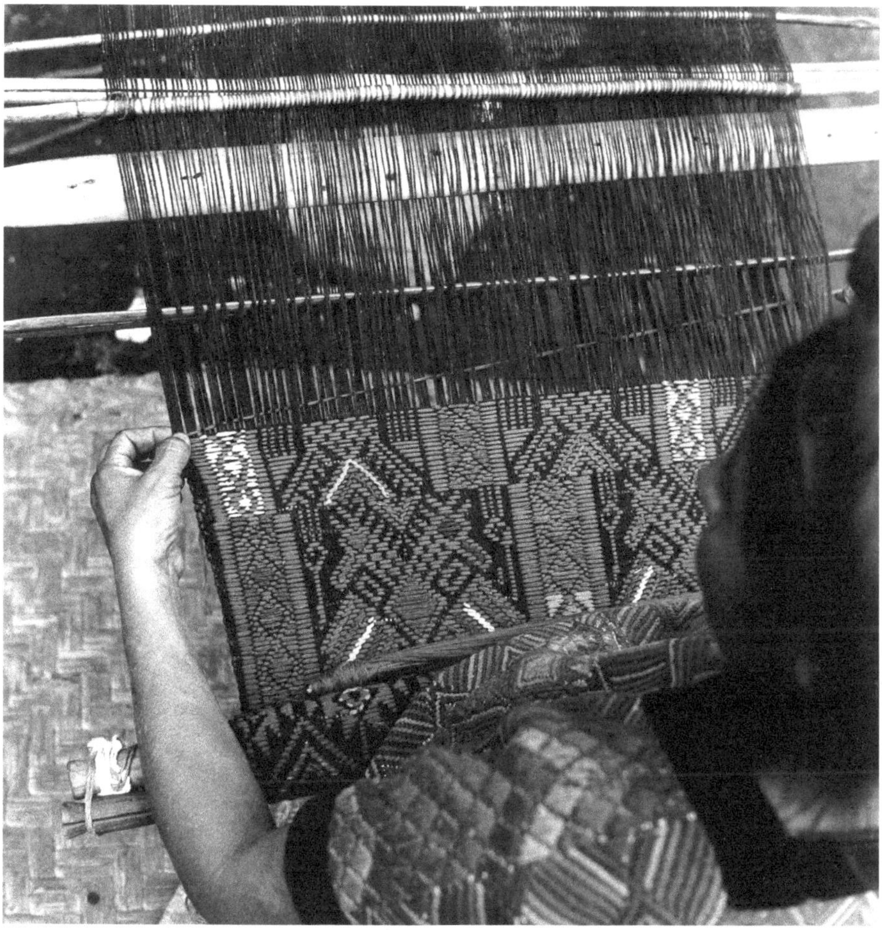

Marilyn Anderson (1937), photographer, *Weaver at Backstrap Loom*, Santa Maria de Jesus, Guatemala c. 1976.

ferent sizes, and were constructed in different, often complex ways according to the type of weaving and patterning being done. Learning to do pattern weaving for the designs presented still another challenge. Understanding the diversity of designs, size, and colors was yet another part of the whole picture of weaving with this loom. This experience changed my life and made me want to share my knowledge, which I did in 1975 through my first book, Backstrap Weaving, *an instructional book which guided the reader to construct and use a backstop loom.*

Anderson received NEA funding in 1976 for a book on textile arts in Guatemala. *For that book,* Guatemalan Textiles Today, *I needed to do photography which would communicate the weaver's techniques and to show the textiles they produced. When I explained my purpose for taking pictures to the weavers, most were welcoming. My box of previously made prints that I always showed them helped convey my respect for their art and demonstrate my goals.*

Marilyn Anderson's books, exhibits, and presentations, seen as a whole, disrupt conventional assumptions about linear time, technological change,

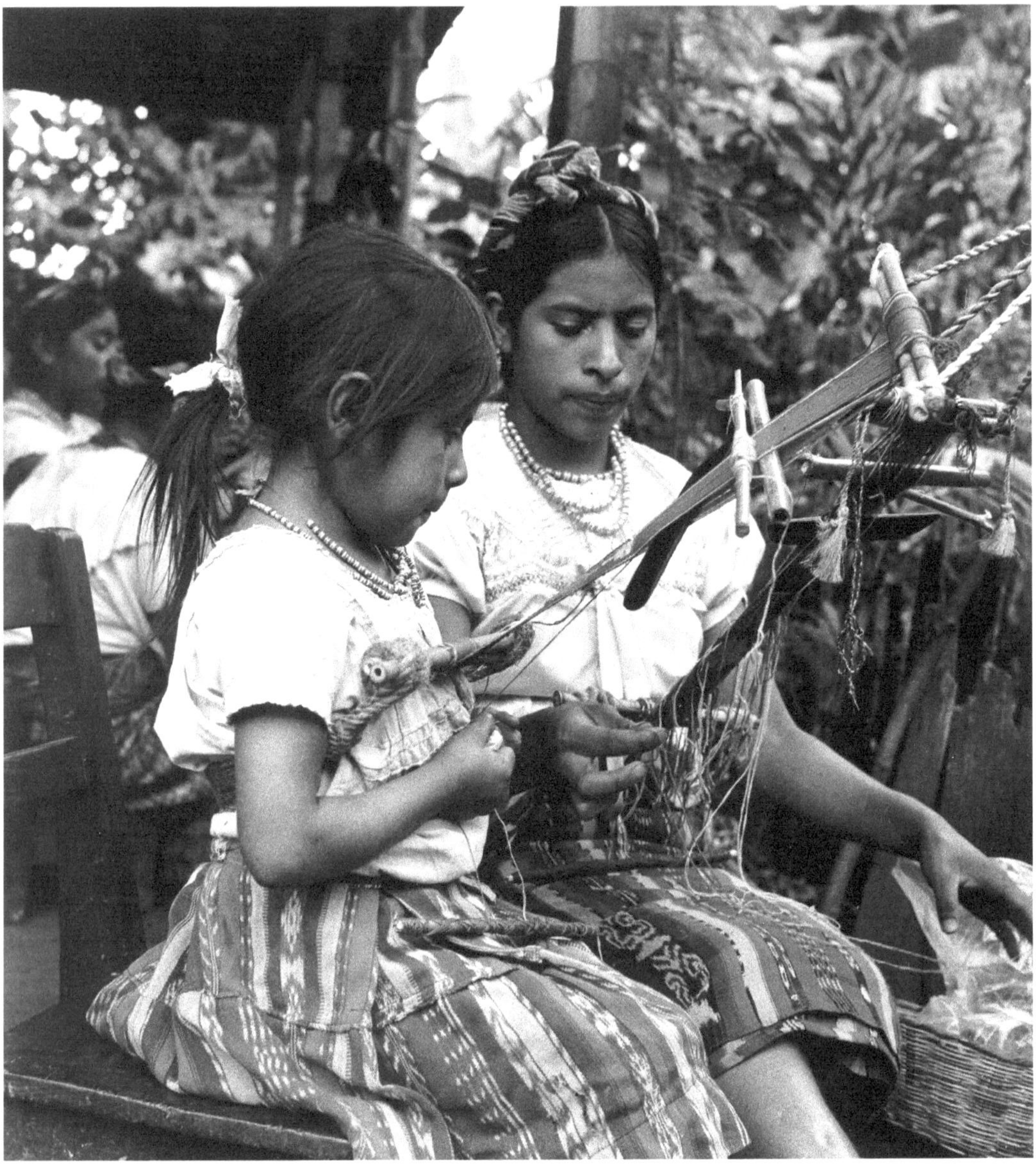

Marilyn Anderson (1937), photographer, *Young Woman and Child Backstrap Weaving*, Jacaltenango, Guatemala c. 1976.

and progress.[6] The inter-relational elements of her work quietly and persistently demonstrate the importance of workers controlling their own labor, whether they are Guatemalan weavers or assembly line workers building electrical motors.

Upon returning from photographing and doing textile research in Guatemala in 1976, and much more now, I realize how privileged I was to do that project. Since then, enormous changes have happened to Guatemala, to the situation of Maya women, the weaving, and to the culture and traditions that enabled it. My

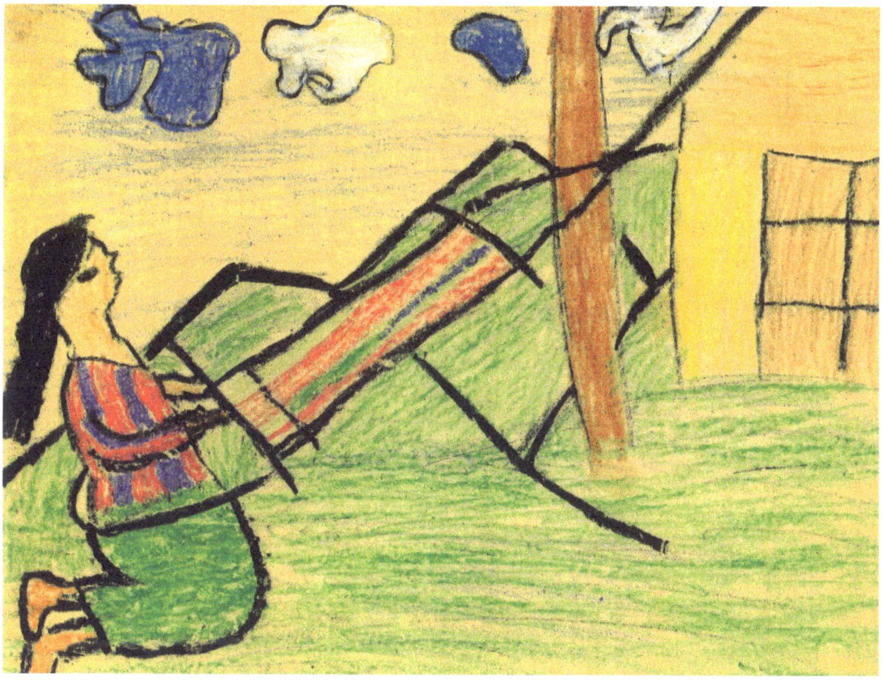

Marilyn Anderson (1937), photographer, *Drawing by a Child,* from one of the art classes Marilyn taught in Jacaltenango, 1968.

boxes of photos, which resulted from my travels and research, show a different Guatemala and the differences between the weaving of that era and the present.

Tragic changes happened in the 1980s, a time often called in Guatemala "La Violencia" (the violent time). These changes involved brutal army repression . . . on the Maya. Because of accusations of cooperation and some participation in the guerilla movement, Maya suffered massacres, bombing, dislocation, and rape. Thousands fled to neighboring Mexico. Reports began to appear documenting these events. One showed a cover photo of a woman wearing the traditional dress of the town where I had lived nearly two years [Jacaltenango, a mountain village without roads, electricity, or plumbing, at that time]. *This photo shocked me into action. In 1983, impelled by the meanings of this photograph, Jon Garlock and I traveled to refugee camps in southern Mexico. This was the first of our several investigative trips. In one, we encountered residents who indeed were from the town where I had lived. As in the 1970s, I carried a box of my previous photos from Guatemala to introduce myself to refugees and to help them to understand my connections to Guatemala. We documented the situation of the refugees through photographing and interviewing and disseminated our findings here in the US through lectures and slide shows. We also brought back drawings done by children in the camps, which showed bombing and destruction of their homes and villages. Some of these drawings were later seen in the film* WHEN THE MOUNTAINS TREMBLE.[7]

Marilyn Anderson and Jon Garlock followed the news from Amnesty International, Human Rights Watch, and the Guatemalan Human Rights Commissions USA/Mexico, and many other sources reporting on the war on indigenous people in Guatemala. Nearly five hundred primarily Maya communities were destroyed. *I learned that many of the towns where I had visited in 1976 to photograph weavers had suffered from army aggression. The "scorched earth" tactics used by the army caused hundreds of thousands of Maya, union leaders and others to flee not only to Mexico, but to the USA and other countries. It also resulted in the displacement of about a million people inside Guatemala.*

A photograph by Jean Marie Simon, in her book Guatemala: Eternal Spring, Eternal Tyranny, *showed how culture, too, was attacked.*[8] *It depicted army training of soldiers to teach them to recognize the traditional dress used in different towns. Maya knew about this army tactic, and women and men from areas designated by the army as "subversive," and during the worst days of army repression, did not dare to wear their traditional clothing—because patterns and colors identified their ethnic group and their community. (During my first return trip to Guatemala since 1980, with a human rights delegation in 1992, a Maya woman told us that was the response in her village of those who had worn traditional dress.)*

In 1985, Anderson and Garlock developed a way of conveying what was happening in Guatemala. They created exhibits using photographic portraits of weavers that Marilyn had taken ten years before and juxtaposed them with text panels, a ribbon of names that Marilyn calligraphed of hundreds of women who had been "disappeared" or had been murdered. *This dialectical format used my portraits with text that was intentionally not descriptive of the portraits. Images were not illustrative of the text and the text was not used as captions to the photos. We also included excerpts from our refugee interviews. Viewer reactions to the exhibit and to the slide show ranged from disbelief that we were truthful (dissemination of news about the reality of the repression in Guatemala was slow to appear in the national press) to those who wept when they saw the photos and read the text.*

Anderson and Garlock designed the exhibit of photos and text panels so it could be packed in a special case and sent via UPS to more than 150 locations in the United States, Canada, and Mexico. They titled the exhibit *Granddaughters of Corn*, words from a poem by Guatemalan poet Otto René Castillo. Eventually, the Unitarian Universalist Service Committee also took charge of a second version of *Granddaughters of Corn* and independently circulated the exhibit. It was designed to be appropriate for an art gallery or for other informal spaces. It was shown in churches, galleries, the corridors of colleges and universities, and in other public spaces such as the city hall of Los Angeles.

In 1986 a publisher invited them to submit a manuscript using photos from the *Granddaughters of Corn* exhibit with additional images and text. Their collaborative effort took on this new dimension. *The text for the book included not only the names of the disappeared and excerpts of our interviews with refugees but also many other sources. Jon and I took great care to verify both . . . the names of the disappeared and the other material we included. We consulted with representatives of Guatemalan groups in exile and human rights organizations as we proceeded to prepare our book. This required trips to Washington, DC, and Mexico City for meetings with the Guatemalan Human Rights Commissions USA /Mexico. We received encouragement from them to proceed with our book and indeed would not have proceeded without their approval. Laborious effort was also needed to obtain the many permissions for use of the quotations we included.*

Their book *Granddaughters of Corn* appeared in 1988.[9] Anderson printed the photographs and Garlock wrote the introduction and edited material from many sources. Their exhibit continued to travel; sometimes two sets traveled to different locations at the same time, reaching over fifty U.S. cities. This is the work of commoning, crossing geographical and political borders, presenting material many Americans prefer not to see or know. It is also an example of how photography, in its inception and dissemination, is **not** used as an imperialist tool. Marilyn Anderson offers another kind of image circuitry. A camera in her hands is a conduit, not a weapon; she photographs out of relationships formed rather than captured. Fluent in Spanish and other languages, she developed a practice, early on, of introducing herself to weavers in Guatemalan villages by showing them pictures taken of weavers in other villages, explaining and assuring people that their craft and communal traditions would be respectfully documented. The images that emerge in her books and exhibits come out of this process of reciprocity and mutual recognition. By the time she was ready to pack her cameras, she had established rapport with village weavers, and then one and another, primarily women, sometimes with their children, would ask, perhaps shyly, if she might have her photograph taken. Her subjects determined how they wanted to present themselves to her camera. They are clothed in the woven garments of their own making. She recalls a later encounter: *In the 1990s, I began to travel to Guatemala again and to photograph and do research. Peace Accords were signed in 1996 and that year I was happy to return to the town* [Jacaltenango] *where I had lived longest. There I found our book* Granddaughters of Corn *in the hands of a young man who taught the reading and writing of the Pop'ti language as part of a national program to support the use of Maya languages. He and I sat down for an hour, and as he slowly turned the pages, we talked about the book and the photographs in it. Because it is in English, we talked mainly about the photos. His appreciation alone made the effort Jon and I had made to make the book seem worthwhile.*

Granddaughters of Corn: Portraits of Guatemalan Women forces the developed-world viewer to work, that is, to make meaning out of each page's photograph and texts. First the eye is drawn to Anderson's stunning photograph, maybe a young mother, or a child, or an elder, maybe at the loom, or

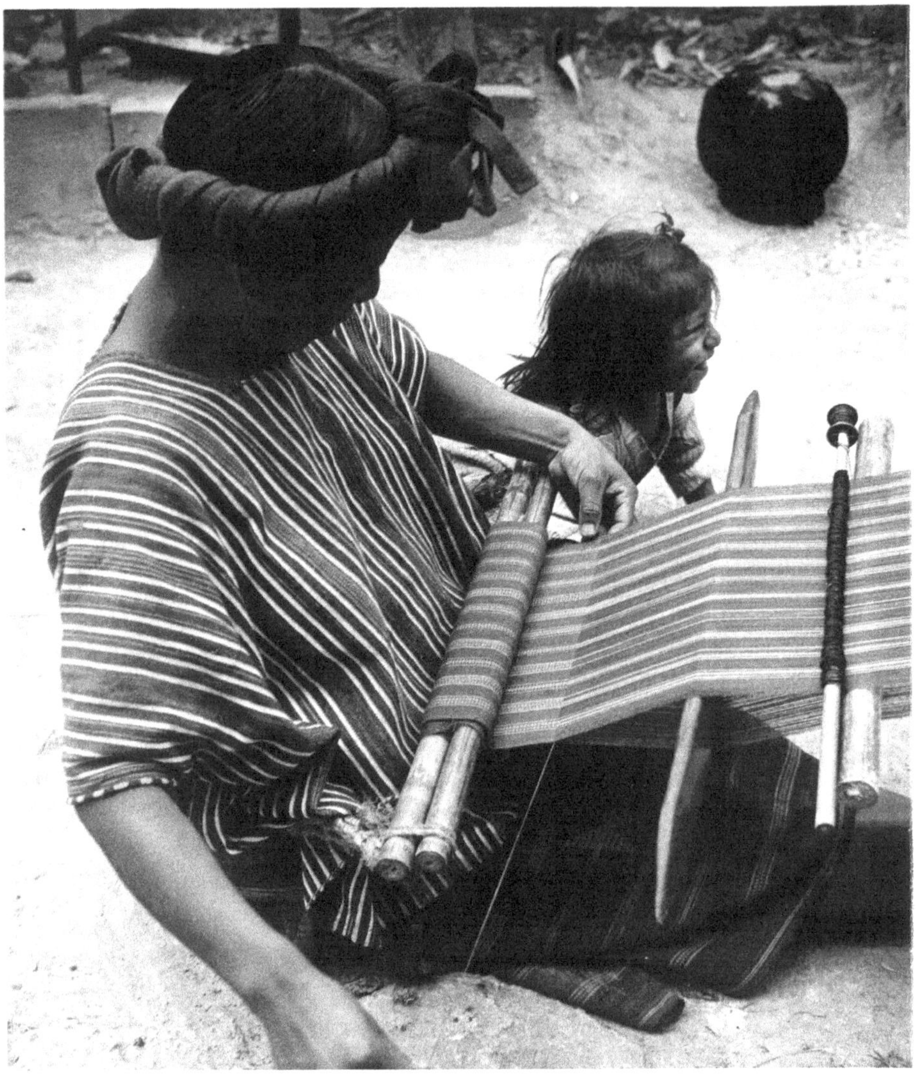

way to market in Guatemala City, April 13 • Olga Marina Paredes Saravia, 50, disappeared in Guatemala City • Jésica Mariel Hernández, 8, disappeared en route to the store, Guatemala City, April 15 • Alma Violeta Rivas del Cid, 15, disappeared in Guatemala City, April 18 • Xiomara Valexca Saraccini Ramazini, 17, disappeared after lunch, Guatemala

From *Granddaughters of Corn*, 1988, courtesy Marilyn Anderson and Jonathan Garlock.

possibly standing in a doorway. These women wear the intricate weavings of their culture—their embroidered *huipils* (upper garment), woven *corte* (skirt), elaborate *cintas* (ribbons, bands, cloths) circling their heads. Next, the eye turns to the parallel texts, not commentary on the image, but a record of destruction: "more than 800 women were raped by soldiers" . . . "By the end of 1980 over 400 teachers had been killed" . . . "When the troops were

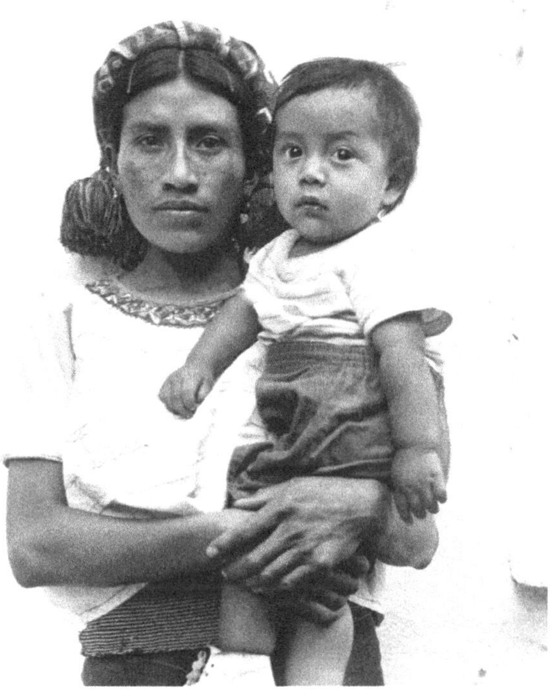

Question: "Who in your family has disappeared?"

Answer: "My father, Rigoberto Morales."
"My brother, Máynor Morales."
"My brother, Otto Raúl Morales."
"My brother, Armando Roberto Morales."
"My uncle, Moisés Morales."
"My uncle, Salomón Morales."
"My aunt, Lilián Aida Morales."
"My aunt, Elizabeth Morales."
"My aunt, Sipriana Ramírez de Morales."
"My cousin, Damaris Marleni Morales."
"My cousin, María Victoria Morales."
"My cousin, Hector Manolo Morales."
"My cousin, Noé Salomón Morales."
"My cousin, Byron Moisés Morales."
"My cousin, Abygail Morales."
"My cousin, Claudia Roxana Morales."[105]

bus station, Guatemala City, July 19 • Karina Zusette Leal Moctezuma, 16, disappeared on her way to school, July 23, Retalhuleu • Two Salvadoran women known as Sara and Antonia were taken from a bar in Amatitlan by armed men driving a blue van with polarized windows in August, 1986 •

in Papachala, soldiers snatch a new born baby from its mother's arms and began to play soccer—with the infant as the ball."[10] And then the eye lowers to the gray ribbon of names, at the bottom of page after page, a steady litany of *las desaparecidas*: *Edna Magaly Cifuentes, 14, peasant Berta Monterroso, 37, Maria Hayda Garcia Micaela Gabriel, 15, peasant Olivia Rodriguez, 19, Maria Argentina Mus, 14, student Lidia Son Monroy, 21, Dolores Piedad Alpirez Irma Y.*

Mundo Humbelina Flores, 34, Juventina Bolanos, 45, Maria Quiej, 58, peasant Adelina de la Cruz, 21, peasant.[10]

Or maybe your sequence of looking could differ. It is difficult not to see the beautiful photograph first. But then you have to decide how to see, what to take in. You must look not just at the beauty but also at the horror: "women were weaving when the army arrived . . . the first thing the soldiers did was to cut down the loom with a machete. And when they had cut down all the warp threads of the loom, they began raping two young women. After raping them, they tortured them. They cut off their hands and cut off their noses and ears in front of their own mother."[11]

Anderson and Garlock include voices from the Guatemalan refugee camps along the Mexican border:

> "Our culture has survived because it was not made in one month or one year. Rather it comes from our ancestors. . . . Even our Indian dress has come under attack in Guatemala because we are obliged to take it off. Why? Because the rich and the army say that all of us Indian people are communists, and subversive. So for our own safety, so that they will not take us, so that they will not kidnap and torture us, we have stopped wearing our Indian dress. This is a painful thing because for us this way of dressing is also our culture. . . ."[12]

One of the last photographs in the book is of a young girl. She is wearing a Western-style dress; it is dirty; her mouth is tight, but her eyes look directly into the camera. And, then, notice—all the fingers of her right hand have been chopped off.

Marilyn Anderson and Jon Garlock created a visual and textual heteroglossia, multiple voices, texts, words, images,[13] a dialectical method and model for conveying beauty and horror without diminishing either.

To understand the development and construction of Anderson's books, exhibits, photographs, and methods for dissemination, it is useful to return to the idea of good work. And what is that? And how is it related to art making?

As an alternative to modernism's "make it new" and a postmodern hyper-individualism of monetized art, Marilyn Anderson offers other artists and informed curators a model and a method that *serves* rather than captures, that *restores* rather than ransacks. It requires a consciousness of ways of knowing, of multiple epistemological layers. This is larger than well-intentioned representation. It involves a linking of art to non-alienated labor. It constructs a commons where labor and art are not bifurcated.[14] Perhaps one has to turn to organized labor, not academic institutions, to recognize the necessity of this intervention.

Marilyn Anderson's subjects and her own artistic practices are living examples of un-alienated labor. When a Guatemalan weaver can produce her richly textured and colored garment without coercion, censorship, or

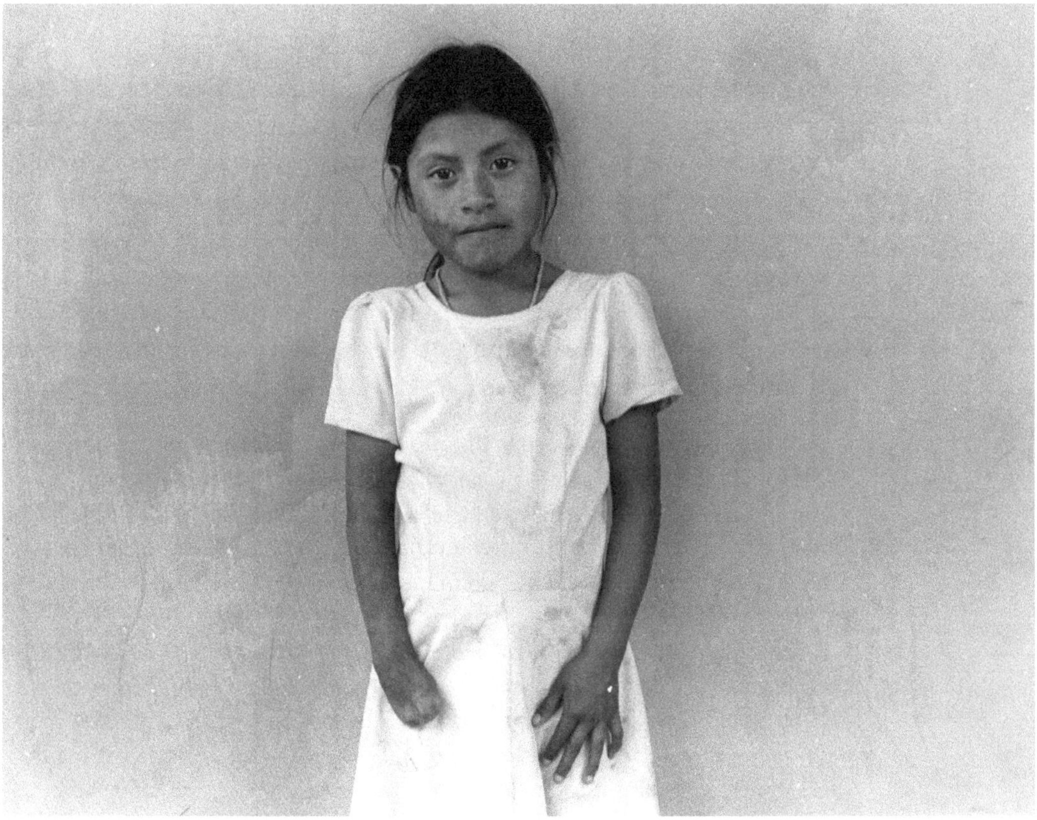

Marilyn Anderson (1937), photographer, *Refugee Girl*, mutilated by Guatemalan Army,"1982.

outside control, when she possesses the space, companionship, and community to learn and teach her skills, and when she can earn an income from her craft in fair trade, she is doing what should be natural to all workers—working well. What U.S. popular media fails to name in current accounts about workers leaving or forced to leave their jobs is the deeper Marxian language of estrangement and alienation.[15] Or, as the un-alienated, un-estranged stone mason in Studs Terkel's *Working* puts it, "It's a pretty good day layin' stone or brick. Not tiring. Anything you like to do isn't tiresome."[16]

In *Guardianes de Las Artes/Guardians of the Arts* (2016), Anderson presents her own woodcut prints of Guatemalan craft workers—weavers, knotters, embroiderers, hat makers, paper cutters, stone carvers, tile makers, silver smiths, potters, glass blowers, mask makers, blacksmiths, and many other forms of "slow art." Her woodcuts of process and products—of making by hand—hats, bags, hammocks, pots, sandals, masks, marimbas—emerge from her subjects' generational memory and knowledge.

With *Guardians of the Arts,* Marilyn Anderson closes a circle. Her forty-three woodcut relief prints are organized by fabrication technique and raw material. Over ten years in the making, based on decades of observations, photographs, drawings, and conversations—years of relationships—and drawing on German and Mexican woodcut traditions, Anderson created a book that not only presents her own artistic virtuosity, but also foregrounds crafts of beauty and utility as well as their makers—men, women, or children, all concentrating (in Anderson's depictions) on the task at hand. She becomes a guardian of the guardians, whose skills have been passed (down and across) generationally in families and villages. This is more than an art book; it is a lesson on how to show multiple ways of knowing, multiple epistemologies, outside institutions. Anderson widens our knowledge and vision with personal story, learning, making, showing. She writes,

> *This book aims to foster deeper appreciation for the beauty and history of Guatemalan arts and crafts. . . . Living in Jacaltenango in the 1960s and '70s, I became curious about how huipils and other crafts are made. In order to understand them, I learned to make a number of them. All my experiences learning how to make crafts helped me later as I made the relief prints that illustrate this book.*
>
> *I was taught to weave by a skilled, patient Maya teacher. . . . As a novice weaver, I learned to build and maintain looms, to execute the proper motions and steps of weaving, and to sustain the backstrap loom's proper tension. . . . [E]veryone in Jacaltenango, young and old, knew how these arts and crafts were made, especially weaving. A neighbor once remarked, "everybody knows how weaving is done."*[17]

Guardians of the Arts calls for slow reading and viewing. Consider the rattan weaver.

Like the depicted maker/weaver whose large hands firmly grasp the developing circle of rattan, we readers/viewers see the action of the craft from a downward perspective, as we notice the embracing position of his body as he works the natural material into a seat for a stool. Anderson explains, "with an ancient twining technique, he twists two or more alternating wefts one by one around the uprights. He and others in the workshop expertly coax the rattan into many different shapes to create several types of furniture which can be of simple or elaborate construction."[18] Into the larger relief, Anderson inserts a small woodcut of the finished stool for the reader, who may not be familiar with the skill and the product. Aesthetics and utility are not separate. While the intense colors of Guatemalan weavings draw our eyes, their crafts, through Anderson's book, call for our respectful attention as well: "Juana Camposeco, my late friend and neighbor in Jacaltenango, taught me to value crafts both as beautiful objects and as useful utensils. While showing me a newly acquired gourd for tortilla storage, she exclaimed: 'How lovely it is!'"[19]

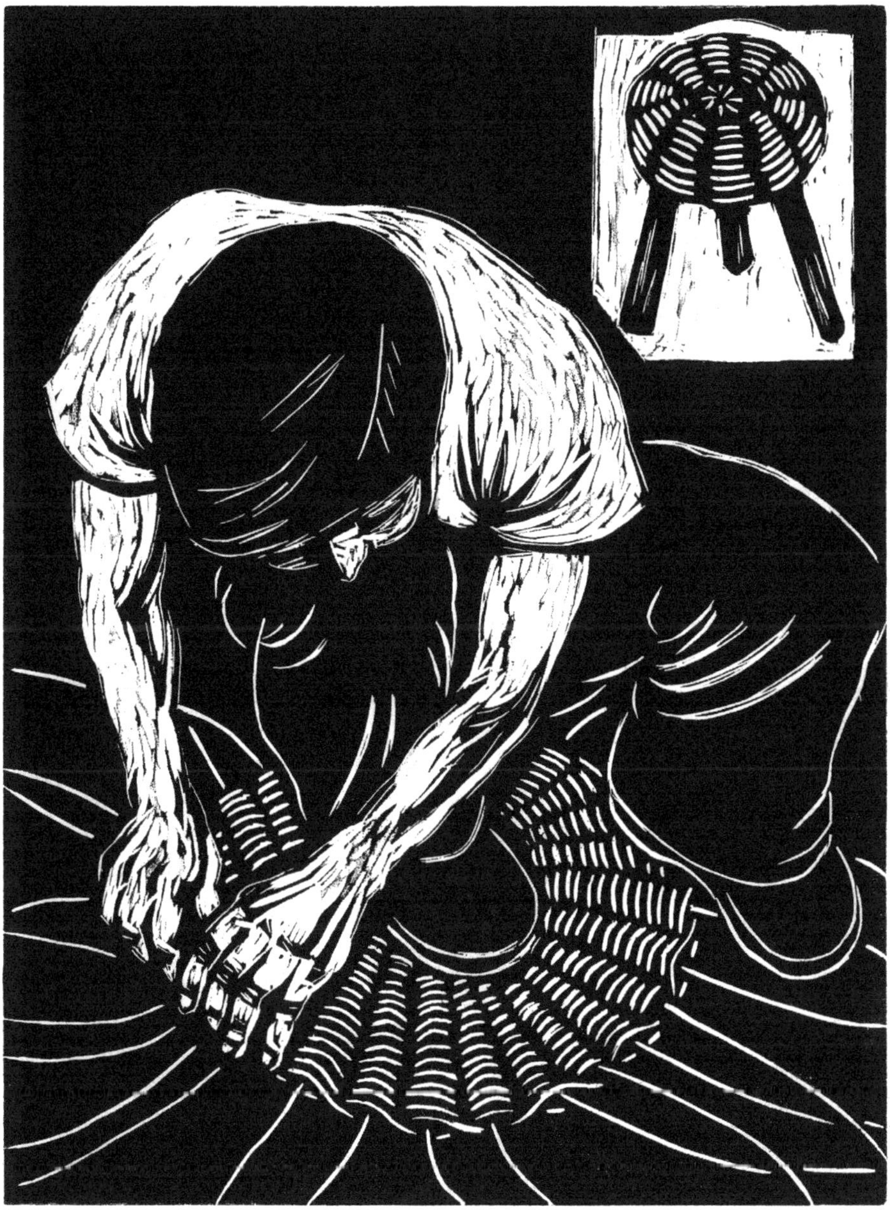

Marilyn Anderson (1937), *Rattan Artisan/Tejedor de mimbrer* from *Guardianes de las Artes*, 2016.

Marilyn Anderson offers another way of seeing and making art. Her body of work testifies to the inseparability of art, craft, and the laboring hand across cultures, histories, and geographies. She also forces us not to look away from the cutting presence of brutality and political domination. Anderson has earned her guardianship.

Photography and the Art of Returning

It is 1915. An itinerant photographer accompanied by a placid pony makes inquiries. "How about a picture of your children on the pony?" This mother wanted such a picture, but "How much? The cost?" Satisfied that some money could be scraped together, and likely without the permission of her husband, she agreed to the picture.

The setting is a cityscape, near their apartment in Union City, New Jersey. The woman pictured here is my grandmother Anna. The baby she holds is my mother, her two brothers astride the pony. This woman, Anna, *desired* a photograph of herself and her children. It must have been a spontaneous decision—no time to wash the kids or change out of her soiled apron. She is an immigrant, illiterate though the daughter of a rabbi, estranged from her family in Europe because she married a Catholic. Powerless, one might say. She cannot take pictures of her children; owning a camera is beyond what's possible. But she looks directly at the photographer. She presents herself and her young children. This is an exchange, not a theft. A hundred years later, this photograph survives.

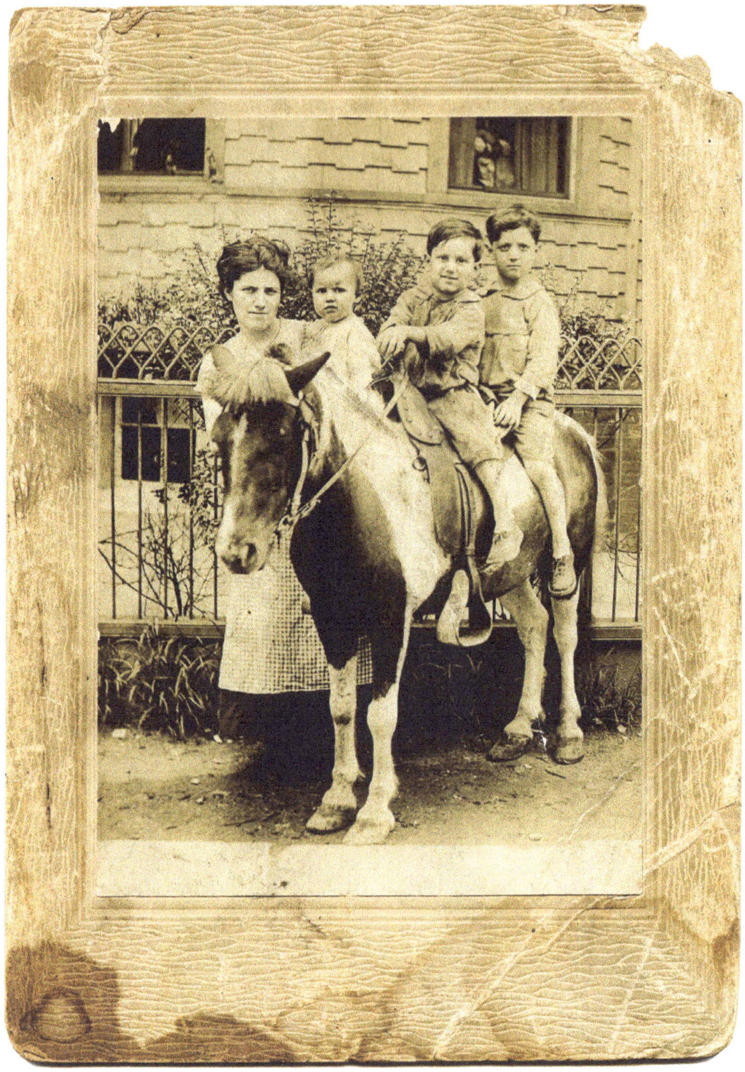

Anna and children, Parisi/Zandy family photograph.

I am the recipient of Anna's pictorial desire. The photograph represents the most commonplace generational wish—to have photographs of one's children. Yet it evokes something larger than family sentiment or easy nostalgia. It speaks to the circumstances around the taking of a photograph and the relationship between photographer and subject. Whose photographic desire dominates? How is the photograph the result of an achieved balance between desires?

This photography section emerges out of multiple, intersecting desires—emotional, intellectual, historical, political, aesthetic, cultural. It harbors my own protective sense toward those who desire images but do not control them, especially as those photos may enter the circuitry of public consumption. This work of returning is also the work of building or rebuilding relationships, a mutuality between photographer and others over a long period of time. This is not the photographic language of shooting and capturing, and certainly not a transaction in a material or political sense. These images are *given*, not *taken*. It is visual trust and visual commoning.[1]

The parallels between the Swedish photographer Jens S. Jensen and the American photographer Milton Rogovin are uncanny. Or perhaps not, if one is willing to trace an alternative art imaginary and a lineage of working-class representation. Over a span of forty years, Jens S. Jensen (1946–2015) photographed people who lived in Hammarkullen, a working-class and immigrant suburb of Gothenburg, Sweden. For an equally long time, Milton Rogovin (1909–2011) photographed people who lived in Buffalo, particularly the Lower West Side, among many other photo series. Key to their parallel body of work is the photographer/artist *returning*—to the same families, friends, and neighborhoods. We see generations of working-class people grow older. We see presence and absence: the grandchild in a small carriage pushed by her grandfather; the grandfather in a wheelchair steered by the grown grandchild. The kid holding on, with one hand, to the rim of a wall; the adult man posing in front of that wall. Jensen and Rogovin, born in different countries a generation apart, never met or knew of each other. What they had in common is an aesthetic of human relationships joined to a skilled photographic eye. As Jens Jensen wrote to Mark Rogovin in 2014, "Yes, it seems like Milton and I have a lot in common!" Through the agency of their photography, the word *common* shifts from noun to verb.

Jens S. Jensen, born in Stockholm in 1946, and Milton Rogovin, born in Brooklyn in 1909, were educated, politically conscious intellectuals who developed affinities with workers and immigrants. They both trained for professions other than photography—Milton was an optometrist; Jens an architect. They both played the cello as amateurs. They both envisioned a photographic process that affirmed ordinary culture over consumerism and elitism. They both photographed workers at home and on the job. Their photography was intentionally instrumental, a secular practice of *tikkun olam,* repairing the world. Their curiosity was generous; they didn't pathologize or categorize.

Jens S. Jensen and Milton Rogovin have differences, of course. Jensen relied more on voice and textuality, using a tape recorder in his work with residents of Hammarkullen. Jensen was his own oral historian; Rogovin worked with oral historian Michael Frisch, matching his steelworker photographs with Frisch's oral histories. Rogovin was also protective of the identities of his subjects. Names of families were listed in his private notes but not revealed in his books. In Rogovin's *Triptychs: Buffalo's Lower West Side Revisited* (later expanded into *Quartets*), there are no names, just years: "1973 / 1985 / 1992"—numbers with resonance for the viewer and the families.

How best to see these two photographers in juxtaposition? Consider how the passage of time speaks in their photography. An ordinary photograph may hold the ephemeral still, but an expansive photograph might hint at the movement within that stillness. Working-class-focused photographers like Jens S. Jensen and Milton Rogovin respectfully reveal movement in that stillness. For those anxious or insistent in placing them into a photographic category, I would recommend a hybrid understanding: part documentary (Jensen's inclination), part portraiture (a category Rogovin rejected). Better, perhaps, to drop the categorical imperative and use paleontologist Stephen Jay Gould's metaphors of arrows and cycles: "time's arrow—a sequence of unique events moving in a definite direction" and "time's cycle—some dependable or lawlike constancy amidst the flux . . . in order to make time comprehensible."[2] Milton Rogovin and Jens S. Jensen demonstrate how photography can visualize arrows and cycles in human lives. I wish for the necessary resources to stage a future joint exhibit of Rogovin and Jensen photographs, visual transnational testimony to human patterns of arrows and cycles.[3]

Milton Rogovin

His Leaves of Grass

December 30, 1909, Manhattan, New York–
January 18, 2011, Buffalo, New York

I never could warm up to the middle class in photography. The artist Käthe Kollwitz . . . said that portraying the poor was the thing that interested her most, and doing it sort of helped her survive.
—Milton Rogovin, *The Forgotten Ones*

In a little house keep I pictures suspended,
. . . it has room for all the shows of the world, all memories!
Here the tableaus of life, and here the groupings of death;
. . . With finger rais'd he points to the prodigal pictures.
—Walt Whitman, "My Picture Gallery," *Leaves of Grass*

Milton Rogovin answered Lewis Hine's call for an "intelligent interpretation of the world's workers, not only for the people of today, but for future ages."[1] Rogovin photographed ordinary people at home and at work (or out of work) in Buffalo, Appalachia, China, Chile, Zimbabwe, many places.[2] He did not *capture* or *contain* his subjects but rather **presented**—evoked—their inherent dignity. Rogovin's photographs, as individual portraits or as sequenced series, are specific yet adhere to something larger—sets of relationships, circumstances of work, expressions of culture—as well as allude to constellations of other Rogovin pictures.

Consider Milton Rogovin's capacious body of work as akin to Walt Whitman's *Leaves of Grass* and its accretions of poetic proclamations, observations, and encounters from 1855 to 1892. Whitman sang his collective self. Milton Rogovin's chorus—and there is a musicality to his images—is a democratic imaginary of Hine's "ever the human document." Melding technical prowess, imaginative aesthetics, and political consciousness, Rogovin saw significance in the ordinary. His continuum is of Lewis Hine and Käthe Kollwitz, his inspiration Bertolt Brecht and Pablo Neruda. Looking down into the lens of his Rolleiflex, asking permission of his subjects who posed themselves, Rogovin produced thousands of portraits of *lives*, not lifestyles.

Born in 1909 in Manhattan, the youngest son of Lithuanian Jewish immigrants who initially lived on One Hundred-Thirteenth Street, Milton experienced the cross-currents of the cultures of home and school. He attended public schools as well as Hebrew school and listened to the stories of Sholom Aleichem and Isaac Loeb Peretz that his mother read from Yiddish newspapers. He writes sympathetically about his mother's efficient household work and recalls living on the second floor of a five-story walkup, where lighting fixtures were fueled by gas and where the ice man would deliver an "ice block" every few days (reminiscent of Ralph Fasanella's father delivering ice). He recalls the pleasures of listening to music on the family's first record player, attending the Yiddish theater, and a rare visit to the Metropolitan Museum of Art and seeing Rosa Bonheur's painting *The Horse Fair* (also an important visual memory for Marilyn Anderson). He graduated from Stuyvesant High School, where he learned to use tools as well as studied academic subjects. After high school his family persuaded him to follow the career path of an older brother and become an optometrist. As a 1931 Columbia University graduate, he did not fit the stereotype of the working-class laborer. Yet, as the son of a bankrupt small store owner who died suddenly, as a young man experiencing and witnessing the no-safety-net suffering of the Great Depression, and through his lifelong self-education in literature, political philosophy, economics, music, and the visual arts, Rogovin taught himself how to see the worlds of working people.

We have these details of Milton Rogovin's early life because he responded to his wife, Anne Rogovin's, suggestion in 1997 that he write his life story. *Not having a television set, we usually spent our evenings reading, writing, or listening to music. Suddenly Anne dropped her newspaper and said, "Milton, I think you should write your autobiography!" At age 87, this was quite a challenge for me.*[3] In *Milton Rogovin: The Making of a Social Documentary Photographer,* art historian Melanie Anne Herzog weaves Milton's written autobiographical reminiscences with analysis of his place in the history of social documentary photography as well as the economic and political circumstances that shaped the Rogovins' lives. Multivocality aptly describes Herzog's integrated biography and also offers a way of seeing Milton's work patterns and photographic projects.

Milton Rogovin experienced the economic fissure of the Great Depression personally with his father's death and the bankruptcy of the family business, but also politically and intellectually by observing and understanding societal structural failure. His developing consciousness moved from the individual aspirations of an immigrant family to a larger vision of solidarity with the least fortunate and most overlooked. *My real education began after I graduated from Columbia. What I saw around me and personally experienced completely changed my way of thinking. I could no longer be indifferent to the problems of people, especially the poor, the forgotten ones. . . . My brother Sam told me about a class in political economy that would be held in a friend's apartment. The teacher, a gray-haired old man, came from the Workers' School run by the Communist Party. This class, plus many others that I subsequently attended, convinced me that socialism was the path we should take to create a more equitable society.*[4]

Rogovin sought an integrated life. He made a living as an optometrist in optical offices in Manhattan at first, then found a job in Buffalo in 1938 where he joined the United Optical Workers Local Industrial Union. He helped raise funds for the Spanish Civil War, listened to music by Prokofiev, Shostakovich, and Sibelius and studied the art of Francisco Goya, Honoré Daumier, and Käthe Kollwitz. In Buffalo he met Anne Snetsky (later her name changed to Setters) and they married in 1942. Anne was a crucial catalyst in the development and continuation of Milton's work as a photographer. She encouraged him to open his own optometry office in Buffalo, which was located near a union hall and union newspaper. Because of her innate warmth, extroverted personality, dogged letter writing, narrative sense in the development of series, and critical eye for the placement of Milton's photographs in galleries and museums, Anne enabled Milton to claim his talent as a photographer, work that wove artistry and activism. This is more than a detail about a supportive spouse. Rather, it illuminates how artists, either from the working class or in solidarity with workers, struggle to give themselves **permission** to become artists. Some have the support of family members, like Kollwitz; some have to balance labor with art making, like Ralph Fasanella and Ruth Asawa. Is this effort to claim oneself as an artist relevant to all artists, or is it particularly shaped by class, race, and gender? And how is class a determining element if the art making is not targeted for consumption and markets?[5]

The Great Depression, the Spanish Civil War, World War II, and the McCarthy era of political prosecution were all shaping forces on Milton Rogovin and his choice of photographic subjects and series. In 1942–43, he was inducted into the Armed Forces, served in the Air Force, acquired a camera, and won an amateur photography contest. *I was transferred from the Air Force to a general hospital unit connected with the Ground Forces and we were immediately scheduled for shipment overseas. A few days before we shipped out, Anne gave birth to our first child, Ellen. I asked for permission to see Anne and Ellen but this request was denied. Our unit soon left for overseas and I didn't see my child, except for photographs, until she was sixteen months old.*[6]

When he returned, he resumed work as an optometrist, joining his brother Sam in their optometry practice, Consumers Eyesight Service, in Buffalo. While raising a young family, he and Anne reached out to others through weekly learning, studying, and discussion sessions in their home. *The beauty of these sessions was that people of various ethnic groups as well as different political beliefs participated.*[7] Notice the word *beauty*. Milton's understanding of **beauty** is always larger than bourgeois aesthetics. *It is important to understand that as a Marxist I am not indifferent to a beautiful body, a cloud formation, or the forms created by peeling paint. But I feel my priority should be to create through my photography a better understanding of the problems facing working people.*[8] Rogovin didn't encourage analysis of himself as a photographer, but rather urged analysis of structural inequalities.

Thwarting or expanding awareness of structural inequalities has never lost its relevancy to American politics—or to the shaping of art. The Rogovin family, including two more children, Mark, born in 1946, and Paula, born in 1947, experienced the burden of political constriction and oppression during the Cold War/McCarthy era. The formation of HUAC (House Un-American Activities Committee) in 1938, the blacklisting of the Photo League in 1947, the execution of the Rosenbergs in 1953, and the continuing climate of investigation and surveillance were external forces that affected the Rogovins' lives. This culminated in 1957 when Milton, age forty-eight, was summoned to appear before one of HUAC's committees and was targeted in Buffalo newspapers as being the "Number One Red" in Buffalo. Actually, he was an optometrist trying to register Black voters.

As a result of these vicious and untruthful attacks, our optometry practice was severely affected. Our patients were afraid to come to our office for fear that they too might be accused of being "reds."

My appearance before the House on Un-American Activities Committee was very painful. Until the last few days before the hearing I was unable to find an attorney to represent me. . . . I refused to answer any questions other than my name and occupation. . . . What was especially painful was the effect the attacks had on my family and our true friends. . . . Children on our street were warned against playing with the "the Rogovin children." People who we knew very well were afraid to greet us openly on the street.

This experience brings to mind a statement that the German graphic artist Käthe Kollwitz wrote in her diary: "There is this curious silence surrounding the expulsion of my work from the Academy show . . . Scarcely anyone had anything to say to me about it. I thought people would come, or at least write—but no. Such a silence, all around us. That too has to be experienced."[9]

And yet we managed to survive. Since Anne refused to sign the "Loyalty Oath" necessary to become a teacher in the Buffalo school system she finally got a job in the suburbs [for the Board of Cooperative Education as a special education teacher]. *When she offered to resign because of the attacks against me, the superintendent urged her to stay on. He too had been attacked during the First World War because of his German ancestors.*

The result of all these attacks on me by the newspapers, as well as the constant surveillance, was that my political voice was essentially silenced. Under those new circumstances, I turned to activities other than political ones . . . Since I had always been interested in classical music, I decided to study the cello; when our son Mark became a teenager he also played the cello and we both joined the Community Music School Orchestra.[10]

Anne and Milton Rogovin engaged in purposeful travel. During Anne's school breaks in the early 1950s, they traveled to Mexico City, where they met artists from the *Taller de Gráfica Popular* (TGP, People's Graphic Arts Workshop). Perhaps influenced by Käthe Kollwitz's artistry, they understood the power of graphic arts as a political and cultural force—as well as the potential beauty of humble linoleum prints and woodcuts. Like Marilyn Anderson's efforts to bring Guatemalan textiles to an American audience, like Elizabeth Catlett's desire to reach out to her Mexican and African American communities, the Rogovins brought TGP prints back to Buffalo. So began their pattern of *commoning* art.

In 1957–58, soon after he was summoned to appear before HUAC, Rogovin joined his friend William Tallmadge, a professor of music at Buffalo State University College, in entering spaces that were not their own, Buffalo's African American storefront churches. Tallmadge, an ethnomusicologist educated at Oberlin College, recorded music during services, while Rogovin photographed the congregants and preachers as they engaged in life-sustaining Black religious expression.[11] Rogovin faced two challenges: as a white outsider in a Black community and as a photographer wrestling with technicalitics of lighting and aperture. *I readily accepted my friend's offer since I felt that once again I could speak out about the problems of the poor, but this time through my photography.*[12] He also wanted his photographs to be technically good, to hold up visually. He respectfully and deliberately consulted other photographers, writers, and church participants to improve the quality of his photographs. *Every Sunday evening at about midnight my friend and I went to the Holiness Church service that was held in an abandoned movie house. . . . For me, this truly was a "learning by doing" process. Since I had never studied photography at any school, I had to learn to use my camera and flash in this poorly lit church. Heretofore most of my photographic work had been with natural light. . . . After we worked together for three months, my friend completed his recordings. But I continued to work in a number of storefront churches for a period of three years. . . . At this time I began to appreciate documentary work in*

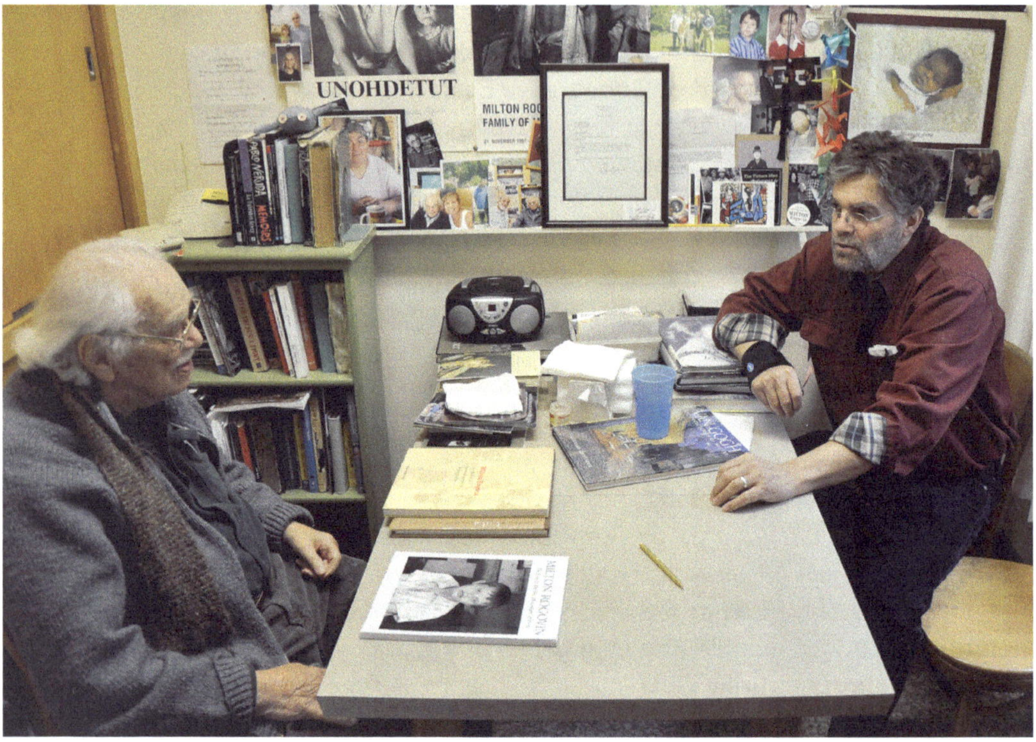

Milton and Mark Rogovin at their kitchen table, Buffalo, New York, 2010? © The Family of Milton Rogovin, www.miltonrogovin.com, photographer unknown.

comparison to casual "shooting." In some ways it is more difficult since each shot had to relate to the general theme I had selected.[13]

Rogovin also engaged the critical eyes of his family. He would post his newly printed photos on the bulletin board above the table where the family shared meals. His older daughter, Ellen, recalls her father asking for comments and suggestions about the photographs: "So we would say, 'I think you should crop the photo here' or crop it in another place. And there would be a discussion of our suggestions. In a very small way, we were all involved in evaluating newly printed photographs." Mark Rogovin adds, "All photos were 'fair game' for praise and criticism. Our mother was very much a part of each critique. She saw these photographs as a family accomplishment."

Rogovin's *Storefront Churches* series marked the beginning of his conception of photography as a thematic or geographic or occupational *series*. It also advanced his practice of listening to the people he photographed, giving them prints, and seeking help from them and others, often prominent photographers and writers, in order to improve his aesthetic and technical work. Mother Tokio, one of the storefront church preachers Rogovin photographed, would exclaim during a service, "You must get ready—you gotta get your ticket now."[14] Her language had a double resonance—urging

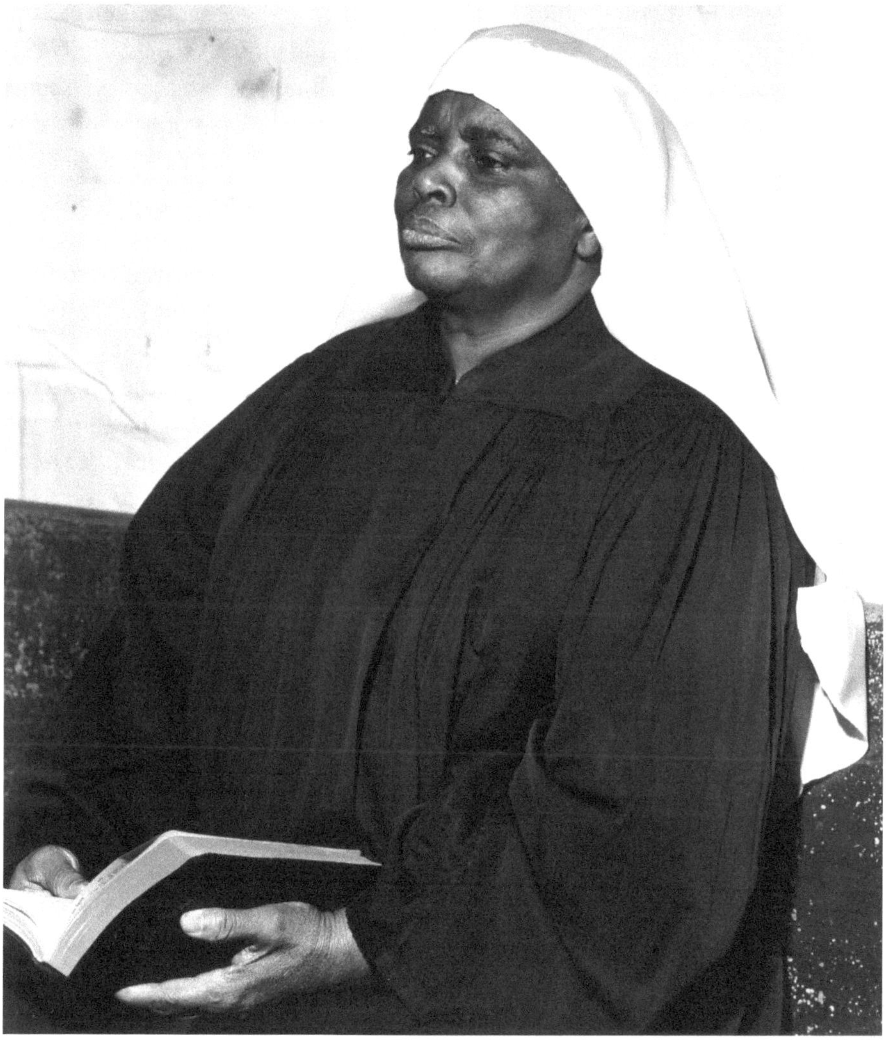

Milton Rogovin (1909–2011), "Mother Tokio," *Storefront Churches*, 1958–1961

her community toward repentance and redemption—and encouraging the nascent photographer to improve the quality of his photographs. *An important criticism came from Mother Tokio. She felt that I made the faces too dark. At first I was rather disturbed by her criticism. Later I realized that in printing the faces of these dark people I must preserve certain qualities that result in a fine photograph instead of a snapshot.*[15]

Rogovin also sought advice from other photographers, particularly Minor White, who was then curator at the George Eastman House (now the George Eastman Museum) and taught photography at the Rochester Institute of Technology. White cofounded *Aperture* magazine and published forty-eight photographs from Milton's *Storefront Churches* series in 1962 that included an accompanying essay by W. E. B. Du Bois (1868–1963). White was also instrumental in shaping Milton's thinking about photographic series, and series within series, rather than just selected individual images. *Every few weeks, I would send him some photographs and he would return them with some commentary. During this time I sent Minor about thirty photographs of a "guest" preacher delivering a sermon at one of the storefront churches. He suggested that instead of using one or two of these photographs as part of the larger series that I consider using a large group of them.*[16]

Rogovin's photographic (cinematic?) practices were inseparable from his life-long intellectual development. He read and was informed by Du Bois's *The Souls of Black Folks* while he was working on the *Storefront Churches* series.[17] *In the chapter "Religion of Our Fathers"* ["Of the Faith of the Fathers"], *Du Bois talks at length about the preacher, the music, and the trance. As a result of Du Bois's brilliant analysis I zeroed in on these three important features that I kept seeing in these churches.* Prompted by some criticism he received from two Black physicians in Buffalo about issues of representation (class concerns?), Rogovin wrote to Du Bois and asked his opinion about the *Storefront Churches* series. *Dr. Du Bois answered promptly and invited me to visit him at his home in Brooklyn. There I showed him my photographs, and he expressed great interest in them and offered to provide an introduction to this series.*[18]

The Storefront Churches series was a critical factor in turning me away from being a casual photographer to becoming a thoroughly committed social documentary photographer. Before starting any new series I would have to be convinced that it had the possibilities of dealing with the problems of people; especially the poor, the disadvantaged, the "forgotten ones."[19]

Viewing Rogovin's pictures involves relinquishing binary thinking about documentary versus fine art photography. Like Lewis Hine and contemporary photographers of labor Earl Dotter, Ken Light, and David Bacon, Rogovin produced aesthetically powerful photographs. These photographers may have their own recognizable style, a visual voice, but they are similar in their consistent focus on their subjects—workers—and not just on their own style or skill as photographers. They photographed people in discernible environments, not in front of a white sheet—as, for example, Richard Avedon's *In the American West* portraits (1985). The visual vocabulary of advertisement is not in the work of Dotter, Light, Bacon, or Rogovin. They photographed workers as dignified subjects, not as caricatures for entertainment or props for commercials.[20]

Rogovin understood the alignment of photographs in particular sequences as evident in the work of Minor White, Alfred Stieglitz, and later, Nathan Lyons. But sequences are not series. Series have implicit narratives, and often those narratives have political import. Series take time. Rogovin continued photographing in Buffalo's storefront churches for three years, long after Tallmadge completed his musicology study.[21]

Milton's awareness of the aesthetic and political potential of photographs grouped in series coupled with the Rogovins' informed reading about the devastation mining brought to the Appalachian landscape and to the lungs of miners shaped their decision to travel to West Virginia and eastern Kentucky over a period of nine hot summers. They began in 1962 by reaching out to the United Mine Workers union leadership and traveled to areas where small mines were located (most of the bigger mines were closed). Milton photographed people in their homes and on their porches, and Anne talked with the women particularly. They recorded some of these conversations with miners and their families and were welcomed because of Anne's exuberant good will and the Rogovins' unthreatening demeanor. The physical conditions were challenging. *With temperatures often in the 90s, and having to sleep in the back of our station wagon, it was no easy matter to make these photographs.*[22] His Appalachia photography (1962–71) was the prelude to Rogovin's worldwide *Family of Miners* photography series (1976–87).

Closer to home, Rogovin began photographing residents of Buffalo's Lower West Side, a six-square-block community. Starting in 1972, Milton and Anne returned to the neighborhood in 1984–85, in 1992 (*Triptychs*), and again in 2000–02 (*Quartets* 2002). Rogovin was always a self-reflective photographer: *It should be obvious to everyone that when we go into an area we do not do so with a "clean slate." On the contrary, we come, like a turtle, carrying our prejudices, our racism, our political orientations. . . . The selection of the Lower West Side or the mining villages of Appalachia is a political choice based on my desire not only to bring to the surface the conditions which exist but also to show that we are dealing with human beings.*[23] Rogovin did not stage people: *I wanted to get close and make the people be the most important thing in the frame. I never directed them or told them where to stand, how to hold their hands or what to wear. The only thing I asked them was to look at the camera. I liked it when I saw their eyes and that's when I knew I was ready to make their picture. Typically I would make two or three exposures. When you look at these pictures, you know there was no monkey business, and that I was not sneaking around trying to steal pictures of people.*[24] In 1975, 150 photographs from Milton Rogovin's *Lower West Side* series were exhibited at the Albright-Knox Art Gallery in Buffalo.

Rogovin's artistic and political rhythms called for focused projects. Bertolt Brecht's poem "A Worker Reads History" spoke to him: "In the evening when the Chinese wall was finished / Where did the masons go?"[25] He decided to photograph people working in the steel mills and foundries in or near Buffalo. In order to acquire the time to develop this new *Working People* series (1976–1987), and with the acquiescence of his family, he sold his optometry practice in 1978 when he was sixty-nine years old. Buoyed by the communal reception of his *Lower West Side* exhibit at the Albright-Knox, Rogovin decided to enter spaces not his own once again. He asked and

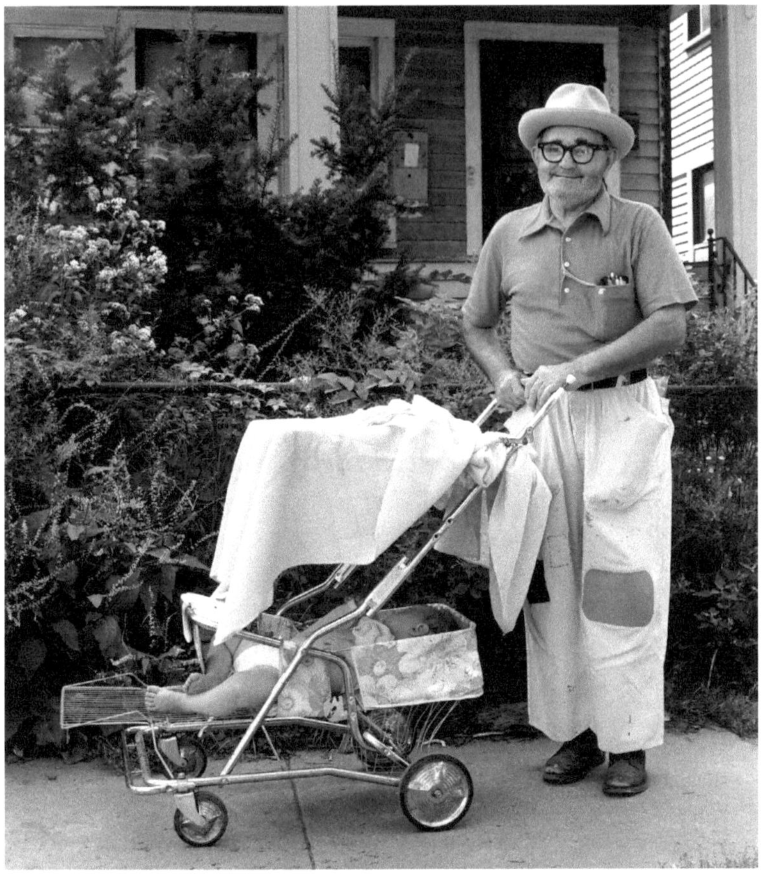

Milton Rogovin (1909–2011), *Triptychs: Buffalo's Lower West Side Revisited*, 1973 © The Family of Milton Rogovin, www.miltonrogovin.com.

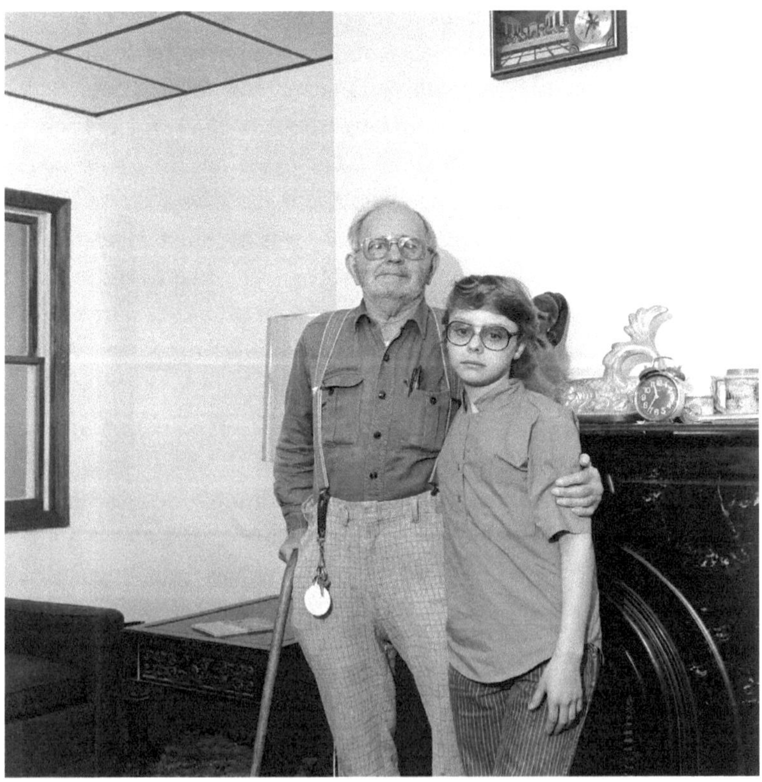

Milton Rogovin (1909–2011), *Triptychs: Buffalo's Lower West Side Revisited*, 1985 © The Family of Milton Rogovin, www.miltonrogovin.com.

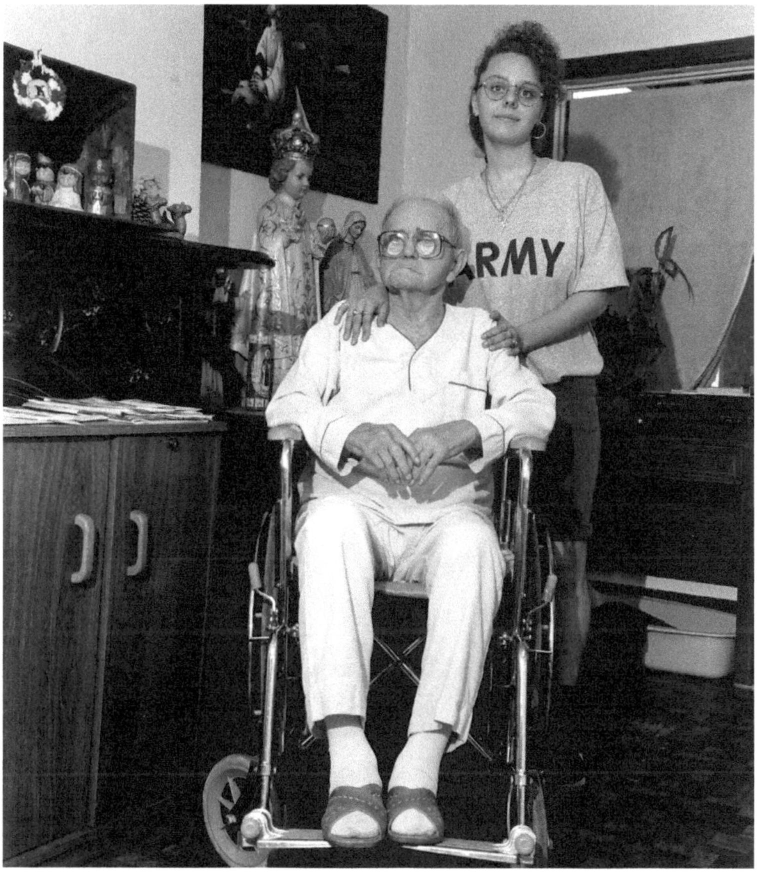

Milton Rogovin (1909–2011), *Triptychs: Buffalo's Lower West Side Revisited,* 1992 © The Family of Milton Rogovin, www.miltonrogovin.com.

received permission from the superintendent of Atlas Steel to photograph workers inside the plant. *A new world opened up to me. I had never been in a steel mill. The place was relatively dark except for the areas where the steel workers worked. . . . The important thing was that I was permitted to work at the steel mill as long as I wanted to. Except for one other plant, Shenango Steel, no other place allowed me access for months and months. . . . But perhaps the most important lesson for me was to learn how to approach the workers. I found out quickly that they were paid by the number of items they produced. Therefore I had to adopt a procedure whereby I did not spend too much time with any one worker.*[26]

Rogovin also made a deliberate choice to seek out and photograph women steel mill workers. *The first thing I did when I went onto the production floor was to look for women workers. Fortunately I came across several who were scarfing, burning, and welding. . . . And so this type of photography is saying something to whoever's interested in looking. Women go to work, and they are doing it in some cases because they must go to work. They should be treated the same as men and given the opportunity.*[27]

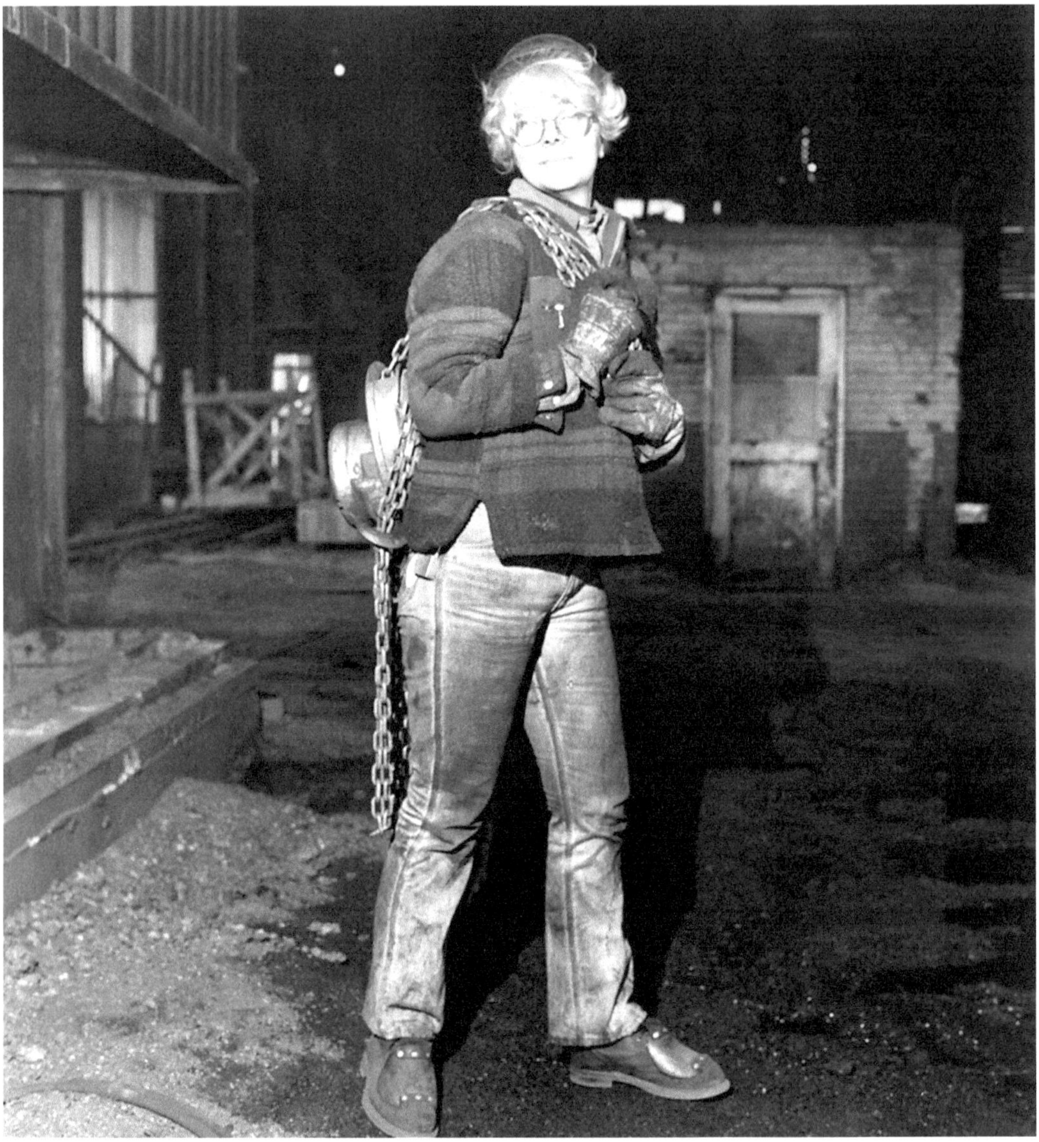

"Mary Daniels," Milton Rogovin (1909–2011), *Working People*, Republic Steel 1978–1987, ©The Family of Milton Rogovin, www.miltonrogovin.com.

Although Rogovin never had a laboring job, he recognized the physicality of labor. Like Lewis Hine, Rogovin demonstrated how photography could document brutal and dangerous physical work *and* create aesthetically powerful images. He photographed Doris McKinney in her "burning outfit" with her "burning torch," working in a "burning bed," whose other job was "hooking steel," a skill she described as an "art" that calls for "muscles."[28] He photographed the labor of "perfecting" ingot molds in his work portraits of "chippers" Benjamin Boofer[29] and Ralph Wils.[30] While some may see their bodies as balletic, others may recognize the physical labor inherent in the

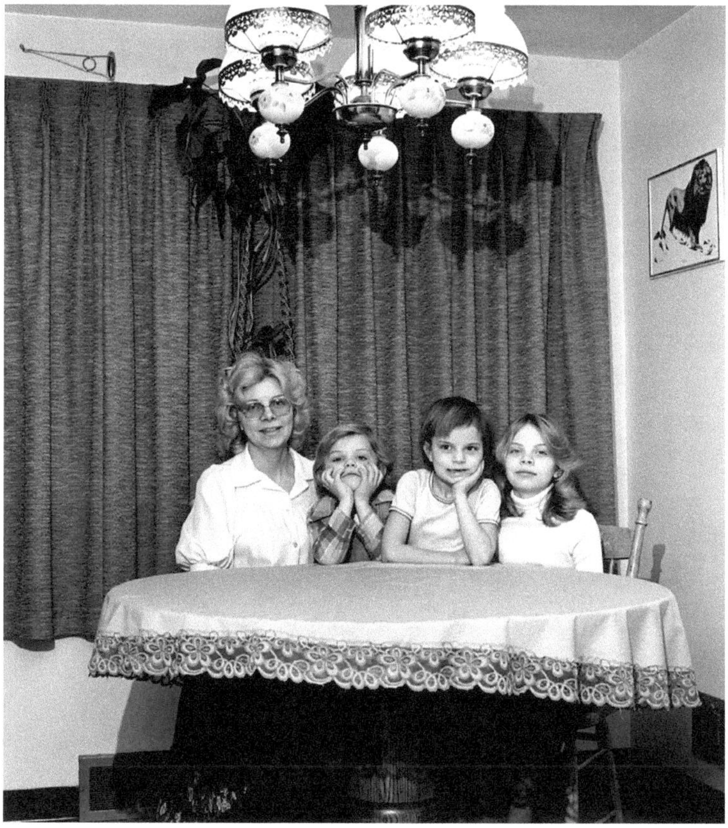

"Mary Daniels," Milton Rogovin (1909–2011), *Working People*, Republic Steel 1978–1987, ©The Family of Milton Rogovin, www.miltonrogovin.com.

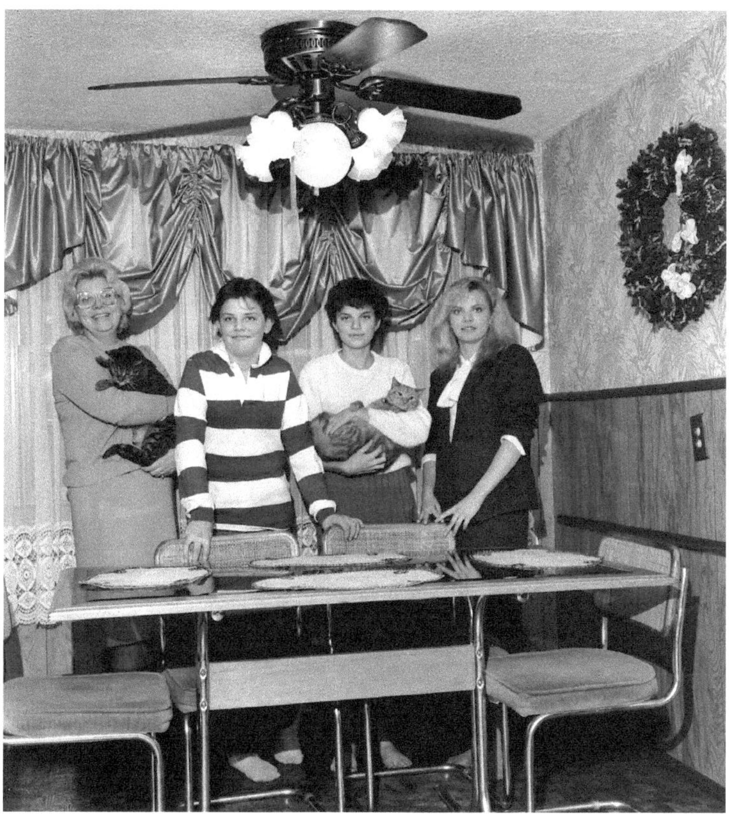

"Mary Daniels," Milton Rogovin (1909–2011), *Working People*, Republic Steel 1978–1987, ©The Family of Milton Rogovin, www.miltonrogovin.com.

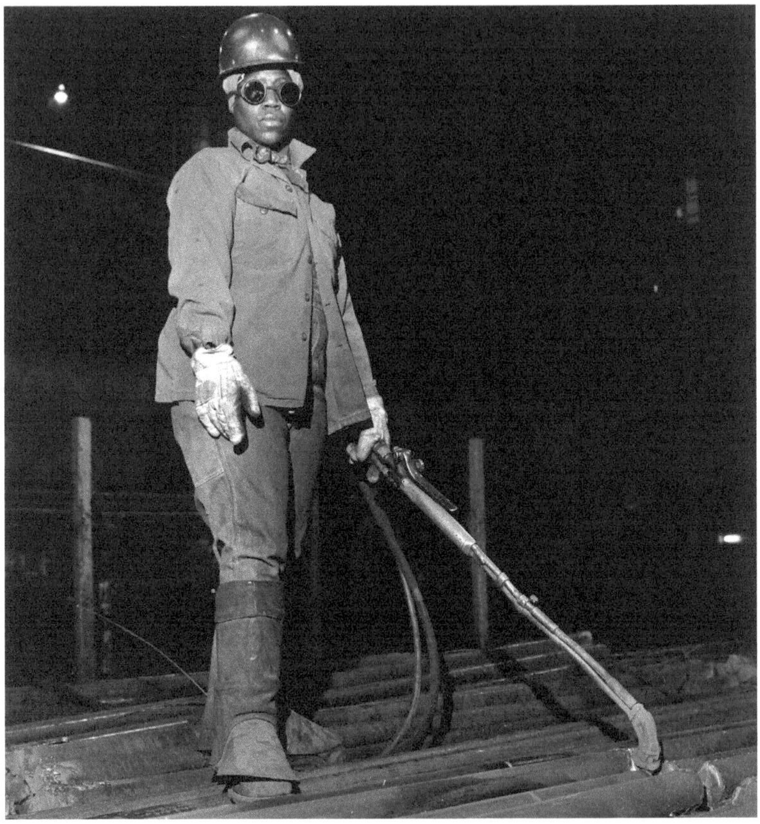

"Doris McKinney," Milton Rogovin (1909–2011), *Working People*, Republic Steel 1978–1987, ©The Family of Milton Rogovin, www.miltonrogovin.com.

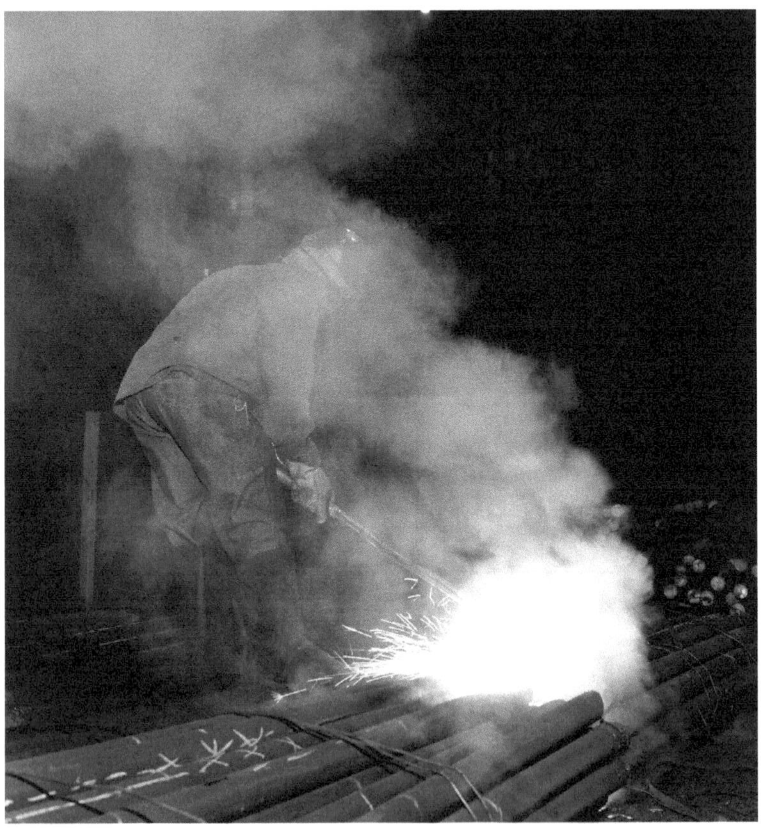

"Doris McKinney," Milton Rogovin (1909–2011), *Working People*, Republic Steel 1978–1987, ©The Family of Milton Rogovin, www.miltonrogovin.com.

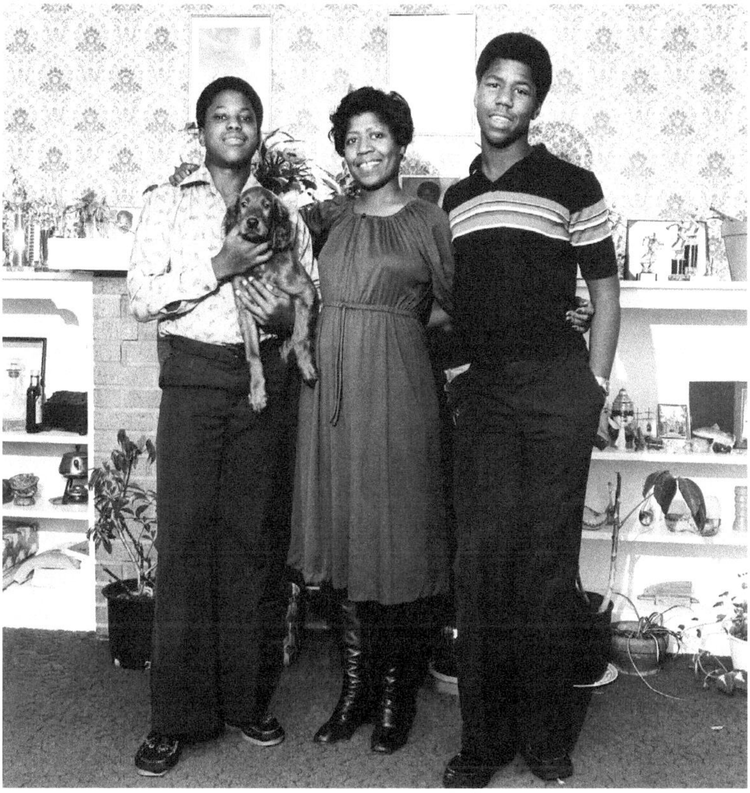

"Doris McKinney," Milton Rogovin (1909–2011), *Working People*, Republic Steel 1978–1987, ©The Family of Milton Rogovin, www.miltonrogovin.com.

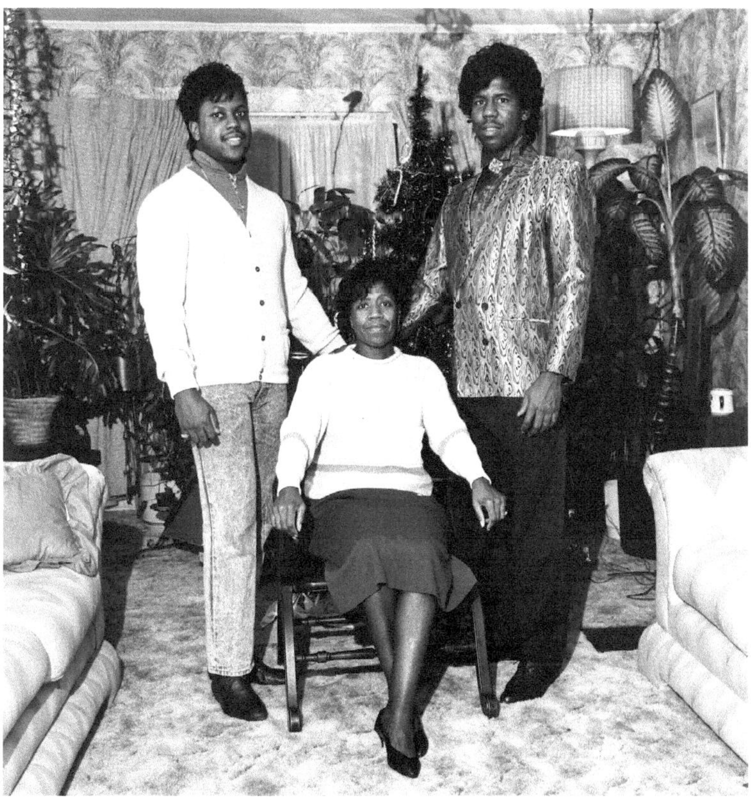

"Doris McKinney," Milton Rogovin (1909–2011), *Working People*, Republic Steel 1978–1987, ©The Family of Milton Rogovin, www.miltonrogovin.com.

products that they produce and we consume. Rogovin recalls perceiving the forms from which castings were made as beautiful objects, and not viewing how from a worker's perspective, the castings *required back breaking labor to prepare for shipping to other steel mills. What to me was an aesthetic experience represented to the workers pain and exhaustion.*[31]

As Studs Terkel once observed, "jobs are not big enough for people." Or, as Rogovin recognized, people are more than their jobs. When he came across a photograph of a steelworker and child feeding ducks outside their home, Rogovin was inspired to ask permission from steelworkers to photograph them at home as well as at work. We have these extraordinary juxtapositions of work life and home life in *Portraits in Steel*, Milton Rogovin's and Michael Frisch's collaborative book. I once assigned this book in my Photography and Writing course at RIT. As a prelude to a discussion of the book, I asked students to write, anonymously, a description of what photographs of their parents/family at work and at home would look like. It was a revelatory exercise in class differences.

Milton Rogovin's decision to photograph steel workers from 1975 to 1978 was unintentionally prescient. A seismic shift in the 1980s, subsequently labeled deindustrialization, altered the lives and livelihood of workers through no fault of their own or for lack of a work ethic. These were the sudden structural capitalistic changes Milton understood well, though. *Little did I realize that I was recording the end of the era of steel production in the Buffalo area. Within a few years after I completed work in the steel plants nearly all of them closed down, leaving thousands of workers jobless.*[32]

Rogovin's photographs contain instrumental power, creating a circuitry of connection across education, class, and race differences. Michael Frisch, a Princeton educated professor of History and American Studies (State University of New York, Buffalo) began his oral histories with former steel workers by placing Milton's on-the-job photographs before them and asking what's happening in the photo: "Tell us a little bit about what your job was"; "tell us about what's going on in there"; "what's happening when that picture was being taken?"[33] Frisch honors the epistemology/knowledge/experience of the worker first.

That same process of using a photograph to connect is key to Rogovin's art of return. When he traveled to Appalachia he contacted union leaders and other activists to reach out to miners and their families. When Rogovin photographed people living in Buffalo's Lower West Side (1972–73–74; 1984–85; 1992; and 2001–02), he returned to the neighborhood accompanied by Anne and a box of photographs and stood on a street corner where there was the most activity. *People would gather around and I'd show them the pictures.*[34] In several of the *Triptychs* (and subsequent *Quartets*), visible on a wall or mantel, there were older Rogovin photographs inside the newer ones. As Mark Rogovin recalled, "it wasn't only a photo that was taken but a strong relationship was built." These photographs of individuals and families attest to birth, rebirth, growth, change, loss, and continuance—the missing and the present. Blank spaces in the sequence, a missing third image, may be a death announcement. The viewer takes a breath and grieves loss too.

Between 2000 and 2002, StoryCorps founder Dave Isay and colleagues Harvey Wang and David Miller traveled to Buffalo and accompanied Milton and Anne Rogovin on photography trips to the Lower West Side: "It was a magnificent experience, watching this tiny white-haired man and his wife striding past drug dealers with a smile and a wave on one corner, embraced with a 'whoop' and a bear hug by a group of burly, tattooed domino players on the next. His subjects—from cops to housewives to hustlers—would take one look at Milton and Anne, back again ten years later, and greet them like long-lost family. . . . At some point we'd pull out the old portraits—from thirty years ago, twenty, ten. It's difficult to describe the intensity of emotions these photographs would unleash in their subjects."[35]

As part of a continuum of labor representation and as a distinctive artist in any history of photography, Milton Rogovin is a pivotal figure. Indeed, the power of his work, its artistry, rewrites the history of photography. Rogovin's Lower West Side Buffalo could be Chicago's or Pittsburgh's. Indeed, his photographs signal hundreds of Lower West Sides—in the United States, but also globally.

Approach a Rogovin photograph with open mind, open eyes, open (unbleeding) heart. Then move from individual photographs to the larger Rogovin solar system. I offer these keywords to glimpse that larger Rogovin vision and his "intelligent interpretation" of the worlds' workers: Precision, Body, Voice, Use, and Beauty.[36]

Precision

This is the language of measurement, what you might expect from a trained optometrist. But there's more. Precision is not just technical, although Milton spoke about it in those terms.

I have a sort of unorthodox way of photographing. I can avoid shadows. I go around with a tripod, no less. Even outdoors, I walk around with a tripod. It gives me a very precise photograph, which I like. . . . I prefer precision. There's a certain sharpness, even in the background. I could blur it out, I know how to do that. But I think it's important to make a statement about the background. It's all part of the photograph. Is that person more important than the ashcan next to him [or the interior of a storefront church or the tools on the wall behind the Chilean worker?]. *I'm not sure, because they're working on each other.*[37] This "I'm not sure" is modest but also indicative of Rogovin verbal precision, of finding language that matches the specificity of his ideas and his vision. There is also precision of choice. There are no "gotcha moments." He didn't walk around

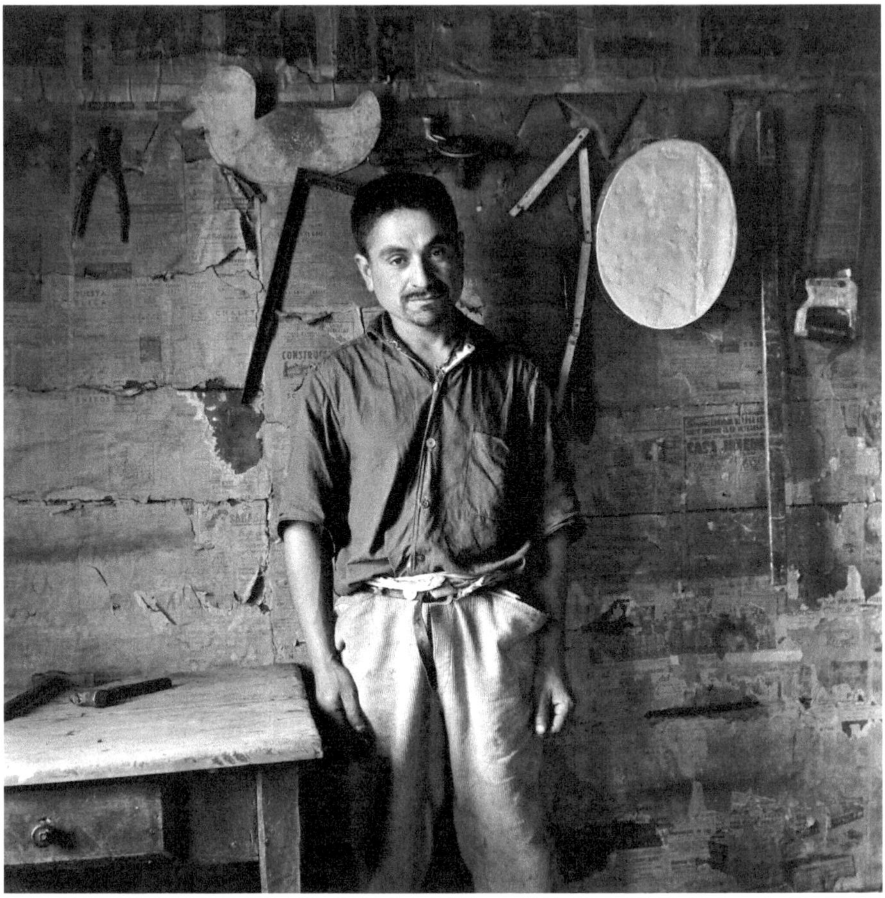

Milton Rogovin (1909–2011), Chile 1967, ©The Family of Milton Rogovin, www.miltonrogovin.com.

looking for the decisive moment, but he was extraordinarily decisive in what and how he photographed.

But precision is not dominance or objectification. He doesn't turn people into things. Even when he photographed things, they become something more than things or just objects. It is the viewer's task to read the object's social and personal meanings, and to understand something about people's lives by seeing the precision of details. Some of these "background" details include religious statues on a table next to a floral bedspread, the exposed varicose veins on the legs of a mother of seven children, the clashing patterns of stripes and polka dots, the white Christmas tree and the Black family, the crocheted pillows, the family pictures, the fullness of small, tidy home spaces. (Bauhausian modernism seems to have skipped the working poor.) To understand is not to judge or categorize. Milton was able to see the everyday poetry in the details—and poetic lines do not necessarily have to be conventionally beautiful, as Walt Whitman well understood.

Precision is also balance—between stillness and motion, between the white sweater and the outstretched arms, between the tools and the worker (reminiscent of the nineteenth-century occupational tintypes of people with their tools), between the deep background of blighted neighborhoods and jobless circumstances and the daily struggle to survive. There's a double aesthetic to see—the balanced power of his compelling photographs and the aesthetics that people with few material resources shape for themselves. A desire for beauty is not the property of any one class. And Rogovin never shames his subjects by how he photographs them.

The Body

Whether they are quiet, in trance, at leisure, not working, hanging out, at work, covered in tattoos, covered in the sweat of work, uncovered in the summer heat, heavy or thin, dancing, sitting on stoops, eating ice cream, holding a Genesee beer, holding a baby, in a wheelchair, pushing a wheelchair, embracing children, leaning on machines, leaning on each other, perched on tidy sofas or in front of newspaper-covered walls, these bodies look with trust at the picture man. Rogovin's bodies speak. Can we hear them? That's Milton's implicit question (and is akin to what Oliver Sacks calls "seeing voices" in relation to the deaf and the language of ASL.)[38]

Rogovin is always interested in the human landscape. But, curiously, in a mid-1980s interview, he declined the category "portrait photographer." Asked whether he considered his photos of people portraits, Milton responded, *No. I guess you call it a portrait like the woman and child in the Chilean series. But if you look at it carefully, you see the walls are covered with newspapers and they're disintegrating. You see that there is some problem there. I don't try to make those things obvious.*[39] I wonder if Rogovin shied away from the "portrait photographer" tag because it suggests studio work, of posing people who wish to purchase flattering images of themselves. After all, as Milton observed, "The Rich Have Their Own Photographers."[40]

Milton Rogovin searched in interior and exterior ways to locate the human landscape compatible with his own intellect and imagination, and where he could work productively. He stepped away from some subjects, because, seemingly, he realized the subject or setting was not right. He commented on how he tried to photograph the workers building the convention center in Buffalo. *I tried several times to photograph these workers and the results were disastrous. For whatever reason, I don't know. After a week or two, I dropped it. Yet when I go back to the workers in the factories, the ones I know how to approach, there's no problem.*[41] Also, if someone said to him, "take my picture," he wouldn't do it.

Even when he photographed people individually, there was a relational element.

We see this in the work/home photographs and in the triptychs and quartets, in East Side and West Side Buffalo, in the Yemeni series, the Native American series, Scottish miners, Appalachia, everywhere in his work. Any assumptions the viewer might make about the working body are challenged by the body at home.

In her oral history with Michael Frisch, published in *Portraits in Steel,* "Mary Daniels" comments on the effect of the sudden closing of the mills (she was a rigger's helper at Republic Steel). Her comments reflect, not an aggrieved victimization, but rather a working-class ethos of solidarity: "When the newspaper article came out about us and the plant closing down—it sounded desperate. People that we know, just friendly neighbors . . . called us up and said, 'Is there anything we can do? Can we lend you some money, can we drive you here, can we do this for you—if you ever need us, we're here.'"[42]

This sense of connection and mutuality is not the revolution, but it is the understood necessity of survival. The conventional notion of "sticking together" is literally apparent in Rogovin's photographs—in family relations, but also on the job and in the neighborhood. Sometimes those bonds are broken—jobs end, the street takes a son or daughter, mother or father. Those are embedded stories Rogovin does not penetrate. They are the white spaces in the triptychs. Instead of the drunk in the doorway or the raised fist of anger, we have in Milton Rogovin's photographs the physicality and aesthetics of human relationships. In the rough physical world of work, people are physically and literally in touch. Rogovin's people touch each other—more than they touch things. The pervasive emblems of technology—cars, phones, computers—are nowhere in Rogovin's photographs. But there are many images of children bunched together outside a house or squeezed onto a couch. Rogovin photographs them shoulder to shoulder. (These squished-together family photographs of bunches of kids and relatives are strikingly recognizable to me.) What makes them more than family snapshots? The dignity of presentation and the rarity of the image—this is not just another casual digital image. Whether people are in their best clothes or not, there is a gravity to the moment of the family photograph. I think of the itinerant photographer and my grandmother Anna's desire to have a photograph of her children. There is a solemnity to that image. With the ubiquity of today's images, what have we lost?

A word about the public bodies of Milton and Anne Rogovin. Anne—with her warm embrace, her generous smile—Milton's dignified bow into the lens of his Rolleiflex—they, as partners, as a couple, built relationships. In their own quiet, insistent way, they presented themselves as more than strangers with a camera. They created a mutuality of seeing, and trust. These are "given," not taken, photographs (as many have acknowledged). Rogovin returned to the neighborhoods with prints, gifts of time frozen.

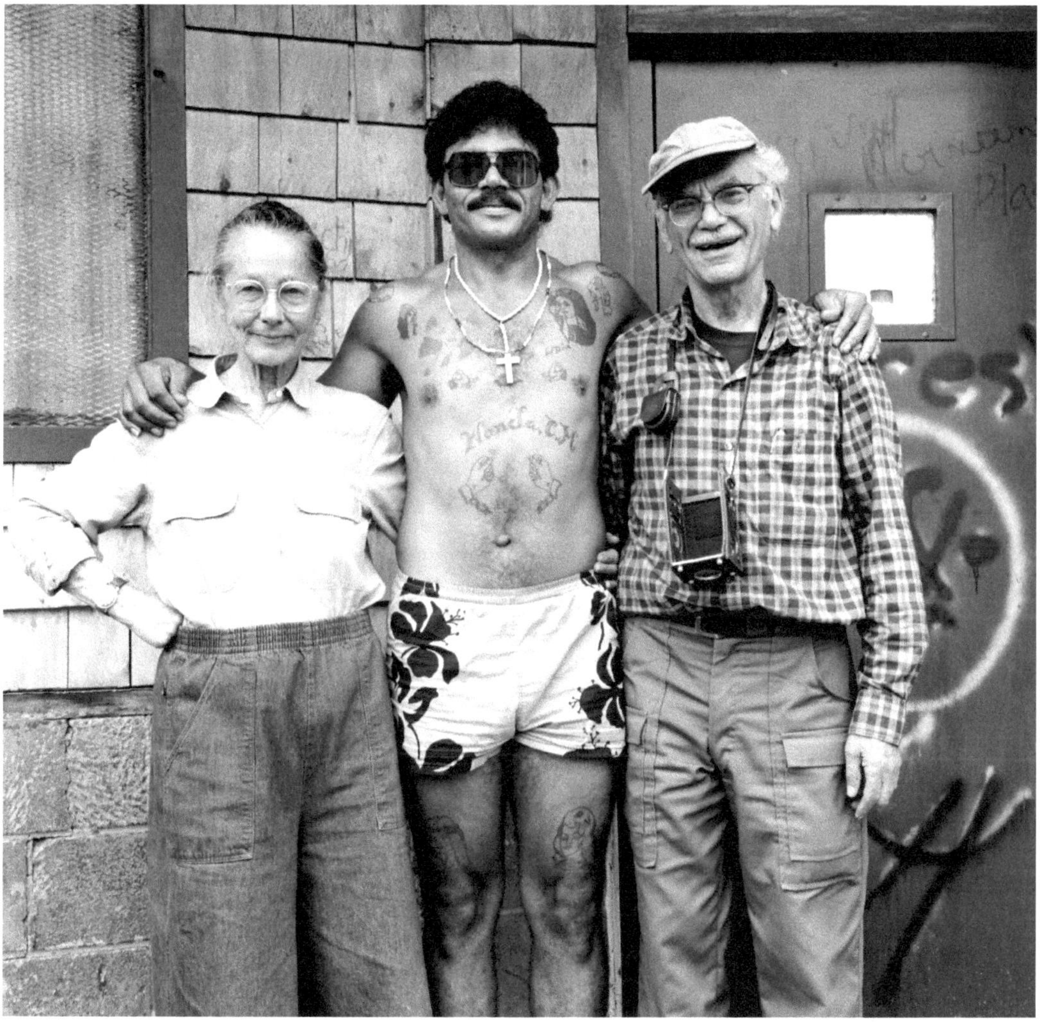

Milton Rogovin (1909–2011), Triptych, 1986 Anne and Milton ©The Family of Milton Rogovin, www.miltonrogovin.com.

Voice

Photographs are mute—or are they? Consider the metaphoric language of Rogovin's photographs and his relationship to language. Milton Rogovin was an intellectually engaged reader. He understood the relationship between photography and knowledge, photography as the practice of knowledge, of ways of understanding the world. This is more than superb technique; it comes from an intellectual engagement with the world. He also knew silence. He frequently recalled his summons before HUAC and how, in his own words, "my voice was silenced." He dreaded the silence of his photographic voice between series. This tension between silence and utterance, absence and presence, vibrates through his body of work. This is not a monologue;

it is a dialogue, indeed, a dialectic—with the implied question, where's the synthesis? These photographs speak privately, locally, but also out of a larger, insistent political conversation about equality and justice. Rogovin's people are a great human chorus, a chant democratic. Can you hear them?

Let's frame these voices/images through a literary imagination. Rogovin and the working-class writer Tillie Olsen were of the same generation but did not know each other. Old Left warriors, deep artists, one writing about "silences," the other about "visibility," they would have discovered a lot of common ground.[43] They answer, as philosopher Susan Neiman writes in another context, the difference between tribalism and universalism. They both emerge as secular Jews from what Neiman describes as "a Jewish universalist tradition" rooted in the Bible.[44] Tillie Olsen in her writing and Milton Rogovin in his photography never succumbed to cynicism or despair. There are no human gargoyles, no tricks, no pretty cameos, no types, no castes, no captures in their work. Their focus is human potentiality and the circumstances that thwart it.

Milton Rogovin read poetry—Brecht's "The Worker Reads History," Thomas Gray's "Elegy Written in a Country Churchyard" ("Full many a flower is born to blush unseen, / And waste its sweetness on the desert air.") He also wrote poetry. Poetry was crucial to his photographic imagination. His daughter Paula Rogovin wrote, "our father lived and breathed poetry. . . . Always, it was a poem which gave greater meaning to a topic."[45] However, if you think about the artistry and vision involved in constructing his body of work, the architectonics of it, the relationship of parts to whole, built over a long period of time, then the model has to be something larger than a single poem, something like a symphony, something like an epic. Consider Walt Whitman's "Leaves of Grass" (with many editions, many tributaries). Rogovin photographs embody a democratic vernacular as Whitman's great voice did. Whitman turned the eye of American poetry away from the British tradition; Rogovin turns the eye of the photography establishment away from the bourgeois gaze of satisfaction, ennui, and self-congratulation.

Use

The Rogovin family speaks frequently about the intentions of their parents in wanting the photographs to be used—in the classroom—and to be seen—in communities, in public spaces as well as beautiful galleries and museums. But the simple word "use" also has other connotations as a verb—to be used, to be exploited, taken advantage of, to be used up, to profit from, to exhaust, to consume. Rogovin's photographs are a counterweight to that imbalance of users and used. They chip away at that implacable stonewall. His photographs direct the eye to those who can be used in a good sense—employed, utilized, not discarded or wasted. They value thrift, the ordinary practices of working-class people, especially the women, of stretching resources. This is not an innate virtue, but a practiced necessity. Rogovin developed a balance of representation—between the micro and macro, between the individual and the family, neighborhood, work, job, nation, world. He traced the patterns of time, its etchings on the human body, on family, and on place. He recognized how time stops, promise ends, the flowering bud is thwarted because of rocky soil or impossible circumstances. His politics turned toward structural change, not charity or individual blame. *I see what happened when people were working diligently, bought homes, invested their life savings, and suddenly—everything collapses. Everybody should know—not just those who are better off. People in our society should know that there are people with problems. It isn't that they are just lazy bums or looking for handouts. These are people who worked hard.*[46]

It's not so much that he "celebrates" the ordinary, but that he understood and appreciated the complexity in the ordinary. As Raymond Williams said, "culture is ordinary: that is where we must start."[47] Or, as Milton commented, *I take the simple commonplace things and photograph them. I just take the usual things and show them to people.*[48] Or, as Whitman said, "the divine average of American democracy." This is how Milton Rogovin answered and practiced "an intelligent interpretation" of the world's workers; this is his working-class eye. Milton Rogovin was himself a worker, a producer, an interpreter. He led a life of praxis, action matching beliefs. He said, *I feel if I didn't do this work, I'd just give up my photography.*

Our eyes are polluted by the fake—by advertisements, by commercials, by reality shows, by false promises. Cameras can't lie, as Lewis Hine once said, but photographers can.

Milton Rogovin's photographs take us closer to what James Agee called "actuality."[49] They are not impostures. That takes us to the last keyword (and you could easily list other words).

Beauty

Rogovin said, "People all over are beautiful if given half a chance."[50] Milton didn't like the word aesthetics—not an art for art's sake kind of photographer. But let's be clear about that. It is one thing not to want technique or composition or form to dilute meaning. It is another thing to have an eye for inherent beauty. And Rogovin shows us how the artistic eye is not counterintuitive to the working-class eye. He understood and practiced the artistry and skill necessary to produce something of beauty. He lived that well and deeply.

Longing for beauty in one's life is a human trait. This was "Sugar."

I visited the Rogovin home in Buffalo on June 18, 2004. His son, Mark Rogovin, and biographer Melanie Herzog and others were present. We sat on his living room couch. A small book stand on the coffee table held albums

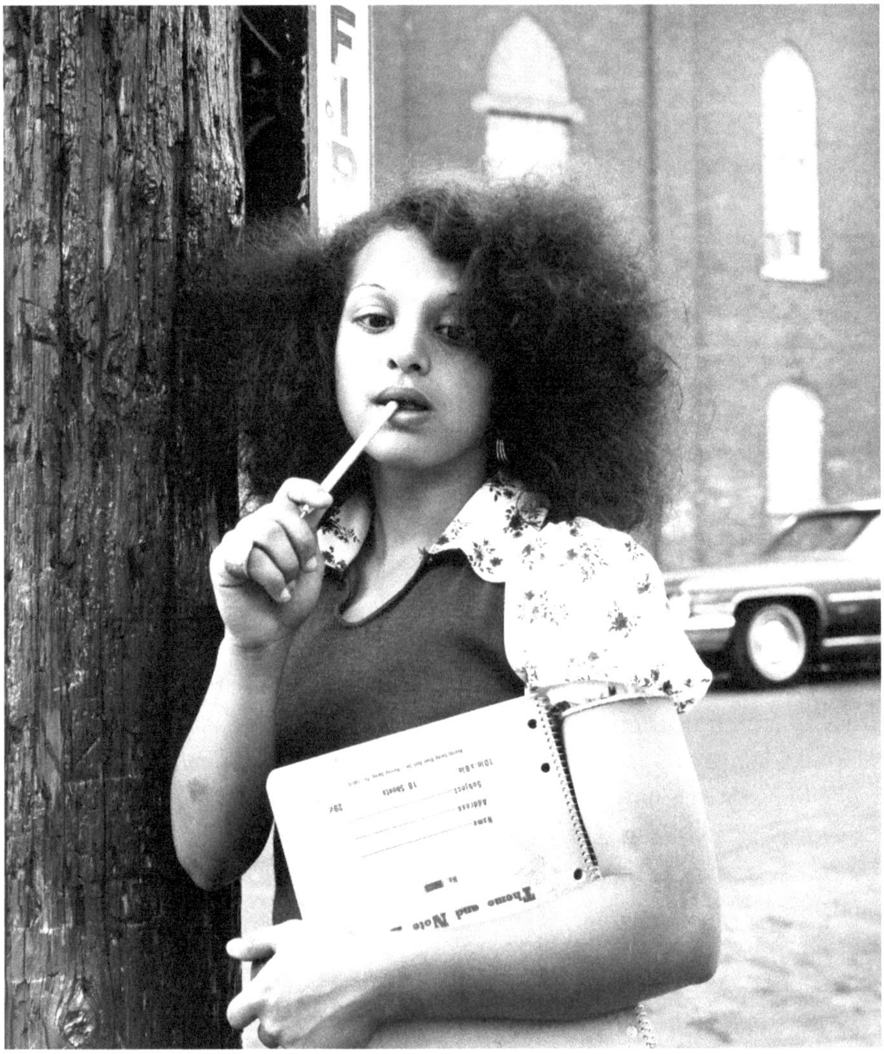

Milton Rogovin (1909–2011), Triptych, 1986 ©The Family of Milton Rogovin, www.miltonrogovin.com.

of photos. Mark offered to turn the pages, but Milton said, "No, I can do it." Mark hovered nearby, calling him "Milton" as if he were father and separate entity. That sense of separation, of looking from a distance, surprised me in Rogovin's response as we looked at photograph after photograph. He would pause over certain pictures, chuckle, maybe reflecting on the specific circumstances of the taking of the photograph. Occasionally, he would wipe the plastic jacket of dust, a tidy stroking. And he would look at certain pictures and say, "beautiful," not, seemingly, in a self-congratulatory way, but as someone with a keen aesthetic sense. Photographer and viewer, at ninety-four years he had earned the right to sit back and see his own images and say "beautiful."

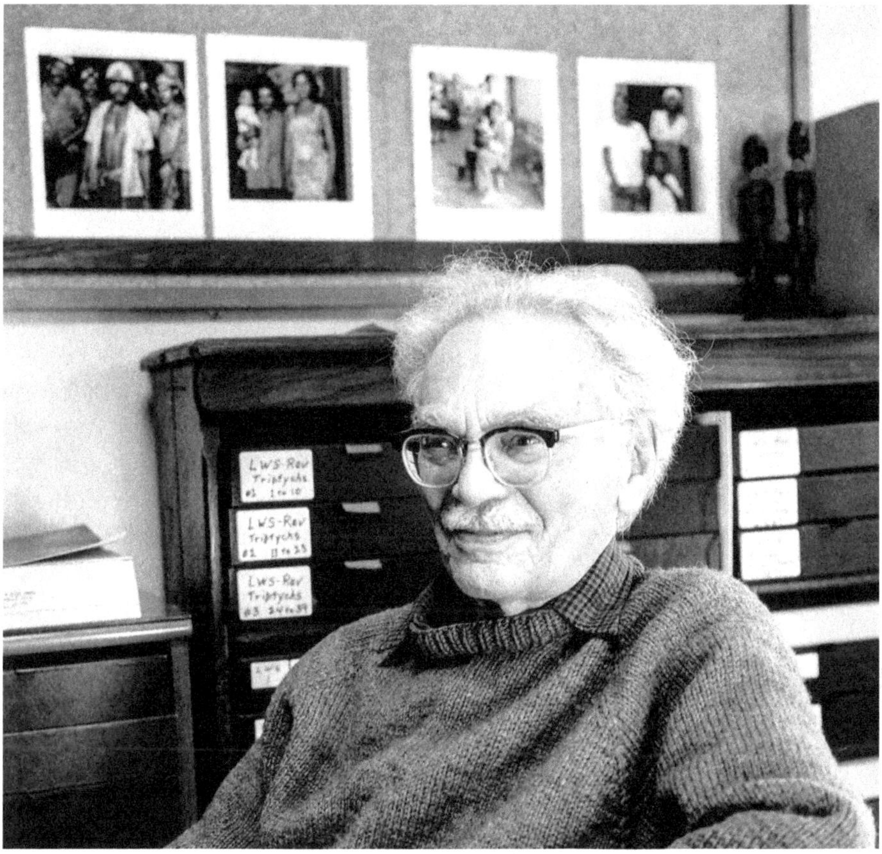

"Milton at Home," 1994, Abe Aronow, photographer. © Abe Aronow.

How do these photographs work on us? Consider James Agee's questions: "Who are you who will read these words and study these photographs, and through what cause, by what chance, and for what purpose, and by what right do you qualify to, and what will you do about it?"[51]

Opening and closing. The camera's shutter. The human eye. The door in and out. The photograph as hinge. Our eyes connect one space to another, moving us into and beyond the frame, our thoughts swinging back and forth.

How do *we* qualify in Agee's sense? When asked about the intent of his photographs, Rogovin responded, that they might "help to feed and strengthen" the communities in which the photographs were taken. (Emerson described Whitman's poems as "fortifying and encouraging.") He understood that his work alone will not make the revolution—it takes collective effort—all those chisels banging away at so many stones.

Established art history categories do not adequately contain Milton Rogovin's body of work, his interpenetration of culture and memory. We need hybrid critical and theoretical practices. Will future art historians and curators recognize Milton Rogovin as pivotal to the history of photography? This

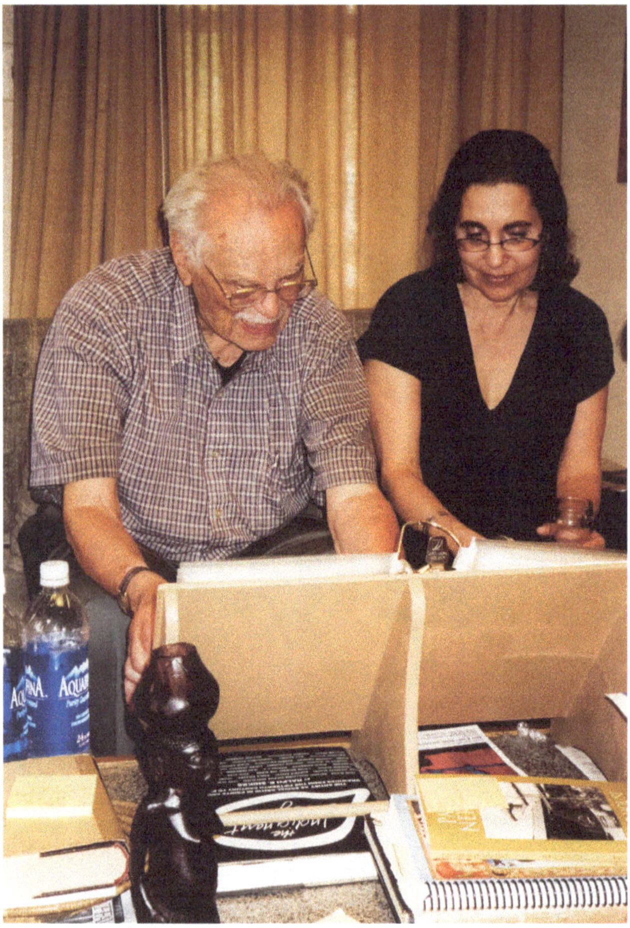

Milton in his Buffalo home with Janet Zandy, June 18, 2004, Mark Rogovin photographer.

is more than an academic concern. It is certainly more than nostalgia for a place or time. It is—to use Lewis Hine's words again—an "urgent need" to reclaim what is "real and actual." It is resistance to big lies—to what has actually been stolen.

Rogovin did not photograph wars or political events. He certainly did not photograph fashion or celebrity. He was deeply politically conscious, but not an ideologue. His critical eye resisted sentimentality, but not emotion. He saw the knowledge embedded in the human body. Rogovin practiced the art of photographic return in his four decades–long Lower West Side series (a body of work most relevant to Jens S. Jensen's Hammarkullen's work in Sweden). Here we see Stephen Jay Gould's timeline of arrows and cycles. But with Rogovin there is always more. Returning was as much a political practice as an aesthetic calling. It is not mechanical reproduction or some Warholian gimmick of repetition. It is visual storytelling.

Rogovin's work, his "Leaves of Grass," expands our understanding of what it means to be a human being. His photographs are about us.

Jens S. Jensen

Hammarkullen

May 25, 1946, Stockholm, Sweden–
July 1, 2015, Gothenburg, Sweden

We must emphasize not the ladder but the common highway.
—Raymond Williams, "Culture is Ordinary"

Kensal Rise Library, built by public subscription on a site donated by All Souls College, Oxford, was ceremoniously opened by Mark Twain in the year 1900. It was closed by Brent Council in 2011 and sold to a property developer called Platinum Revolver. Public pressure to save and protect the library has been so strong . . . that the property restorers . . . (Uplift Property, whose marketing hook is "homes to make you happy") have been forced to produce redevelopment blueprints which include both designated public space and designated library space.
—Ali Smith, *Public Library*

Children's creativity knows no boundaries.
They create their own playground.
—Jens S. Jensen

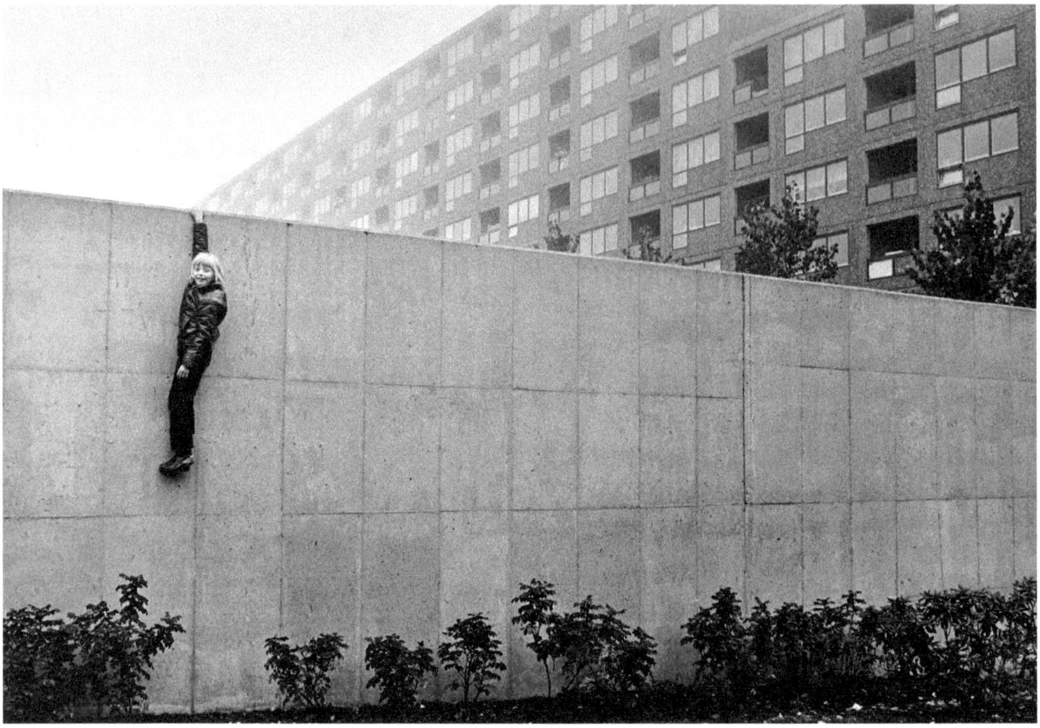

Jens S. Jensen (1946–2015), *Michael, Hammarkullen* 1973, courtesy Jesper Schleimann-Jensen and Jakob Schleimann-Jensen.

A kid hangs with one hand from a grey wall with a big look-at-what-I-can-do grin on his face. He just had this exchange with the photographer: *Why don't you take a picture when I'm hanging on that wall? Sure, but how? I'll show you!* says the boy and disappears around the corner. He then climbs over the edge of the wall, drops one hand, clutches the wall with the other, and shouts: *NOW!*

Jens Jensen recalled this encounter with Michael (the boy with the grin) when his photograph (printed 7×11 meters) was featured in the Museum of Modern Art's 2012 *Century of the Child* exhibit, which Jensen attended.[1]

The striking question is: who is in charge of the photograph? The boy invites Jensen to take the photograph and the boy stages it himself. Jensen explains how it was Michael's own idea. Jensen sees the boy's smile as a kind of thrusting victory despite the milieu, the stark environment surrounding the Hammarkullen apartments where Jensen lived for a time and photographed generations of its inhabitants.[2] Nearly forty years later and about two weeks before the MOMA interview, Jensen meets Michael, a grown man, and photographs him again in Hammarkullen. Michael stretches and touches that same wall, now painted a neutral ochre. The impossibility of hanging again from such a high wall is evident. Bulky recycling bins intrude on the camera's frame. If the first image suggests youthful daring and joy, the

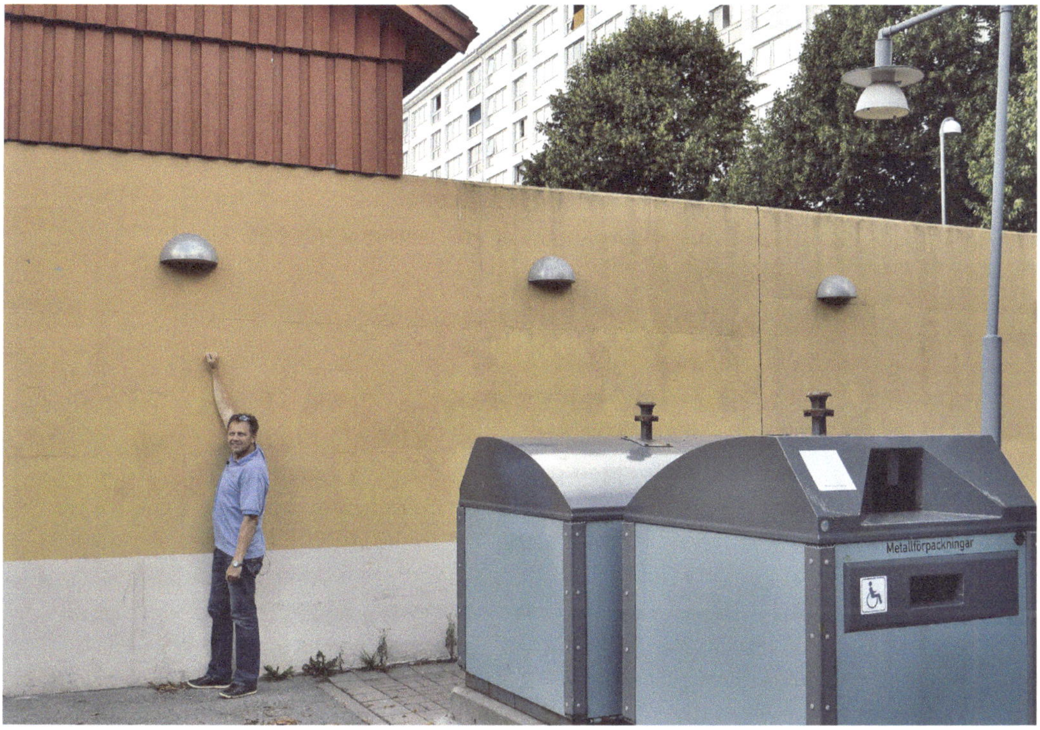

Jens S. Jensen (1946–2015), *Michael, Hammarkullen* 2012, courtesy Jesper Schleimann-Jensen and Jakob Schleimann-Jensen.

second depicts survival and continuation—and trust in the photographer's eye and hand.

In 2013 I saw Jens S. Jensen's *Hammarkullen—40 Years Later*, a photography exhibit at the Hasselblad Center in Gothenburg, Sweden (curated by Dragana Vujanovic). I was struck by the similarities between Jensen's approach, subject matter, and timeline and Milton Rogovin's photographic triptychs. I contacted Jensen and subsequently visited him twice at his home in Gothenburg before he died in 2015 of a late diagnosed cancer.

Born in Stockholm, Sweden, Jens S. Jensen studied architecture at Chalmers Institute of Technology (1965–1971) and lived in Gothenburg, Sweden, since 1965. He also taught "visualization" at Chalmers Architecture in Gothenburg, and writing and photography at the School of Photography and Film at Göteborg University. Recipient of numerous grants and awards, he developed his own documentary projects while contributing to books as well as national and international magazines. Jensen also wrote scripts and was involved in the radio series *En enkel till Tahiti* (*One way ticket to Tahiti*) for National Swedish Broadcasting Company in 1988, and the documentary TV film with the same title, directed by Ulf Aldevinge for Swedish Television, 1991. He exhibited at the Kulturhuset and the Museum of Architecture in Stockholm; Hasselblad Center in Göteborg (1996 and 2013); Museum of

Work in Norrköping; and other museums, galleries, and libraries at some twenty places around Sweden, but also in Denmark, Germany, France, Belgium, Holland, Austria, Hungary, and Moscow. His photographs were included in group shows in Europe, the United States, Canada, and Mexico. His work is represented in museum collections, including the Hasselblad Foundation, Gothenburg, Moderna Museet and Nordiska Museet, Stockholm, the Museum of Work, Norrköping, and the Museum of Modern Art, New York.

Jensen summarized his published books and projects—a resume accented with his own personality and interests:

> 1974: **Hammarkullen** (People and life in the new suburb *Hammarkullen* north of Gothenburg); 1976: **Bilfabriken** (The *Car Factory,* about workers at the Volvo car-plant in Gothenburg.); 1978: ***Dom kallar oss* bilbyggare** (Carbuilders, deep-going documentary about assembly line work at Volvo.); 1982: **Ljuva drömmar** (Sweet *Dreams*—the same people from *Hammarkullen* eight years later.); 1985: **Oavslutat** (*Unfinished,* my relationship to my work, my first son and three women); 1990: **En enkel till Tahiti** (*One Way Ticket To Tahiti*—about my grandfather who went to Tahiti in 1921 and never came back. I follow in his tracks 60 years later to understand what happened); 1995: **Tänk om allting var underbart** (*What if everything was wonderful,* same people from the suburb *Hammarkullen* 20 years later. What happened to their lives—hopes and dreams?); 1999: **Borta bra** (East, *west.* About our longing for something else—but what?) 2006: *Den svarta pärlan* (*The Black Pearl.* A stunning journey through time and space, about a deeply depressed woman filled with guilt and longing, all since childhood. Fiction drama); 2013: *Hammarkullen—40 år senare.* (*Hammarkullen—40 years later*). (What has happened to the people and the suburb Hammarkullen since 1973?)

That's the public dossier. It reveals little about his childhood, family of birth, and artistic desires. As a young man he made a crucial turn—from a career path in architecture to a (less economically secure?) focus on photography and writing, particularly as tools to understand people and himself better through storytelling.

Photography came into my life when I was 12. I had no camera but started to draw and paint negatives on translucent material, create contact prints and develop them myself in the dark cellar of the house. It was like magic to me. When I was 13 in 1959, I got a simple Agfa 6×6 camera from my parents, and I was so curious about how it worked, technically and chemically. I soon began to understand it all and really enjoyed using it as a way of storytelling. So around 19, when I started to study to become an architect (which I became but never have used as a normal profession), I understood what I really wanted to use this knowledge for. I was curious about life and relationships between people and society, and tried to be as open about myself as I could to build confidence and trust between us. I wanted to understand how their lives were, combined with my own experiences and to discover and question my own hidden preoccupations. I also loved to write since I was a kid, so I found a way of combining photo and texts to create a deeper and more alive dimension to my storytelling. Time becomes so important to my work. I try to show the people that I meet, who I am and how I think, and that I want to learn more about their lives by talking and listening to them, and building a deep, open and honest relationship. This, of course, takes time, and during that time things happen and change, which makes it even more important and exciting to continue and dig deeper. Some of the people I got to know quite well forty years ago—and they me—have become a very important part of my own life. What has happened to us, our dreams and expectations, fear and anger . . . love and hate . . . everything. So a large part of my driving force probably is my curiosity about life and relationships in and between ourselves and to our surroundings like family, work, habitation, home, society and so on.

Jensen speaks of his *curiosity*, a word that may have deeper meaning in Swedish than its colloquial American English connotation. Jensen's curiosity inspired an engaged and committed photographic practice. His curiosity is not voyeuristic, quick, or cheap. He began photographing people living in Hammarkullen in 1973, and after commuting to Gothenburg, decided to rent an apartment there that same year. *A lot of people were suspicious of me at first, and thought I was just another bastard who came with a camera.* He didn't know then that the project would span four decades. This was personal, artistic, somewhat political, and, always, dialogic, a conversation with people and place, something more than a documentary project intended for a commercial or academic audience. Jensen probed his own motivations, and, as he respectfully photographed others, his "curiosity" deepened.

In 1971, I finished studying architecture and took up photography full time, even then with thoughts of telling my own story about a suburb. My idea was to describe the suburb from the inside, through the people living there, and at the same time criticize the policies of social planning that consistently compromised many fundamental and self-evident human needs— sacrificed for profitability and efficiency.

I decided, more or less randomly, on Hammarkullen and in the spring of 1973 started going out to the area several times a week with camera and tape recorder. I was quite full of preconceived notions. The idea of making a story about a suburb [affordable but inferior spaces outside European cities] *was probably born already in the late sixties when I was studying architecture at Chalmers in Gothenburg. In several of our tasks, the prerequisites and requirements were dictated by the Million Program's need for fast, cheap and rational solutions. We were often critical of this and discussed and read a lot about the rapid expansion of large cities. In the debate books that were published at that time, the suburbs were often described from the outside and from above by so-called experts, and less often from the inside by the residents. . . . My idea then was to try to describe the town from the inside, through the people who lived there, and at the same time criticize the social planning policy that has consistently come to put many fundamental and obvious human needs second to demands for profitability and efficiency.*

Hammarkullen, Thursday, 8 March 1973.

First visit. 11.30–13.30. Warm, sunshine—walked about the white [color of buildings] *area, the houses and the town centre. Took some photos, just to feel the shutter release. Everyone was happy. Spoke to people at the accommodation service: "People like it here. There's a boxing club. Youth problems are no greater than elsewhere about town." It was quite deserted, apart from the centre. Saw only a few preschoolers and mothers with prams. It was absolutely idyllic this day. Went home with something to think about—after all, I had quite preconceived notions about Hammarkullen—expected it would be god-damned awful in every way. Yet today, everyone seemed happy. At least on the outside.*

Nevertheless, the first pictures were quite traditionally suburban: harsh, desolate images of lifeless high-rise buildings, solitary mothers with prams seen from a distance and any contact I had with people was only in passing. I was observing it all from the outside, contrary to what I wanted. After all, I wanted to be a part of the life and aromas in the apartments. At the same time, I found it difficult to just walk into a stairwell, ring a doorbell, explain my business and ask if I could come in and talk and take photos. The first ones to make me formulate my intentions and, in some way, stand up for what I was trying to achieve, were the children. They simply stood straight in front of the camera and demanded to be photographed. They wondered what I was up to and in which newspaper they could see the pictures the next day. Gradually, I got to know a few families and they were almost tired of constantly hearing from others how terribly they lived. The criticism that should have been directed at politicians and planners had instead hit the residents and made them feel downgraded as a worse kind of people. My view of Hammer Hill [Hammarkullen] *also changed, from being fixated on the brutal environment to seeing the people who lived behind the anonymous facades.*

But the problem remained. I left the area in the evenings, and did not participate in the real life there. In June, my mother killed herself.

In his book on tracing his mother's father's journey to Tahiti (*En enkel till Tahiti* 1990) and recounting how that grandfather never returned to Sweden, leaving three children behind, Jensen writes: "A still June morning on Edsviken north of Stockholm, I row a small oak slowly towards the shore. In the stern my father sits curled up and cries quietly. One of his arms hangs over the railing and he looks steadily at his wife in the water beside the boat, keeping an awkward grip on her arm."[3] His mother had been missing for ten days; the pocket of her jacket, when they found her body, was filled with stones.

Jens Jensen titled one of his books *Unfinished*. It is perhaps the most private and self-revealing as it includes descriptions of his love relationships as well as his mother's suicide in 1973. This is the same time period when he started his first Hammarkullen project. Work answers grief.

Shortly afterwards, I moved out to Hammarkullen—perhaps as a kind of escape from all the darkness—and it was only then that I actually got down to work in earnest. I didn't have to take the tram home every evening and could take part in everyday life in a completely different way than before.

Eventually I got to know about twenty families. We often sat at each other's houses and talked about work, living and free time—about dreams and hopes for the future, and about light and darkness. I also got to know the teenage gang, and behind the walls and masks of what the media called "the heavy elements" it turned out to be a gang with fantastic cohesion and great initiative. In the end I was almost like one of the gang even though I was ten years older.

Jensen's 1973 photograph of these five teenage boys, as seen through a window, became the cover image of Jensen's first Hammarkullen book.

Seven years later, he photographed the same group, then rephotographed them in 2010.

In January 1974, I moved back to the apartment in town. It felt desolate after the intensive and enjoyable time in Hammarkullen, and I had probably already made up my mind to stay in touch one way or another and follow up the work. It had become a part of my own life. I made transcripts of all the tapes, printed the photographs and went through the material with those involved. In the end, I turned it into a book and an exhibition.

It wasn't as problem-free as it sounds. There was a period of intense despair; I had doubts about my material and my ability to do anything reasonable with it. Real and imaginary expectations haunted me and I totally lost perspective over what I was doing. I came close to burning the whole lot. But in the end, I decided, at least, to finish the work as best I could. The result was the book Hammarkullen.

Jensen used his talents to build something larger than a social critique of public housing or a portfolio of perfect visual images. As a socially conscious architect, he understood how human needs were not necessarily integrated into the economics of quickly built mass housing. As a politically aware artist, and a very good listener, he recognized the many iterations of human experience those structures harbored. Refugees, immigrants, and working-class Swedes rented apartments in Hammarkullen, which Jensen describes as a *mirror image of the world* where *people from conflict-filled regions* would settle. What Jensen achieved is a model of how to tell a story as an outsider by observing (as photographer), by respectful listening (as an oral historian), and by learning (as a humanistic intellectual) about the currents and changes in people's lives. Out of a Lewis Hine photographic lineage of immigrants and labor, Jensen presented the unfolding of human lives over a long period of time. He brought a metaphysically infused class consciousness to his picture stories, which were never reducible to sociological categories or pathologies. His practice was a form of decentering the self in order to understand not only the self but others better.

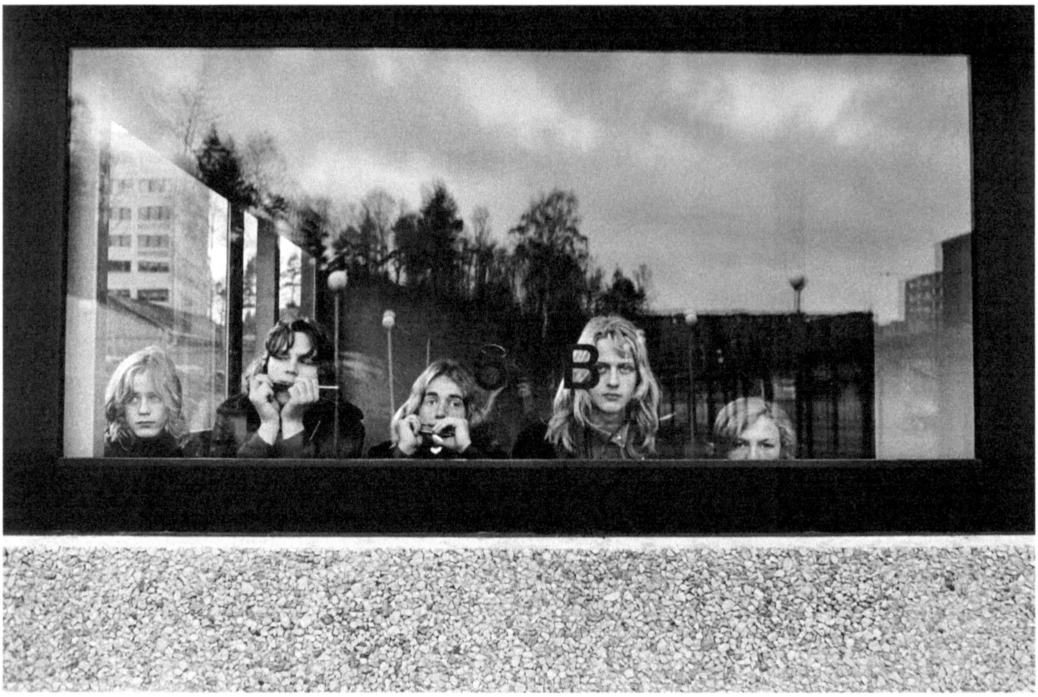

Jens S. Jensen (1946–2015), *The Five, Hammarkullen* 1973, courtesy Jesper Schleimann-Jensen and Jakob Schleimann-Jensen.

In a series of photo/text spreads in a 1972 Swedish photography publication, Jensen called for a "vibrant residential area" in Gothenburg. Vibrancy not only suggests the tone he wished to achieve in his photographs, but also his awareness of human complexity and vitality whatever the living circumstances. In *Jens S Jensen: Samlat verk* (*Collected Work*), professor and curator Niclas Östlind traces the development of Jensen's early interest in the impact of buildings on people's daily lives. Östlind's description of Jensen's degree project at Chalmers University, which focused on the "historical and contemporary importance of public libraries," attests to Jensen's implicit understanding of common space. In collaboration with fellow student Olle Ribbing, Jensen recognized the distance between the intentions of tax-funded libraries as places for everyone and the actuality of libraries being underused because of how they are managed and controlled. (Or, to put it another way, scheduling library hours for the convenience of library administrators and employees rather than for the work schedules of parents.) Reminiscent of Ruth Asawa's advocacy for artists' involvement in art education, Jensen and Ribbing challenged staff hierarchies in libraries and presciently advocated for more people's participation in decisions about library materials. Influenced by Marshall McLuhan, Jensen and Ribbing saw the "library as its own medium that mediates contact between the small, shrinking, directly experienced environment and the larger growing outside world, which is experienced

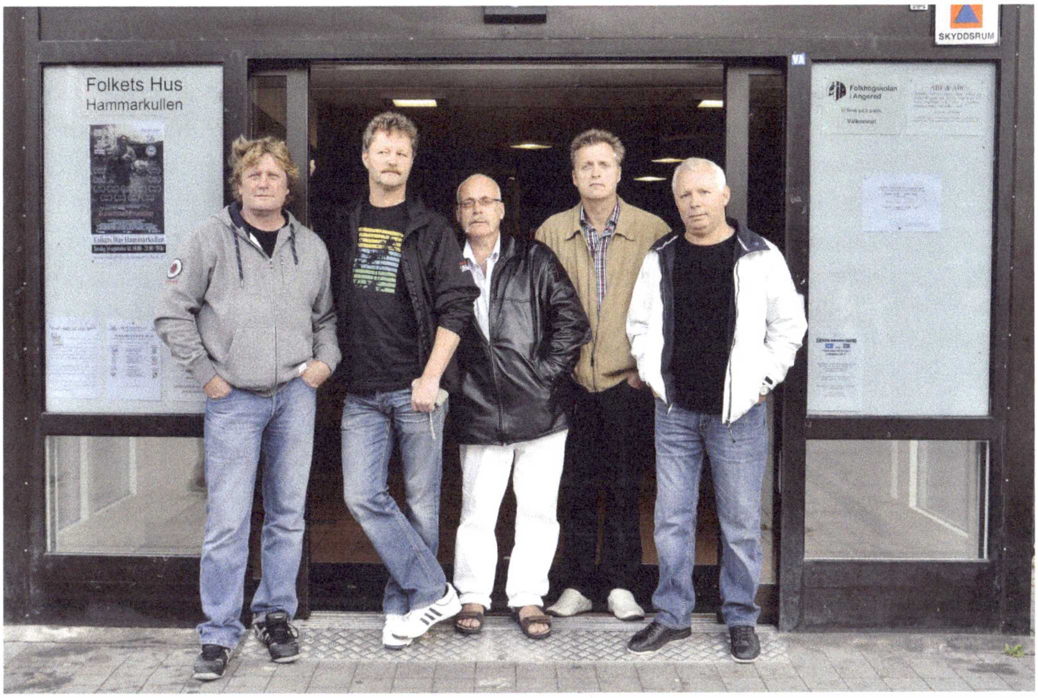

Jens S. Jensen (1946–2015), *The Five, Hammarkullen* 2011, courtesy Jesper Schleimann-Jensen and Jakob Schleimann-Jensen.

through electronic media." Whichever Gothenburg location attracted his attention, Jensen was theorizing and practicing a view of culture as ordinary, which does not mean sameness or simplicity, nor does it mean the cultivations of the economically elite.[4] Jensen does not separate the static noun of common space (a library, for instance) from the active verb of *commoning*, the vibrant interactions of people within those spaces.

Like Milton Rogovin, Jens Jensen photographed people at home and at work. Given greater managerial control and security concerns, it is likely not easy today for photographers to have access to interior industrial production sites. But in the mid-1970s (as did Rogovin around the same time period), Jensen managed to photograph and interview workers at the immense Volvo production plant in Torslanda, an inland near Gothenburg, resulting in two books, *Bilfabriken* (1976) and *Dom kallar oss bilbyggare* (1978). I saw an exhibit of some of this work at the Gothenburg City Museum in 2018, *Jobba, leva, bo: Bilder av ett samhälle* (Work, Live, Life: Images of a Society). The exhibit emerged from the Jensen family's donation of negatives and images to the Gothenburg City Museum combined with contemporary voices and new photos of people from Hammarkullen and the Volvo plant. The curator, Niclas Östlind, draws this distinction between Jensen's photographs being exhibited in a cultural museum as compared to an art museum: "it is not a retrospective focusing on the photographer as auteur. . . . The theme[s] of the exhibition are the issues that Jensen investigated in his work. With texts and photographs he unfolded and discussed how labour and living influence people's lives, and how they are strongly connected to socio-political structures and questions of class."[5] Östlind is attuned to workers' voices, preferring vocal variations to nostalgic reminiscence while honoring "Jensen's dialogue-oriented working method." By juxtaposing Jensen's recorded interviews with more recent stories collected by museum staff as well as in collaboration with Mixgården, a youth club in Hammarkullen, Östlind demonstrates how presenting life's arrows and cycles is fundamental to Jensen's artistry. Östlind chose to put images flat on a wall rather than "fetishizing" the framed vintage print. The result is a chorus of workers' voices accompanying their multiple images.

That chorus also includes other Swedish designers and curators associated with Jensen's work—what they recognized and how they framed and interpreted it. Greger Ulf Nilson, the designer of the award-winning catalog that accompanies the *Hammarkullen—40 Years Later* exhibit, offered this poem at the opening of the exhibit:

> *I know the guy hanging on the wall.*
> *It's Jens.*
> *It's Jens, when he grew up in Hammarbyhöjden.*
> *Or:*
> *It's me.*
> *I'm the one hanging there.*
> *It's that wall in Högdalen that I'm hanging on to.*
> *Or.*
> *It's you,*
> *You're the one hanging there.*
>
> *I think that everyone who grew up in a suburb in Sweden or anywhere in the world,*
> *Recognizes the guy who hangs there on the wall.*
> *We remember that day vividly, it lives with us forever.*
> *Jens has made it visible.*
> *Jens has also made life in Hammarkullen visible.*
>
> *It is important.*[6]

Nilson caught the folding and unfolding of lives and photographs in his catalog design. The outer section unfolds to a poster-size reproduction of the kid Michael hanging from the wall. The inner section holds color-pencil drawings of Hammarkullen apartment layouts and some of Jensen's early and later Hammarkullen photographs. The body of the catalog is in Swedish and in English, public descriptions juxtaposed with Jensen's own words drawn from his written diary.

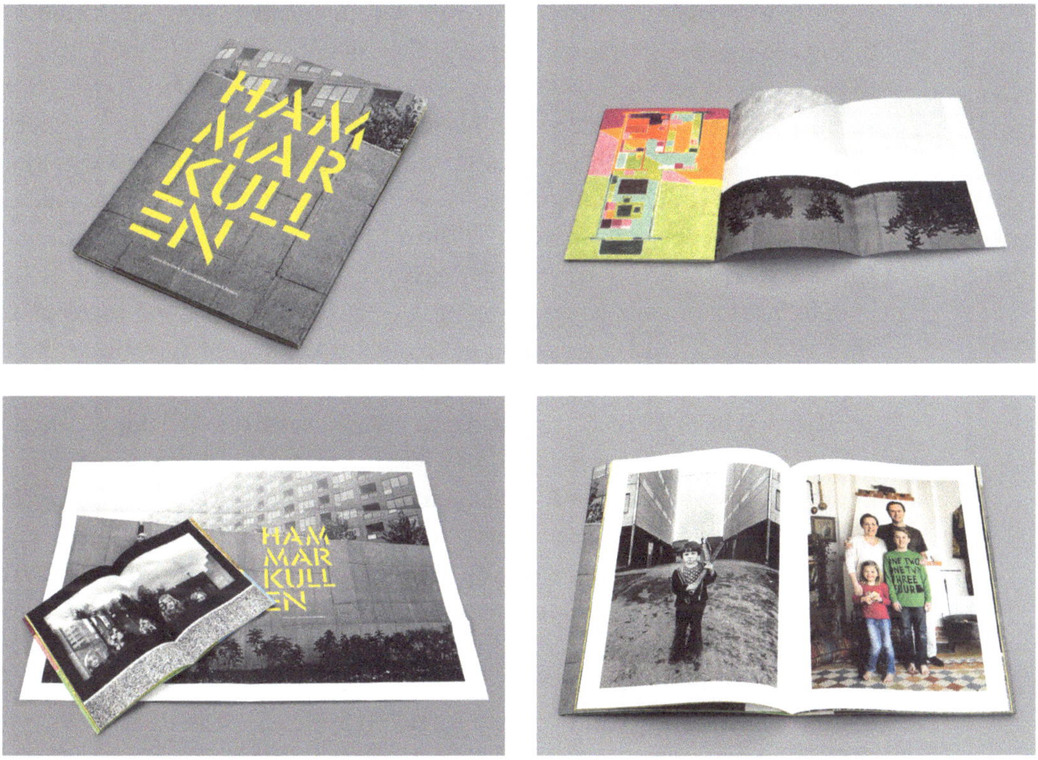

Greger Ulf Nilson, Designer, *Hammarkullen.* This catalog was published in conjunction with the exhibition *Jens S. Jensen—Hammarkullen 40 years later* at the Hasselblad Center, Gothenburg, Sweden, August 30–October 13, 2013, editor, Dragana Vujanovic, Hasselblad Foundation, photography and text © 2013 Jens S. Jensen, Art Direction & design: Greger Ulf Nilson, Dustjacket: Jen S. Jensen, Cover: 2 × 63m2 (This was the standard layout for a two-room flat): by Greger Ulf Nilson, Translation: Andrew Yong, Printed by Göteborgstryckeriet, 2013. Reprinted with permission from Dragana Vujanovic, Chief Curator, Hasselblad Foundation.

Folding and unfolding are also keywords that metaphorically represents Jensen's approach to his work and life, encounters with himself and others, folding and unfolding. He allowed space for interior dialogue as well, the push–pull of oppositional forces within. Jensen's father, Arne Schleimann-Jensen, was a Danish civil engineer and a successful inventor of electronical components. Jensen's sons, Jakob and Jesper, describe their paternal grandfather as strict and pragmatic, and their paternal grandmother, Maj Bengtsson (later Schleimann-Jensen), as someone who "had a sorrow that she kept within" from when her own father left the family (to travel to Tahiti) after his wife and son died. Maj gave birth to four children, three sons (Jens became an artist and the other two became engineers and took over their father's business), and a daughter, who became a physician.[7]

Jakob and Jesper Schleimann-Jensen see their father, Jens, as shaped by both parents, "the strict and pragmatical ways of his father (although maybe this was also what invoked Jens's rebellious side) and the softer, longing and somewhat melancholic side from his mother." They recognize their father's "bright intellect" and charisma. Jakob writes: "He had a natural way of getting to know people and getting personal with them very fast and easy, which I find very rare for being a Swede. He also spoke English, Danish, French and German fluently which made it very easy for him to bind similar bonds with people internationally when traveling. He could get to know people of all ages and backgrounds easily. And people from all kinds of cultures seemed to like him."

Class and birth place shape artistic development. Jensen was able to sustain himself as an artist because of his own inspirations and will, and also because he was born in socialist Sweden. Jensen was critical of state-sponsored mass housing, but his health care did not depend on his employment. According to his son Jakob, Jens was able to support himself through his work. "I don't think he ever had a full time employment in his whole life. . . . He wasn't very skilled at selling his own photographs to collectors, etc. . . . He didn't get much money for his books . . . The main income he had was state funded culture contributions and something called 'writer's wage' that was a set amount yearly from the state . . . In general he didn't have a big income."

Jensen's pattern of returning to Hammarkullen (initially in 1973, then eight years later, then twenty years later, then forty years later) was not one, preconceived, artistic project. It evolved as Jensen listened to his inner voice, continued his relationships with some of the original Hammarkullen residents, and confronted happenstance in his own life. After his large Hammarkullen exhibit at the Hasselblad Center in 1996–97, he thought he was done with the project. *One generation was enough and there was so much else I wanted to do.*

On 8 March 1997, exactly 24 years after I had taken those first pictures in Hammarkullen, something happened when I was cycling home at night. "Unknown 40-year old man" was the note in the hospital journal. And this was me; I still have no idea how I got there. Parts of my body were broke and I had lost one of my most important resources—language. At first, I did not know who I was. Later, a doctor explained there had been a mighty force against my head. Fortunately, I quickly returned to my old self, but what happened that night 16 years ago remains in darkness; all I have is a black hole. And yet, I was soon working on new projects.

Jensen did regain his language skills. He called what happened to him "the accident" rather than "an assault." He produced two books, *Black Pearl* and *Borta bra*, as part of the process of reacquiring his language skills. Although Jensen completed mock-ups and interviews, his last project, *Hammarkullen: 40 Years Later* does not include an accompanying book because of publisher conflicts and his own declining health. What emerged from the photographs, exhibits, interviews, and videotapes is, however, a view of photography as a visual language of time. This language is not the grammar of decisive moments, shoots, or captures. It is a lived language with continuations (cycles) and disruptions (arrows). Also, for the storyteller Jens Jensen, visual and spoken languages are intertwined. Östlind describes Jensen's "balancing act" as a photographer and oral historian: "He never published anything against anyone's will, but he also writes that it has sometimes been difficult to include certain things even though the people explicitly said it was okay. [In Jensen's own words] *That's a bit of the dilemma with my work—it's an interaction built on respect and mutual trust. I am talking about people who opened up to me primarily as fellow human beings. At the same time, I will make the whole thing public. Sometimes, I feel like I'd like to keep all the nice and close connections I've had to myself, and be content with that. But I continue.*"[8]

Jensen's interactive process is evident in his continuing relationship with Nettan (Anette Jansson Frisk), a Hammarkullen resident he rescued when she was twelve years old. His ongoing conversation with Nettan, grouped under "You Damn Saved My Life!" NETTAN 1973–2013, includes conversations with her in 1973 when Nettan was twelve, and then later conversations in 2009 through 2013.

Conversation with Nettan, 12 years old, 1973:

> *Why are you sniffing?*
> *I don't know—I have no idea about that.*
> *What do you feel when you sniff?*
> *You feel strange . . . feel thin . . . just like nothing.*
> . . .
> *Do you ever think ahead—how you would like it?*
> *Well, I just take the day as it comes.*
> *Do you care about something?*
> *Nah . . .*
> *Don't you care about yourself?*
> *Well, I suck at everything. I'm not interested in anything. I never think.*
> *Does anyone care about you?*
> *I don't know . . . not at home anyway, that's what they tell me.*
> *They probably don't mean that*
> *Yes.*

From conversations with Nettan 2009–2013:

"It is July 2009, and I am visiting Nettan in Ugglarp south of Falkenberg. She actually lives in Anderstorp, but now we sit in the evening sun in the garden outside the house she rents for a week every summer, and talk about old memories."

> *Oh my God. The first thing I remember about Hammarkullen is that it was grey, grey. Concrete and tall houses in long rows.*

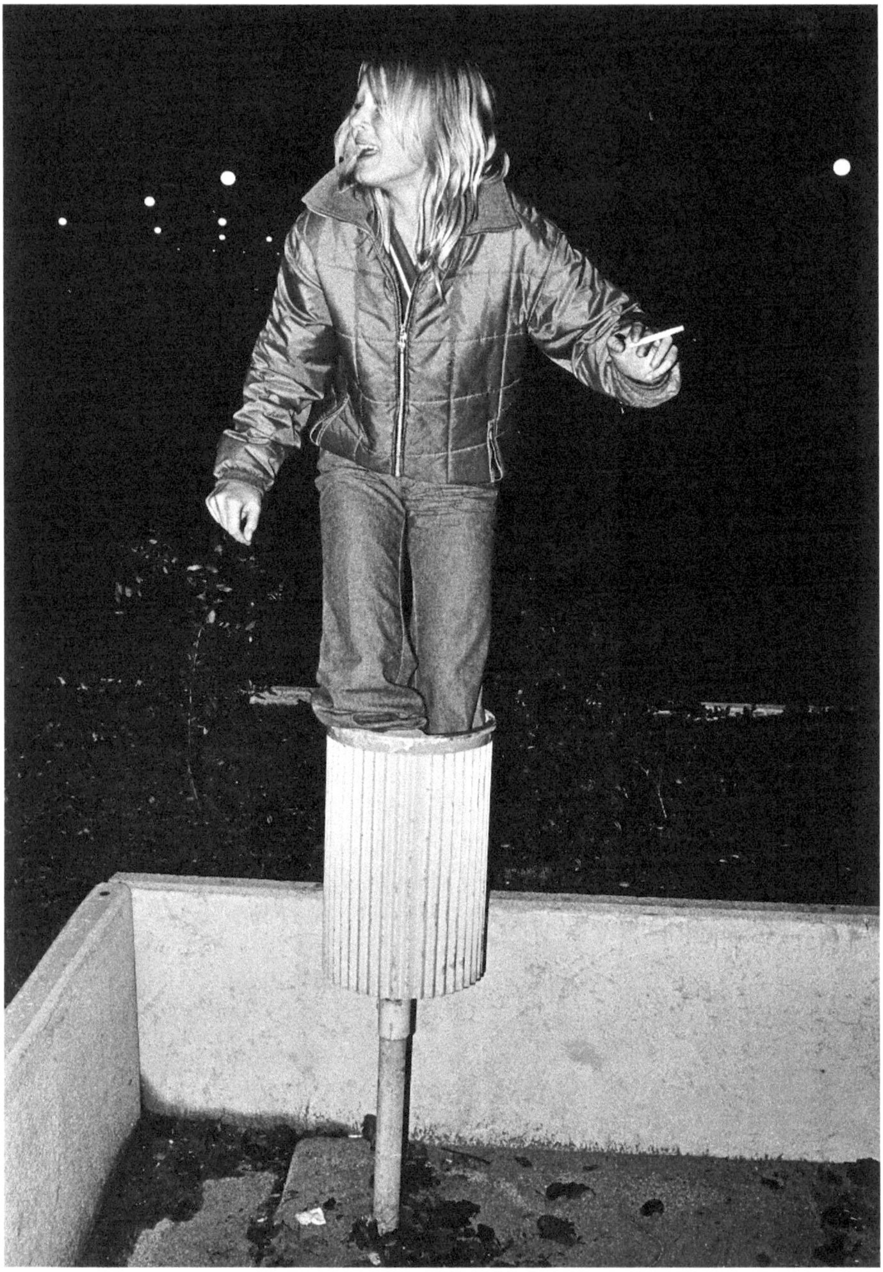

Jens S. Jensen (1946–2015), *Nettan, Hammarkullen*, 1973, courtesy of Jesper Schleimann-Jensen and Jakob Schleimann-Jensen.

You were only eight years old and still remember. In 1969 it was you who came among the first?

Yes, that's my entire upbringing. In the fifth and sixth grades, things started to happen. . . . And you found me in some fucking shelter there.

Yes, at Sandeslätt.

I should be really happy about that today. You fucking saved my life!

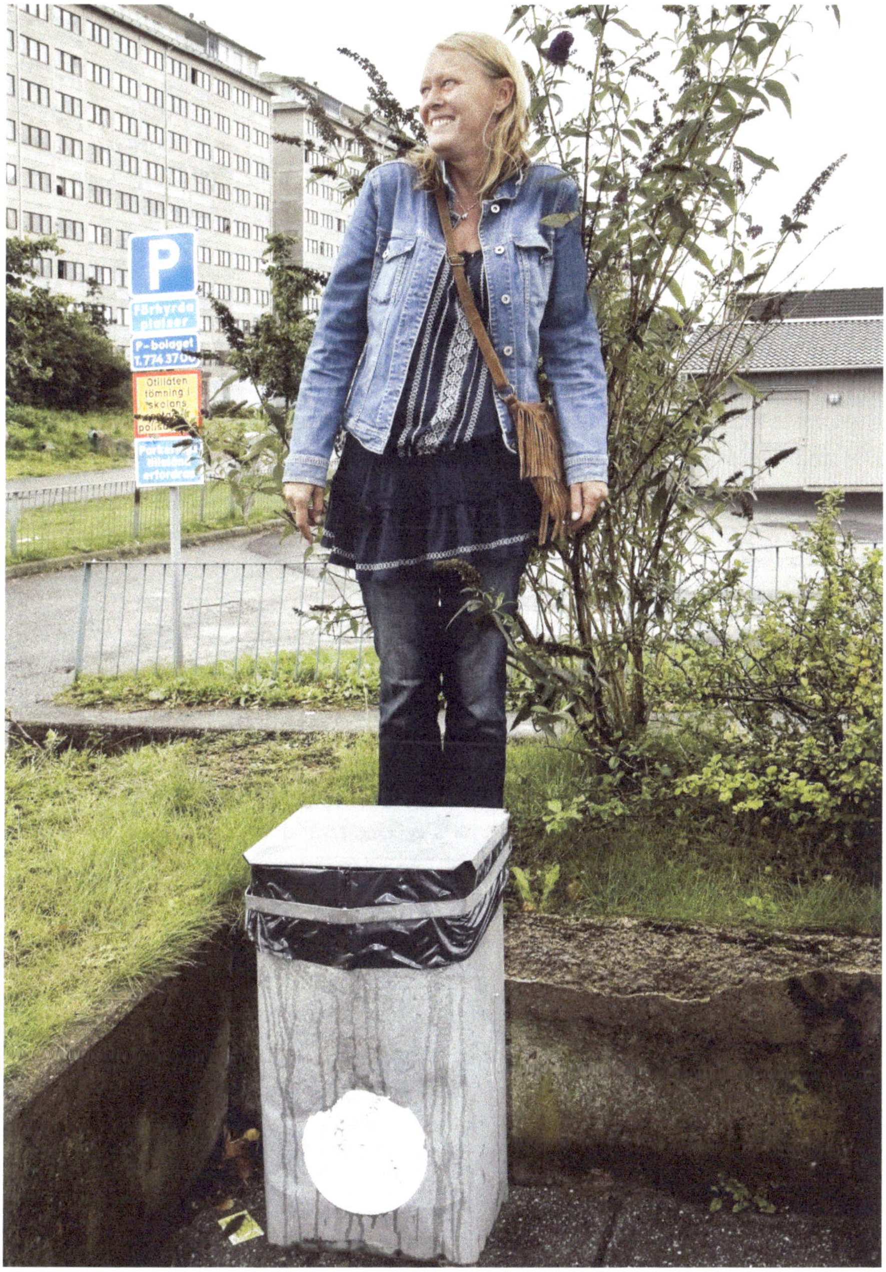

Jens S. Jensen (1946–2015), *Nettan, Hammarkullen*, 2011, courtesy of Jesper Schleimann-Jensen and Jakob Schleimann-Jensen.

Nettan visits Jens a year later in 2011. *We sit and have coffee at my house in Kortedala.* They reflect on the deaths of her parents and her early years in Hammarkullen. Nettan describes herself at twelve years as an *idiot.* Jensen responds, *You were a child. A brave child, but still.* Jensen sums up their last encounter in March 2013 at a restaurant in Gothenburg: *[we] talk about everything that happens in our lives, and what she has told me during the forty years we have known each other.*

> *Yes, a lot of darkness . . . but the brightest memories . . . do you have any? Apart from Göran and the children, it is when I returned to Gothenburg a couple of years ago. . . . You're my best friend, Jens . . . you mustn't die before me.*
>
> *Okay . . . Well, I promise to stay alive as long as I can!*

Jensen concludes: *This is where I end the conversations with Nettan this time, and we will always be . . . very close friends.*

Folding, unfolding, listening, voicing, all keywords that describe Jensen's approach and body of work. His process upends any preconceived notions of the photographer as dominator. Rather, through his photography, he saw the possibilities of *refuge*, a keyword also. Refuge was evident in his interactions with immigrants, whether from Nordic or non-Nordic regions of the world, who sought safe shelter in Hammarkullen's stark public housing. Refuge also was understood by him as those safe havens that humans create for each other and through their cultural and artistic practices.

Jens S. Jensen's body of work is a significant strand of Sweden's photographic history. He also crosses geographic borders and enlarges definitions of national identity. Jens S. Jensen and Milton Rogovin can speak to a new generation of photographers—are there listeners? Neither Jens Jensen nor Mark Rogovin, Milton's son, lived long enough to continue their initial e-conversation. On March 5, 2014, Jens wrote to Mark: "What I really would enjoy, would be to meet you somewhere in the world, and keep on talking for hours about everything! . . . Many warm thoughts to you, and to your parents who have meant so much for so many people!"

Jensen did not separate the personal and private from the social and structural. He sought self-understanding, the shaping circumstances of life's tragedies and occasional joys, by expanding his awareness of other people's lives through his genuine and generous curiosity. Antonio Gramsci framed this interpersonal approach in educational terms: "to know oneself better through others and to know others better through oneself."[9] Perhaps this sums up Jensen's dialectical and dialogic ethos and method. However, Gramsci takes us only so far. There's still the wall of the unknowable, the impenetrability of others' lives. In the meantime, we hang onto the wall, dangling with one hand.

The Art of Commoning: Murals

Ultimately, it is the community residents and passers-by who most greatly appreciate the involvement of the artist. Unless one is actually witness to the enthusiasm, curiosity, and serious discussions of these newly involved art-lovers, one does not realize the vitality and the potential of the mural as a public art form.

—William Walker and Others, Artists' Statement[1]

We are going to unite for peace, freedom, jobs for all, and a clean, unpolluted world to share. How will this come about? The murals will tell the story. You don't believe me? Keep your eyes open.

—Pete Seeger[2]

Murals are catalytic. They rouse emotion, history, and longing. They answer barriers and borders. They contain collective memory. Murals—situated in communities and neighborhoods around the world—speak to and exist in relation to working-class lives. The instrumentality of murals is larger than representation. Murals fuel communities.

Alan W. Barnett, in his comprehensive *Community Murals,* describes murals as an "authentic people's art." Barnett tells the story of a "young man who stood for a long time gazing at the portraits of Black leaders and artists on the *Wall of Respect* in Chicago. When the young man was asked what he was doing, he replied, 'I'm getting energy.'" The *Wall of Respect* mural emerged in the late 1960s as part of the civil rights struggle and was painted by the visual arts workshop of the Organization of Black American Culture (OBAC). Barnett also recognizes Mark Rogovin's mural, *Break the Grip of the Absentee Landlord*, created by Mark and local youth in 1973, as "a drama of walls and hands" where "slumlords looming over tenements firmly clutch their property."[3]

The makers of murals, unintentionally perhaps, practice a theoretically informed art. They may not have read M. M. Bakhtin's ideas on architectonics and answerability regarding literary texts, but they are aware of the necessity of seeing the relationship of parts to the whole—architectonics—and the inclusion of the viewer as agent in *completing* the visual manifestation—answerability.[4]

On a more prosaic level, murals resist barbarism. They expand historical consciousness. They fill loopholes in citizens' understanding of actuality, of lived reality. They evoke response. This recognition of the power and potency of murals is no more than a brushstroke, a modest preface to Mark Rogovin's activism and artistry. Readers will notice that I have not paired Mark Rogovin with another muralist. I invite readers to do that work in their own neighborhoods and communities.

THE MURAL

There is no admission price
standing
between us and these colors
There is no frame
other than the sky, the rain, the sun,
the people, the polluted air.
There is no guard
reminding us

not to touch
not to stare too long
not to lean against
not to piss on it.

Is this a work of art?

. . .

You better believe it!
This is where it all came from!
GO ASK THE CAVEMEN.

—Carlos Barón[5]

Mark Rogovin

Activism as Artistry

July 31, 1946, Buffalo, New York–
September 30, 2019, Forest Park, Illinois

an active aesthete, a fighter for the harmony of life
—Alexander Bogdanov, *Art and the Working Class*

And so my life is a sort of shaggy dog story
—Mark Rogovin

Mark Rogovin had a voice of unbridled enthusiasm, affection, informed opinions, and urgency. He spoke in, and profusely used, exclamation marks, a fitting punctuation to describe Mark's inseparable artistry and activism.

Where does a rich and complex artistic talent go if its mission is to repair the world rather than enhance the self? Mark Rogovin was a muralist, a filmmaker, a curator, a float builder, a banner and button maker, a producer of ephemeral public art, a citizen-historian, an author, a keeper and advancer of his father's photographic legacy, an educator, a carpenter, a progressive institution builder, and a very good neighbor.

Mark observed the working lives of his father and mother, Milton and Anne Rogovin, as he and his two sisters lived the palpable oppression of 1950s McCarthyism in Buffalo, New York. His legacy from his father, a trained optometrist and internationally known photographer, and his mother, a special education teacher as well as author and artist, is of an intellectuality grounded in race and class struggle, expressed through art making. Mark expanded his political inheritance as he studied art and practiced art activism. Combining a large political imagination with art school training, he earned a BFA from the Rhode Island School of Design and assisted muralist David Alfaro Siqueiros in Mexico City and Cuernavaca on the enormous mural *March of Humanity on Earth and Toward the Cosmos* (1964–1971). From Mexico he traveled to Chicago in 1968 as the Democratic National Convention erupted in violence. He earned a degree from the Art Institute of Chicago but rejected institutional art practices. Instead, he immersed himself in producing communal art in and with impoverished Chicago neighborhoods.

Mark possessed what Raymond Williams observed as "the rare capacity to articulate and to form, to make latencies actual and momentary insights permanent."[1] Plainspoken, sometimes profane, Mark Rogovin would likely disdain Williams's theoretical language, but he would certainly recognize Williams's observation about how cultural work can be practiced. Given his stewardship of Milton Rogovin's photographs, a role he cherished, Mark was well aware of the importance of museum and gallery recognition and the apparatus of cultural production. Beyond exhibitions, the Rogovin family wanted the photographs to have agency in promoting equality and justice. They also were protective of the people photographed. Their agreement with the Library of Congress included a stipulation that a member of the Rogovin family had to sign off before a photo could be used for books or other purposes.

As an artist, Mark chose not to focus *in* on his own capacious talents, but to channel his art making into collective practice by drawing others *out*. Organizer, instigator, and imaginative political pioneer, Mark was a *founder* in numerous ways—as someone who could transform found objects into something politically meaningful and useful, and as a builder of community structures. He was a founding father—not as an individualistic entrepreneur, but as a communal orchestrator. Mark founded the Public Art Workshop (PAW, 1972), a community and art mural center, and coauthored the book *Mural Manual: How to Paint Murals for the Classroom, Community Center, and Street Corner* (1975).[2] He made floats and street props and, with the National Alliance against Racism and Political Repression, worked to free Angela Davis and other political prisoners. In 1981 he cofounded the Peace Museum and was its director for four years. In 1997 he led a nationwide organization to celebrate the centennial of actor, singer, and activist Paul Robeson and coauthored *Paul Robeson: Rediscovered*.[3] For many years he worked closely with the Illinois Labor History Society on restoring its monument to the Haymarket Martyrs and coauthored the publication *The Day Will Come*.[4]

The arc of Mark Rogovin's life offers a historically significant model of how to connect powerful artistic energy with political struggle. His life's work was not for sale. It was not marketable. It was outside capitalism—however that's possible.

We hear the distinct rhythms of Mark's voice in this condensed interview with art historian Rebecca Zorach:[5]

In 1953 my parents started to go to Mexico, and because my parents were radicals, they went to Mexico City to meet up with the Taller de Gráfica Popular (TGP).[6] Now some of that history is murky to me because I was a child back then, very young. I don't know whether they knew Elizabeth Catlett before they went or met her while there, but the other person who went with my parents on their trips was a person from the FBI; they were following my parents! In Washington DC, there are photographs taken by the FBI of my parents getting off a plane in 1954. So what my parents would do, is they would go and spend time with artists like Raúl Anguiano, they would go out to some of the places where the indigenous people were living, and Raúl would draw and my father would photograph, my mother would actually draw as well. And they would go with Pablo O'Higgins and some of the other artists. When my parents would come back to Buffalo, the TGP would send them back with bulging black portfolios of prints . . . and my parents would take all the art down from the house, and they would put up all the art. There were already prices on them. Siqueiros: 35 dollars. Posada: 15 dollars. And people joke and they say if my parents had been smart, we'd be really rich. We'd have a better Posada collection than the Art Institute of Chicago. All of these great artists! Amazing, amazing stuff.

My parents went year after year to the TGP, and that's how the connection with myself and Elizabeth Catlett came about. She was teaching at Academia San Carlos in 1964 and 65 and I was there and the second time I was there to study, she started to hit me heavy with the mural thing and gave me a letter which I then put in front of Siqueiros. The mural I was an assistant on eventually became part of this massive space in Mexico City, but we were working in Cuernavaca in this incredible studio and we were working with a scale model that was a scale of this future building in Mexico City, so we were working with 11 × 13 foot asbestos panels. The scale model was based on drawings and paintings but mainly gesture drawings that Siqueiros did while in prison.

I left Mexico in 1968, and so I show up in Chicago, and I was coming for graduate school at the Art Institute of Chicago, and I knew nobody in town, but I had a letter that said visit so and so in an apartment here, so I show up at this couple's place and a woman comes to the door and she says, "oh yes, I know so and so" and she says, "well you know what just happened?" and I said, "of course, the whole world knows what just happened."

I arrived two days after the Democratic Convention, and she says, "well, if you can't find a place, you're welcome to stay here until you find somewhere to stay," so I go into this little tiny apartment, and there, all around the walls were wounded people, with bloody knees, and other injuries . . . [W]hat was happening was that the cops were not only beating people up on the street, but hauling people out of hospitals and beating them up again. It was frightening! Progressive doctors were doing whatever they could, either in the hospitals or literally on the street, and many other places had become sort of "safe houses."

I found an apartment in South Shore, and started at the Art Institute. I did not like the Art Institute. While I was at the Art Institute, I would take a bus back and forth from the Art Institute to South Shore, and, son of a bitch, I'm looking out the window, there is Bill Walker and the Wall of Respect at 43rd Street as I was heading towards South Shore, so I just jumped off the bus and had a little bit of conversation with Bill and our conversation kept on going for many, many years. But one of the things that I also did at that point was I started to document with color slides the mural, the Wall Of Respect and Wall Of Truth, as I had done in Mexico.

Despite his training, travels, parental legacy, and relationships with world-renowned artists, Mark tended to demystify the art world and the process of art making. He was adept at seizing opportunities to bring art to the people, such as the Public Art Workshop. In 1972 he found a vacant building at 5623 W. Madison Street that he felt would be "idyllic" for a community mural resource center on the West Side of Chicago.

It [the building] *had a wonderful first story; the second story housed an international mural resource center and all of that material, all of the archive is at the Chicago History Museum, and it's finally, after 15 years, now available to the public. We kept track of murals around the world, and this was at an early stage. There are no slides there. It's our bookkeeping and all that kind of stuff . . . and it shows our proposals that we wrote. We got National Endowment for the Arts (NEA) grants, we were this freaking tiny hole in the wall; we had CETA* [Comprehensive Employment Training Act] *people for x number of years and here's this big NEA and we wrote to them and they wrote back at a certain point and they said, "you're exactly what we want to fund!" And they said, "change this and change this and change this." We got it in the same day! So OK, our interests were serving the community. It was a 100% Black community, except for me. And I mean the community used to be Ukrainian and Jewish, and then as the landlords let the properties go in terms of repairs, it became a Black community. There were times when I was in my old apartment where I could stand on the back porch and look out into the alleys and see moving vans night or day. Just routine in poor neighborhoods. Diagonally across was an elementary school, Robert Emmet Elementary School, that had just lost their art program, and so we knew we wanted to do things both within the school and at our shop and with murals in our neighborhood. At that point, I was employed part-time by Urban Gateways. They brought artists to schools or schools to concerts. It's still alive and they do it well, a very, very, excellent program for decades. I went to classrooms in five counties through that program, and I was either doing workshops for students or workshops for teachers, which I liked even more because you knew they could affect more within the schools. We learned a lot working with those programs,*

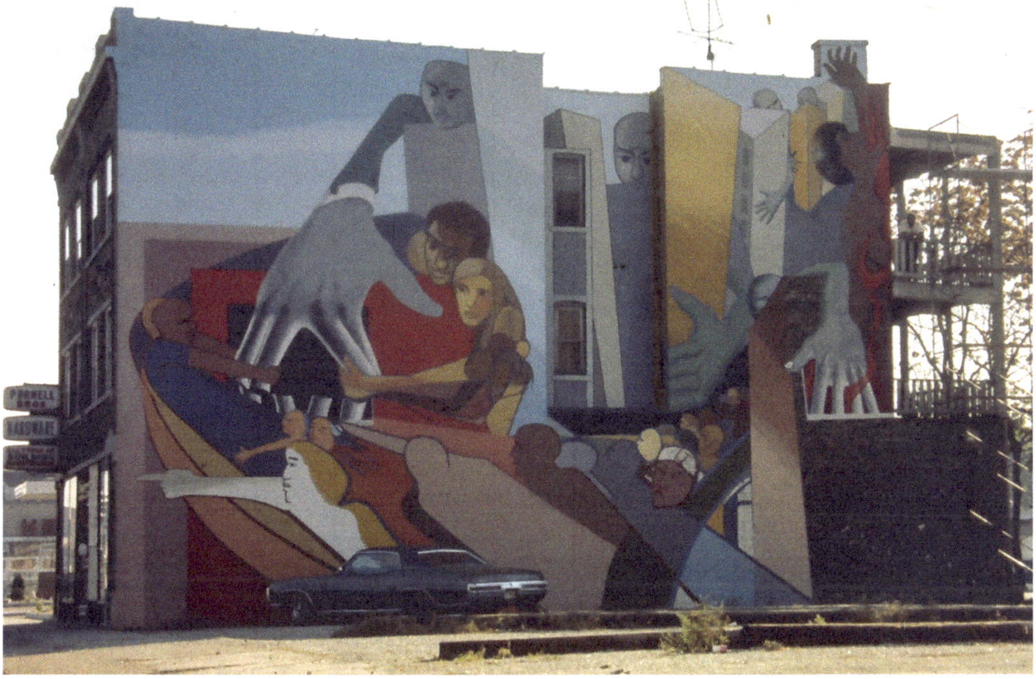

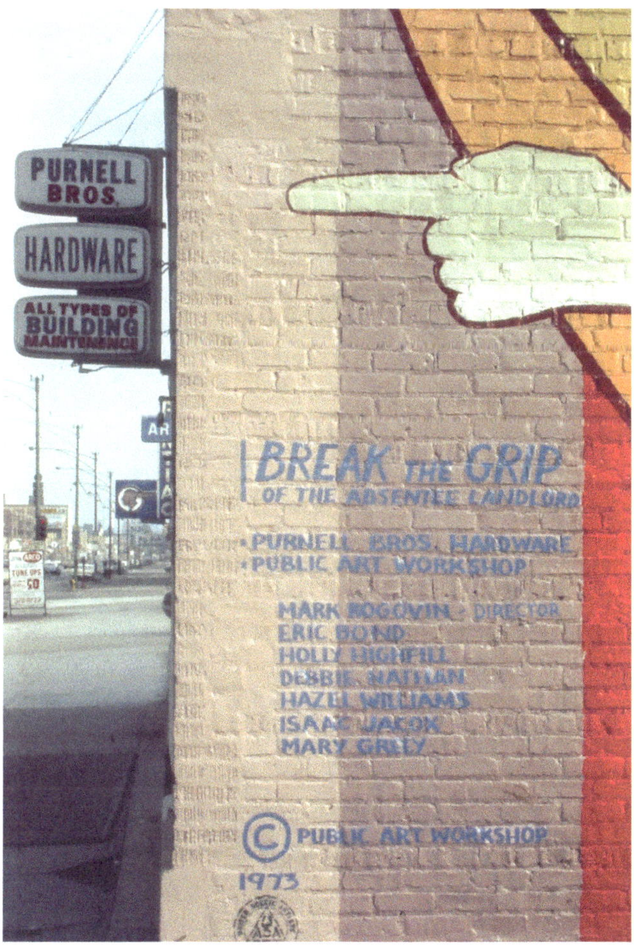

Above: Mark Rogovin (1946–2019) and the Public Art Workshop, *Break the Grip of the Absentee Landlord* (full view), 5219 W. Madison St., 43' × 60', 1973, Mark Rogovin photographer, © The Family of Mark Rogovin, www.markrogovin.com.

Left: Mark Rogovin (1946–2019) and the Public Art Workshop, *Break the Grip of the Absentee Landlord* (corner detail), 5219 W. Madison St., 43' × 60', 1973, Mark Rogovin photographer, © The Family of Mark Rogovin, www.markrogovin.com.

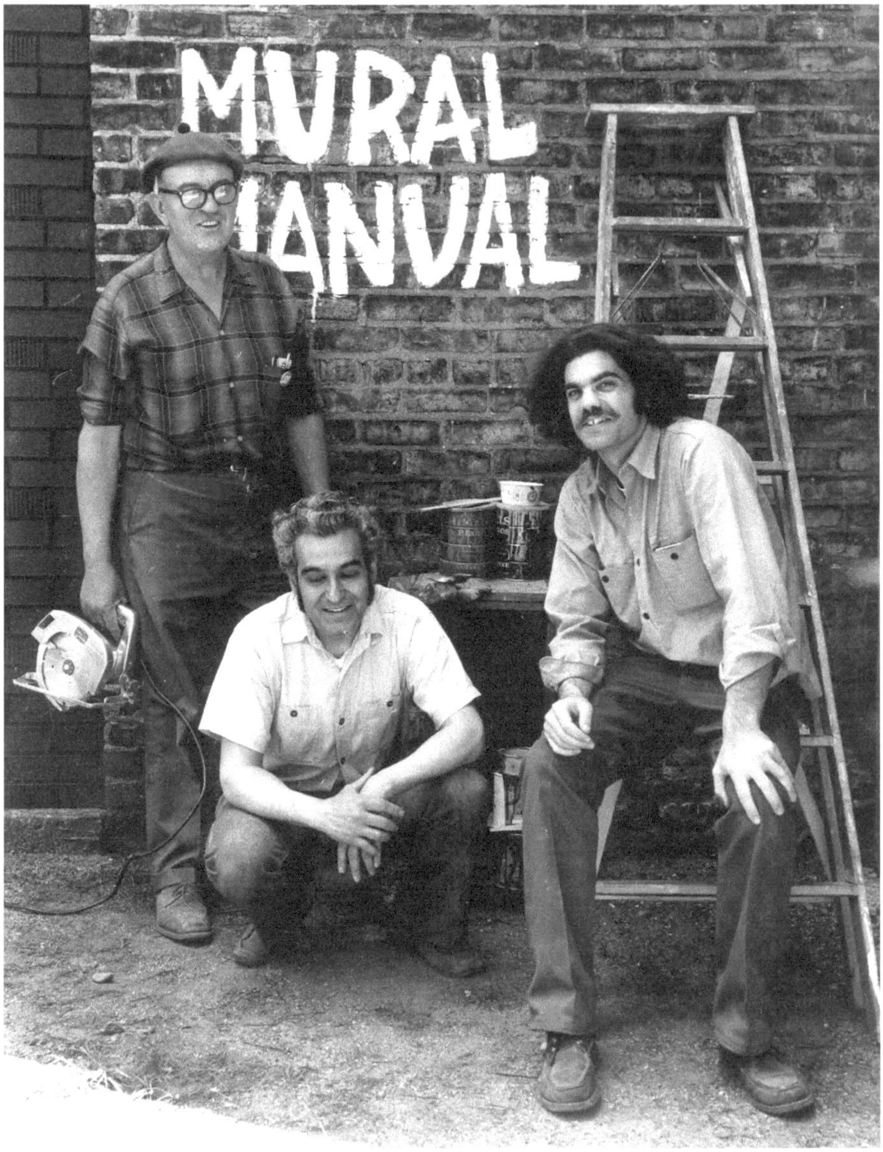

Mural Manual Cover (photographer unknown), © The Family of Mark Rogovin, www.markrogovin.com.

all of those programs. We also did some murals and we did one mural that's called Break the Grip of the Absentee Landlord.

There [are] *a lot of older murals, like a fun one which is called Bored Of Education. We did some murals in our neighborhood and that was the main area that we focused on. We also developed the concept of portable panel murals, and I brought one portable panel mural to an international festival and we developed in the* Mural Manual *step-by-step guidelines for how to do the portable panel pieces and be able to move them from site to site. These were with Masonite. Among other things, on the second floor we had the archive but we also wrote the book* The

Mural Manual. *Within six months* [of the opening of] *the Public Art Workshop, I started getting calls from old friends of mine saying, "well, you have to develop a manual," and I said, "Hey, you know, we've just begun learning how to paint murals, how can we develop a manual?" I pulled a couple of people together and we wrote an 86-page booklet and it's a very, very valuable document. We even had a paint section, which is not useful today, of course, but we had a little history section which obviously needs to be updated . . . but how to look at a wall, and many people don't care about this, I still do, if you've got windows, do you just pretend that they don't exist or do you weave them into the concept, into the drawing. And really, some people just have their own approach and that's just fine.*

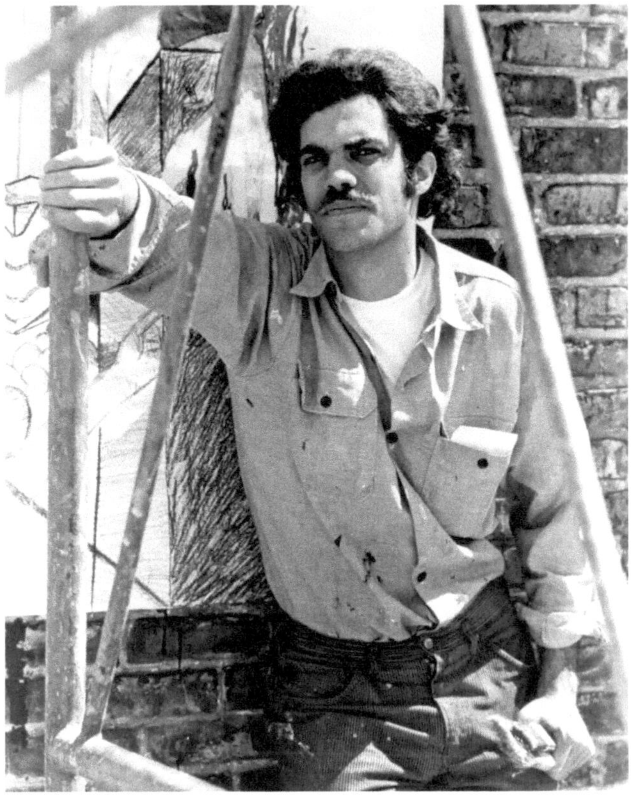

Mark Rogovin (1946–2019), (photographer unknown), © The Family of Mark Rogovin, www.markrogovin.com.

People took bunches of them [Mural Manual] *to Nicaragua, I sent half a box to Cuba, but mainly we sold them around the US. We had developed a thing called Mural Resources, and it was a four-page, sometimes six-page flyer where we offered books, booklets and reproduced pieces for people. This was at the beginning of the whole renaissance of murals, and so any books that I found on Siqueiros I would buy six or eight copies and I would write to SPARC (the mural center in LA) and say, "I'm holding a copy for you," or there was another book which is so incredible, it's this thick, which I would only get small quantities of because there were very few, and it was an inventory of the murals in Mexico,* Inventario Del Muralismo Mexicano, *and it's a profound document . . .*

Mark Rogovin and his family were very conscious of the role of the artist as teacher and of the pedagogical possibilities of art making. His protean nature embraced occasions to produce materials for passing on artistic techniques. One example is his pamphlet on silhouette murals.

And you know, that silhouette booklet, there were again a lot of people who said, "I really like this approach." I'm in Urban Gateways, and I developed that concept and I wrote the booklet and then I wrote another version of it, which was much, much more sophisticated, where we would take and instead of just plain here it is—instead of just plain taking a projector and doing this, we would take

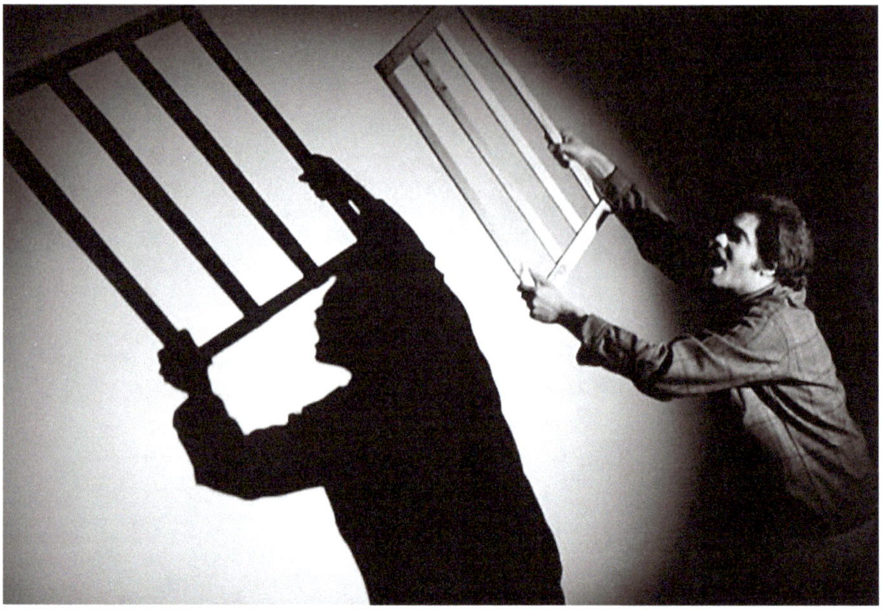

Mark Rogovin (1946–2019), demonstrating silhouette techniques, (photographer unknown). © The Family of Mark Rogovin, www.markrogovin.com.

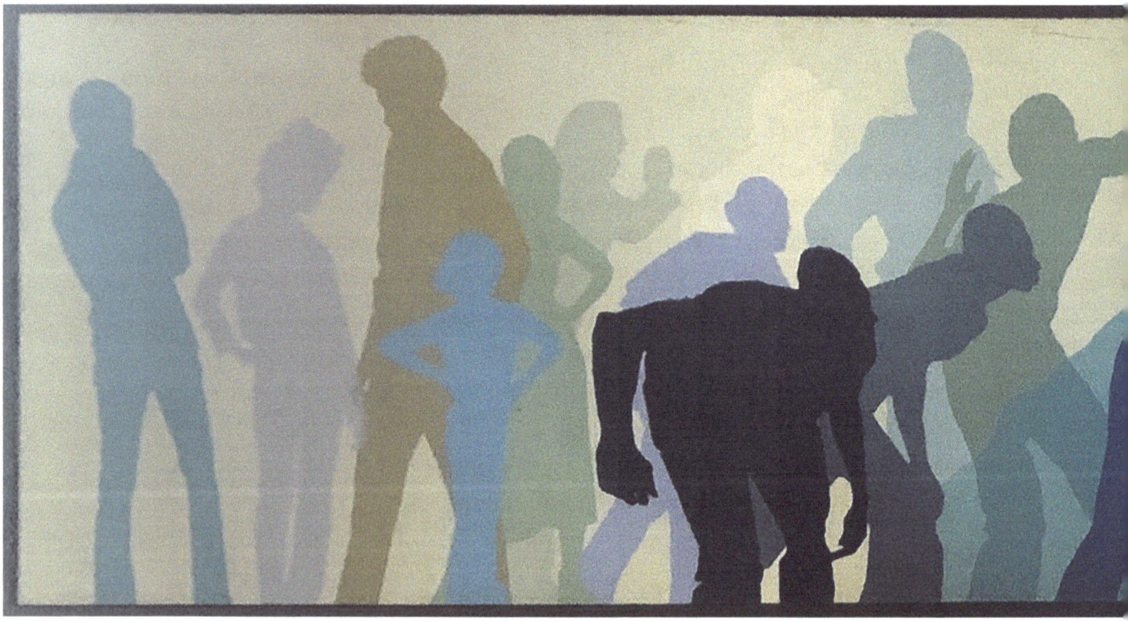

Mark Rogovin, (1946–2019), *Peace Mural Mock Up,* 98 × 25 × 1.5. © The Family of Mark Rogovin, www. markrogovin.com.

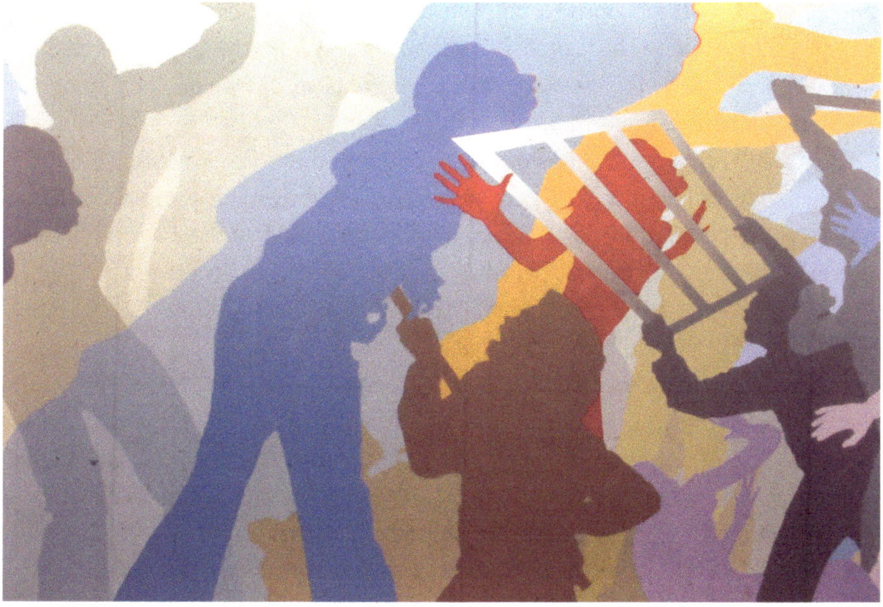

Mark Rogovin, (1946–2019), *Peace Mural,* © The Family of Mark Rogovin, www.markrogovin.com.

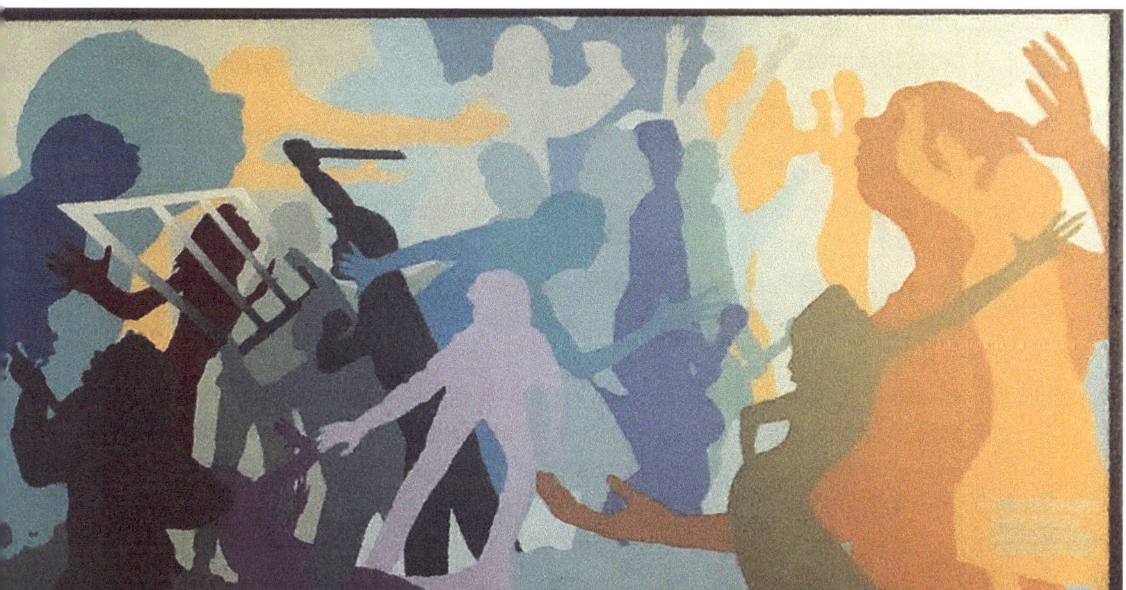

and photograph the shadows and then re-project upside down, backwards, and so it became more sophisticated. I've got boxes and boxes of slides, all black and white, and you've got this person in this beautiful pose, or I would just photograph them, but usually just the shadow. It's interesting.

Rogovin and his young co-muralists produced the *Peace Mural* (8'×36') in 1980; its original host home was the first floor lobby of Columbia College in Chicago. Its dedication coincided with the launching of the Peace Museum. Studs Terkel was master of ceremonies for the dedication event.

In a 1972 letter to his parents, Mark wrote, "Every mural is something special, never routine, never boring, never stagnant!"

Rogovin was also part of the *Murals for the People* (1971) exhibit at the Museum of Contemporary Art Chicago. *It was quite something. It was really a great time for us, we had a chance to talk to the public; people could walk into our studio area and I developed this piece on Angela Davis and it was a piece that was meant to travel. I don't remember how many venues it went to but I remember one where Sally Davis, Angela's mother, came and it was a precious event.*

We did write this paper, "We the artists . . ." The artists asked if I would draft the statement, if I would be the "coordinator" or "spokesperson" or whatever for this project at the Museum of Contemporary Art. I think that I did a draft of the mural statement, and everybody had their input and it served for many years. This was one of the first projects that employed artists to be there on a full-time basis, and that the public could meander from project to project and talk with us. It was really wonderful. It was wonderful for us and wonderful for the public and the press and it was a great experience. Plus we got to purchase whatever paint we wanted and so we ordered the polytech acrylic, which was the best acrylic in the world and by far the most expensive acrylic in the world, and when we finished, [Museum of Contemporary Art Chicago, MCA] *continued to supply the mural movement in Chicago for endless projects! It was great stuff.*

When asked about activities at the Public Art Workshop, especially its involvement with neighborhood kids, Mark responded in a spirit that would echo Ruth Asawa's work in San Francisco's city schools: *Yeah, we had after school classes. We went into Robert Emmet Elementary School, the school I mentioned where they had cut the art program. We taught a class in photography for the deaf. We had converted an unused basement into a gorgeous five-enlarger darkroom. And we had to make some slight additions or changes, so a light would come on if somebody needed to come or go through the main door instead of knocking. We had two very, very skilled teachers. So the students produced some superb work in the afterschool art program and then we produced some murals in our area. The Peace Mural was done there, all the beautiful movement of the young people was photographed there.*

Another thing was that we worked for the peace and justice movement around the city. It was mainly myself but I did banners; I'm a great banner maker although

I don't do them anymore, my hands are too shaky. And picket signs, I did some trade union stuff and peace and justice stuff.

Now, I have to tell you some other fun things that I did. Nobody knows that I ever did this. I developed these things called "truth balloons"—around an election, I took bumper sticker stock and I developed these designs.

They were beautifully printed and really, really interesting, and I went on the El, I got on the El at like five in the morning and I put these up on two El lines on every single one of a certain image [of] *a certain person, basically it was calling somebody an idiot or something like that, and it was one of those truth balloons kind of thing. It says, "this is what Jimmy said about Mike," and then "He's a fraud but so am I." These are all the work on the El. And then, I came back to the Public Art Workshop, got my camera and returned to the El, and photographed them. You know, it was sort of trying different things, playing with different things.*

Regarding the Peace Museum, Mark describes how the idea evolved from a place to archive peace/war resistance materials, and after many meetings of activists over the years, to an actual building that opened in 1981. *The Peace Museum took seven years from a concept to the day we opened. We always knew that we wanted to engage young people; there was no question. The museum opened in '81, in '83 we had a show called* The Unforgettable Fire, *on drawings by survivors of Hiroshima [and] Nagasaki, and we get a phone call from the Chicago Board of Education, and they said, "would you accept a busload of students?" and I of course said, "absolutely, when are you coming? We'll have somebody walk your students through." And I hung up the phone and I called the staff together and I said, "Wow we have made it!"*

We did not usually push people into activism; we did not see that as our mission. We wanted it very much and what we would hope for was that it would lead to activism. When we had the exhibition of drawings by survivors of Hiroshima [and] *Nagasaki, it was because there was an elderly man who was a volunteer at the Peace Museum, and we used to have occasional meetings and this guy said to me, "my son lives in Japan, fluent in Japanese, and he is translating a book called* The Unforgettable Fire *which is on the drawings by survivors."* [The book came about because] *one day a survivor walked into NHK TV in Japan, and brought in a drawing that he had made for the head of the station, and the guy was so moved by this image, that he put out a call for drawings by survivors. I flew to Hiroshima and Nagasaki and I flipped through or edited through about 2,000 drawings, and they had a size constraint too, they were all about this size, about let's say 16 × 20 inches. And they were amazing drawings, many of them in black and white. Why? Because that's what these survivors saw: char, burnt buildings, burnt flesh and that's what they saw, and there were some other photographs or drawings.* Mark comments on the complicated questions associated with representation and intention: *And I learned so much trying to figure out, what is our role? [Was] it to have people head out the door when they finished and say this shit can't happen again. This can't happen again. These were kind of second learning things for us.*

Mark Rogovin was a raconteur; one event, encounter, happenstance spilled into another, networks of people, famous and ordinary, populate his stories. One activity, really a mission, was sustaining his father Milton Rogovin's photography in exhibits, museums, books, and films. *I love the role that my father and my sisters entrusted to me: making certain that our father's photography is accessible and not used in any commercial or demeaning way. Our parents worked for 50 years on series after series, respecting the multitude of people they encountered—from coal miner to Chilean mother and child, to a family from the Lower West Side being photographed for three decades. Never once was the person being photographed looked upon as lesser than my folks or without respect.*

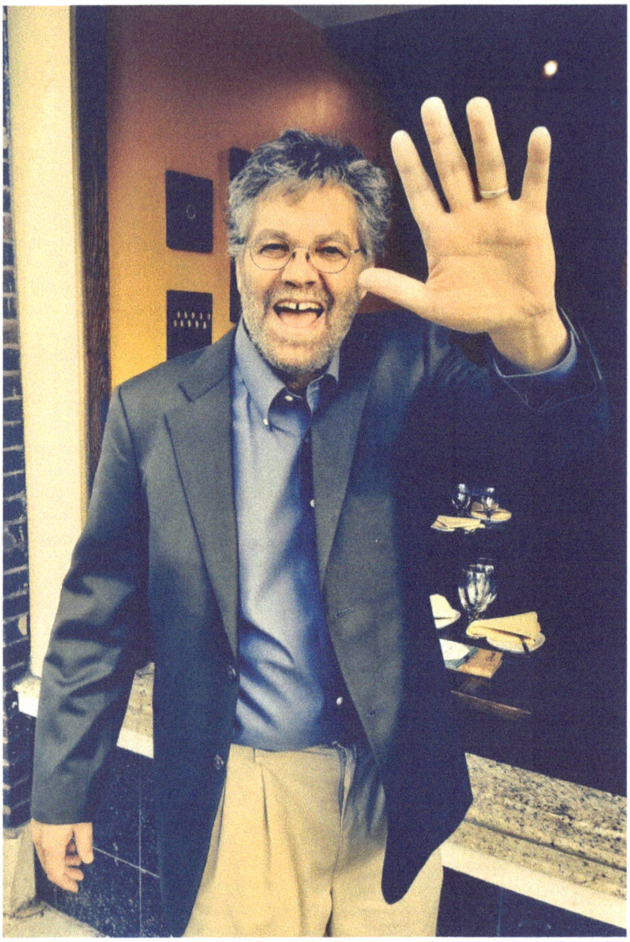

Mark Rogovin (1946–2019), Michelle Melin-Rogovin, photographer, 2015, ©Michelle Melin-Rogovin.

Mark had a meta understanding of the ephemeral and the permanent. On one hand, there was his love of posters, especially international posters. *This is something very important that I have always believed, and that is you did not always have to have pristine works of art, that if works of art had pushpin holes in the corners or were scraped off walls during the French Revolution. Hey! You know? That was a goddamn revolution, you know? Let's learn from it, you know?* On the other hand, Mark had his eye on permanency and history—and the importance of bringing labor history and political struggles into the classroom. For forty years Mark was involved in the preservation of the Haymarket Monument in Forest Home Cemetery. Inserted inside a copy he sent to me of *The Day Will Come: Honoring Our Working Class Heroes, Stories of the Haymarket Martyrs* was a note in his looping, dramatic handwriting: "wanted you to see one of my casual projects—ready for that tour?" In 2011 Mark gave me that tour of the markers, graves, and histories of Haymarket activists buried in Forest Home Cemetery.

Mark Rogovin, the son of artists, activists, anti-imperialists, internationalists, thinkers, and doers, led an eventful and consequential life that would take multiple libraries to contain. But he would not want it contained; indeed, that it could not easily be archived, housed, or numbered is the essence of his democratic artistic practice. In 2019 he died from complications of frontotemporal dementia. His grave location in Forest Home Cemetery is 779-Section M.

One day I'd like to write a real book . . . there's a lot of stories, a lot of history. What I should do someday is to just write all these little incidents down.

History and Beauty, Crowds and Multitudes

What is a labour victory? I maintain it is a two-fold thing. Workers must gain economic advantage, but they must also gain revolutionary spirit, in order to achieve complete victory. For workers to gain a few cents more a day, a few minutes less a day, and go back to work with the same psychology, the same attitude toward society is to achieve a temporary gain and not a lasting victory. For workers to go back with a class-conscious spirit, with an organized and determined attitude toward society means that even if they have made no economic gain, they have the possibility of gaining in the future.

—Elizabeth Gurley Flynn, Paterson Strike Speech, New York Civic Club Forum, January 31, 1914

The children asleep would become the children awake. That's what art does.

—Letter from Studs Terkel to Ralph Fasanella, June 30, 1988

In depicting sidewalk encounters, street traffic, markets, marches, demonstrations, and communal gatherings of celebration and loss, American painter Ralph Fasanella (1914–1997) and British/French sculptor Raymond Mason (1922–2010) envisage the choreography of human interactions. The center for Ralph Fasanella is the worker—especially the cohesion of collective labor struggle. That center does not collapse or reconfigure into a mob. It is always grounded in the actuality and rhythm of individual working lives. The center for Raymond Mason is human love, companionship, and longing for beauty. That center does not dissolve into sentimentality. Both artists understood the difference between commercialized nostalgia and **memory** (mixed with pain, untold and indeterminate stories). They offer the possibility of adhesive human relationships. Both depict individuals within larger frames—waiting to step onto a streetcar or watching a baseball game. They hold in common: red brick facades, human density, rhythm of daily lives, rhetoric of the body, empathetic imagination, acute sensitivity to human potential and human waste, architectural sense of balance and relationship, and art as healer.

I came upon the artistic work of Fasanella and Mason unexpectedly. One evening in the winter of 1982, I attended a talk about the 1912 Lawrence "Bread and Roses" strike.[1] The speaker was historian Peter Linebaugh. The walls leading to the forum were covered with reproductions of Ralph Fasanella's Lawrence paintings. It was one of those "what is this?" moments—seeing working-class history as art. It evoked an unaccustomed sense of affirmation, even joy. It answered a then unexpressed need to see representations of working-class people, their labor struggles, their neighborhoods, buildings and factories, streets and bridges, and their bodies at work.

My encounter with Raymond Mason's sculpture came later, in 1997. I was attending a conference in Birmingham, England, and, as was my conference-attending custom, sought a respite from academic talk by walking in the city center. There in Birmingham's Centenary Square was a large, dense, complicated sculpture of humans, their artifacts and tools, still but seemingly moving, with the billowing smoke of a midland factory behind them. It was another unexpected public art encounter. That the sculpture was titled *Forward* was a fitting answer to labor's call for solidarity. Again, I felt an unfamiliar affirming emotion that someone recognized the lives of working-class people in his art.

Fasanella and Mason created accessible art. Sometimes it wasn't welcomed. One of Fasanella's paintings, *The Great Strike (IWW Textile Strike)*, 1978, purchased by the Building and Construction Trades Department of the AFL-CIO, hung in a hearing room of the U.S. House Subcommittee on Education and Labor. It was removed after the 1994 elections, when the Republican party took control.[2] Raymond Mason's crowded statue, *Forward,* an optimistic tribute to his hometown Birmingham, was unveiled in 1991 and destroyed by vandal fire in 2003.

Through their art Raymond Mason and Ralph Fasanella answer mobs with multitudes. They recuperate the crowd, offering the possibility of human cohesion instead of division and hatred. Artist-workers, they expand our understanding of history and beauty.

Ralph Fasanella

History Painter

September 10,[1] 1914, Bronx, New York–
December 16, 1997, Yonkers, New York

What in fact can a work of art contain? At this hour of simplification, the reply seems to be—the least possible. Here, once more, I'm "against the movement," because for me the reply is everything. And it seems just as evident for me that I should address it to everybody.
—Raymond Mason, *At Work in Paris*

Art in this country belongs to and is controlled by a specific group of people. . . . [A]rt with spiritual depth and social meaning is homeless in this society.
—Lucy R. Lippard, *Mixed Blessings*

Most people live a life of beauty. Not the Hollywood beauty, but the nice dish on the table, the beauty of a body. I am observant about that and I put it down in my paintings.
—Ralph Fasanella

Waiting for the bus, pushing a baby stroller, playing stickball, looking out a window, sewing, listening, talking, smoking, hanging out, marching, riding the subway, weeping, fixing dinner, eating ice cream, pitching a ball, skipping rope, and working, always working—under the shadows of apartment buildings, factories, churches, and state officialdom—working-class people sustain their families and each other. These are Ralph Fasanella's people. He presents their lives through perceptive details: the weight of an ice block on a man's back, a woman's hands shielding her sorrowful face, the resignation in the shoulders of people at machines, and the claimed relaxation of a Sunday afternoon. At first glance, because of the dimensions of the paintings and the domination of his New York City buildings, the people may seem small, but look again. Through the language of the body at rest and in action, Fasanella tells anyone ready to look: "Hey, they may seem small in relation to all this, but their lives are not small."

I've always been involved with masses of people. Oh, I looked at guys, I had my heroes, baseball heroes, fighters, politicians, sure. But I don't like big shots. When it got right down to it I always looked at people in the total mass. He may be a great guy, but I look over on the side, I say, "What's this little guy here, who's trying to learn something just like me? I might as well talk to him. He's part of the mass, like me." And these people aren't stupid, either.[2]

Even in his early, dark, shadowy and unpopulated paintings—*Wall Street* (1947) and *Sheridan Square* (1945)—Fasanella inserts sparks of human light. The cacophony of city streets and the rituals of festas come later, not as a departure in style but as a development of the "wail" Fasanella hears, grabs, and converts to visual form. *Oh, there are parts of the city that make me uncomfortable. Wall Street, maybe, parts of the Lower East Side where there's no light. But if you stay with it long enough, even that, the poetry comes out . . . I love my New York, I know, most of my work has a message, most of it's critical. But I've got to have my poetry some of the time . . . I'm not a one-dimensional guy, after all, I may paint flat but I don't think flat.*[3]

For all their awareness of political and economic oppression, Old Left artists like Milton Rogovin, Tillie Olsen, and Ralph Fasanella still believed in human—individual and collective—**possibility**. In *Tell Me a Riddle,* Tillie Olsen poetically sums up this ideal:

> *No man one except through others*
> *Strong with the not yet in the now.*
> . . .
> *And every life . . . shall be a song.*[4]

What if socially informed artworks were viewed through the lens of *possibility* as well as critique? This could expand art discourse, reveal class bias in labels like "primitive" or "urban exotic," and encourage access, inviting working-class people to see art that would nourish them. *Most working people don't go to museums. . . . They are frightened at the bigness. They feel left out. Going to a museum is like going into a rich man's house. They may have a lot of respect for art, for culture, but museums are like an obstacle course for them.*[5] Ralph Fasanella answers those class-biased inhibitions. His paintings welcome people home. He affirms emotional knowledge.

Marc Fasanella, the painter's son, named after Ralph's political hero Vito Marcantonio, purposefully includes *optimism* in the title of his book about his father. He speaks to the core meaning of Ralph's life and work: "Living alongside a self-taught intellectual who had achieved the freedom to pursue his muse—to think independently, experiment, fail, innovate, reconfigure, and recommit to his work in an endless dialogue with the world he inhabited—defined for me 'the good life' . . . . [I]n the context of the twenty-first century, it became clear that he held out a fundamental hope for a universal human society. For many years I thought it was his critique of modern civilization that would earn him a noted place in the history of art. I now know that his positive spirit, his sanguine imagery, and his fundamental optimism were what gave him strength and imbued his work with a singular visual and intellectual depth of meaning."[6]

Intellectual optimism is earned and should not be confused with bourgeois personal aspirations. Fasanella's worldview is collective, not individual. Born in the Bronx in 1914, fourth of six children of Ginevra and Giuseppe Fasanella, Southern Italians who immigrated to the United States around 1911, Ralph Fasanella embraced the culture and fought the restrictions of working-class, Italian, New York City neighborhood life.[7] When Ralph, christened Raphaele, was about five years old, his family moved to 173 Sullivan Street in Greenwich Village, an emotional and geographic ground of being for his early paintings.

What does it mean for an artist to come out of a working-class family? (A question germane to Raymond Mason as well.) Ralph's father, Joe, worked as a longshoreman and later had a small business delivering blocks of ice to tenement families with the reluctant help of his son Ralph. This was before refrigerators, when people had "ice boxes." That memory, his observations of workers' labor, and his reading of Pietro di Donato's *Christ in Concrete* inform Fasanella's four *Iceman Crucified* paintings.[8]

Ralph's mother, the central, sustaining figure in his painting *Family Supper* (1972), raised six children while working as a buttonhole maker in a coat factory and was an active, politically informed trade unionist. Ralph learned resilience and labor struggle from his mother, who in dialectical relationship to his father, was literate, resourceful, and, ultimately, the family provider. The parents' marriage was strained by differences between Ginevra's outspoken socialist politics and friendships and Joe's disappointment in his ice-delivering American dream. Joe left the family intermittently, returning permanently to Italy in 1954, the same year Ginevra died in Arizona.

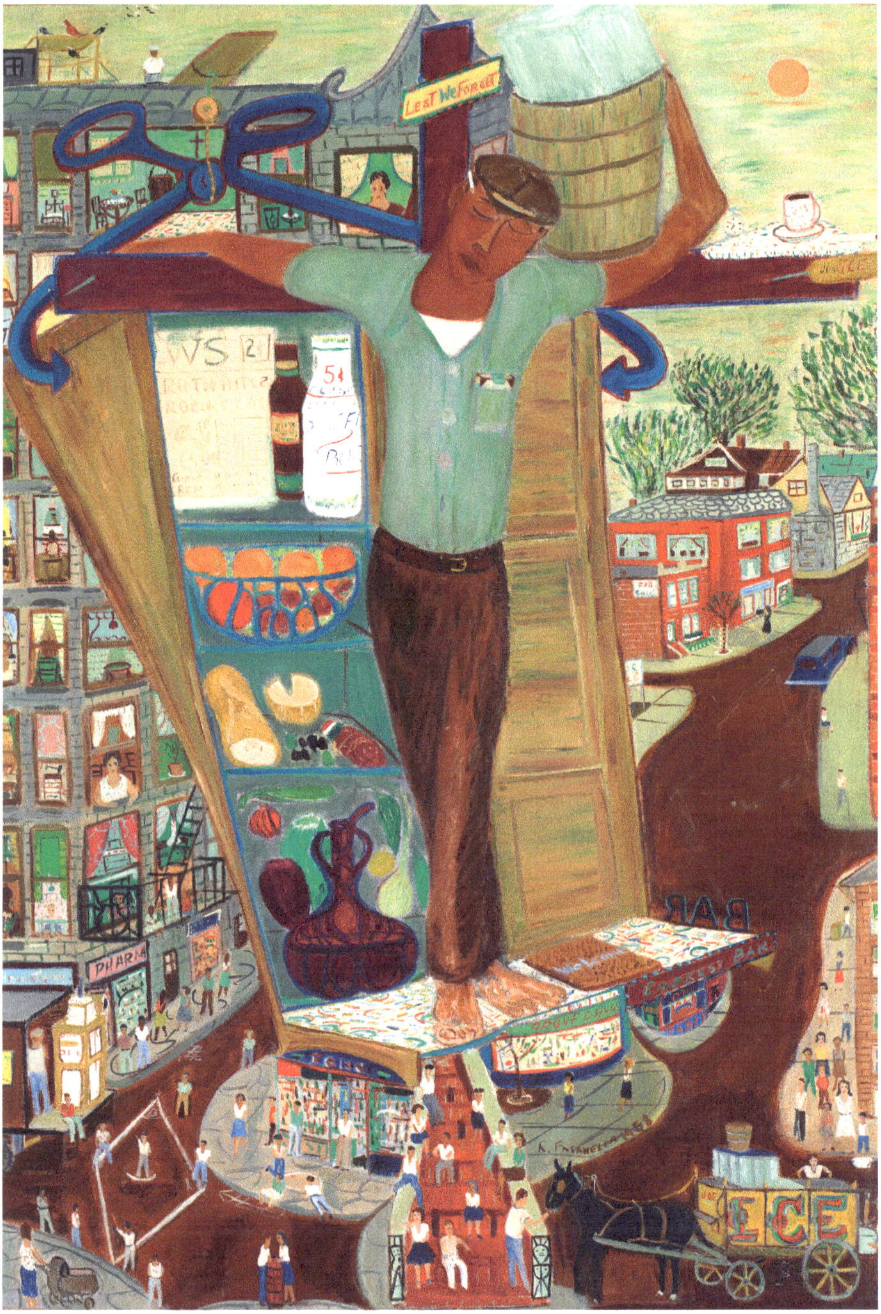

Ralph Fasanella (1914–1997), *Iceman Crucified #4*, 1958 (oil on canvas, 36 × 25 in. [91.44 × 63.5 cm]) Smithsonian American Art Museum, Gift of the estate of Ralph Fasanella, 2013.69. Photograph courtesy of Museums.co. © Estate of Ralph Fasanella.

A tough street kid, amateur boxer, frequent truant, and baseball fanatic, Ralph engaged in petty criminality, what some might see as immigrant/working-class survival skills, and was arrested initially in 1925 for theft and sent to New York Catholic Protectory three separate times. *Protectory Games* (1962) and *Lineup at the Protectory* (1961) attest to that experience directly, but also to the underbelly of imprisonment in American culture, a theme, along with ominous surveillance, that surfaces repeatedly in many of his paintings. Quitting public school in the eighth grade, his self-taught education came through libraries, organizing, working in factories, his family, and political activism. He joined the Young Communist League (YCL) in the early 1930s, drawn to its praxis of intellectuality, social adhesiveness, and political action. He also studied at New York Workers School in Manhattan in the 1930s. (Milton Rogovin also attended Workers School sessions around the same time, but perhaps not in the same location.) During this period, he helped his mother publish a small Italian-language anti-fascist newspaper. Books and newspapers appear frequently in his paintings, a visual thread recognizing the importance of workers' self-education on one hand and the use of media as propagandistic political control, on the other. See his *McCarthy Press* (1963), *The Great Strike (IWW Textile Strike)* (1978), *Ron's Rollin'* (1985), *The Daily News Strike* (1993), *Farewell, Comrade—The End of the Cold War* (1992–1997). Fasanella writes back through his inventive intertextual topography. Follow his visual geography of texts through newspaper headlines, banners, slogans, signs, advertisements, street signs, mottoes, graffiti, sidewalk chalk games, police barricades, union posters, as well as frequent representations of books. Newspaper headlines surround the women garment workers in *Dress Shop* (1972). Fasanella inserts into the measured and timed workplace the news flashes New Yorkers might have been (and still are?) accustomed to seeing in Times Square. My mother remembered how she and my father were enjoying a Chinese dinner at an upper-floor restaurant in Times Square when they looked out and saw the news flash—Pearl Harbor Attacked, December 7, 1941. History impinges on working-class private lives. Fasanella understood that.

After the war, Fasanella observed another bombardment—of consumer messages, slogans, and ads. He found ways to recuperate the banal language. Embedded in the sky of *Gray Day* (1963), commemorating the execution of Ethel and Julius Rosenberg, consumers are urged to SAVE (4%), an ironic message he also places in the red sky of *McCarthy Press* (1963). Crowds gather, weep, and mourn, but their call to "Save the Rosenbergs" is denied.

Did Ralph Fasanella have Charlie Chaplin's film *Modern Times* (1936) in mind when he painted his own *Modern Times* (1966)? His painting has a ground/space, inside/outside tension, encompassing baseball, draft resisters, returning soldiers, a pope, scientists, the UN, an aircraft carrier, an Intercontinental Ballistic Missile, abstract modern art, and various atomic symbols

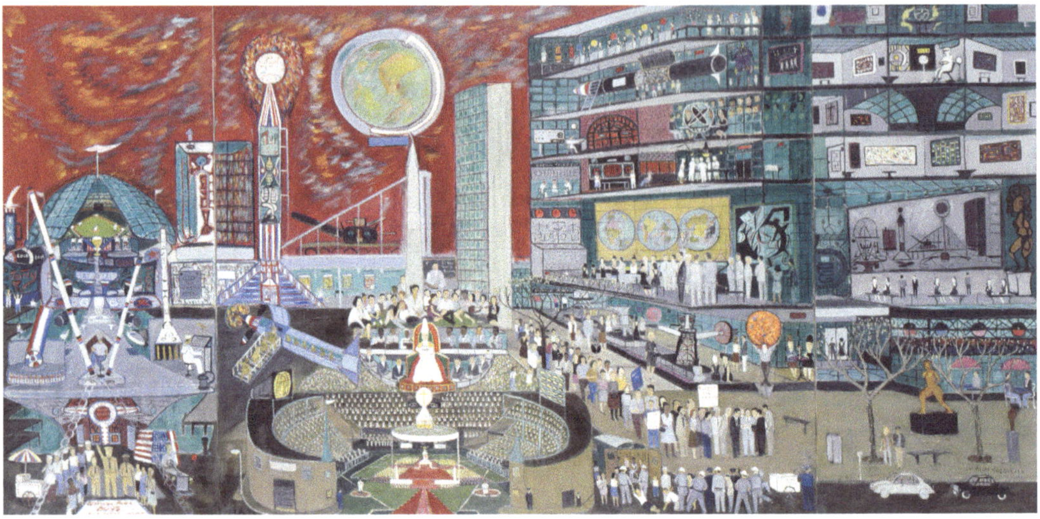

Ralph Fasanella (1914–1997), *Modern Times*, 1966 (oil on canvas, 49¾ x 104 in. [126.4 × 264.1 cm]) Smithsonian American Art Museum. Gift of Maurice and Margo Cohen, Birmingham, MI, 2002.10. Courtesy of Museums.co. © Estate of Ralph Fasanella.

of destruction. Here are the systems of war and death—the processing of soldiers leaving or returning from Vietnam, rows of flag-draped coffins, a hovering black helicopter before a blazing red sky, and pockets of draft resisters dragged into police vans. Although a crowded canvas, there's a bit of unoccupied space on the exposed art museum floor, where unviewed abstract paintings hang—not Fasanellas. Outside, notice a statue of a working stiff literally holding up the world. Nearby, a strolling couple; inside, ladies lunch. The convenient obtuseness of the privileged. The painting conveys technologized blind spots, not mutual vision (and not Raymond Mason's "interactive gazes.") Fasanella is sympathetic toward both the anti-war protestors and the departing soldiers—"welcome home boys" and "refuse the draft." He exposes the thin lines separating ART and CULTURE and WAR—the gray walls of the modern art museum and the gray floors of the war industry, the corporate/government/technical liaisons producing knowledge of destruction. And yet, perhaps dialectically, perhaps out of his own quirky humor, Fasanella shows us more: a naval aircraft carrier that segues into a baseball stadium; a 25-cent rocket amusement ride is embedded with a baseball catcher positioned below a 7 Up ad, while bursting from the rocket's cone is a large, signed baseball surrounded by reverential flames. Centrally locating is a long shot and close-up of a visiting pope celebrating mass in Yankee stadium, surrounded by his religious "fans" as well as attentive outfielders. Fasanella's *Modern Times* is more sweeping than Chaplin's. Fasanella is less concerned with Tayloristic measuring of workers' motions and more focused on grasping and presenting technological linkages. Fasanella disrupts linear time and offers instead an imaginative simultaneity of times, comparable to Arthur Miller's shifting present/past conversations in Willy Loman's head (*Death of a Salesman*). Fasanella includes, but goes beyond, individual psyche. Here are the **systems** of war and death, a Blakean vision, and Fasanella's own riff on modernity—not as progressive leap, but as a continuation of militarism, what he witnessed when he volunteered to fight fascism in Spain.

The disquieting red sky in his *Modern Times* echoes 1930s newsreels of blitzkrieg bombing in Spain.[9] For Fasanella and some 35,000 other transnational volunteers who formed what became known as the Abraham Lincoln Brigade, the Spanish Civil War was not ambiguous. It was about fascism and the fight to stop it. Spain democratically elected a Republican socialist government. In 1936 General Francisco Franco, aided by Mussolini and Hitler, led and eventually won a military fascist coup. Fasanella joined about two hundred other volunteers and boarded a French vessel that left the port of New York in early 1937. They entered Spain by walking across the French Pyrenees in winter, at night, with little food. When he reached a training base in Albacete, Spain, Fasanella volunteered for dangerous transport duty, bringing food and military supplies to the front and wounded fighters back to base camp. Fasanella remained in Spain until late summer 1938.[10] The Spanish Republic dissolved the Brigade in October 1938 and surrendered in April 1939. Peter N. Carroll includes a chapter on "Alienated Artists" in his history of the Abraham Lincoln Brigade. He describes Fasanella as "short, broad, and tough," who "easily won friends and respect from his comrades in the Regiment de Tren." When a new Republican commanding officer attempted to impose military discipline, like saluting, on the volunteers, Fasanella, who abhorred petty authority, found his way to Barcelona and soon decided it was time to board a ship out of the region. Carroll notes that even aboard the British ship that would return him to New York, "he managed to organize a seaman's strike, which won better food, beer, and American cigarettes."[11]

Back home, he turned his attention to and channeled his energies into organizing labor. "The great word solidarity has arisen," Walt Whitman proclaimed in "Democratic Vistas" (1871).[12] For Fasanella *solidarity* is action, not just an aspirational song. Between 1938 and 1945 Fasanella worked as a union organizer, primarily for the United Electrical, Radio, and Machine Workers of America (UE) and helped organize the Sperry Gyroscope Company in Brooklyn and the Western Electric plant in Manhattan. In a series of paintings, Fasanella pays homage to the small storefronts and union halls that are/were the foundations of the industrial union movement, not to the big guys—bureaucratic union structures—but to the actual labor environment on the shop floor, as shown in *Bench Workers (Morey Machine Shop)* (1954). Fasanella understood the educational potential of unions to empower workers as depicted in his early *Union Hall* (1949) and later *Organizing Commit-*

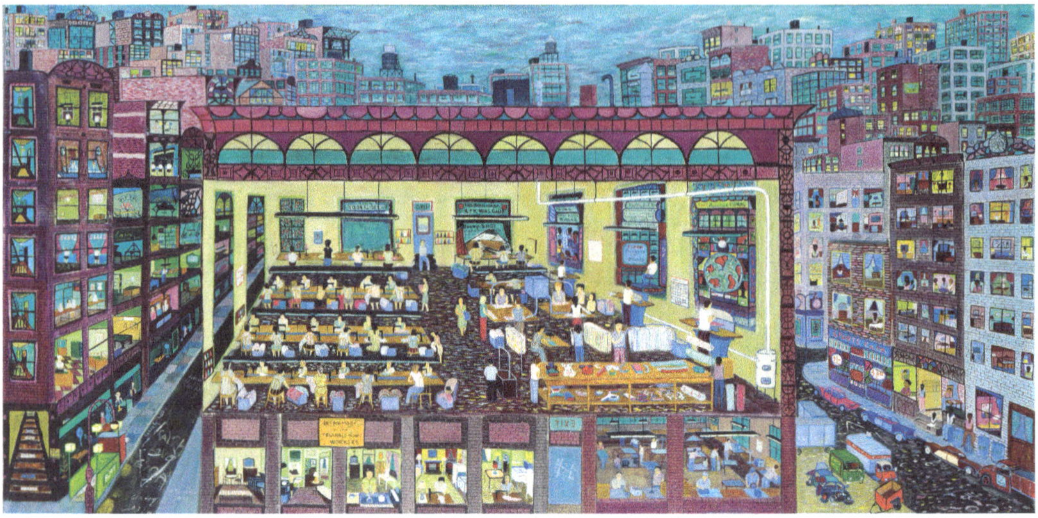

Ralph Fasanella (1914–1997), *Dress Shop*, 1972 (oil on canvas, 45 × 90 in. [114.3 × 228.6 cm]) Fenimore Art Museum, Cooperstown, NY, Museum Purchase, N0003.1983. Photograph courtesy of Museums.co. © Estate of Ralph Fasanella.

tee—Dedicated to John L. Lewis (1980) and *Labor Education Union Hall* (1986). We see workers as listeners, learners, and thinkers. It's not just a men's world either. His sweeping *Dress Shop* (1968–72) includes male pressers and cutters, but mostly women at sewing machines on one level of the painting, and at a lower level, at home preparing food and caring for the household, the double work lives of women. And he hadn't forgotten to remember workers' history; outside the dress shop building is the sign "In Memory of the Triangle Shirt Workers."

On a smaller scale, consider his late painting *Luncheonette* (1987). The gray-haired woman frying an egg on the left of the painting could have been a portrait of my mother, who prepared and served food at Skipp's Luncheonette in Lyndhurst, New Jersey. When high blood pressure forced her to quit, Skipp closed the luncheonette.

Fasanella materializes Whitman's abstraction of solidarity through his knowledge of the multidimensional potential of unions and union halls—rooms for meetings but also for music, lectures, dances, and books. See *Build Your Union* (1991). His painting *Local 65* (1950) shouts and whispers: "union," "union book store," "Be Happy Go Union," "Join Today." District/Local 65 was a protean, "catch-all" union. Along with organizing, picketing, and striking, the union had cultural agency, including theater, workshops, dances, excursions, cooperative consumer shops, and photography exhibits and publications. It was also a racially integrated union.[13]

Fasanella completed his huge, celebratory, brightly exuberant *May Day* in 1948.

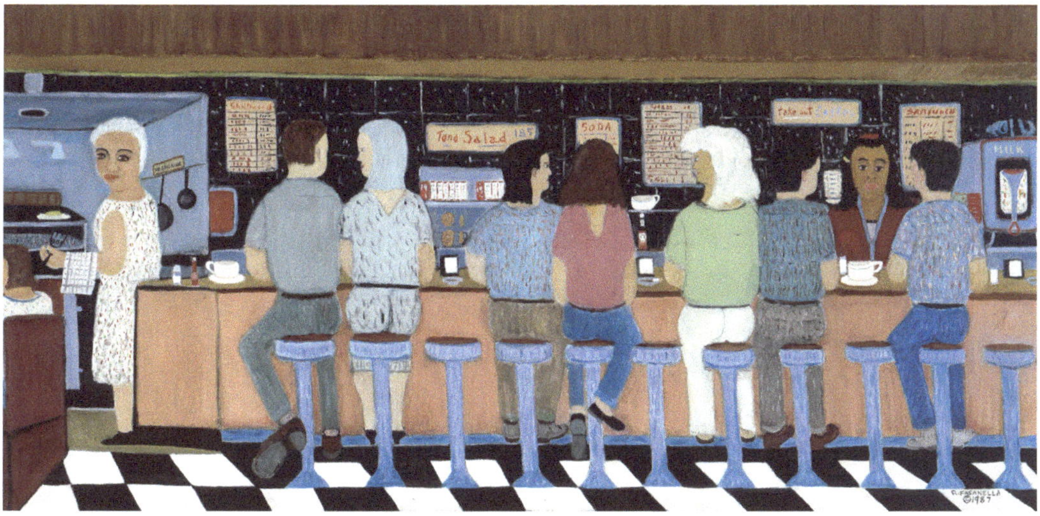

Ralph Fasanella (1914–1997), *Luncheonette*, 1987 (oil on canvas, 28 × 60 in.) Private Collection. Photograph courtesy of Museums.co © Estate of Ralph Fasanella.

Now remember I was painting only three years at the time. That's all. And this is a big canvas for a guy to do. But that concept I had, of the world of tomorrow, was clear in my mind. It was sweat and joy doing it, a tremendous amount of, oh, I guess you'd call it "joy energy."[14]

Fasanella conceived and painted **definitional ceremonies**, what anthropologist Barbara Myerhoff described as "performances of identity, sanctified to the level of myth."[15] Fasanella showed how ordinary people "witness themselves" (to borrow Myerhoff's language). Fasanella's political witnessing, rooted in economic justice for all, is distinctly different from political mobs and their false golden calf idols. Embedded in Fasanella's collective gatherings are potential human values of community and cohesion, not differences.

Books and music and painting, these are the things I grab. So this May Day has room for all that. It's full of music. Sounds, and echoes, and spaces in between.[16]

And then there is baseball. A player at bat, a pitcher warming up, multiracial fans in the stands, umpires conferring; it is April and baseball season begins. That's the Fasanella cover of the April 1975 issue of *TV Guide (cost, twenty-five cents)*. Fasanella presents the tension between motion and stillness, a challenge for any painter.[17] Baseball is also a definitional ceremony—simultaneously communal and individual. Especially in smaller local stadiums, it is affordable commons and a choreographed display of skill, craft, and grace.

As a union organizer, Fasanella fought for better pay and working conditions. He also recognized workers as multidimensional, needing leisure time, roses as well as bread. Yet he was critical of "pie in the sky" materialism and its ubiquitous advertisements. His enormously detailed and developed paintings prick American Dream bubbles, the trap of things, the traps of

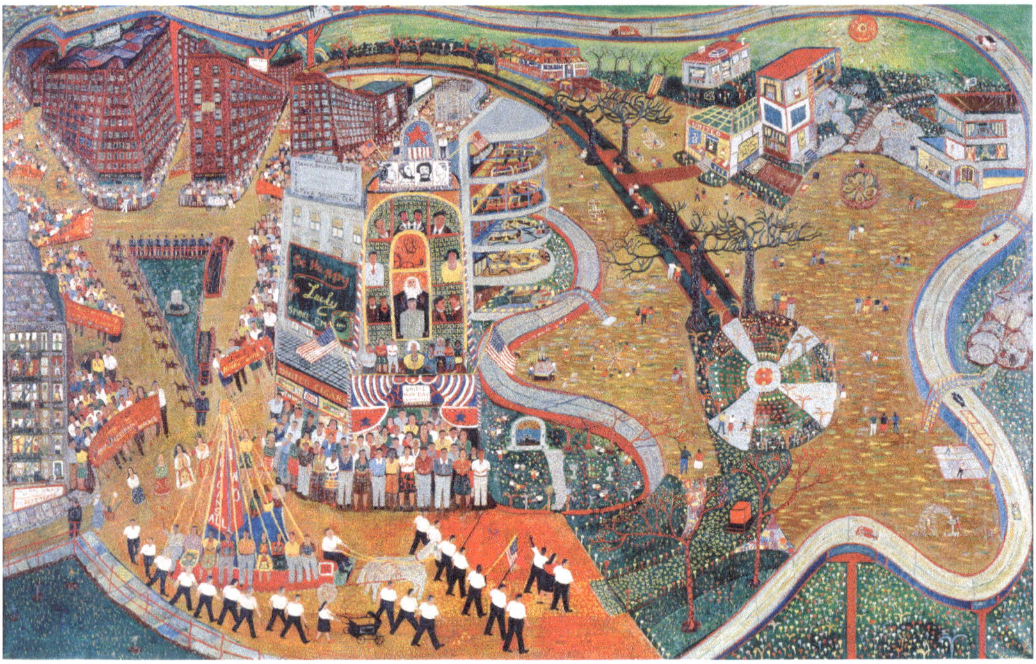

Ralph Fasanella (1914–1997), *May Day*, 1948 (oil on canvas, 54½ x 84¼ in. [138.4 × 214 cm]) Fenimore Art Museum, Cooperstown, NY, Gift of Ralph and Eva Fasanella, N0052.194, photograph by Richard Walker. Photograph courtesy of Museums.co © Estate of Ralph Fasanella.

capitalism. He sought what Walt Whitman called *adhesiveness*, or in Ralph's less poetic language: *Well, we have to live together you know. People live with people and grow with people.*[18]

In commentary about his beginnings as a painter, there are two not necessarily conflicting stories. The subordinate one explains Fasanella's great sense of visuality—his eye for color and form. *Now it didn't come from nowhere. It comes from somewhere. I always had images as a kid, you know? Walking around and seeing figures and constant stories all the time. And when I worked in jobs full of monotony, I was making ideas in my mind.* He also recalled seeing some drawings or etchings of human figures by William Blake. *Yeah. I saw something by Blake and it gave me something inside. I didn't know what, but it excited me.*[19] The second, more dominant and public story is that Fasanella took up drawing at the suggestion of a friend to relieve what appeared to be arthritis in his hands. It's a good story. And I have no reason to think it is not true. My skepticism is not because of fussiness with the biographical record, but because of an investment in what lies beneath that record. Working-class artists, writers, and organic intellectuals do not necessarily have permission or acceptance from their families, and, more importantly, economic support, freedom, and space from the demands of material subsistence, to claim for themselves the name **artist**. Certainly, becoming "bohemian" (especially for a girl) was not an option in my conservative working-class family. So we need an excuse, eh? Drawing eases pain in the fingers—OK, it does.

In the mid-1940s, and with support from his brothers and especially his sister Tess, Fasanella structured his days around painting, reading, and working. In 1950 he married Eva Lazorek, who became a schoolteacher, and they parented two children. During the Cold War/McCarthy years, Fasanella was blacklisted and jobs were scarce. Eva's teaching job helped support the family. She later became his business manager. Fasanella painted and worked, worked and painted, for a time working at his brothers' filling station, and later as co-owner of his own gas station. See *Happy & Bud's Service Station* (1968).

Fasanella chased after the ideal but worked through the actual. Like the Rogovin family, the Fasanellas were harassed by the FBI in the early 1950s. It was difficult for Ralph to find and hold a job. The conservative AFL (American Federation of Labor) challenged politically progressive unions like Ralph's United Electrical Workers. *They Red-baited us—we took them right on. When a guy came in, we took this approach. I'd say to a guy, "Listen, you come to this union, there's a couple of things you can't do. Number one, you ain't allowed to Jew-bait. You ain't allowed to Red-bait, you ain't allowed to color-bait. . . . if you want a rank-and-file union, come in here."*[20] Yet there is always that Fasanella light in the darkness, the sense of possibility that he found in Vito Marcantonio, a left-wing congressman from East Harlem, the only member of Congress who opposed U.S. intervention in the Korean War. *An unbelievable man, Marc. When this man spoke at a rally, you should have him taped. This man was a Beethoven when he spoke. Music!*[21] Fasanella loved the guy and painted his political energy decades later in *Marcantonio for Mayor.* When Marcantonio died suddenly on August 9, 1954, Ralph painted within four weeks of his death the communal wail of grief and his personal sense of loss in *Death of a Leader* (1954). Fasanella respected Marcantonio's knowledge of history and his practice of racial solidarity: *Always took a principled position no matter where he was. . . . And he always stated his position. Beautiful how he did it. He'd say how he remembers when his family came over and they were called guineas and greaseballs and all that shit, and he says, "I don't like the words 'spik' and 'nigger' because my people took the same kind of beating and I don't buy that stuff."*[22]

How, after working for decades in relative isolation (although he had a determined capacity to paint with a lot of commotion around him), was the painter Ralph Fasanella "discovered/uncovered?" His biographer Paul S. D'Ambrosio traces how Fasanella's painting of *Marcantonio Campaign—Lucky Corner* (1972) caught the eye of Frederick Fried, folk art scholar and former labor activist, which led to contacts in the New York art world as well as the New York State Historical Association in Cooperstown, New York, which led to a feature article in *New York* magazine written by Nicholas Pileggi, "Portrait of the Artist as a Garage Attendant in the Bronx."[23] During this same auspicious autumn, fifty Fasanella paintings were exhibited at a labor center, Automation House on East Sixty-Eighth Street, from October 24 to November 4, 1972, followed by an exhibit in a Toronto gallery in spring 1973 and a major show at the Xerox exhibit center in Rochester, New York, in fall 1973. Patrick Watson's book, *Fasanella's City,* appeared in autumn 1973.

Well-intentioned art historians, curators, and writers attempt to categorize Ralph Fasanella's art and usually miss the mark. The problem lies with the absence of a theoretical vocabulary that addresses working-class aesthetics as well as, perhaps, an unnamed assumption that workers do not *have* aesthetics. Fasanella's capacious visual imagination infuses energy, movement, voice, action, and a kind of grace onto his canvases. But his paintings are not the nostalgic and static scenes of greeting-card folk art. "Fasanella is not an easy artist for some people, not because his work is inaccessible, but because it is too accessible. . . . If, as some people believe, folk art is a distillation of happy memories of a bucolic past, then Fasanella doesn't fit the bill. If folk art is the expression of the most important human passions in a form that transcends the rigid canons of academic art, then Fasanella must stand as one of the most important creative forces of our time," remark art historians Jay Johnson and William Ketchum.[24]

Consider the vocabulary of literature and architecture to interpret the grammar of Fasanella's paintings. He paints like a bard, a visual troubadour telling a communal story. He presents a visual epic by placing individuals inside larger, sweeping historical contexts. He is a storyteller, a visual narrator juxtaposing private and public worlds. He is also architectural. He designs and builds. He notices the relationships of parts to whole in his depictions of buildings, particularly his cathedrals/churches and skyscrapers, but also the skyscape in relation to the streetscape. He constructs architectonics, sets of relationship and tensions, an interconnectivity that opens to an aesthetic event.[25] Because he is painting from inside working-class experience, he achieves a visual vocabulary of representation that reveals without violating, objectifying, or colonizing his subjects. A Gramscian intellectual, organic, not functionary, he devised ways of carrying home, family, and community aspirations out and into a wider world. His "Lest We Forget" is not comfortable nostalgia. His work is about connection, agency, praxis, and liberation.

Fasanella does not fit easily into academic or art writing conventional categories. I prefer "communally taught" to "self-taught." Casting him as an outsider artist is obviously from a bourgeois art history/market perspective. Seeing his practice as *inside* a long lineage of narrative and history-focused paintings is another vantage point. Fasanella painted confluence, intersection, and struggle for human liberation against military, political, and economic domination. These are not simple binaries; they are interconnected loops. In Ralph Fasanella's cosmology, labor history is inseparable from art history.

Fasanella's canvases encompass: assassinations (Kennedy brothers, Martin Luther King Jr., Medgar Evers, Malcolm X); shootings (Kent State, Jackson State); killings of civil rights activists (Chaney, Goodman, and Schwerner); executions (Ethel and Julius Rosenberg); political shifts (McCarthyism, Atomic Age, the '60s); newspaper headlines; advertisements to consume *and* save; demonstrations (Vietnam, civil rights); names to remember in history (Abraham Lincoln, Ronald Reagan, Tom Paine, FDR, Barry Goldwater, Frederick Douglass, Sacco and Vanzetti, Eugene V. Debs, John Lewis, Vito Marcantonio); not just politics, but politics mixed with the mundane (Agnew Out, Mets In); and a distinct Fasanella geography of sandlots and stadiums, cityscapes and utopian suburbs, factories and storefronts, love goddesses and religious icons. Politics, for Fasanella, is not *out there*—atomized and separate from daily life—but rather closer to home, actions that affect people's lives, especially the poor and the working classes. Fasanella's figures are not generic peasants painted to amuse the owning classes. They may line up, demonstrate, parade, and observe, but they never devolve into a mob—although police, often on white horses, loom at close range.

Ralph Fasanella was a citizen-painter. He found a perfect match for his democratically shaped artistic vision in the 1912 "Bread and Roses" strike in Lawrence, Massachusetts. Lawrence's history is emblematic of capitalist America extremes: the titanic wealth of a few mill owners who sucked and squeezed labor out of thousands of workers. In 1860, the Lawrence Pemberton mill, cheaply and hurriedly built, suddenly collapsed, burying 670 workers, including women and children.[26] In 1905 William M. Wood built his empire of American Woolen Company mills, expanding from the mile-long first mill in Lawrence to twenty-seven miles. Yankee workers in Lowell and Lawrence, facing declining working conditions, left the mills and were replaced by hungry European immigrants recruited with false promises of the golden land. The crux of the strike in 1912 was how the mill owners responded to a new state law reducing hours for women and children from fifty-six to fifty-four hours a week—they cut wages. Faced with the impossibility of living on reduced wages, mill workers saw no alternative but to strike on January 12.

The internationalism of the strike led by the "Wobblies"/ Industrial Workers of the World (IWW), the *necessity* of solidarity despite ethnic, language, and religious differences, the alliances with other unions to protect the children, and the courage of the frontline women workers all spoke to Ralph Fasanella. He arrived in Lawrence in October 1975 and lived monastically and periodically at the YMCA over the next four years. He absorbed the city, talked and listened, evoked people's memories, studied the mill architecture, learned the intricacy of cloth-producing machinery, and found his epic subject through preliminary drawings, street paintings, and then, major canvases:

Lawrence 1912—The Bread and Roses Strike (1977), *The Great Strike (IWW Textile Strike)* (1978), and *Meeting at the Commons—Lawrence 1912* (1977).

Fasanella approached his study like a union organizer **and like a historian**: *I began to walk around town. I built a kind of route, stations of my own. I knew my landmarks. I was beginning to absorb the streets and buildings. At all different hours, all different shifts, all different times. Sunny days, cold days, mood days . . . I would walk into the buildings by myself. I knew how to skip the guards, factory bosses. I could always find a way of walking very naturally to get into the buildings. . . . I never left the area of about five square blocks away from the mills.*[27]

Fasanella's powerful Lawrence paintings recover inter-ethnic workers' labor movements. Fasanella distills the epic struggle between labor and owners onto a series of canvases that visually narrate the conditions of the mills, the greed of the owners, the specific stages in the production of textiles, the physical environment of bricks and bridges, the presence of children as laborers, the use of police and militia to attack their own class, the leadership of the IWW, and the transformation of separate immigrant identities into a mass of workers united in struggle against oppression. The paintings embody solidarity and struggle. The Lawrence Strike of 1912 should be part of the historical consciousness of every American. In evoking the resilience of the 20,000 textile workers in a city of 90,000, and the bridging of differences of more than thirty different ethnicities speaking forty-five different languages, in the face of every business, government, judicial, and military tactic used against the strikers, the paintings demonstrate the *possible*. This is not romanticism; this is submerged historical reality revealing human possibility through artistic creativity.

"I never left" sums up not just Fasanella's sojourn in Lawrence, but also his artistic and political trajectory. He never obfuscated America's failure to live up to its democratic ideal, nor did he abandon possible democratic change through struggle. What distinguishes working-class art, and Fasanella's body of work in particular, is its depiction of power relationships between the non-owning classes and, as Richard Wright put it, "the Bosses of the Buildings and the Lords of the Land."[28]

All artists face problems of audience, of literally getting the work out to be seen or heard or read. Whether today's social media improves the challenge of audience access or complicates it, is for another writer to probe. Certainly, for Fasanella and my own generation of working-class artists, coming from the working class complicates the circuitry of access. There is no legacy of personal, academic, and professional connections or insight into the language and hierarchy of institutions. When, after painting in obscurity for more than two decades, Fasanella was "discovered" in the *New York* magazine article, he finally had buyers who could offer prices far beyond the yearly wages of Fasanella's working-class subjects. Understandably, after pumping gas and various other jobs for so many years, Fasanella must have

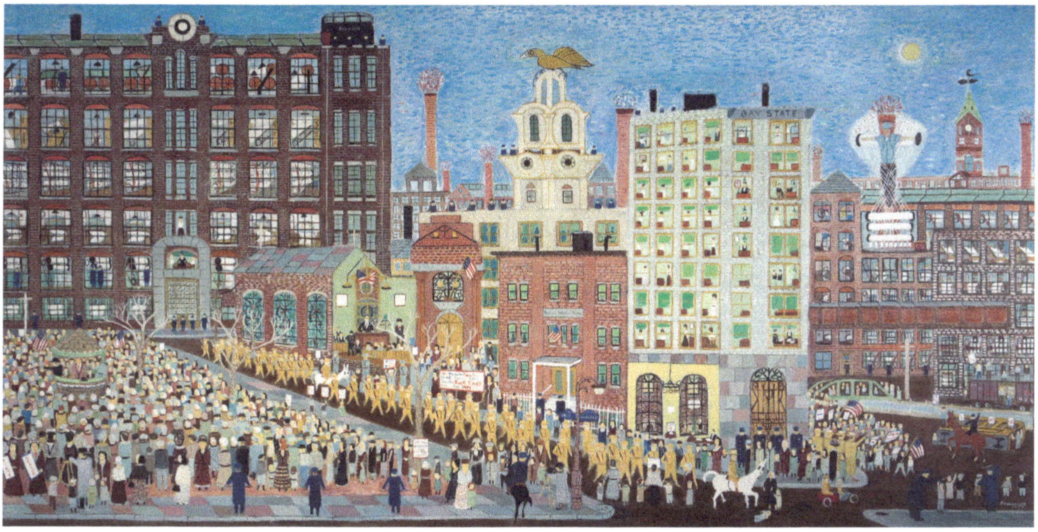

Ralph Fasanella (1914–1997), *Lawrence 1912—The Bread and Roses Strike*, 1977 (oil on canvas, 45 × 90 in.) Lawrence Heritage State Park, Department of Environmental Management, Commonwealth of Massachusetts, and the City of Lawrence, Massachusetts. Photograph courtesy of Museums.co. © Estate of Ralph Fasanella.

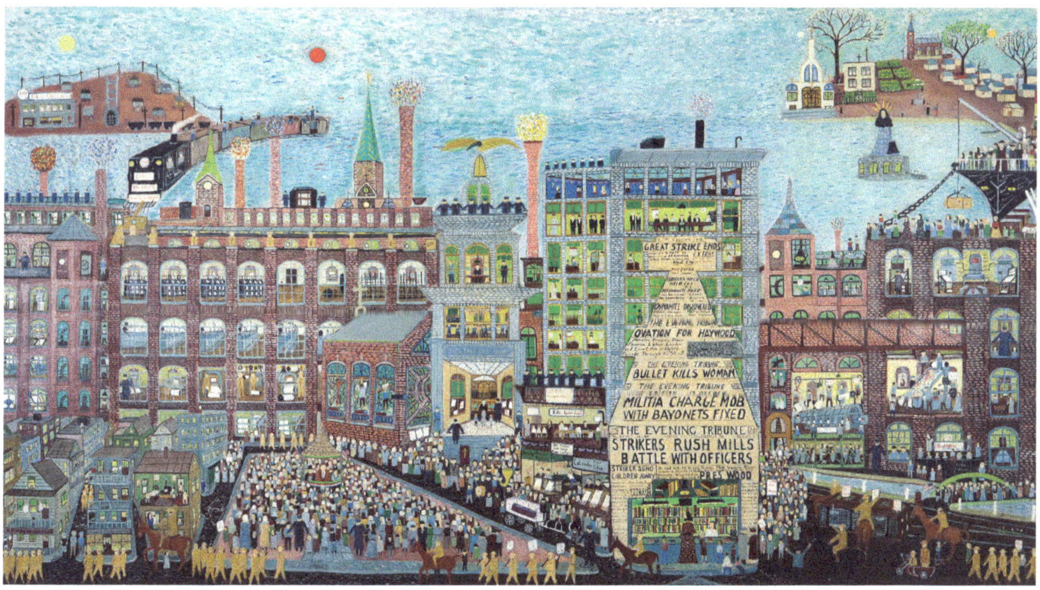

Ralph Fasanella (1914–1997) *The Great Strike* (IWW Textile Strike), 1978 (oil on canvas, 65 × 118 in. [165.1 × 299.72 cm]) Building and Construction Trades Department, AFL-CIO. Photograph courtesy of Museums.co. © Estate of Ralph Fasanella.

welcomed not only the appreciation of his work, but the possibility of some economic freedom. On the other hand, once the paintings are collected and privatized, where is the working-class audience? Are working-class subjects in these paintings then colonized and corralled in the living rooms of the economic elite? Even if Fasanella paintings find their way into museum collections, who will view them?

Eva and Ralph Fasanella addressed this conundrum with the help of Ron Carver, a union and community organizer who founded Public Domain to raise money to purchase Fasanella paintings from private collectors and place them in public spaces. Carver took a leave from his job as an organizer for the United Electrical Workers (UE, Fasanella's old union) because he fell in love with Fasanella's paintings: "I was overwhelmed with emotion at Fasanella's depiction of ordinary people—many of them painted en masse, with tiny brushstrokes—but with such verve and heart."[29] Carver finessed a way to bring a traveling Fasanella exhibit, *Urban Visions,* to his home base, New Bedford, Massachusetts, and its Whaling Museum, located near Carver's union hall. Carver describes the mutual embrace of Fasanella and New Bedford: "he got to know the fishermen, the 'lumpers' who unloaded the boats, the painters, and carpenters." Fasanella talked to public school and art students, urging them to "paint from your belly, from your life, your heritage. . . . [W]hy do you paint as if you are from New York City?"

Carver recalls Fasanella selling his *Lawrence 1912—The Bread and Roses Strike* to a private collector for a substantial sum and his own reaction: "'You can't do that,' I almost screamed—before I stopped and congratulated him. . . . That is the most important labor painting in America. . . . *Bread and Roses* is *our* painting, it represents our heritage. . . . 'Give me a year to raise the money and I will buy the painting and donate it to a public building in Lawrence, Massachusetts, where it belongs.' Ralph talked it over with Eva and agreed to give me a year." That is how Public Domain was launched in 1986. It is also a story of the humble poster. "At all our events, Public Domain sold posters to help raise funds to purchase the paintings . . . Fasanella insisted that we print enough posters to give one to each student in every classroom he visited. When unions donated money for the project, he asked for hundreds of posters to give to their members." That's called commoning art.

It is possible to have a Fasanella reproduction in your home. Posters, notecards, the covers of books, and websites make his art accessible to the people he wanted to reach. This is not about building a Fasanella commercial industry. No souvenir mugs. Rather, it is testament to the public purpose of his art, how it rouses consciousness of working-class history and culture.

Class oppression is cultural as well as economic. I have encountered progressive Left academics who are unself-consciously classist in their dismissal of working-class epistemology, working-class knowledge acquired through lived experience. They may be adept at quoting Marx and super cautious about the language of race, but blinkered when it comes to recognizing the dominance of their own middle- or upper-class perspective. Once, at a conference on class in Bellagio, Italy, I was one of the invited speakers, the token academic from the working class. One of the participating academics offered me temporary use of his "extra" apartment by saying, "It's not very clean, but you won't mind, you're from the working class." I call that encounter "They Didn't Speak Gramsci."

In *The Conspiracy of Good Taste,* Stefan Szczelkun writes about the effect of classism on working-class people: "What I learned was the central and murderous denial of our intellectual capacity which is at the heartless core of class oppression." Calling for a "liberatory people-oriented culture," Szczelkun urges a reconnection "to the hidden working-class personal and cultural histories that produce us and find ways to heal ourselves from the terrible legacy of hurt left by class oppression."[30] In any analysis, it is crucial to complicate single oppression apertures. The best way forward in my mind is to nurture doubt and risk learning what you do not know. It is not easy to insert race, ethnicity, gender, and sexuality into the complicated mix, but, at least, there is some meager awareness. Class oppression is another matter. We are still living with the damage of McCarthyism. Class is conveniently unnamed and cloaked.[31] Ralph Fasanella intuitively understood and surely recognized the not so hidden hurt and pain in the lineage of oppression. His art is not a luxury, but an essential. It comes out of the light as well as generates the light. Art can heal. bell hooks sees art as "one of the rare locations where transcendence can take place and have a wide-ranging transformative impact."[32]

Follow Ralph Fasanella's great open and expansive painting *Family Supper* (now installed at the Ellis Island Immigration Museum). Begin at the bottom, at street level, the corner of Sullivan and Bleecker Streets. Notice the neighborhood shops—Charles Russo meats, Dapolita Fruits—an Italian, working-class neighborhood, guys hanging out on the corner, women shopping, kids reading the funny papers, and the ice man delivering ice. We move into building 173 and up the dark stairs and into the bright heart of working-class relational life—the kitchen. It is immaculate. At the center is the mother surrounded by her children. The table itself is set for a continuing ritual, sharing pastry, fruit, and talk. One of the grown children, maybe Ralph, jabs a cigarette into an ashtray. Seated around the oval table, the figures may seem static, but that is a false impression. It is the viewer's task to imagine the loud conversation, the fight to be heard, to make one's point. Talk, coffee, pain, sorrow, happy times remembered, struggle, sustenance, betrayals, hopes, these are the linguistic rhythms of working-class lives. Telling the family story through the careful placement of artifacts also suggests the larger historical narrative. The trundle bed indicates tight sleeping quarters. The immigrant's trunk labeled with the flag of Italy reveals not only his parents' arrival, but

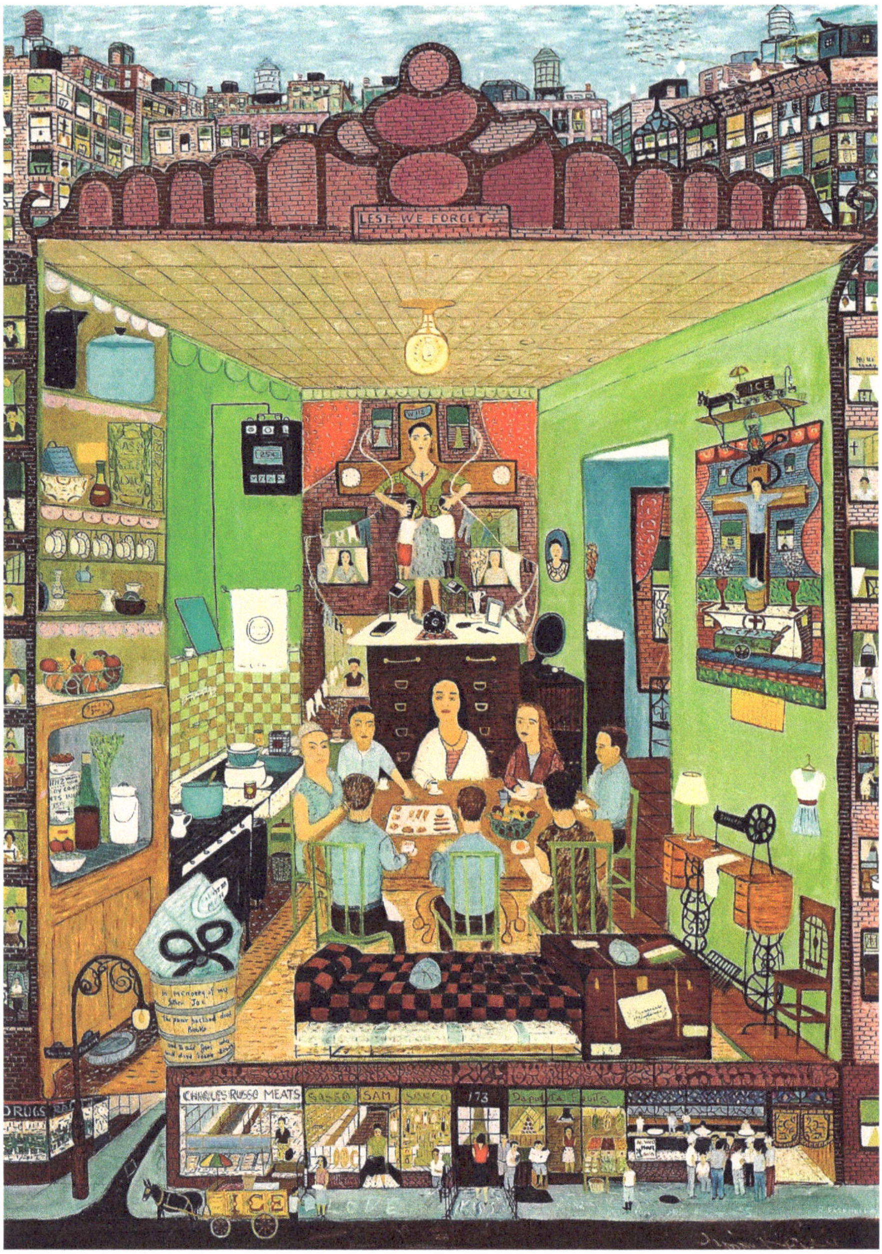

Ralph Fasanella (1914–1997) *Family Supper*, 1972 (oil on canvas, 72 × 50 in.) National Park Service, Ellis Island Immigration Museum. Photograph courtesy of Museums.co. © Estate of Ralph Fasanella.

the emptying out of Southern Italy between 1880 and 1924 because there was no paying work, no future. The wine, olive oil, cheese grater, pasta pot, espresso cups, juice squeezer, cans of tomatoes, these are the basics—not just for physical survival—but for the continuance of culture. Behind the family is the precious Victrola, a rare family photograph on the wall; nearby, viewed from open windows, are neighbors, other women. And always the reminder of the necessity of work. Joe Fasanella's individual life is typified through the iconic ice tongs, and also generalized as Joe Everyman. The wooden barrel is labeled "In memory of my father Joe/the poor bastard died broke/and to all Joes." Beneath the surface of *Family Supper* is Joe's anger and Ralph's loss of a father, and the intellectual distance between his parents. Those matters are private, not for public consumption. Instead, Fasanella extends the average Joe into the crucified working immigrant. Joe Fasanella is not Christ Incarnate, but Jesus the proletariat. But Joe's story is not the only story. Fasanella recognizes the many, especially women, who don't give up, who enjoy their children and the pleasures of family supper.

In dialectical relationship to Joe is the mother figure—larger, centered—the family provider and sustainer. Ginevra Spagnoletti Fasanella is literate, resourceful, political, and a union steward. Her trundle sewing machine is symbolic of the multiple dimensions of women's lives—home and work—sewing clothes for her children, stitching button holes for her employer. Behind the seated family is another painting of the mother, not crucified, but loosely threaded to a cross by a clothesline. She cradles the heads of her children, who stand on chairs with schoolbooks at their feet, seemingly nursing and gaining nourishment and comfort from her clothed body. This is homage to Ginevra, not only his love for his mother, but also his respect for women's work. The iron ice tongs are transformed into the fluid lines of the clothesline. Her feet stand on the marble top of the dresser where comb, brush, picture frame, vase with flowers, and a book are neatly placed surrounding the centered alarm clock, the omnipresent signifier of work.

The setting of *Family Supper* evokes "storia," public and private history. Culture marks every corner. Fasanella demonstrates the aesthetic of relationality, of one human being to another, of connections in time and place, presently and historically. It is *not,* as John Berger avers in "Fasanella and the Experience of the City," the absence of interiority. Berger writes, "The windows *present* the life or lives of their building. They present their interiors in such a way as to show that they were never interiors. Nothing has an interior. Everything is exteriority."[33] Even John Berger, whose work I deeply respect, can fail to acknowledge his own assumptions as he gazes into Fasanella's windowed interior scenes. He confuses privacy, which is an entitlement of economic privilege, with interiority, which is not dependent on physical space. The family kitchen table is personal and historical. As Fasanella recognized, *In our house, very few little books we had, and our knowledge was at the table.*[34]

Imagine a union organizing campaign with posters of Ralph Fasanella's paintings displayed in the parking lots and entrances to the work sites. Imagine a classroom lesson on Workers Memorial Day (April 28) focused on Fasanella's workscapes. Imagine an emphasis not on art markets, but on the efficacy of art to rouse consciousness and invite engagement. Think of Fasanella and the other artists in this book and their efforts to *common* art as a counterweight to monetized art.

Ralph Fasanella recognized the human need for bread and beauty. He was a solo artist with an immense, collective imagination.

Raymond Mason

Embodied Art and Experience

March 2, 1922, Birmingham, England–
February 13, 2010, Paris, France

For myself I believe that sculpture is essentially an art for crowds, and must be conceived and executed with this in mind. The great sculpture of all times has been an art in which everyone could find something of himself. But if the artist thinks of the people, they must think of the artist: great art is always the result of such reciprocal identification.

—Jacques Lipchitz

An object is not a sculpture. An object is simple, whereas a sculpture is symphonic.

—Raymond Mason

I was a working-class boy living in the simplest of working-class areas, and my father as a taxi-driver earned so little that a world financial crash could probably have had little effect once arrived at our low level.[1] Born in Birmingham, England, the only child of two loving parents, Raymond Mason observed road traffic, building shapes, color relationships, and the rhythms of sidewalk encounters by looking out the downstairs window of his parents' home on Wheeleys Lane.

Because of his asthma, likely aggravated by living in the industrial Midlands, he stayed home from school frequently. From that window frame, always observant, Mason drew the inside/outside world he witnessed. A working-class rooted artist, formally educated by winning art scholarships, informally educated through encounters with other artists, especially in Paris, keenly self-taught, Raymond Mason became a painter, superb draughtsman, and sculptor of human density. He left Birmingham for Paris in 1946 but always carried with him the vivid visual memory of Wheeleys Lane: *Our house in that all-brick street was the typical three tiny rooms, one above the other, joined by an almost vertical staircase. At the back, it gave onto the common courtyard and the common lavatories and wash-house. This courtyard was the province, the state, almost the entire world for us youngsters living in the adjoining houses. . . . Looming on that other side of our narrow street was a giant red-brick factory . . . it was a peaceful giant . . . an immense presence which must have marked my childhood . . . and many of my large sculptures share a characteristic abrupt climb-up.*[2] His parents' gifts to him were the conviviality of his mother, daughter of a publican (pub owner/manager) and his father's working-class know-how. *At least Dad was never out of work and this was certainly due to the fact that in his early days in Scotland he had been a gifted and noted motor mechanic, driving some of the earliest cars on the road . . . [H]is boss Mr. Wheatley was too smart not to know that if they lost "Andy" they might as well close down the garage.*[3]

In recalling his visit to the studio of the British sculptor Henry Moore, Mason indirectly comments on working-class know-how: *In my last year in England, on 7 March 1946 to be precise* [while Mason was still in London], *I walked up to Hampstead to visit Henry Moore. It was as though I had wanted to pay tribute to the art of my country through its most distinguished representative. In the small studio, I found him on all fours trying unsuccessfully to light a small coal stove. While I waited respectfully, a thought crossed my mind: how was it that Henry Moore, a miner's son, was incapable of lighting a coal fire? I offered to do it for him, which he accepted with relief, and soon the first flames sprang up.*[4] Mason was not shy about critiquing the work of other artists, including Henry Moore, but he respected Moore's early works, as sculptor and draughtsman, and likely appreciated Moore's well-known shelter drawings of people clustered in the London underground in the early days of World War II.[5] In a conversation with Moore some forty years later during a Moore retrospective in Paris, Raymond also noticed and admired Moore's drawings of sheep, about which he later wrote, "*nuzzled up to the windows of his studio, the work of an aged man who couldn't move about much any more.*[6] The window, the frame, the hinge of eyes looking out and drawing in—all are reminiscent of Mason's childhood purview in Birmingham. Yet Moore, the British Art Council's preferred sculptor, *stiffened and in a hardened voice* chastised Mason in that conversation, saying, *I'd like my name to go down in history for rather more important things.*[7] Such a small detail about two complicated and briefly intersecting lives, yet permeated by differences of shifting class consciousness.

Raymond Mason wrote about art in an engaging colloquial voice, often in French, sometimes in his distinct British/"Brummie" English. A working artist living in Paris, initially quite impoverished, he soon developed associations with other postwar artists, Alberto Giacometti at first and later Balthus. His excellent drawing skills were enhanced by his architectural sensibility and his intuitive ability to absorb his immediate environment. He understood art making as *action,* the physicality of sculpting, but also the movement of art in time and in relation to other human beings. He parsed the differences between academic studies and the intellectual and physical practice of making art. To read Mason's commentaries on other artists is to enjoy a short course in art history. He perceived, for example, the imaginative, compositional, and humanistic leap of Giotto's early Renaissance frescoes. Giotto's "interacting gazes" inform Mason's own sculptures, and his interrelational aesthetic. Much has been written about the male gaze on the female body in Western art, but not enough notice has been given to "interactive" looking. Seeing others, viewing interactions, noticing reciprocity, being alert to unexpected encounters and sparks, all fuel the possibility of mutuality, a democracy of seeing. While political and labor affiliations are crucial to understanding the work of Ralph Fasanella, Raymond Mason offers something wider, a politics of humanism. *The vivifying moments of European art* [Mason wrote] *are due to a Giotto, a Caravaggio, a Manet, who felt the urgent need to draw closer to their fellow men and to represent what they saw.*[8]

Let's consider Raymond Mason a reliable narrator of his own public life. Among his writings we have his distinct voice in "My Early Artistic Life in Birmingham," written on the occasion of his retrospective exhibition in his native city of Birmingham in 1989, his interview for BBC Radio 3 with Richard Cork in 1985, an informative conversation with Cynthia Nadelman conducted in 1984, and his lively compilation, *At Work in Paris: Raymond Mason on Art and Artists (2003).* How many artists use the words *work* and *art* in the titles of their books? How many artists produce books about artists and art making? From his earliest days, Raymond Mason was conscious of his own *Künstlerroman*, his own development as an artist, not to mention his felicitous leap to writing and speaking in French.

How does a talented working-class boy leave his familiar surroundings and find a place in the world? To start: scholarships. In 1937 he won a scholarship at the age of fifteen to the Birmingham College of Arts and Crafts. In 1939 that study was interrupted when World War II broke out and he voluntarily joined the Royal Navy. *I felt capable of finishing off the war with the Germans single-handed—a sentiment fortunately shared with most of the other chaps of my age.*[9] He was invalided out in 1942 because of poor eyesight and returned to Birmingham Art College when, in 1942, he won a painting scholarship to the

Royal College of Art (then evacuated from London to Ambleside in the Lake District). He stayed at the Royal College of Art for just a term, returning to Birmingham with a developing awareness of lineages of art making practices, such as fifteenth-century Italian frescoes in relation to color sculptures. In 1943 he studied at the Slade School then evacuated to Oxford, where it was temporarily blended with the Ruskin School of Drawing and Fine Art. There he developed a friendship with fellow artist-student Eduardo Paolozzi, a native of the Edinburgh dockyard district of Leith, Scotland, where his Italian family operated an ice cream shop. Mason earned some money as a fire watcher in the Ashmolean Museum in Oxford, locked up for the night with the museum's Mediterranean sculpture. It was during this period that he moved from painting to sculpture. That movement, though, is said too simply and may be more a continuation than a shift. Poet and literary scholar Michael Edwards deepens our understanding of Mason's artistic development: "It was not simply that Mason, having begun as a painter, was led to colour his sculptures—though that in itself is no small affair in the history of modern art. Many of his sculptures are pictorial reliefs, and very few are fully free-standing. . . . His work occupies a new ground, in fact, a space explored for the first time, with unflagging persistence and with prodigiously varied inventiveness, between the pictorial and the sculptural."[10]

Mason worked alone, but was not a loner. While throughout his life Mason sculpted solitarily without assistants or models, he also had a talent for introducing himself and cultivating relationships. One of those early catalytic relationships was with Sven (Harry) Blomberg, son of the Swedish consul in Birmingham. Blomberg, while ostensibly working as a minor office executive in his father's tube-making company, preferred to read Russian literature and study art in evening classes, where Mason met him. Mason recognized a familiar subject in Blomberg's art: *he was already painting pictures which made a great effect on me. This super-dilettante, with his cushy home in Solihull . . . [H]is interest was the dirty, dipping streets of lower Birmingham, painting their gleaming damp bricks in deep reds with dark skies and the black accents of doors and windows.* Mason saw, through Blomberg's paintings, how the streets of home can be beautiful. He also was pricked with realization of class differences; when dining at the Blomberg home, he first ate asparagus beginning at the white end like celery and *noticed the consul and his family eating the green.*[11]

Harry shared a flat with Raymond in Birmingham, and they jointly presented their art in a small exhibit where Harry, as Mason explains, was *turning out his beautiful cityscapes, yet, although charmed and convinced, I did nothing but portraits* [which helped pay the rent], *still-lifes and an occasional view from the window, as though I felt my inferiority.*[12] Why inferior? Mason could see that Blomberg's paintings were more accomplished than his own student-level studies. But inferior suggests something more than a fledging artist comparing his work. Coupled with the remark about proper asparagus eating, these asides reveal Mason's process of learning and unlearning, as working-class scholarship students who move from home to the larger world well know. Class, as E. P. Thompson famously wrote, is not a category or thing, but a relationship.[13] Class is *seen* in juxtaposition, in unexpected comparisons. But for Mason (and many other working-class cultural workers), working-class identity is not necessarily a burden to be discarded (except, importantly, for improved economic circumstances); rather, its *structures of feeling*, as Raymond Williams articulated, is a reservoir of knowledge and experience.[14] Raymond Mason thought with his hands—as was no doubt true for his mechanic father and as is true for the other artists in this book.

As Mason developed his art, he drew on that working-class reservoir to imagine and shape his public sculptures, especially of crowds—handling produce in public markets, shoulder to shoulder on crowded streets, publicly grieving at the site of a mine disaster, and, produced late in his life, fleeing from collapsing buildings (*Twin Towers Ablaze* 2003). Raymond Mason's sculptures developed from the early solitary head of a man and an empty street, to lovers in a bucolic arbor, to people clumped together, to queueing up to an opera theater, to leaping onto a Barcelona tram, and to serendipitously mixing on city streets as seen from a Parisian café or a coffee shop window in New York's St. Mark's Place. Like Ralph Fasanella, Mason maintains individual presence within a crowd and conveys movement within the stillness of representation. Curator Jane Farrington sees Mason as working within an English narrative art tradition.[15] Michael Edwards has meticulously studied the particulars of his sculptures,[16] and new writing on Mason is forthcoming,[17] but few have given enough attention to Mason's class of birth as a shaping element in his craft. To be clear, this is not an ideological flattening of his work or an attempt to put him in yet another category (throughout this book I question the dominating imperative of academic categorization), but rather to recognize the reality and value of working-class lived experiences. Such experiences are grounded in the nature of work and an adhesiveness, sometimes solidarity, of *necessity*, helping each other because survival depends on that mutuality; these are shared structures of feelings. Mason understood the circuitry of his sculptures in relation to non-elite audiences, how an artwork speaks to working-class people and how it might be dismissed by elite critics. Perhaps I would be hesitant to make this case about art making and class if more curators, historians, and critics of differing races and ethnicities came from the working classes, which does not seem to be the case, past or present.[18] Mason answered queries about his art being too populist by drawing attention to the speaker of the critique: *I shouldn't think critics like an artist who has a direct contact with the public; they must vaguely feel that they are going to be out of work. They like to explain things, and work that doesn't need that, either they don't like, or it doesn't interest them.* And, hinting at an unnamed class prejudice against representing (not caricaturizing) what Mason calls "the common man," he adds, *it isn't so much the vulgarity of my treatment of sculpture; I think it is the vulgarity of my subject.*[19]

William Louis-Dreyfus, businessman, lawyer, and art collector, however, recognized the power and potential of Raymond Mason's sculptures to speak to ordinary people:

> wherever Raymond's work is put, the general public . . . not the self-styled sophisticated collector . . . not necessarily the professional well-versed people, . . . but the people who walk the street to and from work, the people who pass by on a stroll, the people who visit the people who are not especially conscious of art or sculpture are deeply affected. Those people, in numbers that would surprise you, flock to see Raymond Mason's work wherever it has been made available to them . . . It speaks to them with a feeling they recognize. . . . I think it is significant that people who are generally not attuned to art or the art world seek out Mason's work, stop to look at it, visit with it[;] I'm reminded of those who stood at the Globe Theatre, rowdy and mostly illiterate, to listen to the Shakespeare plays unfold.[20]

Although William Louis-Dreyfus's observations were delivered in the spirit of appreciation and not intended as theoretical analysis, they usefully identify Mason's audience/artist circuitry, how his art speaks to people outside the milieu of white-walled art galleries, markets, and academic institutions. Mason practiced his own distinct answerability, more than a call and response, much more than bourgeois "appreciation." He respected his plebian audience and subjects and created visual spaces they could imaginatively enter.[21]

Raymond Mason insisted that *a sculpture is not an object . . . it's a vehicle for containing something.*[22] What is that something? Why describe a sculpture as a *vehicle*? Mason, son of a wizard car mechanic, was as drawn to recreating events, moments, scenes, and settings as he was to sporty cars. His sculptures, however, are more than reflections or representations or documentations. Mason is probing something more elusive yet pervasive and essential. Mason practiced a complicated yet accessible aesthetics, an aesthetics of *actuality*. To render actuality is no small task. In his anguished preface to *Let Us Now Praise Famous Men*, James Agee speaks about approaching actuality: "This is a book only by necessity. More seriously, it is an effort in human actuality, in which the reader is no less centrally involved than the authors and those of whom they tell."[23] Raymond Mason's mature sculptures approach *human actuality*. His sculptural figures are not statues; his painted epoxy resins blur the line between painting and sculpture.

In his 1984 interview with Cynthia Nadelman, Mason traced his evolution as a sculptor: *The movement towards accessibility is also the movement towards color. To go back, originally I was a painter, so when I started doing sculpture, the color crept in quite quickly . . . When I met Giacometti . . . I was already bored stiff with abstraction, the self-invented forms. I was only too glad to move towards the whole human condition . . . by then I was already seized by the activity of the Parisian street—the street scene with these crowds all animatedly walking in front of stone facades, strongly punctuated with doors and windows . . . I worked on these street scenes, and they finally culminated in a giant sculpture called "The Crowd," where 99 figures were all locked together in a sort of seething mass. Then I came to the conclusion that if I wanted to move on, bronze was not really the material. Because my scenes* [as converted into bronze] *were no longer scenes but pieces of metal, and the lightness and light which the plaster so beautifully suggested were lost. When I encountered epoxy resin—which, to look at, is exactly the same as plaster but with tensility and lightness and strength—it seemed the ideal way of making my sculpture from plaster permanent. You can't do anything with the sculpture in plaster, they have to be translated to something else. And there it was. . . .*[24] Mason's commentary on the materiality of epoxy resin resonates with Josef Albers's theory of *matière* so important to another sculptor, Ruth Asawa. Albers's exercises at Black Mountain College focused less on the literal material and more on the *relationship* between the viewer's eye and the material, hence expanding the viewer's haptic sense.[25]

Through all of antiquity, the Middle Ages, the Gothic period, the early Renaissance, and a lot of the baroque period, sculpture was polychrome. . . . So why were they colored? My conclusion is that the whole point of these sculptors or whatever they called themselves was not "sculpture." It was to project whatever they wanted to say to an audience as richly and as humanly as possible. They painted over their subtly wrought forms in strident color applied with vigor. The form had to be tight in order to hold the color and the color very free so as not to hide the form. They neglected nothing to make them warmly human. A sculpture in color is more human than one in marble or in bronze.

Mason's analysis calls to mind the religious statues placed prominently in Catholic family homes of my generation. These figures of the Virgin Mary or Joseph or Jesus were dusted and respected, small shrines of religiosity sparked by painted figures.

That's why I moved toward color. One of the reasons. Because I want the work to be accessible to everybody. This seems a natural imperative to me. I don't even think of myself as producing art. What I really like to do is to share my notions with my fellow men.

Any attempt to bring the world to oneself and stamp it all over with your style or your name is the hallmark of a second-rate art. . . . I wanted things more real, more physically present. My big works are conceived in size so the spectator could imagine himself actually in the work, participating in the action. And then, with all the depth of the high reliefs, and because they are in color, the slightest movement of the spectator produces a sort of reply in the sculpture. All this bristling around, this metamorphosis, for me, sort of gives an aliveness to the whole work. My goal is not the animation of space but to animate my figures, just as I color them to speak more directly to an audience.[26]

When I say I want to have a direct contact with the public, under no conditions am I trying to do popular art. The most popular art is supposedly one in which one simplifies one's forms, but I have no intention of watering down my esthetic intentions at all. In fact, I don't think you interest the public by simplifying your forms. I think the way to talk to anybody is to multiply the complexity of the sculpture to the point where there is something for everybody. Not simplify it—on the contrary, to really open it up.

. . .

I do not work on two sculptures at the same time. I do not make sculptures in series. I work on a sculpture when I am seized by a subject that is big enough for me to work on for two or so years and big enough to interest everybody. And that doesn't come up all the time. I suppose I work more like a novelist who, when he finishes a novel, does not start another novel the next day. What I am actually doing in my bigger works is describing an event. As they are big, they unfold in time. I mean, the spectator has to move around. And all the work is calculated so that every movement of the spectator is captured and puts everything into motion. It is, in a way, like a three-dimensional fresco. Three-dimensional so that every nuance of the whole image has a coherence. Art in its complexity is naturally the fusion of the outer world with the inner mind, and the intellectual structure of the work is important to me. But all is subservient to the general theme.[27]

Notice how useful Mason's analysis is to viewing not only his own work, but also to understanding art encountered in museums, for example, Pedro de la Cuadra's *Redemption of the Captives*, 1599, a polychrome wood sculpture of late sixteenth century Spain, in New York's Metropolitan Museum of Art.

Raymond Mason saw beauty in the commons and the commonplace. He loved markets, a people's choreography of buyers and sellers, an amplitude of fruits, vegetables, cheeses, meats, sauces, fresh breads, flowers, and whatever inviting surprise awaits at the next stall. Markets, those lovely alternatives to Amazon shopping, exist all over the world and often thrive. In Mason's sculptural hands, his tribute market, *The Departure of Fruit and Vegetables from the Heart of Paris, 28 February 1969,* is a secular procession, akin to Fasanella's *Festa,* a voluptuous depiction and a resistance to another misguided attempt at urban renewal. When Mason learned that Les Halles, Paris's central market, was to be closed, he responded, *The market for fruit and vegetables, wonders of nature, which opened at night under the stars in the historic centre of the most beautiful city in the world, far transcended the mere question of commerce.*[28]

In his *Departure of Fruit and Vegetables*—notice the produce gets equal billing with the people—Mason brought together two elements of human existence: labor and pleasure. *It was a place of joy. Powerful and vast since it made an endless number of people happy, and many tears would flow at the thought that it would cease to be. The work there was hard. The cold and rain to be endured were also hard. However, its magic was such that this hardness*

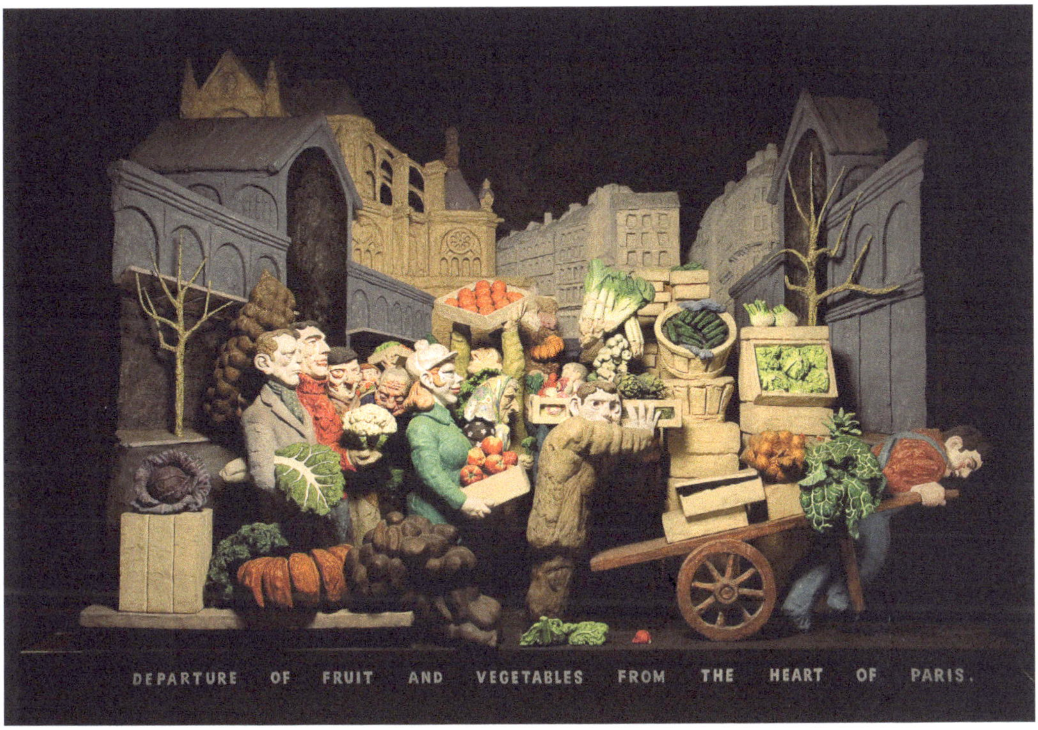

Raymond Mason (1922–2010), *The Departure of Fruit and Vegetables from the Heart of Paris. Feb. 28, 1969* (1969–1971). The William Louis-Dreyfus Foundation ©2025 Artists Rights Society (ARS), New York/ADAGP, Paris.

transformed itself into a strange gentleness, and the most fearsome character became peaceable. Of course, it was the pleasure of working together, but it was subtly ennobled by the fresh beauty of that country produce.[29] Here are Mason's creative insights about reciprocity and working-class integrated lives. The vicissitudes of labor—"cold and rain"—are not separate from the pleasures of mutuality, community, and useful work. Notice how he converts working-class actuality into art.

Mason rented a studio near the market, creating many preliminary pen and ink drawings, and developed the sculpture over two years. His vision was of an integrated place—the sixteenth-century church of St. Eustace shadowing and embracing the market, the density of bodies lifting and pushing and holding, the evocative ripe fruits and fresh vegetables, the humans in work and street clothes. All the senses are evoked. Can the odors germane to city markets be enclosed in a sculpture? Mason created architectonics, so many parts organically related to the whole, a vision larger than individual transactions.

Such a long association of ideas and things had produced an interpenetration of forms and habits which I discovered little by little in elaborating my sculpture. . . . The certainty I had acquired that a great web had held together the subject I wanted to bring to life again had made me decide to sculpt and paint not only the heart of Paris but also all the things that were to be found there—at their very heart. I would separate each cauliflower cluster, each artichoke leaf, as I would count each window on the streets of Montmarte and Montorgueil. Like a reservoir of ink, night would have to spread out everywhere, defining the drawing. . . .[30]

Mason enlarges his intentions and descriptions of the closed market by also placing it and himself within contemporary art movements: *A work of art. Does one always know what one can put into it? In these days of simplification, the answer seems to be—the least possible. For me, the answer has always been more perplexing—everything. People explain to me in a friendly way that I am going against the current. Well, yes, I am against the current. Endlessly I hear talk about the movements, the trends in art, of those who are making painting and sculpture move forward, of the avant-garde, who have already reached the year 2000. The perpetual movement which artists must follow.*

But for me, art, on the contrary, should be the means of intercepting thought in its flight, of merging it with matter, giving it weight and body precisely in order to stop time, to hold out against the centuries.

I wish that my little procession from Les Halles did not ever have to leave for good.[31] After the fruit, vegetable, and flower vendors departed, the butchers and the meat market were the last to leave. Mason's pen, ink, and water color painting is an apt remembrance.

Art answers oblivion. Art stops time. Does photography inspire art? In his interview with Cynthia Nadelman, Mason adamantly refused *any link up between art . . . and photography*. But photography, as he also acknowledged, can trigger, perhaps inspire, creative work. I wonder whether he was aware of Robert Frank's *The Americans,* originally published in Paris in 1958, when he conceived of a sculpture *Le Voyage* (1966), a car trip involving seated male and female passengers in a painted plaster car, subsequently criticized by his art (not car) dealer and abandoned by Mason.[32]

It was a photograph accompanied by a news article that inspired Mason's most labor-conscious and emotionally charged work—*A Tragedy in the North, Winter, Rain and Tears* (1975–77). On the 27th of December 1974, an explosion ignited a fire in the Saint-Amé pit, number 3, a coal mine shaft 2,100 feet deep, soon killing 42 workers, injuring 5, leaving 120 children without fathers.[33] Mason describes not only his reaction to the event, but also his strategies as an artist to convey through his figures—in their facial expressions and body language, awaiting or gravely hearing news of survivors—and with his architectural eye—the rain-etched pavement bricks and looming structures, the atmospherics of working lives performing, of necessity, dangerous work.

Shortly after Christmas 1974, on a warm sunny day in the South of France, I read in a local newspaper about the mining disaster in Liévin, a small town in the

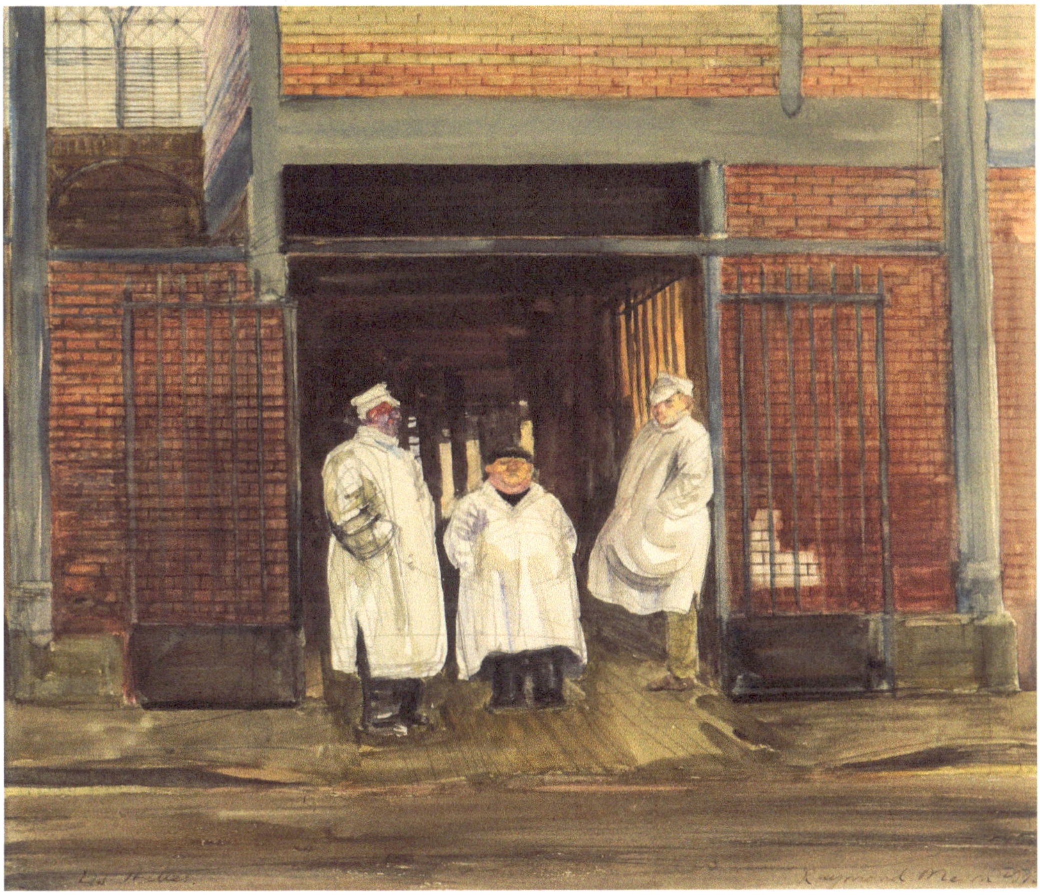

Raymond Mason (1922–2010), *Butchers at Les Halles*, 1972. The William Louis-Dreyfus Foundation ©2025 Artists Rights Society (ARS), New York/ADAGP, Paris.

Pas de Calais. An accompanying news photo showed brick buildings of the mine and on the cobble-stones agleam with rain, an anxious milling crowd.

I was born and brought up in similar surroundings and at once felt nearer to this painful scene in the North than the near-idyllic one of the festive Provençal interior in which I was sitting. On that very day I began a small low-relief based on the newspaper photo and subsequently painted it in the colours I felt would be appropriate. On the base of that relief, Mason wrote, *The Tragedy of Liévin. 27 Dec. 1974.The North, winter, rain, tears, rain. Love of one's own. REALITY. R.M. Ménerbes (Vaucluse).*

The following spring I happened to be passing through the Pas de Calais and decided to visit Liévin's tragic mine. I made the colour drawing at that time and on the spot. Once again, I was seized by the poignant beauty of simple nineteenth-century industrial architecture and I decided to undertake a large work based on the tragedy which would also be an act of fidelity to my own past.

Immediately, on beginning work, I felt obliged to eliminate the pit-shafts to concentrate on the human figures. Moreover, although I come from a district in England of bricks and paving stones, I know nothing about mines and I felt some hesitancy about so specific a subject. I thus enlarged it into an industrial catastrophe and finally chose as title A Tragedy in the North, Winter, Rain and Tears.

So to indicate the mine, there remains only the slag—heap [shadowed behind the pumping structures of the mine], *that black man-made mountain, that enigmatic symbolical pyramid whose sloping sides are echoed repeatedly in the composition, be it in the gables of the buildings, the climb-up of the curbstones, the arms of the young woman in front of the torn features of her face. The slag-heap finally appears in direct contrast to the white handkerchief of the woman to the left. . . .*

In a scene of tragedy, the unwilling actors recognize each other in their suffering. The bonds of such feeling are translated by their looks, which criss-cross space forming axes as active as those of lines and volumes. Mason's reflection on situating his figures in relational positions, an implicit visual reciprocity of "interactive gazes" within the art work, also opens a shared experience and identity for the viewer. Mason's artistic sense enlarges the event, a sensibility Ralph Fasanella also possessed and understood, especially in his Lawrence paintings. This obviously differs significantly from random street crowds. Mason focuses on the immediate aftermath of the explosion. Yet there is more. The sculpture evokes another kind of definitional ceremony, distinct to the event, yet familiar to the viewer—of loss, personal and collective. What is not presented but has to be imagined are the continuing definitional ceremonies of multiple funerals for fathers, brothers, and neighbors, and a future without sustaining wages. The sculpture becomes a commons of shared grief, artistically and experientially.

I should say here that I want people to look at a large sculpture of mine not as an object, but rather to have the impression of being in the work and of participating in the action. And what matters just as much to me is not uniquely the subject of the work, but the people's understanding of it. Even though this is a condition difficult to fulfil, and thus considered today almost irrelevant, it is an essential aspect of a work of art.[34]

Mason's language, his reference to a *work* of art, has resonance in the demanding physical labor involved in sculpting, as his bad back reminded him, and also in how art *works* on the viewer and in the world. Still, there's more. Mason *inserts* human labor into his art. We see the marks of labor on the male figures in the sculpture—the tall miner from Poland and the stunned, smoke-streaked face of the miner who survived the disaster. We see it in Mason's sensitivity to the hands of these workers, their size and necessary power. Mason drew and sculpted his own hand, a geography of complexity and potential strength. *The hand,* he once wrote, *seems to play an important role in my work.*[35] We see that role in how his sculptural hands

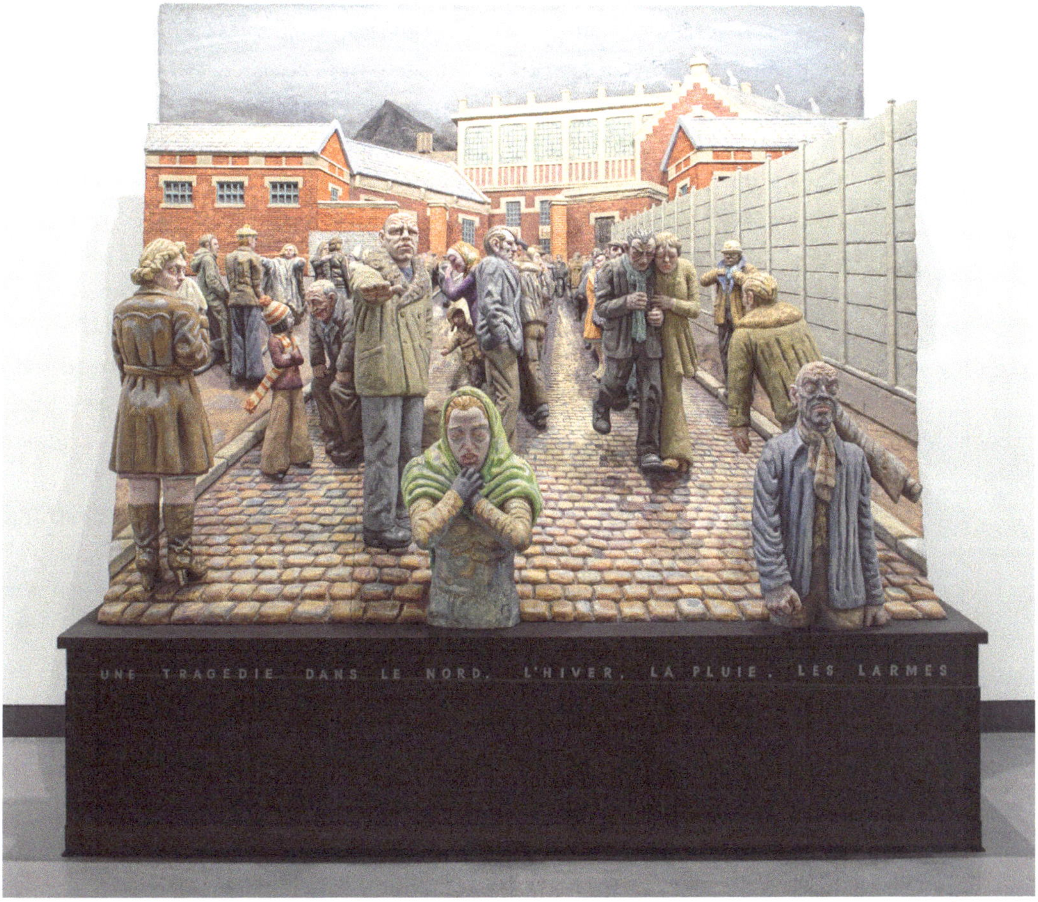

Raymond Mason (1922–2010) *Tragedy in the North. Winter, Rain and Tears*, 1977 (1975–77). The William Louis-Dreyfus Foundation ©2025 Artists Rights Society (ARS), New York/ADAGP, Paris.

are marked, how they literally hold up vegetable-laden crates in Les Halles, how they point, grasp, express grief. Hands are not silent. In one of his early paintings, *Mother and Child* (1944), the quiet tones of blue and purple and the white of the infant's swaddling are contrasted with the large brown hands of the nursing mother, almost like those of a laborer, holding the baby's head and guiding her engorged breast into the infant's mouth. Its combination of tenderness and exaggerated features is reminiscent of Alice Neel's own figurative Madonnas.[36] Mason recognized the labor of mothers.

Mason's sculpted bodies are indented and ridged, some lightly, others more deeply, as in his depictions of the Luberon and Southern France's sun-absorbing vineyards. Compare, for example, his sculpture *The Back* (1963) and his studies for *The Falling Man* (1962) with his sculpted landscapes, *The Luberon I and II* (1974) and especially *The Grape Pickers* (1982). We can count the vertebrae and ribs of the grape picker's lean, muscled, and shirtless back. The surrounding fields echo the back's geography, and vice versa, conveying Mason's sense of art as amplitude, fullness, potential. Mason understood the power of art and the obligations of the artist. Whether city or countryside, human or natural, his worlds are symphonic.

In his expert analysis of Mason's work, Michael Edwards groups Mason's sculptural sequences in the mid-1970s as "long moments": *Monument for Guadeloupe* (1976), *The Aggression at 48 Rue Monsieur-le-Prince on 23 June 1975* (1976), and *A Tragedy in the North. Winter, Rain and Tears* (1975–77).[37] Mason interrupted work on *A Tragedy* to create, in smaller scale and freestanding, *The Aggression*. It depicts an assault on someone from Mason's own Parisian neighborhood, an ophthalmologist whose stabbed body is being carried away presumably to an ambulance by medical personnel. Surrounding the body are curious onlookers, including a little girl standing in a woman's heeled shoes, a concerned couple, a woman passing by eating an ice cream cone, and, nearby, a screaming woman, the doctor's wife. This is not a definitional ceremony but rather the awkward and arbitrary circumstances of assault.[38] This too is indicative of Mason's understanding of someone's reality—unexpected harm, erupting violence, and escalating anger.

Monument for Guadeloupe, the third sculpture in this sequence, was commissioned as a specific historical reminder of resistance to enslavement and was intended to stand in a prominent place in Pointe-à-Pitre, Guadeloupe. Within two weeks of the commission, Mason completed a maquette in painted plaster. It depicts the moment in 1802 when resistance leader Louis Delgrès, facing approaching Napoleonic troops, chose collective death over reinstituted slavery by igniting an explosion, killing himself, hundreds of other resisters, and attacking soldiers. A pregnant woman named Solitude figures in Mason's depiction of individual bodies rising up in the explosion and in resistance to enslavement. For reasons beyond Mason's control, the commission was withdrawn and the actual sculpture was never built. Michael Edwards sees Mason's sculpting of this explosion as a tremendous loss to the history of art (and to historical accounts of slaves' own resistance): "The explosion of *Monument for Guadeloupe* is . . . the stilling of a moment that cannot hold, the sculpting of forms on the edge of not being, the conceiving of an extreme in sculpture beyond which it is impossible to go."[39] As distinct as Mason's sculptural vision is, we have seen these forms and gestures before—in his own drawings of thrusting arms, in Käthe Kollwitz's raised arm *Never Again War* lithograph, and in the exploding bodies and broken limbs of Picasso's *Guernica*. As for a mother choosing death for her child over enslavement, there is Toni Morrison's *Beloved*.

Mason depicts human darkness in relation to the potential of light. Like Fasanella's scenes of beach pleasures in relation to city work (*Coney Island*, 1965), Mason's beach people, sun worshippers, and sand settlers appear in colorful bathing suits on holiday in *The Costa Brava* (1967). The politics of these works is recessed, much more so for Mason than Fasanella. We have to interpret the human need for respite as a counterpoint to the grimness of modern or postmodern despair and technologized labor. This is an open art of possibility, as we've seen in Mark Rogovin's politically joyful murals and in his father's generation of Old Left writers and artists.

I have been fortunate to encounter two Mason public sculptures—*Forward* in Birmingham before it was destroyed and the Georgetown Plaza sculptures. I remember the pressure on my eyes to look here and there actively, a different way of seeing than glancing at a museum wall. I have studied his high and low reliefs only through reproductions in books. With those I imagine a stage and a curtain opening. For *The Aggression* it is theater in the round. For *Tragedy in the North,* it is Shakespearean tragedy told anew. With *St. Mark's Place,* the human heteroclite comedy. Mason acknowledges his structural/sculptural/theatrical inclinations: *it would consist of a windowed box in which I could stage the scene and place the various* dramatis personae.[40] Raymond Mason stagecraft is literally evoked in his 1959 drawings for the set and curtain design for a revival of Racine's *Phèdre* (first performed in 1677, a French version of the Greek and Roman story of gods manipulating humans). Mason evoked horror and terror as well in *Les Epouvantées* (1963). He attempted to take in **everything**, the arbitrariness of violence and the consequences of dangerous work, **and** the celebratory and processional, prosaic and profound, encouraging viewers to step out of the darkness of the private ego and enter the sunny street and the possibilities of common spaces. Notice the consistency of his observatory power, seeing from within and without, from the window of his family's flat on Wheeleys Lane in Birmingham to the mature expansiveness of his public art.

Raymond Mason received the Order of the British Empire award in 2002 and the title Commandeur de l'Ordre des Arts et des Lettres in 2008, public recognition only partially illuminating Mason's complexity, his friendships with other artists, dealings with galleries, his "Brummie" sense of humor, his private life (when he married Janine Hao, he became stepfather to her three daughters), and the full range of his artful practices, particularly his drawings in ink and watercolor.

His work offers public art that is more than large formations. It is needed "because," as John Berger wrote in relation to sculptor Jacques Lipchitz, "we are surrounded by thousands of discredited public monuments—mostly hypocritical war memorials—and because the whole bias of our culture is towards the fragmentary and private, we tend to underestimate the civic social nature of sculpture."[41] It is also needed, because as Berger recognized in writing about Mason, as counterpoint to the class biases against representational sculptural aesthetics. Mason often evoked what he knew was unfashionable—the value and importance of beauty—not as cosmetic lies

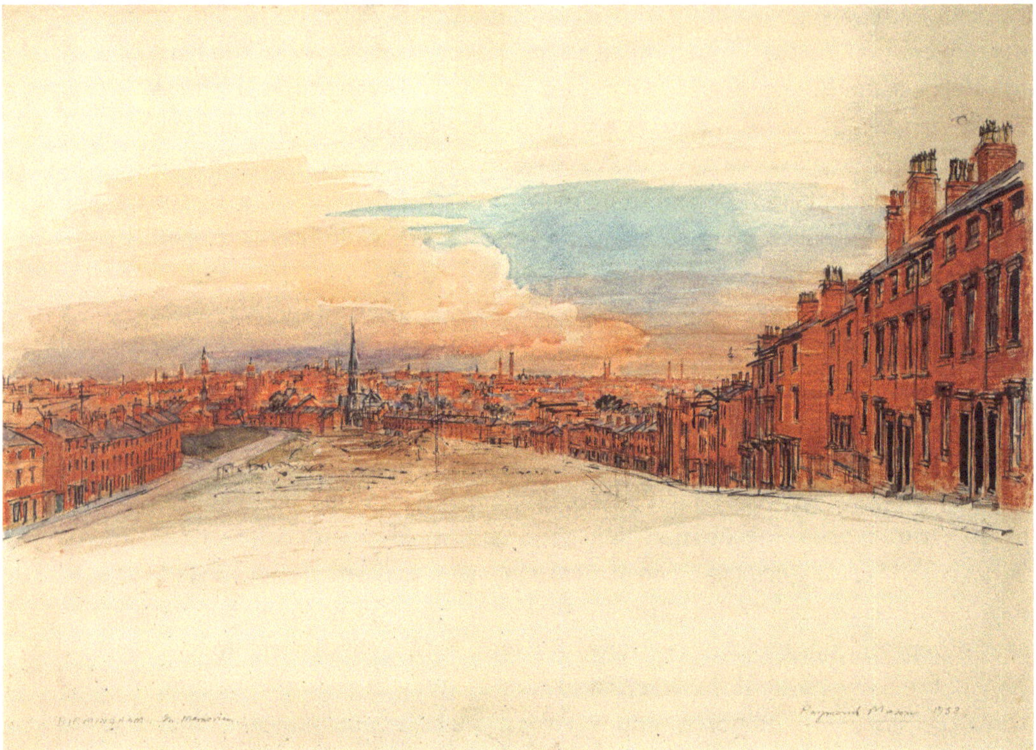

Raymond Mason, 1922–2010 "*Birmingham, In Memoriam*," 1958 (oil on canvas) The William Louis-Dreyfus Foundation ©Artists Rights Society (ARS)/New York/ADAGP, Paris

or advertisements, but as embodied in workers' lives of "endurance and companionship."[42]

In 1958 Raymond Mason's mother died. He returned to Birmingham to mourn her, to close the Wheeleys Lane family home, and to witness the receding of a familiar place, industrialized Birmingham. During a rainy week there, he completed several watercolors, channeling grief into art making, saying simply, *it was a necessity.*[43] Returning to Paris, he painted in oil *Birmingham, In Memoriam,* a quiet, beautiful demonstration of how color (oranges, reds, blues, browns) and composition, a street view, can evoke a range of human emotions—pain, loss, and joy.

In turning to sculpture as public art rather than solely focusing on paintings that would be housed in private homes and institutions, Raymond Mason offers another paradigm of how to be an artist. It is a large vision—being *seized by a subject*, having an acute focus on a single big work at a time, composing diverse elements in harmony, infusing energy into a still form (see his spirals, torrents, waves), developing an inclusive vision (especially for the ordinary and humble), possessing historical consciousness of art and of events, and presenting time as past, present, and future simultaneously. (This is another parallel with Fasanella.)

Mason's Birmingham sculpture *Forward* masterfully encompasses his capacious treatment of time, not just as an abstraction, but as tangible industrial and technological change pressing on human lives. My 1997 snapshots of *Forward* (sadly, not reproducible for this book; other images are available online) attest to Mason's sculptural vision of Time—cycles and arrows once again. British art writer James Hamilton began collaborating with Mason on the "genesis [and] purpose" of *Forward* after it was "burnt out by a boy with a match, an act that appalled the 81-year-old artist, but stiffened his resolve to carry on."[44]

Mason is a master teacher of artists' grammar—the centrality of drawing (especially his graphic density, his black ink cityscapes), composition, structure, color, and form. Raymond Mason's artistry is a wide invitation, taking us from the world of art markets and institutions to the landscape of humanity and to the *necessity* of humanism. Respect for the inherent dignity of his subjects, a capacity to carry his birthplace with him, consciousness of community, and a great love for beauty mark the life of Raymond Mason. He called Beauty *the great subject* itself and resolved *never to turn my back on the community at large, standing hungry for art and beauty.*[45] Mason recognized the longing for beauty that is inside everyone. *I've already repeated this word several times and I do so without a blush. That, in case our contemporary art world has forgotten, is what art is all about.*[46]

Conclusion

"Everyone has the capacity to make art," says Micah Pegues, a video producer employed by the Metropolitan Museum of Art in New York, one of 640 Met staff members who exhibited art in the Met's biannual show, *Art Work: Artists Working at the Met* (November 2024), which included paintings, sculptures, embroideries, photographs, digital arts, assemblage, drawings, and much more.[1] Art made by staff has been a Met tradition since 1935, but 2024 was only the second time that this staff exhibit has been open to the public.

Remember the plumber denied entry in 1897? What would he make of such an exhibit? What do *we* make of the channels between institutional securing and preserving and inspired workers producing and shaping? Art making answers art viewing.

This book, through its process of architectural/textual **building**, and archeological/research **excavating**, invites this circuitry of looking and making—across class lines.

THE GARDEN STATE

My poem "The Garden State" traces movement from Manhattan back to New Jersey. It is a loop that never closes.[1]

Drums as big as a man
Drums whose innards,
corroded by chemicals so toxic
they'd eat through steel,
greet you
as you leave Manhattan for New Jersey
The Garden State.

The soil is spongy here, water too clear
Elizabeth, New Brunswick, Menlo Park, Edison
homes to the workers of Manhattan
Camden, not Mannahatta.

Leave Lincoln Tunnel, twist around the curve
to Jersey City, Weehawken, Hoboken, Union City
cross Hudson Boulevard
and you're on Route Three.

Boxy corporate headquarters
squat on soil
that once was sewage,
and before that, swamp.

Where my uncles went crabbing every summer,
dipping their nets in stagnant water,
where the race track and Giant Stadium now stand
where once the swish of punk stalks
sounded.

Where one rush hour, long ago,
before the stadium, before the sewage,
even before the chemicals,
two men were killed on Route Three.
"Manslaughter" "Collision"
said the newspapers.
They were working men
coming home.
One was a carpenter, the other
was my grandfather.

Even then Route Three crossed Seventeen
Even then Seventeen flooded.
Rainwater from the hills of
Hackensack, Wood Bridge, Hasbrouck Heights
hit the four lanes of Seventeen.

It would get so deep and so dark, you'd swear the car was swimming.

Before the fast-food stands and wedding caterers
Small industries grew and died.
Trubeck Laboratories manufactured perfume, expensive perfume,
Arpege, White Shoulders, Chanel No. Five
at the crossroads of Three and Seventeen.

The chemicals
ran
through
exposed pipes
and drained
into
open drums.
No shower, no soap
could wash away the smell.

My father worked at Trubeck's
he brought home perfume samples,
chemical burns.
and always
the smell.

They killed him
younger than his own father.
And just as unexpected.

They are all dead now.
Grandfather, father, uncles,
and, now, son.

There are no markers along their route.

Except

In the backyards of these small New Jersey towns
in tiny plots
grow tomatoes so big, so tasty, they'd make a meal.
And eggplants, cauliflower, zucchini, cukes
the size of small babies
Fruit trees droop with pears, cherries, apples,
Botanical Gardens
Bloom.

Acknowledgments

I am one of those whose life is sustained by books. Books are integral to my process of writing and to my understanding of artistic formation. They nourish the never-ending process of learning and unlearning—for everyone. I am grateful for the privilege of owning books.

I moved to Rochester, New York, in 1970. It is a city of stubborn poverty and deep culture. I am grateful for those who practice and expand the visual arts here: for the art classes I once took at the Memorial Art Gallery's All of Us workshop, described as "an art program for people who couldn't afford art school," that was then housed in an old city jail, which is now the well-established Writers & Books; for community art initiatives such as the mural project Wall\Therapy; and for community art galleries, particularly, RoCo, Rochester Contemporary Art Center, and the Mill Art Center and Gallery.

I acknowledge with appreciation:

Those who taught me about making art: Kathryn Bevier, Lyn Belisle, Connie Ehindero, and Lanna Pejovic.

Those whose friendships sustain me: Chojy Schroeder, Sylvia Gasoi, Maria Scipione, Chris Fusilli, Marianne Oliveiri, Bonnie Garner, Terry Easton, Michele Fazio, Jeanne Bryner, Sue Doro, Edvige Giunta, Tom Zaniello, Gail Hosking, Samuele Pardini, Peggy McNamara, and my new/old friend Ellen Rubinstein.

Those colleagues in Working-Class Studies: Christie Launius, Michelle Tokarczyk, Michael Zweig, Sarah Attfield, Laura Hapke, and Barbara Jensen.

This book is an orchestration, not a solo performance. I thank the artists and their families for their assistance, generosity, kindness, and patience:

Marilyn Anderson and Barbara Day; the Rogovin family—Milton's daughters, Ellen Rogovin Hart and Paula Rogovin, Mark's wife, Michelle Melin-Rogovin; Marc Fasanella and Stephen Del Prete at Museums.co; Jens S. Jensen's sons, Jakob Schleimann-Jensen and Jesper Schleimann-Jensen; and Greger Ulf Nilson for his *Hammarkullen* catalog design images. I thank the Asawa-Lanier family, particularly archivist and arts manager Vivian Tong and Henry Weverka, and I thank Meg Partridge, Director of the Imogen Cunningham Trust. I thank the artist Charles Roth for his talent and foresight in creating *Class Lines: Craftsmen.* I thank Abe Aronow for his portraits that evoke innate human dignity, not celebrity.

This book involved a complicated network of individuals and institutions who supplied images, content, and support. I thank Alexis Ellers, who was crucial to securing Rogovin images and had great patience with my limited technical skills. Melanie Anne Herzog's books on Milton Rogovin and Elizabeth Catlett were invaluable. I am grateful for: Peter Linebaugh's scholarship on The Commons and the virtue and necessity—of Commoning; Rebecca Zorach for her interview with Mark Rogovin; the Kollwitz Museum in Koln, Germany, especially the patient assistance of Christian Nitz; the professionalism of Siobhan Donnelly from the Artists Rights Society for permissions and licensing; Mary Anne Costello and the generosity of The William Louis-Dreyfus Foundation; Cynthia Nadelman for her interview with Raymond Mason and her many kind responses to my inquiries; Thames & Hudson for permission to quote from Mason's *At Work in Paris*; the invaluable Niclas Östlind, University of Gothenburg Professor of Photography, who generously shared his book on Jens S. Jensen with me; Dragana Vujanovic, Chief Curator, Hasselblad Foundation, for permission to include images from the *Hammarkullen* catalog; Sarah Jesse, Director of the Memorial Art Gallery, for permission to photograph the museum's Catlett sculpture; and Cesar Bracamonte from the Miami-Dade Public Library System for the Catlett images.

I thank the staff at the University of Illinois Press for their professional work, especially project editor Tad Ringo, book designer Jim Proefrock, and cover designer Jason Gabbert. I appreciate Roberta Engleman's careful indexing. I was fortunate to have Natalie Reitano's expert copyediting, and I thank her for knowing where Upstate New York is located. I appreciate how the University of Illinois Press treated the many and diverse images in this book. I would advise the reader, though, to see the art works themselves, especially the very large Fasanella paintings.

I thank Lumiere Photo for their digital image work.

I thank Paul England for his designer's eye and neighborly friendship.

Special thanks to Larry Merrill, whose photographs of *Woman Fixing Her Hair* ensured the inclusion of images of the Catlett sculpture located in Rochester's Memorial Art Gallery.

I acknowledge Tate Shaw. This book would not exist in its present form without Tate, who navigated Box and capably calmed technical waters. Tate, thank you, thank you.

I send love and gratitude to my daughter Anna and granddaughters Norah and Ebba, and to my husband Bill Zandy, who has been steadfast with technical, intellectual, and loving companionship.

I thank my parents, who gave me gifts that cannot be counted or measured.

Notes

Preface

1. Bus service ended April 7, 2023. "DeCamp to End Commuter Bus Service to New York City from New Jersey," *New York Times*, March 21, 2023, https://www.nytimes.com/2023/03/20/nyregion/nj-nyc-decamp-bus.html.

2. Pablo Picasso was commissioned by the Spanish Republic to paint a mural for its pavilion at the 1937 Paris International Exposition of Art and Technology in Modern Life (Paris World's Fair). After the attack on the Basque town of Guernica on April 26, 1937, by low-flying German planes strafing streets and civilians with machine-gun fire, Picasso had his subject. He began sketching images of destruction. His completed painting (25 feet long, 11 feet tall) was exhibited throughout Europe and the United States, raising funds for Spanish refugees from Franco's fascist regime. It remained at MOMA until after Franco's death and is now at the Museo Reina Sofia in Madrid.

The literature on the Spanish Civil War was unknown to me in 1964 but is widely accessible today. See, for example, Xabier Irujo, *Gernika, 1937: The Market Day Massacre* (Reno: The University of Nevada Press, 2015); Giles Tremlett, *The International Brigades: Fascism, Freedom and the Spanish Civil War;* and *The Volunteer* (founded by the Veterans of the Abraham Lincoln Brigades, https://albavolunteer.org/.

3. All the artists in this book connect their private art making to public and historical events—for example, Raymond Mason's *Tragedy in the North*, Ralph Fasanella's *Lawrence Bread and Roses Strike of 1912*, and Käthe Kollwitz's etchings of the sixteenth-century Peasant War in Germany.

4. Hilary Mantel, *Giving Up the Ghost* (London: Harper Collins, 2003), 49–50.

Introduction

1. TimesMachine, February 4, 1897, NYTimes.com. As referenced in Dorothy Moss, *The Sweat of their Face: Portraying American Workers* (Washington, DC: Smithsonian Institution, 2017), 50.

2. Truman Chambers, "How an Art Museum Betrays Its Social Class Bias." *Hyperallergic*, June 15, 2021.

3. Doreen Carvajal, "Artistic Insight Comes Through Different Eyes." *New York Times*, March 1, 2020, C3.

4. Ken Grossinger, *Art Works: How Organizers and Artists are Creating a Better World Together* (New York: The New Press, 2023), 107–08, 112. Compare these efforts with the Met's 1969 exhibit *"Harlem on My Mind": The Cultural Capital of Black America, 1900–1968.*

5. Annie Lanzillotto, "Healing through Colors," *Frame of Mind,* a podcast from the Metropolitan Museum of Art, March 2, 2022.

6. Michael Findlay, *The Value of Art: Money, Power, Beauty* (New York: Prestel, 2012) and *Seeing Slowly: Looking at Modern Art* (New York: Prestel, 2017).

7. See Ronni Baer, *Class Distinctions: Dutch Paintings in the Age of Rembrandt and* Vermeer (Boston: Museum of Fine Arts Publications, 2015).

8. Mike Watson, "Let's Talk about Class and Art," *ArtLeaks Gazette,* September 2017.

9. John Dewey, *Art as Experience* (New York: Penguin, 1934, 2005), 9, 7.

10. Ariella Aïsha Azoulay, *Potential History: Unlearning Imperialism* (New York: Verso, 2019), 140.

11. Peter Linebaugh, *Stop, Thief! The Commons, Enclosures, and Resistance* (Oakland: PM Press, 2014), 7.

12. Peter Linebaugh, *The Magna Carta Manifesto: Liberties and Commons for All* (Berkeley: University of California Press, 2008), 103. On the endurance of the commons see also Jay Walljasper, On the Commons, *All That We Share: A Field Guide to the Commons* (New York: The New Press, 2010), and Rebecca Solnit, *A Paradise Built in Hell: The Extraordinary Communities That Arise in Disaster* (New York: Viking, 2009).

13. See Jane Jacobs's paean to sidewalks: "Lowly, unpurposeful and random as they may appear, sidewalk contacts are the small change for which a city's wealth of public life may grow." *The Death and Life of Great American Cities* (New York: Random House, 1961; Modern Library, 2011), 95.

14. Linebaugh, *Magna Carta,* 103.

15. Linebaugh, *Stop, Thief!*, 13.

16. I am a member of the Mill Art Center & Gallery in Honeoye Falls, New York (Kathryn Bevier, director), where I exhibit regularly in group shows and practice encaustic painting and figure drawing. I am also a member of Rochester Contemporary Art Center (RoCo; Bleu Cease, director), where I exhibit in member shows, 6 × 6 and attend lectures. RoCo balances original and distinct exhibits with community outreach. The September 2024 exhibit was *RG Miller: Tsi Non:we Entewaha'hara'ne / Our Path Forward.*

17. See Janet Zandy, ed. *What We Hold in Common* (New York: The Feminist Press, 2001).

18. I have been inspired by *commoning* without necessarily using the word. I recall the excitement of discovery when anthologies of Black women's writings

were published in the early 1980s such as Barbara Smith's *Home Girls* (New York: Kitchen Table: Women of Color Press, 1983) and the pioneering *This Bridge Called My Back: Writings by Radical Women of Color*, edited by Cherrie Moraga and Gloria E. Anzaldúa (Persephone Press, 1981, rpt. 1983, Kitchen Table: Women of Color Press). These collections opened spaces for others. Note also the history of the Combahee River Collective.

19. This multivocal approach evokes Gramsci's prison writings, developed as network or web, not as directives. *Antonio Gramsci: Selections from Cultural Writings*, ed. David Forgacs and Geoffrey Nowell-Smith, trans. William Boelhower (Cambridge: Harvard University Press, 1991), 10.

20. For that difference, see Edward W. Said, *The World, the Text, and the Critic* (Cambridge: Harvard University Press, 1983).

21. *The Routledge International Handbook of Working-Class Studies,* edited by Michele Fazio, Christie Launius, and Tim Strangleman (New York: Routledge, 2021), 343–358.

22. Raymond Mason, writing about Giacometti, in *At Work in Paris* (London: Thames & Hudson, 2003), 64.

23. James Agee and Walker Evans, *Let Us Now Praise Famous Men* (Boston: Houghton Mifflin, 1941), xvi.

24. *Azoulay, Potential History: Unlearning Imperialism*, 43, 82, 2, 57.

25. Raymond Williams, *Resources of Hope* (London: Verso, 1989), 113.

26. Williams, *Resources*, 114.

27. Williams, *Resources*, 114. See his more abstract excavation of the meaning of community in *Keywords: A Vocabulary of Culture and Society* (New York: Oxford University Press, 1983), 73–76.

28. Williams, *Resources,* 117.

29. See Manning Marable, *How Capitalism Underdeveloped Black America: Problems in Race, Political Economy, and Society* (Boston: South End Press, 1983), and his many other books examining the crucial intersections of race, class and power. For a Rochester, New York, context of race, class, and education see my reviews of Justin Murphy's *Your Children Are Very Greatly in Danger: School Segregation. In Rochester, New York* (*Radical Teacher*, 124, 68–71, 2022) and Bolgen Vargas's *Let Our Children Soar! The Complexities and Possibilities of Educating the English Language Student* (*Radical Teacher*, 127, 87–89, 2023).

30. Mark Fisher, *Capitalist Realism: Is There No Alternative?* (Winchester, UK: ZerO Books, 2014), 80.

31. Quoted in "Foreword," Paul Von Blum, *The Art of Social Conscience* (New York: Universe Books, 1976), ix.

32. Dewey, *Art and Experience*, 53.

33. Robert Henri, *The Art Spirit* (New York: Harper & Row, 1923), 77. Raymond Mason caught not only the beauty of well-arranged fruits and vegetables in his sculpture, *The Departure of Fruit and Vegetables from the Heart of Paris, 28 February 1969,* but also the choreography of workers arranging and shoppers carrying—consider his cauliflower bouquet, for instance.

34. Quoted in *Elizabeth Catlett: A Black Revolutionary Artist and All That It Implies* (Chicago: University of Chicago Press, 2024), 14.

35. "The Wound-Dresser," *Leaves of Grass and Selected Prose,* 244. Also, a piece for chamber orchestra and baritone singer by composer John Adams (1988) is based on Whitman's poem. See Patrick Bringley, *All the Beauty in the World: The*

Metropolitan Museum of Art and Me, which shows how his job as a museum guard becomes a "wound healer" after the death of his brother Tom (New York: Simon & Schuster, 2023).

36. Lynda Barry, "Interview," the *New York Times Magazine*, September 11, 2022, 15–17.

37. John Berger, *Berger on Drawing,* edited by Jim Savage (Co. Cork, Ireland, Occasional Press, 2005), 77.

38. John Berger, *Art and Revolution* (New York: Pantheon, 1969), 9.

Drawing, Printing, and Sculpting the Labor of Mothers

1. Zachary Small, "Therapeutic Creative Expression," *New York Times*, June 16, 2020, C1, C5.

2. *The Washerwoman (La Lavandière)*, painted 1860–62. Art historian Robert Rey describes the context of this painting: "From where Daumier lived, at 9 Quai d'Anjou, he could see buildings on the opposite bank of the Seine rising like a scraggy cliff. Right underneath his window, on the near bank, were moored some of those *bateaux-lavoirs*—covered barges which served as community washhouses. . . . Here women bustled about all day amid the racket of the paddles. At sunset they climbed up from the river's edge, bent under the weight of bundles of wet laundry. These women . . . often brought their children with them for the day . . ." *Honoré Daumier* (New York: Abrams, n.d.), 124–25. Consider Rey's language: "bustle about" rather than scrubbing and rinsing. He does not comment on why these women had little choice but to bring their children with them to work. He does use the words "bent" and "weight."

Käthe Kollwitz

1. Käthe Kollwitz, *The Diary and Letters of Kaethe Kollwitz*, 47. All quotations from Käthe Kollwitz directly are in English translation, not her original German. Notice that the title of this book does not include the *umlaut*, the diacritical marking indicating a sound shift in German.

2. Kollwitz, *Diary and Letters*, 40.

3. Dr. Karl Kollwitz was put in charge of the tailors' *Krankenhasse,* a system where members paid a small fee, a *Kasse*, for supportive medical care. *Diary and Letters,* 41. The apartment house where the Kollwitz family lived and worked for fifty years was destroyed by Allied bombing on November 23, 1943. Letters, photos, many drawings, and mementos could not be saved from the fire.

4. Kollwitz, *Diary and Letters*, 4.

5. See *Outbreak* [*Losbruch*] in the *Peasant War* series (*Bauernkrieg,* 1902–1908).

6. See Edward Said's distinctions between the two in *The World the Text and the Critic*, and as referenced in the introduction.

7. Alternatively, Williams calls this epistemology, "structures of experience" in *Marxism and Literature* (Oxford University Press, 1977), 132. Current critical language about representation and identity insufficiently encompasses Kollwitz's life and work. In a broader sense, we need to recognize the unacknowledged bourgeois class perspective in art historical practices and develop instead a class-conscious epistemological approach to art study, especially from a worker-class perspective.

8. See Herbert Bittner, *Käthe Kollwitz: Drawings* (New York, Thomas Yoseloff/Sagamore Press, 1959), which included this appreciation by Romain Rolland (in French translated into English) in 1927: "The work of Kaethe Kollwitz which reflects the ordeal and the pain of the humble and simple is the grandest German poem of the age. This woman of virile heart has looked on them, has taken them into her motherly arms, with a solemn and tender compassion. She is the voice of the silence of the sacrificed." Bittner describes Kollwitz as a "great dramatist" who "invents her own stage, in the sense of the Greek tragedy, on which her *dramatis personae* tread the boards," 1. See also Carl Zigrosser, *Prints and Drawings of Käthe Kollwitz* (New York: Dover, 1969).

9. The evolution of her body of work and her creative processes were evidenced in a major retrospective exhibition, *Käthe Kollwitz*, at the Museum of Modern Art in New York City, March 31 through July 20, 2024, presenting about 110 drawings, prints and sculptures, preparatory studies, and working proofs, and curated by Starr Figura with Maggie Hire. See the exhibit catalog *Käthe Kollwitz,* edited by Starr Figura, with contributions by Kirsty Bell, Maggie Hire, Dorothy Price, and Sarah Rapoport (New York: The Museum of Modern Art, 2024).

10. Kollwitz, *Diary and Letters*, 43.

11. A reproduction of this sketch is included under "Formative Years" in Janice R. MacKinnon and Stephen R. MacKinnon, *Agnes Smedley: The Life and Times of an American Radical* (Berkeley: University of California Press, 1988). Read Agnes Smedley's *Daughter of Earth* 1929, (rpt. The Feminist Press, 1975) in relation to Kollwitz's drawings. See also Agnes Smedley, "Germany's Artist of the Masses," *Industrial Pioneers* (September 1925). Smedley acted as a go-between for the German artist Kollwitz and the Chinese artist Lu Xun (1881–1936), who purchased several of her works. "Lu Xun literally imposed Kollwitz onto the history of Chinese modernity," writes Estelle Bories in "The Influence of Kathe Kollwitz on Chinese Creation: Between Expressionism and Revolutionary Realism," in Jerome Bazin, Pascal Dubourg Glatigny, Piot Piotrowski, *Art Beyond Borders: Artistic Exchange in Communist Europe (1945–1989)* (New York and Budapest: CEU Press, 2016), 459.

12. *Daughter of Earth*, 17. See Peter Hitchcock, *Dialogics of the Oppressed,* (Minneapolis: University of Minnesota Press, 1993) and his analysis of answerability and the writing of Agnes Smedley.

13. MacKinnon and MacKinnon, *Agnes Smedley*, 351.

14. Kollwitz, *Diary and Letters,* 100.

15. Kollwitz, *Diary and Letters,* 18.

16. Kollwitz, *Diary and Letters,* 28.

17. Kollwitz, *Diary and Letters*, 25.

18. Kollwitz, *Diary and Letters*, 37.

19. Kollwitz, *Diary and Letters*, 28.

20. Kollwitz, *Diary and Letters*, 39.

21. In March 1848 demonstrations erupted in several German states in reaction to high unemployment, poverty, and political repression. The uprising was suppressed; over two hundred workers were killed by government troops. Known as the March Revolution, this was one of a series of rebellions across Europe.

22. Martha Kearns, *Käthe Kollwitz: Woman and Artist* (New York: The Feminist Press, 1976), 42.

23. Kearns, *Käthe Kollwitz,* 47.

24. John Berger, *Berger on Drawing,* ed. Jim Savage (Cork, Ireland: Occasional Press, 2008), 70, 77. Although a small compilation of Berger's writings, it offers large reflections on the act of drawing that illuminate Kollwitz and other artists in this book, including the American painter Ralph Fasanella and his art making practice of "catching and grabbing." See further reference to Berger and drawing in the Introduction.

25. Kollwitz, *Diary and Letters*, 23.

26. Kollwitz, *Diary and Letters*, 42

27. Kollwitz's sources include "Weaver-Song" or "The Silesian weavers," a poem by Heinrich Heine. It was translated into English by Friedrich Engels and published in 1844 in Karl Marx's *Vorwarts (Forward)* newspaper. Hauptmann's source was likely Alfred Zimmerman, *The Rise and Fall of the Industry of Linen Weaving in Silesia* (Breslau: W.G. Korn, 1885). As clarified in the Käthe Kollwitz Museum Köln text, Kollwitz's cycle is not a literal representation of actual events in 1844, but rather a fictitious revolt in a contemporary setting with workers in clothing appropriate to the industrialization of Prussia after 1850 (https://www.kollwitz.de/en/cycle-weavers-revolt-overview).

28. Adolf von Menzel (1815–1905) was a German painter sympathetic to the working classes. See his *The Steelworks* and *The Knife Grinder,* reproduced in Edward Lucie-Smith and Celestine Dars, *Work and Struggle: The Painter as Witness* (London: Paddington Press, 1977).

29. Kollwitz, *Diary and Letters,* 43.

30. Kollwitz, *Diary and Letters*, 44.

31. Kollwitz, *Diary and Letters*, 3.

32. Kearns, *Käthe Kollwitz,* 108.

33. Kearns, *Käthe Kollwitz,* 148.

34. When in 2016 I visited the Kollwitz Museum in Berlin, her sculptures were on the top floor and her print series was on the ground floor. I recall a quotation where she said she would have been a sculptor if circumstances allowed. Christian Nitz, staff member of the Kollwitz museum in Cologne, confirmed that when Kollwitz was evacuated to Moritzburg in 1945, she said to her host, Prince Heinrich of Saxony, that "If I could live once more, I would work exclusively as a sculptor." The museum documents 43 sculptural projects, with 19 surviving sculptures, and 15 reproduced in bronze (email correspondence with Christian Nitz, September 29, 2021).

35. Kearns, *Käthe Kollwitz,* 133.

36. Kearns, *Käthe Kollwitz,* 135.

37. See also Ralph Fasanella's paintings of mourners and coffin inscriptions, particularly his late painting, *Farewell, Comrade—The End of the Cold War* (1992–1997), and his earlier tribute to the Rosenbergs, *Gray Day*, 1963.

38. Kearns, *Käthe Kollwitz,* 164.

39. Kearns, *Käthe Kollwitz,* 193.

40. See Rabbi Earl A. Grollman, *Living with Loss, Healing with Hope* (Boston: Beacon Press, 2000), and his books on grief and loss from a Jewish perspective.

41. Kearns, *Käthe Kollwitz,* 208.

42. Kollwitz was all too familiar with state censorship of art. Wilhelm II criticized her *Weavers' Revolt* series as "gutter painting" in 1898. After the flourishing of avant-garde art and music during the Weimar Republic, Hitler's ascendancy meant the crushing of art that did not project his Germanic Ideal, that was degenerate, depraved, distorted—and Jewish. The Nazis coupled anti-Semitism with culture

control. In the Nazis' Germany of 1939, paintings as well as books were burned. "Degenerate Art" (*Wikipedia).*

43. Kollwitz, *Diary and Letters*, 87.

44. Kearns, *Käthe Kollwitz,* 227–31.

45. See Allan M. Jalon's four-part series, "All Roads Lead Back to Kathe Kollwitz," in *Forward*, December 1, 2019, and especially the influence of Kollwitz on Peter and Elka Schumann's Bread and Puppet Theater in Vermont.

46. This drawing was published by the Women's International League for Peace and Freedom to resist aerial and smoke bomb tests. Also compare Kollwitz's *Saatfruchte sollen nicht vermahlen warden* (derived from Goethe's *Wilhelm Meister* and translated from the German as "Seed Grain Shall Not Be Milled") and its depiction of a woman with massive arms and hands sheltering three small children with contemporary graphic artist Sue Coe's ironically named *Bomb Shelter?* (a print protesting the Iraq war in 1991), which depicts a black bomb torpedoed over a kneeling woman, large hands covering her face, bent over the body of the dead child she was unable to protect.

47. From an interview with Jose da Silva, the *Art Newspaper,* September 23, 2021, https://www.artnewspaper.com.

48. Kollwitz, *Diary and Letters*, 78.

Elizabeth Catlett

1. Catlett's biographer Melanie Anne Herzog speculates whether this sculpture in Rochester's Memorial Art Gallery (MAG) may have been a model for a larger carved wood piece with the same title in the collection of the Metropolitan Museum of Art dated 1993 (email exchange, August 16, 2021). In a conversation with Jessica Marten (Curator in Charge/Curator of American Art, at the Memorial Art Gallery, July 21, 2021), I learned that the Catlett sculpture was acquired at auction in 2014 with the approval of the Art Committee Board of the museum. I thank Sarah Jesse, director of the Memorial Art Gallery, for permission to include photographs of Catlett's *Woman Fixing Her Hair.* Consider juxtaposing this statue with another Catlett figure, *Tired*, terracotta, made in 1946. What if audiences could see—and understand—artworks dialogically instead of individually?

2. Quoted in Melanie Anne Herzog, *Elizabeth Catlett: An American Artist in Mexico* (Seattle: University of Washington Press, 2000), 14–15.

3. In conversation with Jackie Adams, Columbia Museum of Art, "The Ritual of Elizabeth Catlett: A Conversation Celebrating the CMA Opening of The Art of Elizabeth Catlett from the collection of Samella Lewis," Columbia Museum of Art, Columbia, South Carolina, October 14, 2022, 43:03, YouTube video, https://www.youtube.com/watch?v=voXbVvzq5Ug.

4. Quoted in Samella S. Lewis, *The Art of Elizabeth Catlett* (Claremont, CA: Hancraft Studios, 1984), published in collaboration with the Museum of African American Art, Los Angeles, 6.

5. "We wear the mask that grins and lies, / It hides our cheeks and shades our eyes,— / This debt we pay to human guile" (1895). Paul Laurence Dunbar was educated at Howard University.

6. Quoted in Herzog, *Elizabeth Catlett: An American Artist in Mexico*, 15.

7. Audre Lorde, *Zami: A New Spelling of My Name* (Trumansburg, NY: The Crossing Press, 1982), 68–71, reprinted in Janet Zandy, *Calling Home: Working-Class Women's Writings* (New Brunswick: Rutgers University Press, 1990, 1993), 79–82.

8. Quoted in Lewis, *The Art of Elizabeth Catlett*, 8.

9. Although the lawsuit was unsuccessful, it called attention to the layers of racial inequality within educational systems. Thurgood Marshall was involved with the case. Herzog, *An American Artist in Mexico*, 18.

10. Lewis, *The Art of Elizabeth Catlett*, 9–12.

11. Quoted in Herzog, *Elizabeth Catlett: An American Artist in Mexico*, 19–20. See Tillie Olsen's short story "I Stand Here Ironing."

12. Quoted in Herzog, *Elizabeth Catlett: An American Artist in Mexico*, 21.

13. Quoted in Melanie Anne Herzog, *Elizabeth Catlett: In the Image of the People*, catalog in conjunction with an exhibition organized by The Art Institute of Chicago, November 13, 2005 to February 5, 2006 (Chicago: The Art Institute of Chicago, 2005), 32.

14. Winner of the Yale University Series of Younger Poets Award in 1941 and author of the historical novel *Jubilee* (1966). See Maryemma Graham, *The House Where My Soul Lives: The Life of Margaret Walker* (New York: Oxford University Press, 2022).

15. Lewis, *The Art of Elizabeth Catlett*, 93. This represents my view of a diverse feminist movement as well.

16. Museum of the African Diaspora, interview, "Samella Lewis on Elizabeth Catlett," November 27, 2018.

17. Quoted in Lewis, *The Art of Elizabeth Catlett*, 94.

18. "The Ritual of Elizabeth Catlett: A Conversation."

19. Quoted in Lowery Stokes Sims, "Elizabeth Catlett: A Life in Art and Politics," in *Elizabeth Catlett Sculpture: A Fifty-Year Retrospective* (Neuberger Museum of Art, Purchase College, State University of New York, 1998), 11. See also *Reimaging America: The Arts of Social Change, eds.* Mark O'Brien and Craig Little (Philadelphia: New Society Publishers, 1990), 244.

20. Paulo Freire, *Pedagogy of Hope: Reliving Pedagogy of the Oppressed* (New York: Continuum, 1997) 46, 31. See also J.V. Decemvirale, "*La Maestra's* Fugitive Pedagogy in Mexico," in *Elizabeth Catlett: A Black Revolutionary Artist and All That It Implies*, ed. Dalila Scruggs (Chicago: University of Chicago Press, 2024), 138–42. As an art teacher, Catlett was unwilling "to train students to be apolitical commodity-makers for the wealthy." Decemvirale, "*La Maestra*," 140.

21. "My Advice to Young African Americans," April 26, 2010.

22. Quoted in Samella S. Lewis, "Elizabeth Catlett," in *Elizabeth Catlett: Works on Paper, 1944–1992* (Hampton, Virginia: Hampton University Museum, 1993), 8–9. See also James M. Wechsler, "Taller De Gráfica Popular: The Life and Drama of Mexico," in *Mexico and Modern Printmaking: A Revolution in the Graphic Arts, 1920–1950*, ed. John Ittmann (Philadelphia: Philadelphia Museum of Art, 2006), 208–223.

23. See Jacob Lawrence's *The Migration Series* (1940–1941) in relation to Catlett's *The Black Woman Series (1946–47)* in New York's Museum of Modern Art.

24. See Kate Rushin's poem "The Black Back-Ups," which begins "This is dedicated to" and concludes with "This is for the Black Back-Ups / This is for my mama and your mama / My grandma and your grandma / This is for the thousand thousand Black Back-Ups. . . . " Originally published by Firebrand Books (Ithaca, NY: 1993), reprinted in Nicolas Coles and Janet Zandy, *American Working-Class Literature* (New York: Oxford University Press, 2007), 800–02.

25. Richard J. Powell and Jock Reynolds, *To Conserve a Legacy: American Art from*

Historically Black College and Universities (Addison Gallery of American Art, Andover, MA: The Studio Museum in Harlem, distributed by MIT Press, 1999), 183.

26. See Janet Zandy, *Unfinished Stories: The Narrative Photography of Hansel Mieth and Marion Palfi* (Rochester: RIT Press, 2013).

27. See Michelle Alexander, *The New Jim Crow: Mass Incarceration in the Age of Colorblindness* (New York: The New Press, 2010), and the National Black Women's Justice Institute's "The New Jane Crow: Women's Mass Incarceration" and their work to preserve the mother/child relationship; see also the prison abolition movement, especially the advocacy of Ruth Wilson Gilmore.

28. See James Allen, Leon Litwack, Hilton Als, and John Lewis, *Without Sanctuary: Lynching Photography in America* (Santa Fe: Twin Palms, 2000).

29. See Herzog, *Elizabeth Catlett: In the Image of the People,* and the detailed reproductions of Catlett's visual "poem," *The Black Woman* Series, in Scruggs, *Elizabeth Catlett: Black Revolutionary Artist and All That It Implies* (Chicago: University of Chicago Press, 2024).

30. The Civil Rights Congress (CRC) was founded in Detroit in 1946 and was concerned with the legal defense of civil rights activists. See Paul Robeson and William L. Patterson's historic petition to the United Nations, *We Charge Genocide* (December 17, 1951), delivered to the UN in New York (by Robeson) and in Paris (by Patterson). The petition linked racial oppression in the United States to the UN's definition of genocide: "the oppressed Negro citizens of the United States, segregated, discriminated against, and long the target of violence, suffer from genocide as the result of the consistent, conscious, unified policies of every branch of government."

31. See "Art as Collective Process," Herzog, *Elizabeth Catlett: An American Artist in Mexico*, 94–107. Note also the influence of Käthe Kollwitz's graphic portraits on Catlett's portrayal of mothers fearing for their children.

32. Quoted in Herzog, *Elizabeth Catlett: An American Artist in Mexico*, 5, and see Stuart Hall, "Cultural Identity and Diaspora," in *Identity, Community, Culture, Difference, ed.* Jonathan Rutherford (London: Lawrence & Wishart, 1990), 224.

33. See Raymond Williams on the concept of community in "The Importance of Community," in *Resources of Hope*, and his *Keywords*, 75–76. The word community has been flattened by overuse. Historically and presently, we witness the healing bonding that forges community, especially after tragic and unexpected occurrences, and yet we also see the cavalier use of the word in reference to alliances among groups with noncommunal values.

34. Herzog, *Elizabeth Catlett: An American Artist in Mexico*, 79.

35. Herzog, *Elizabeth Catlett: An American Artist in Mexico,* 108; Lewis, *The Art of Elizabeth Catlett,* 97–101, and *Freedomways* 1, no. 1 (Spring 1961): 74–80.

36. Herzog, *Elizabeth Catlett: An American Artist in Mexico,* 120.

37. Herzog, *Elizabeth Catlett: An American Artist in Mexico,* 143.

38. See Floyd Coleman, *A Courtyard Apart: The Art of Elizabeth Catlett and Francisco Mora* (Biloxi, Mississippi: Mississippi Museum of Art, 1991).

39. Quoted in Samella S. Lewis, ed., *African American Art and Artists,* rev. ed. (Berkeley: University of California Press, 2003), 134–35.

40. From her speech before the National Conference of Negro Artists, April 1, 1961, quoted in Lewis, *The Art of Elizabeth Catlett,* 99.

41. See Raymond Williams on "confronting a hegemony in the fibres of the self" in *Marxism and Literature* (New York: Oxford University Press, 1977), 212.

Ruth Asawa

1. This is excerpted from a recommendation that Albers wrote on behalf of Ruth Asawa so she could return to Black Mountain College (BMC). The Louis Comfort Tiffany Foundation turned her down, but with the help of others, she found a way to continue her studies at BMC. See Josef Albers, *Interaction of Color* (1971; New Haven: Yale University Press, 2013). Quoted in Marilyn Chase, *Everything She Touched: The Life of Ruth Asawa* (San Francisco: Chronicle Books, 2020), 58.

2. Paul J. Karlstrom (with Mark Johnson), "Interview with Ruth Asawa and Albert Lanier," conducted for the *Archives of American Art,* Smithsonian Institution, June 21 and July 5, 2002, in *The Sculpture of Ruth Asawa: Contours in the Air, Timothy Anglin Burgard,* Daniell Cornell et al. (Fine Arts Museums of San Francisco in association with the University of California Press, 2006, 2020), 151.

3. See Käthe Kollwitz's "Seed Corn Must Not Be Ground."

4. For a larger cultural context see Leonard Koren, *Wabi-Sabi for Artists, Designers, Poets & Philosophers* (Point Reyes, California: Imperfect Publishing, 2005), especially Shiro Kuramata's wire chair, 38–39. See also the Japanese tradition of weaving baskets in Louise Allison Cort and Nakamura Kenji, *A Basketmaker in Rural Japan* (Weatherhill, Inc.: New York and Tokyo, in association with Smithsonian Institution, Washington, DC, 1994).

5. From a letter (December 29, 1948), quoted in "Foreword," Jonathan Laib, *Ruth Asawa* (New York: David Zwirner Books, 2018), 7.

6. Genzaburō Yoshino, *How Do You Live?* 1937, 1982, trans. Bruno Navasky (New York: Algonquin Young Readers, 2021).

7. Laib, *Ruth Asawa*, 7.

8. In an important instance of artists/photographers witnessing the U.S. government's harm to Americans of Japanese descent, we have the internment camp photographs of Ansel Adams, Dorothea Lange, Hansel Mieth, and Otto Hagel, among others. See John Armor and Peter Wright, *Manzanar: Photographs by Ansel Adams, Commentary by John Hersey* (New York: Vintage, 1988)—especially Hersey's writing. Less known are the Manzanar photographs of Toyo Miyatake, a professional photographer from Los Angeles, who was forced to move with his family to Manzanar. He exhibited his Manzanar photographs with Ansel Adams, *Two Views of Manzanar,* in Los Angeles in 1978. See *Impounded: Dorothea Lange and the Censored Images of Japanese American Internment*, eds. Linda Gordon and Gary Y. Okihiro (New York: W. W. Norton, 2006). Lange photographs reveal the horse stall living quarters assigned to the Japanese families as well as their laborious cultivation of gardens. Less well known are the photographs of Hansel Mieth and Otto Hagel taken at the Heart Mountain Relocation Center in Park County, Wyoming, where nearly 11,000 Japanese Americans were incarcerated during the bitterly cold January of 1943. Mieth and Hagel were on assignment for *Life* magazine, which, despite government clearance, decided not to publish their photographs. See Janet Zandy, *Unfinished Stories: The Narrative Photography of Hansel Mieth and Marion Palfi* (Rochester: RIT Press, 2013). See also "Resistance or Loyalty: The Visual Politics of Miné Okubo," in Nicolas Lampert, *A People's Art History of the United States: 250 Years of Activist Art and Artists Working in Social Justice Movements* (New York: The New Press, 2013).

9. Karlstrom, "Interview with Ruth Asawa and Albert Lanier," 148–49.

10. Karlstrom, "Interview with Ruth Asawa and Albert Lanier," 150.

11. Chase, *Everything She Touched,* 28.

12. A personal class note: I also attended a state teacher college, Montclair, commuted to school, managed tuition with a scholarship from my father's company, but, unlike Ruth and her pivotal Black Mountain College experience, became a teacher rather than an artist because I was *allowed* the requisite practicum, student teaching, and because teaching was the aspirational path for girls of my generation and class background. Such are the class forces that shape and often limit choice. On the other hand, I did not have to sign a loyalty oath or look for a noncoastal interior school; such are the racial differences.

13. See Jacqueline Hoefer, "Ruth Asawa: A Working Life," in *The Sculpture of Ruth Asawa*, 35.

14. Karlstrom, "Interview with Ruth Asawa and Albert Lanier," 151.

15. See Helen Molesworth (with Ruth Erickson), *Leap Before You Look: Black Mountain College 1933–1957* (New Haven: Institute of Contemporary Art/Boston and Yale University Press, 2015), and Amanda Fortini, "Why Are We Still Talking About Black Mountain College?" the *New York Times*, July 7, 2022.

16. John Dewey, *Art as Experience* (1934; New York: Perigee, 2005), cited elsewhere. See also *Leap Before You Look*, 79.

17. Daniell Cornell, "The Art of Space: Sculptural Installations," in *The Sculpture of Ruth Asawa*, 181.

18. Chase, *Everything She Touched*, 86.

19. Karlstrom, "Interview with Ruth Asawa and Albert Lanier," 152.

20. Chase, *Everything She Touched*, 82. Regarding dancing dogs: "Sir, a woman's preaching is like a dog's walking on his hind legs. It is not done well; but you are surprised to find it done at all." Anne and Irvin Ehrenpreis, *Boswell's Life of Samuel Johnson* (New York: Washington Square Press, 1965).

21. See Josef Albers on the haptic sense as related to a sense of touch in *Interaction of Color*, 8. Helen Molesworth writes, "Haptic objects intertwine visuality and tactility so thoroughly that they are inextricable from each other." *Leap Before You Look*, 66. (Haptic quality is a good way to describe the outcome from painting with encaustic wax, my preferred medium.)

22. Albers, *Interaction of Color*, 1.

23. Karlstrom "Interview with Ruth Asawa and Albert Lanier," 147.

24. Karlstrom, "Interview with Ruth Asawa and Albert Lanier," 153.

25. Karlstrom, "Interview with Ruth Asawa and Albert Lanier," 154–55.

26. Chase, *Everything She Touched*, 161.

27. Chase, *Everything She Touched*, 112.

28. Sally B. Woodbridge, "The Alvarado Art Workshop, 1968–1973," In *The Sculpture of Ruth Asawa: Contours in the Air*, 258.

29. Quoted in Chase, *Everything She Touched*, 157.

30. Zack Hatfield, "Tending the Metal Garden" *New York Review of Books*, September 21, 2017.

Marilyn Anderson

1. Ariella Aïsha Azoulay, *Potential History: Unlearning Imperialism* (Brooklyn, NY: Verso, 2019). Artists like Marilyn Anderson are reminders to the art world establishment of the need for a reimagined and rethought infrastructure for art history. We need better theoretical tools not only in evaluating Anderson's place in art history, but because she offers a path that other artists might follow. See Azoulay's analysis of Hannah Arendt's use of *Homo faber* (human as maker), 89–90.

2. Marilyn Anderson's (unpublished) autobiographical memories are printed here in italics, with permission from the author.

3. Quoted from Marilyn Anderson, *Guardianes de las Artes/Guardians of the Arts: Prints of Guatemalan Artists and Artisans* (Antigua, Guatemala: Ediciones del Pensativo, 2016), 14.

4. Jonathan Garlock is a labor historian and activist. In Rochester, NY, he co-coordinates a Labor Film Series, which he founded in 1989, that is screened at the Dryden Theater, a partnership between Rochester Labor Council and the Eastman Museum. He revitalized Rochester's Labor Day parade (paused during the pandemic). He and Marilyn Anderson developed a photo/history exhibit, *Rochester: A Community of Workers* (archived at Cornell University Library's Kheel Center), and with Cornell labor historian Linda Donahue, he produced *Rochester Labor History Map/Guide*. He is a historian of the Knights of Labor, America's largest nineteenth-century labor organization, mapping thousands of assemblies, published in his *Guide to the Local Assemblies of the Knights of Labor* (Westport, CT: Greenwood Press, 1982). He serves on the executive board of the Rochester Labor Council and chairs its Education Committee, coordinating work-based curriculum projects of the Rochester Education Alliance of Labor (REAL).

5. See Azoulay's *Potential History: Unlearning Imperialism* for commentary on "community of *fabri*" and on companionship and co-citizenship, 89–91, 109, 235.

6. See Leo Marx, "Does Improved Technology Mean Progress?" *Technology Review* (January 1987): 33–41. Echoing Karl Marx, Leo Marx asks, "progress toward what?"

7. *When the Mountains Tremble* is a 1983 documentary film of the war on indigenous Maya by the Guatemalan military government, directed by Pamela Yates and Newton Thomas Sigel (Skylight Pictures).

8. Jean-Marie Simon, *Guatemala: Eternal Spring, Eternal Tyranny* (New York: Norton, 1987).

9. Marilyn Anderson and Jonathan Garlock, *Granddaughters of Corn: Portraits of Guatemalan Women* (Willimantic, CT: Curbstone Press, 1988). Documents in relation to the making of *Granddaughters of Corn* are in the archives of the Nettie Lee Benson Latin American Collection, University of Texas Libraries in Austin, Texas. See Aryeh Neier and Amrit Singh, "Guatemala: Democracy Imperiled," *New York Review of Books,* February 13, 2025, 12–14, for an informative summary of Guatemala's political history, particularly documentation of violence against Maya people.

10. Anderson and Garlock, *Granddaughters of Corn*, 52, 72, 48, 27.

11. Anderson and Garlock, *Granddaughters of Corn*, 74.

12. Anderson and Garlock, *Granddaughters of Corn*, 104.

13. See M. M. Bakhtin, "Discourse in the Novel," in *The Dialogic Imagination,* ed. Michael Holquist, trans. Caryl Emerson and Michael Holquist (Austin: University of Texas Press, 1981), especially the useful glossary explanations of heteroglossia and dialogism. By citing Bakhtin I'm inviting an application of literary theory to artistic production in its widest sense. See also Peter Hitchcock's *Dialogics of the Oppressed* (Minneapolis: University of Minnesota Press, 1993), especially his analysis of *positioning*. Anderson crossed cultural barriers through her own earned epistemology. An earned positioning is also relevant to Elizabeth Catlett and Käthe Kollwitz.

14. Anderson answers Azoulay's charge in *Potential History* that "modern art is not a historical category but an imperial condition." Azoulay also highlights a

rift between "scholars interested in labor and those interested in art." See introduction of this book. She elaborates: "the persona of *homo faber*—the idea that humans establish their world through the activity of making, beyond the need to make a living through labor—is completely absent from studies of the labor question in French and British Africa, as if Africans were always and only menial and low-skilled laborers. Whereas in art historians' accounts, individual artists are singled out without regard to how communities were proletarianized and forced to labor, and therefore to minimize the use of various skills to build their world and care for it" (82).

15. In a fragmentary piece written in 1844 but not published until 1927, Karl Marx theorized estranged laboring: "that the work he does is not his own, but another's and that at work he belongs not to himself, but to another" (www.marxist.org).

16. Studs Terkel, *Working* (New York: Pantheon, 1972, 1974), xlvi. See also Alan Trachtenberg's essay "Ever-the Human Document," in Alan Trachtenberg, et al., *America and Lewis Hine* (New York: Aperture, 1977), 134. The artists in this book offer that intelligent interpretation of workers through various artistic modes and tools. It is not coincidental that so many are drawn to Bertolt Brecht's question, "who built the pyramids?" ("A Worker Reads History"). See also Milton Rogovin in relation to Brecht and Hine.

17. Anderson, *Guardianes*, 18.

18. Anderson, *Guardianes*, 64.

19. Anderson, *Guardianes*, 142.

Photography and the Art of Returning

1. This is distinctly different from the photographer as determined "shooter." In his conversation with Lawrence Weschler on image convergences, where photographs are paired with art-historical references, Joel Meyerowitz comments on photographing firemen briefly at rest after the September 11 attack on the Twin Towers: "there was a certain hostility pervasive at the site, because firemen didn't want their pictures taken. . . . You can see one guy in the center here, he's basically telling me no. He actually said to me, 'No,' and I basically said, 'yes. It doesn't matter what you say, I'm doing this'. "Echoes at Ground Zero": A Conversation with Joel Meyerowitz," in *"Everything that Rises": A Book of Convergences* (San Francisco: McSweeney's Books, 2006), 15.

2. Stephen Jay Gould, "Introduction Universal Triptychs," in *Triptychs: Buffalo's Lower West Side Revised, Photographs by Milton Rogovin* (New York: W. W. Norton, 1994), 11. See Stephen Jay Gould, *Time's Arrow Time's Cycle: Myth and Metaphor in the Discovery of Geological Time* (Cambridge: Harvard University Press, 1987). Note his caveat regarding the theme of time's arrow and time's cycle and the necessary intelligibility of both. Other photographers have returned to the same place and people over a period of time; see Joanna L. Cresswell's "Scenes of Return," *Lensculture*, https://www.lensculture.com/articles/scenes-of-return-scenes-of-return. What is distinct about Jensen and Rogovin is their relationships to their subjects; indeed, the word "subject" as "other" does not fit the ethos of their work. They also seem far removed from Cresswell's language about the "power of taxonomies." The key difference is relationships not categorizations.

3. I met with Jens's son Jakob Schleimann-Jensen and photography professor Niclas Östlind in Gothenburg to discuss the possibilities of such an exhibit.

Although the idea was received positively, circumstances curtailed the project—Niclas Östlind was on leave; Jens S. Jensen had died; then Mark Rogovin (an organizer extraordinaire of his father's work) died; and COVID changed everyone's travel plans.

Milton Rogovin

1. Alan Trachtenberg, "Ever-the Human Document," quoting Lewis Hine from a 1909 lecture on social photography in which Hine foresaw a "field for photographic art [that] lies untouched in the industrial world" and an "urgent need for intelligent interpretation of the world's workers, not only for the people of today, but for future ages." *America & Lewis Hine: Photographs 1904–1940* (New York: Aperture, 1977), 134.

2. In 1983 Rogovin received the W. Eugene Smith Award for documentary photography, enabling him to expand his "Family of Miners" series. He and Anne traveled to China, Cuba, Czechoslovakia, Germany, Mexico, France, Scotland, Spain, and Zimbabwe.

3. Quoted in Melanie Anne Herzog, *Milton Rogovin: The Making of a Social Documentary Photographer* (Tucson: Center for Creative Photography, University of Arizona, Seattle: University of Washington Press, 2006), the catalog/book that accompanied the exhibition *Milton Rogovin: Photographer,* August 28–October 1, 2006. Herzog is also biographer of artist Elizabeth Catlett, included in this book. See https://www.miltonrogovin.com for biography, series chronology, books, films, and other resources. Milton Rogovin photographs are also archived in the Library of Congress, Center for Creative Photography/University of Arizona, the Getty Center, and other museums and galleries. See also Janet Zandy, "The Working-Class Eye of Milton Rogovin," *New Labor Forum* (Spring 2011): 41–47.

4. Quoted in Herzog, *Milton Rogovin*, 28.

5. Artist Betye Saar recalls a conversation with her stepfather about wanting to become an artist: "Now, what are you studying art for? How are you going to make any money like that?" Class and race limited Saar's formal artistic education but didn't stop her. See profile by Hilton Als, "Home Bodies," the *New Yorker,* November 27, 2023, 67–70.

6. The Air Force became a separate military branch after the war ended. My father, Charles Ballotta, also served in the Air Force and was stationed in Germany when I was born in 1945. He didn't see his first born, Janet, until he returned many months later.

7. Quoted in Herzog, *Milton Rogovin*, 33.

8. Quoted in Herzog, *Milton Rogovin*, 86.

9. *Diaries and Letters of Kaethe Kollwitz,* ed. Hans Kollwitz, trans. Richard and Clara Winston (Chicago: Henry Regnery Company, 1955), 125 (Herzog, n. 22, 166). See also the Käthe Kollwitz chapter in this book.

10. Quoted in Herzog, *Milton Rogovin*, 36–37.

11. See *Urban Holiness Service: Elder Charles D. Beck,* Folkways Records, FR8901, 1957, for Tallmadge's recordings and Rogovin's early photographs in the Storefront Church Series.

12. Quoted in Herzog, *Milton Rogovin*, 43.

13. Quoted in Herzog, *Milton Rogovin*, 43–58.

14. Quoted in Herzog, *Milton Rogovin*, 43–55

15. Quoted in Herzog, *Milton Rogovin*, 51.

16. Quoted in Herzog, *Milton Rogovin*, 51–52.

17. When I was teaching my course Photography and Writing at RIT, I would ask photography students, "what are you reading?" Often I saw blank stares, but occasionally a student would notice how literature could *inform* their photography. I also assigned Melanie Anne Herzog's biography, *Milton Rogovin: The Making of a Social Documentary Photographer*, and Milton Rogovin and Michael Frisch, *Portraits in Steel* (Ithaca: Cornell University Press, 1993) in my writing courses.

18. Milton Rogovin and W. E. B. Du Bois, "Storefront Churches: Photographs," *Aperture* 10, no. 2 [38] (1962): 62–78.

19. Quoted in Herzog, *Milton Rogovin*, 54.

20. For analysis of worker visual representations: Janet Zandy, "Seeing Dirt, Seeing Beyond Dirt: Photographs by and about Workers," *Exposure 43, no. 2* (Fall 2010): 33–40, recipient of the 2010 Society for Photographic Education Conference Award for Excellence in Historical, Critical and Theoretical Writing. For pedagogy, see Janet Zandy, "Photography and Writing, A Pedagogy of Seeing," *Exposure* 41, no. 1 (Spring 2008): 26–32.

21. Regarding narration and photography, see Walter Benjamin, "The Storyteller," in *Illuminations*, ed. Hannah Arendt, trans. Harry Zohn (New York: Schocken Books, 1968), and Walter Benjamin, "A Short History of Photography," in *Classic Essays on Photography*, ed. Alan Trachtenberg (New Haven: Leete's Island Books, 1980), 199–216. Consider how Benjamin's distinctions between storytelling and information apply to Rogovin's photographs.

22. Quoted in Herzog, *Milton Rogovin*, 60.

23. Quoted in Herzog, *Milton Rogovin*, 84.

24. Quoted in Herzog, *Milton Rogovin*, 92.

25. Rogovin inserted Brecht's poem into his acknowledgements page in *Portraits of Steel.* Studs Terkel also quotes "A Worker Reads History" ("Who Built the Pyramids?") in the preface to *Working: People Talk About What They Do All Day and How They Feel About What They Do* (New York: Pantheon, 1972).

26. Quoted in Herzog, *Milton Rogovin*, 105.

27. Quoted in Herzog, *Milton Rogovin*, 107.

28. Rogovin and Frisch, *Portraits in Steel*, 181–95.

29. Rogovin and Frisch, *Portraits in Steel*, 81–100.

30. Rogovin and Frisch, *Portraits in Steel*, 115–27.

31. Quoted in Herzog, *Milton Rogovin*, 109.

32. Quoted in Herzog, *Milton Rogovin*, 113.

33. Rogovin and Frisch, *Portraits in Steel*, 81, 115, 194.

34. Robert Coles, Stephen Jay Gould, and Joanne Wypijewski, *Triptychs: Buffalo's Lower West Side Revisited: Photographs by Milton Rogovin* (New York: W.W. Norton, 1994), 37.

35. David Isay, David Miller, and Harvey Wang, *Milton Rogovin: The Forgotten Ones* (New York: The Quantuck Lane Press, 2003), 12–13.

36. See Raymond Williams and his "fields of meaning" in *Keywords*. Rogovin keywords are adapted from Janet Zandy, lecture, "What Is a Working-Class Eye? The Photographs of Milton Rogovin," Gage Gallery, Chicago, June 23, 2011.

37. From an interview by Cheryl A. Brutvan, in *Milton Rogovin: The Forgotten Ones*, catalog for the Albright-Knox Art Gallery 1985 exhibit (Seattle: University of Washington Press, 1985), 16–17.

38. Oliver Sachs, *Seeing Voices: A Journey into the World of the Deaf* (Berkeley: University of California Press, 1989).

39.Brutvan, *Milton Rogovin: The Forgotten Ones,* 17.

40. See *The Rich Have Their Own Photographers*, a film by Ezra Bookstein, Telling Image Films, 2009.

41. Brutvan, *Milton Rogovin: The Forgotten Ones,* 19.

42. Rogovin and Frisch, *Portraits in Steel, 223.*

43.Tillie Olsen, *Silences* (New York: Dell, 1978). Olsen was concerned with the "relationship of circumstances—including class, color, sex; the times, climate into which one is born—to the creation of literature."

44. Susan Neiman, *Left is Not Woke* (Hoboken, NJ: Polity Press, 2023). Rogovin's photographs and Olsen's writings answer misguided academic theory that reifies victimization. Neiman argues that "the woke themselves have been colonized by a row of ideologies that properly belong to the right" (127).

45. *Milton Rogovin, The Lens and the Pen: Photographs & Poems, ed.* Craig Smith (Arroyo Seco, New Mexico: Palisade Press, 2009), 11.

46. Brutvan, *Milton Rogovin: The Forgotten Ones,* 21.

47. Raymond Williams, *Resources of Hope*, 4. See Jens S. Jensen's photographic understanding of the ordinary as well.

48. Brutvan, *Milton Rogovin: The Forgotten Ones,* 21.

49. From Agee's preface: "This is a *book* only by necessity. More seriously, it is an effort in human actuality." James Agee and Walker Evans, *Let Us Now Praise Famous Men*, xvi. The complexity of representing "actuality" is key to all the artists collected here. See, particularly, Raymond Mason and his creation of sculpture in relation to actuality.

50. Brutvan, *Milton Rogovin: The Forgotten Ones,* 11.

51. Agee, *Let Us Now Praise Famous Men*, 9.

Jens S. Jensen

1. Jensen's photograph, *Boy on the Wall, Hammarkullen, Gothenburg,* 1973, is in the permanent collection of the Museum of Modern Art in New York (MOMA). It was featured in MOMA's exhibit *Century of the Child: Growing by Design, 1900–2000*, research for which began in the child-centric Scandinavian countries where the curators saw Jensen's photograph of the boy hanging from a wall in a Stockholm museum. Aidan O'Connor and Juliet Kinchin, "Boy Meets Wall: Hanging Out with Jens S. Jensen," *Inside/Out,* October 11, 2012.

2. The **Million Programme** (Swedish: *Miljonprogrammet*) is the common name for a public housing program implemented in Sweden between 1965 and 1974 by the governing Swedish Social Democratic Party to ensure housing at a reasonable price. The aim was to build a million new dwellings during a ten-year period. At the time the Million Programme was the most ambitious building program in the world, developed in a nation with a population then of eight million (en.m.Wikipedia).

Hammarkullen, built 1968–1971, is situated in Angered, one of ten city districts in Gothenburg. Its large-scale (brutalist?) buildings housed many refugees and immigrants. Jensen explored how imposing structures do not necessarily quell human vibrancy. Hammarkullen public housing reminds me of the Projects in Union City, New Jersey, where my cousins lived—concrete everywhere, no green space. For the first ten years of my life, my family rented a three- room apartment in a house in Union City near the Projects.

3. Quoted in Niclas Östlind, *Jens S. Jensen: Samlat verk* (Collected Works). Östlind, curator and professor at HDK-Valand-Academy of Art and Design, University of Gothenburg, sent me his book on Jensen, which I read through Google Translate.

4. Raymond Williams, "Culture is Ordinary," in *Resources of Hope*. "I was not oppressed by the university but the teashop," Williams writes, and a view of culture as "extraordinary fussiness, this extraordinary decision to call certain things culture and then separate them, as with a park wall, from ordinary people and ordinary work" (5).

5. Jobba, leva, bo: Bilder av ett samhälle (Work, Live, Life: Images of a Society). https://vartgoteborg.se/jens-s-jensens-fotosamling-till-goteborgs-stadsmuseum, gupea.ub.gu.se.

6. Correspondence with designer Greger Ulf Nilson, email, November 18, 2024.

7. Correspondence with Jakob Schleimann-Jensen and Jesper Schleimann-Jensen, email, September 4, 2023, and January 4, 2025.

8. Quoted in Östlind, *Jens S. Jensen: Collected Works*.

9. David Forgacs, ed., *An Antonio Gramsci Reader, Selected Writings 1916–1935* (New York: Schocken Books, 1988), 59.

The Art of Commoning: Murals

1. William Walker, Eugene Eda, John Weber, and Mark Rogovin, *The Artists' Statement,* quoted in *Toward a People's Art: The Contemporary Mural Movement,* Eva Cockcroft, John Weber, and Jim Cockcroft (New York: E. P. Dutton, 1977), xiv.

2. Mark Rogovin, Marie Burton, and Holly Highfill, *Mural Manual* (Boston: Beacon Press, 1975), vi.

3. Alan W. Barnett, *Community Murals: The People's Art* (Philadelphia: The Art Alliance Press, 1984), 11. See also Kiriakos Iosifidis, *Murals on Huge Public Surfaces Around the World (Frankfurt, Germany:* Publikat, 2009); Lee Bofkin, *Global Street Art* (Buffalo, NY: Firefly Books, 2014); Francis V. O'Connor, *WPA: Art for the Millions* (Greenwich: New York Graphic Society, 1973).

4. *Art and Answerability: Early Philosophical Essays by M. M. Bakhtin,* eds. Michael Holquist and Vadim Liapunov, trans. Vadim Liapunov (Austin: University of Texas Press, 1990): "architectonics can be understood as concerned with questions of building, of the way something is put together." (Or, as Mark Rogovin questioned, "do you include the windows when you are planning to paint a mural on the side of a building?") "Architectonics is like architecture insofar as it is about building wholes through the manipulation of relations between parts. But architecture suggests the creation of static structure. The matter of architectonics is active in the sense that it is always in process. . . ." (xxiii).

5. Excerpt quoted in Barnett, *Community Murals,* 382–383. Born in Chile, professor emeritus of Theater Arts at San Francisco State University, founder of La Pena Cultural Center in Berkeley, Carlos Barón claimed, "A People Without Murals are a De-Muralized People."

Mark Rogovin

1. Raymond Williams, *Marxism and Literature* (New York: Oxford University Press, 1977), 210.

2. Mark Rogovin, Holly Highfill, Marie Burton, *Mural Manual: How to Paint Murals for the Classroom, Community Center, and Street Corner* (Boston: Beacon Press, 1972). See also Mark Rogovin, Rhoda Morrison, and Karen Peugh, *Silhouette Murals* (Illinois: Public Art Workshop, 1976).

3. Joe Powers and Mark Rogovin, *Paul Robeson Rediscovered: An Annotated Listing of His Chicago History from 1921 to 1958* (Chicago: Columbia College Chicago, Paul Robeson 100th Birthday Committee, 2000), and Barbara Armentrout and Sterling Stuckey, *Paul Robeson's Living Legacy* (Chicago: Columbia College Chicago, 1999).

4. Mark Rogovin, ed., *The Day Will Come: Honoring Our Working Class Heroes: Stories of the Haymarket Martyrs* (Chicago: Illinois Labor History Society, 2011). See the online Haymarket Martyrs tour at the Illinois Labor History Society: http://illinoislaborhistory.org/haymarket/haymarket-tour-intro.html.

5. Edited and reprinted with permission from Rebecca Zorach. Published on Facebook, September 15, 2014, based on a series of meetings between Zorach and Mark in 2013 and 2014. See *Never the Same—Archiving, Curating, Documenting, Teaching*, an archival project concerned with politically and socially engaged art in Chicago, organized by Daniel Tucker and Rebecca Zorach. See also Rebecca Zorach, *Art for People's Sake: Artists and Community in Black Chicago, 1965–1975* (Durham: Duke University Press, 2019), and Abdul Alkalimat, Romi Crawford, and Rebecca Zorach, *The Wall of Respect: Public Art and Black Liberation in 1960s Chicago* (Evanston: Northwestern University Press, 2017). See also Nicolas Lampert, *A People's History of the United States: 250 Years of Activist Art and Artists Working in Social Justice Movements* (New York: The New Press, 2013).

6. The *Taller de Gráfica Popular* (Popular Graphic Art Workshop) was a collective of printmakers founded in 1937 by Leopoldo Mendez, Luis Arenal, and Pablo O'Higgins in Mexico City. It became a lodestar for artists who supported labor and social justice through the visual arts, including the sculptor Elizabeth Catlett. See Catlett chapter in this book.

History and Beauty, Crowds and Multitudes

1. This exhibit, with presentations by photographer Earl Dotter, painter Ralph Fasanella, playwright Manny Fried, journalist Paul Cowan, and historian Peter Linebaugh, was held at the Harley School in Rochester, New York. This was a Bread & Roses project, supported with public funding from the New York State Council on the Arts, corporations, labor councils, and union members, January 4–February 19, 1982.

2. It now hangs at AFL-CIO headquarters in Washington, DC. Fasanella painted several iterations of the Lawrence 1912 strike. This Lawrence painting contains newspaper headlines, "Bullet Kills Woman" (Anna LoPizzo, a bystander), and a visual tribute to the Lawrence Public Library.

Ralph Fasanella

1. Fasanella claimed Labor Day as his birthday.

2. Quoted in Patrick Watson, *Fasanella's City: The Paintings of Ralph Fasanella with the Story of his Life and Art* (New York: Ballantine Books, 1974), 51.

3. Fasanella's earliest paintings from the mid 1940s are sparsely populated cityscapes and apartment interiors with a few broad-stroked, static figures. As his skill and confidence developed, so do his people, as individuals and as part of a mass. Quoted in Watson, *Fasanella's City*, 61.

4. Tillie Olsen, *Tell Me a Riddle* (New York: Dell Publishing, 1961), 109, 110.

5. Quoted in Peter Carroll, "Ralph Fasanella Limns the Story of the Workingman," *Smithsonian* 24, no. 5 (August 1993): 58–69, 68.

6. *Ralph Fasanella: Images of Optimism*, with an essay by Leslie Umberger, chronology by Paul S. D'Ambrosio (Portland: Pomegranate, 2017), 119. See my review of this book for the *Journal of Working-Class Studies* 3, no. 1 (2018): 160–62. Fasanella's optimistic energy is also apparent in a young readers' book, *I'm Gonna Paint! Ralph Fasanella, Artist of the People,* Anne Broyles, illustrated by Victoria Tentler-Krylov (New York: Holiday House, 2023).

7. See Paul S. D'Ambrosio's biography based on extensive interviews with the Fasanella family, *Ralph Fasanella's America* (Cooperstown, NY: New York State Historical Association, 2001), and his useful Fasanella chronology in *Images of Optimism*.

8. Pietro di Donato, *Christ in Concrete* (New York: Signet, 1939; rpt. 1993). See "God Job" in Janet Zandy, *Hands: Physical Labor, Class, and Cultural Work* (New Brunswick: Rutgers University Press, 2004), and an earlier version of this essay, "Ralph Fasanella: Epic Painter of the Working Class" in *Hands,* 157–69.

9. James D. Fernández comments on the newsreels of the 1930s, which celebrated innovations in the field of aviation that later gave way to "nightmarish scenes projected in darkened movie houses all over the world; of the bombers of the Condor Legion—the same planes which soon would be flying over London . . . 'watch and listen,' booms the newsreel narrator, as death rains down from the sky on the defenseless civilian populations of Madrid, Barcelona or Guernica," in "When Did World War II Start? And When Will It End? Reflections Inspired by Guernica," *The Volunteer* 40, no. 4 (December 2023): 10–12.

10. See D'Ambrosio, *Ralph Fasanella's America,* for Fasanella's service in the International Brigades, including excerpts from family letters, 32–36. For a comprehensive history, see Giles Tremlett, *The International Brigades: Fascism, Freedom and the Spanish Civil War* (London: Bloomsbury, 2020).

11. Peter N. Carroll, *The Odyssey of the Abraham Lincoln Brigade: Americans in the Spanish Civil War* (Stanford: Stanford University Press, 1994), 341.

12. Walt Whitman, "Democratic Vistas," in *Leaves of Grass and Selected Prose*, ed. John Kouwenhoven (New York: Random House/Modern Library, 1950), 477.

13. Local 65 has/had its own "communities of interest," including a camera club and newspaper, *New Voice*. For commentary on photography and District 65's camera club from the 1940s through the early 1960s, see Janet Zandy, "Seeing Dirt, Seeing Beyond Dirt: Photographs by and about Workers," also referenced in Milton Rogovin chapter.

14. Quoted in Watson, *Fasanella's City*, 88.

15. Barbara Myerhoff, *Number Our Days* (New York: Simon and Schuster, 1978), 31–33.

16. Quoted in Watson, *Fasanella's City*, 18.
17. *TV Guide*, "Baseball: This Year's Winners," April 5–11, 1975.
18. Quoted in Watson, *Fasanella's City*, 44.
19. Quoted in Watson, *Fasanella's City*, 10.
20. Quoted in Watson, *Fasanella's City*, 96.
21. Quoted in Watson, *Fasanella's City*, 104.
22. Quoted in Watson, *Fasanella's City*, 107.
23. Nicholas Pileggi, "Portrait of the Artist as a Garage Attendant in the Bronx," *New York* 5, no. 44 (October 30, 1972): 37.
24. Jay Johnson and William C. Ketchum Jr., *American Folk Art of the Twentieth Century* (New York: Rizzoli International Publications, 1983), 94.
25. See Michael Holquist and Vadim Liapunov, "The Architectonics of Answerability," in their introduction to *Art and Answerability*.
26. I draw this historical labor summary of Lawrence, Massachusetts, from William Cahn, *Lawrence 1912: The Bread and Roses Strike* (New York: The Pilgrim Press, 1954; repr. 1980), 46.
27. D'Ambrosio, *Ralph Fasanella: Images of Optimism*, 121.
28. Richard Wright, *12 Million Black Voices* (New York: Thunder's Mouth Press, 1941; repr. 1988) 26.
29. Ron Carver, "The Public Domain Story," Smithsonian American Art Museum, 2014. http:/American art.si,edu.exhibitions/online/fasanella/Fasanella_Carver.pdf.
30. Stefan Szczelkun, *The Conspiracy of Good Taste* (London: Working Press, 1993), 1.
31. Michael Zweig attempts to untangle and analyze intersecting oppressions in *Class, Race, and Gender: Challenging the Injuries and Divisions of Capitalism* (Oakland: PM Press, 2023).
32. bell hooks, *Art on my Mind: Visual Politics* (New York: The New Press, 1993), 8.
33. John Berger, "Ralph Fasanella and the Experience of the City," in *About Looking* (New York: Pantheon Books, 1980), 96–102.
34. Quoted in Watson, *Fasanella's City*. 147.

Raymond Mason

1. Raymond Mason, "My Early Artistic Life in Birmingham," in *Raymond Mason: Sculptures and Drawings*, eds. Jane Farrington and Evelyn Silber (London: Lund Humphries in association with Birmingham City Museum and Art Gallery, 1989), 11, 12.
2. From Mason's "My Early Artistic Life in Birmingham," reprinted in *At Work in Paris: Raymond Mason on Art and Artists* (London: Thames & Hudson, 2003), originally published in French by Edizioni d'Arte Fratelli Pozzo, 2000. English version translated by Andrew Doughty in collaboration with Raymond Mason. Further quotations from Mason's "My Early Artistic Life" are from the Thames & Hudson version, 10.
3. Mason, "My Early Artistic Life," 9.
4. Mason, "Henry Moore," *At Work in Paris*, 21. The fair-minded Mason elaborates on Moore's struggle to light the coal stove by explaining that Moore was awaiting a call from the maternity hospital about the birth of a long-hoped-for child, a daughter.
5. See David Alan Mellow, "'And Oh! The Stench': Spain, the Blitz, Abjection

and the Shelter Drawings," in *Henry Moore*, ed. Chris Stephens (New York: Skira Rizzoli, 2010), 52–63.

6. Mason, "Henry Moore," *At Work*, 27.

7. Mason, "Henry Moore," *At Work*, 27.

8. Mason saw Giotto as fundamental, "the first great artist of Western art," in "Giotto," *At Work,* 206–7.

9. Mason, *At Work,* 14.

10. Michael Edwards, *Raymond Mason* (London: Thames and Hudson, 1994), 11.

11. Mason, *At Work,* 15.

12. Mason, *At Work*, 15.

13. E. P. Thompson, *The Making of the English Working Class* (New York: Vintage, 1966), 11.

14. Raymond Williams writes, "Structures of Feeling: We are talking about characteristic elements of impulse, restraint, and tone: specifically, affective elements of consciousness and relationships: not feeling against thought, but thought as felt and feeling as thought: practical consciousness of a present kind, in a living and interrelating continuity" (*Marxism and Literature*, 132). See my Käthe Kollwitz chapter, where I consider her work as "structures of feeling" or experience.

15. Jane Farrington, "Raymond Mason and the English Narrative Tradition," in *Raymond Mason: Sculptures and Drawings*, 39–47.

16. See Michael Edwards's beautifully illustrated *Raymond Mason*.

17. Note the exhibit curated by Leo Costello and Sarah Wilson, "To Speak of Everything: The Art of Raymond Mason," New York Studio School (January 10–February 20, 2023), and the Raymond Mason archives and collection of the William Louis-Dreyfus Foundation.

18. See Elaine Velie, "Only 8% of UK Artists Come from Working-Class Background," *Hyperallergic,* December 14, 2022: "Overall, people from the higher middle classes are four times more likely to be in a creative job than people from the working class, and that hasn't changed over 40 years," from Andrew Miles, University of Manchester, lead author of a study published in the *British Sociological Foundation*. This research also shows the intersectionality of class with race and gender.

19. "The Torrent of Life," a conversation between Richard Cork and Raymond Mason, originally produced for BBC Radio 3 by Judith Bumpus and first broadcast in April 1985, quoted in *Raymond Mason: Sculptures and Drawings*, 37.

20. William Louis-Dreyfus, address to the United States Commission on Fine Arts regarding the installation of Mason's *L'Enfant and Washington* at Georgetown Plaza, 1989 (meeting of recently elected President Washington and Pierre Charles L'Enfant). https://wldfoundation.org/about_wld.php.

21. For a theoretical excavation of Mason's work in light of Louis-Dreyfus's recognition of its answerability and Mason's audience, see M. M. Bakhtin, *Art and Answerability*.

22. "The Torrent of Life," 34.

23. James Agee and Walker Evans, *Let Us Now Praise Famous Men*, xvi.

24. Cynthia Nadelman, "Introduction and Interview with Raymond Mason," *Raymond Mason: Painted Sculptures and Bronzes 1952–*1985, March 28–April 30, 1985, Marlborough Gallery catalog. Nadelman's interview with Mason was reprinted soon after Mason's exhibit at the Pompidou, "Entretien avec Ray Mason," in the *Petit Journal, Galeries Contemporaines, Musee national d'art modern, Centre Georges Pompidou,* September–November 1985.

25. See Josef Albers, *Interaction of Color,* 50th Anniversary Edition (rpt., New Haven: Yale University Press, 2013), and his conception of "haptic sensations," 8. See also Ruth Asawa's recollection of Albers's teaching: "One of the problems that he gave in school, was never to see anything in isolation; that you can define space and you can define an object by defining the space around it," in Marilyn Chase, *Everything She Touched: The Life of Ruth Asawa* (San Francisco: Chronicle Books, 2020), 45.

26. For a contemporary example of animated artistry, see Federico Solmi and his use of video game technology in, for example, his satiric *The Good Samaritans.* Solmi *animates*/combines video-game technology, drawings, and paintings with a biting satirical eye. See Renato Miracco and Bianca de la Torre, *Federico Solmi* (New York: Charta Press, 2010).

27. With appreciation to Cynthia Nadelman for permission to quote extensively from her interview with Mason.

28. Mason, "The Departure of Fruit and Vegetables," *At Work,* 123–26. Mason's sculpture can be seen today in the Church of St. Eustache.

29. Mason, *At Work,* 123–26.

30. Mason, *At Work,* 123–26.

31. Mason, *At Work,* 123–26.

32. Sarah Wilson, "Raymond Mason—An Exalting Life," in *Sculptures and Drawings,* 27.

33. Flora Lewis, "French Open Disaster Inquiry as Mine Deaths Spur Outcry," *New York Times,* December 29, 1974.

34. Mason, *Sculptures and Drawings,* catalog notes, 96–101.

35. Mason, "Video Text," *At Work,* 186.

36. Reproduced in Edwards, *Raymond Mason,* 10.

37. Edwards, *Raymond Mason,* 115.

38. Edwards, *Raymond Mason,* 124–27.

39. Edwards, *Raymond Mason,* 130.

40. Mason, "St. Mark's Place," in *At Work,* 135.

41. John Berger, *Art and Revolution: Ernst Neizvestny and the Role of the Artist in the U.S.S.R.* (New York: Pantheon, 1969), 70–71.

42. John Berger, "Pull the Other Leg, It's Got Bells On It," *The Shape of a Pocket* (New York: Vintage, 2003), 147–54.

43. Mason, "My Early Artistic Life," 17.

44. James Hamilton, "Raymond Mason (1922–2010): A Personal Tribute," *Sculpture Journal* 19, no. 2 (December 2010).

45. From a footnote in the original version of "My Early Artistic Life," where Mason comments on ordinary people's responses to representational art and his own nascent work: "This reverence for the artistic gift still exists and it is the major crime of art establishments to disregard, deride, and partially dry up this marvellous source which has flown since the beginning of time. Certainly, encountering this spontaneous esteem from the poor workers of Birmingham of my childhood, made me resolve never to turn my back on the community at large, standing hungry for art and beauty" (*Sculptures and Drawings,* 13).

46. Mason, "My Early Artistic Life," 16.

Conclusion

1. Maya Pontone, *Hyperallergic*, November 26, 2024.

The Garden State

1. Originally published in *Paterson Literary Review* 43 (2015).

Bibliography

Agee, James, and Walker Evans. *Let Us Now Praise Famous Men: Three Tenant Families.* 1941. Reprint, Boston: Houghton Mifflin, 1980.

Albers, Josef. *Interaction of Color.* New Haven: Yale University Press, 1971.

Alkalimat, Abdul, Rebecca Zorach, and Romi Crawford, eds. *The Wall of Respect: Public Art and Black Liberation in 1960s Chicago.* Evanston: Northwestern University Press, 2017.

Anderson, Marilyn, and Jon Garlock. *Granddaughters of Corn: Portraits of Guatemalan Women.* Willimantic, CT: Curbstone Press, 1988.

Anderson, Marilyn. *Guardianes De Las Artes/Guardians of the Arts: Prints of Guatemalan Artists and Artisans.* Guatemala: Ediciones del Pensativo, Coleccion Vesarte, 2016.

Anderson, Marilyn. *Guatemalan Textiles Today.* New York: Watson-Guptill, 1978.

Armentrout, Barbara, and Sterling Stuckey. *Paul Robeson's Living Legacy.* Chicago: Columbia College Chicago and Paul Robeson 100th Birthday Committee, 1999.

Azoulay, Ariella Aïsha. *Potential History: Unlearning Imperialism.* Brooklyn, NY: Verso, 2019.

Baer, Ronni. *Class Distinctions: Dutch Paintings in the Age of Rembrandt and Vermeer.* Boston: MFA Publications, 2015.

Bakhtin, M. M. "Discourse in the Novel," in *The Dialogic Imagination, edited by* Michael Holquist, translated by Caryl Emerson and Michael Holquist. Austin: University of Texas Press, 1981.

Barnett, Alan W. *Community Murals: The People's Art.* Philadelphia: The Art Alliance Press, 1984.

Barry, Lynda. "Interview." *New York Times Magazine*, September 11, 2022, 15–17.

Benjamin, Walter. *Illuminations.* Edited by Hannah Arendt. Translated by Harry Zohn. New York: Schocken Books, 1968.

Benjamin, Walter. "A Short History of Photography." In *Classic Essays in Photography, edited by* Alan Trachtenberg. New Haven: Leete's Island Books, 1980.

Berger, John. *Art and Revolution.* New York: Pantheon, 1969.

Berger, John. *Berger on Drawing*. Edited by Jim Savage. Co. Cork, Ireland: Occasional Press, 2015.

Berger, John. "Pull the Other Leg, It's Got Bells On It." In *The Shape of a Pocket*. New York: Vintage, 2003.

Berger, John. "Ralph Fasanella and the Experience of the City." In *About Looking*. New York: Pantheon, 1980.

Bittner, Herbert. *Käthe Kollwitz: Drawings*. New York: Thomas Yoseloff/Sagamore Press, 1959.

Bories, Estelle. "The Influence of Käthe Kollwitz on Chinese Creation: Between Expressionism and Revolutionary Realism." In *Art Beyond Borders: Artistic Exchange in Communist Europe (1945–1989), edited by* Jérôme Bazin, Pascal Dubourg Glatigny, and Piot Piotrowski. 1955. Reprint, New York and Budapest: CEU Press, 2016.

Bringley, Patrick. *All the Beauty in the World: The Metropolitan Museum of Art and Me*. New York: Simon and Schuster, 2023.

Brutvan, Cheryl A. "Interview with Milton Rogovin." In *Milton Rogovin: The Forgotten Ones*. Seattle: University of Washington Press, 1985.

Cahn, William. *Lawrence 1912: The Bread and Roses Strike*. 1954. Reprint, New York: Pilgrim Press, 1980.

Carroll, N. Peter. *The Odyssey of the Abraham Lincoln Brigade: Americans in the Spanish Civil War*. Redwood City, CA: Stanford University Press, 1994.

Carroll, N. Peter. "Ralph Fasanella Limns the Story of the Workingman," *Smithsonian* 24, no.5 (August 1993): 58–69.

Carvajal, Doreen. "Artistic Insight Comes Through Different Eyes." *New York Times*, March 1, 2020, C3.

Carver, Ron. "The Public Domain Story." Smithsonian Art Museum, 2014.

Chambers, Truman. "How an Art Museum Betrays Its Social Class Bias." *Hyperallergic*, June 15, 2021.

Chase, Marilyn. *Everything She Touched: The Life of Ruth Asawa*. San Francisco: Chronicle Books, 2020.

Coles, Robert, Stephen Jay Gould, Joanne Wypijewski, *Triptychs: Buffalo's Lower West Side Revisited: Photographs by Milton Rogovin*. New York: W. W. Norton, 1994.

Cornell, Daniell, and Timothy Anglin Burgard, *eds. The Sculpture of Ruth Asawa: Contours in the Air. 2nd ed.* San Francisco: Fine Arts Museums of San Francisco in association with University of California Press, 2006.

Costello, Leo, and Sarah Wilson. "To Speak of Everything: The Art of Raymond Mason." New York Studio School, January 10–February 20, 2023.

Cushing, Lincoln, and Timothy W. Drescher. *Agitate! Educate! Organize! American Labor Posters*. Ithaca: ILR Press, 2009.

D'Ambrosio, Paul S. *Ralph Fasanella's America*. Cooperstown, NY: New York State Historical Association, 2001.

da Silva, Jose. *The Art Newspaper*, September 23, 2021.

Dewey, John. *Art as Experience. 1934. Reprint,* New York: Perigee, 2005.

di Donato, Pietro. *Christ in Concrete*. 1939. Reprint, New York: Signet, 1993.

Edwards, Michael. *Raymond Mason*. London: Thames and Hudson, 1994.

Fasanella, Marc. *Ralph Fasanella: Images of Optimism*. Portland, Oregon: Pomegranate, 2017.

Fazio, Michele, Christie Launius, and Time Strangleman, eds. *Routledge International Handbook of Working-Class Studies*. New York: Routledge: 2021.

Fernández, James D. "When Did World War II Start? And When Will It End? Reflections Inspired by Guernica" *The Volunteer 40, no. 4* (December 2023): 10–12.

Findlay, Michael. *Seeing Slowly: Looking at Modern Art.* New York: Prestel, 2017.

Findlay, Michael. *The Value of Art: Money, Power, Beauty.* New York: Prestel, 2012.

Figura, Starr, ed. *Käthe Kollwitz.* New York: The Museum of Modern Art, 2024.

Fisher, Mark. *Capitalist Realism: Is There No Alternative?* Winchester, UK: Zer0 Books, 2008.

Forgacs, David, and Geoffrey Nowell-Smith, eds. *Antonio Gramsci: Selections from Cultural Writings.* Translated by William Boelhower. Cambridge: Harvard University Press, 1985.

Freire, Paulo. *Pedagogy of Hope: Reliving Pedagogy of the Oppressed.* New York: Continuum, 1997.

Gould, Stephen Jay. *Time's Arrow Time's Cycle: Myth and Metaphor in the Discovery of Geological Time.* Cambridge: Harvard University Press, 1987.

Gould, Stephen Jay. "Introduction: Universal Triptychs." In *Triptychs: Buffalo's Lower West Side Revisited: Photographs by Milton Rogovin.* New York: W.W. Norton, 1994.

Grollman, Earl A. *Living with Loss, Healing with Hope.* Boston: Beacon Press, 2000.

Grossinger, Ken. *Art Works: How Organizers and Artists Are Creating a Better World Together.* New York: The New Press, 2023.

Hatfield, Zack. "Tending the Metal Garden." *New York Review of Books,* September, 21, 2017.

Henri, Robert. *The Art Spirit.* New York: Harper & Row, 1923.

Herzog, Melanie Anne. *Elizabeth Catlett: An American Artist in Mexico.* Seattle: University of Washington Press, 2000.

Herzog, Melanie Anne. *Elizabeth Catlett: In the Image of the People.* Chicago: The Art Institute of Chicago, 2005.

Herzog, Melanie Anne. *Milton Rogovin: The Making of a Social Documentary Photographer.* Seattle: University of Washington Press, 2006.

Hitchcock, Peter. *Dialogics of the Oppressed.* Minneapolis: University of Minnesota Press, 1993.

Holquist, Michael, and Vadim Liapunov. "The Architectonics of Answerability." In *Art and Answerability: Early Philosophical Essays by M.M. Bakhtin.* Translated by Vadim Liapunov and Kenneth Brostrom. Austin: University of Texas Press, 1990.

hooks, bell. *Art on My Mind: Visual Politics.* New York: The New Press, 1993.

hooks, bell. *Yearning: Race, Gender, and Cultural Politics.* Boston: South End Press, 1990.

Isay, David, David Miller, and Harvey Wang. *Milton Rogovin: The Forgotten Ones.* New York: The Quantuck Lane Press, 2003.

Ittmann, John, ed. *Mexico and Modern Printmaking: A Revolution in Graphic Arts, 1920–1950.* Philadelphia: Philadelphia Museum of Art, 2006.

Jacobs, Jane. *The Death and Life of Great American Cities.* New York: Random House, 1961; Modern Library, 2011.

Jalon, Allan M. "All Roads Lead Back to Käthe Kollwitz." *Forward,* December 1, 2019.

Jensen, Jens S. *Hammarkullen—40 Years Later.* Hasselblad Center, August 31–October 13, 2013.

Johnson, Jay, and William C. Ketchum. *American Folk Art of the Twentieth Century.* New York: Rizzoli, 1983.

Karlstrom, Paul J., with Mark Johnson. Interview with Ruth Asawa and Albert Lanier. Archives of American Art, Smithsonian Institution, June 21–July 5, 2002.

Kearns, Martha. *Käthe Kollwitz: Woman and Artist.* New York: The Feminist Press, 1976.

Kollwitz, Hans, ed. *The Diary and Letters of Käthe Kollwitz.* Translated by Richard and Clara Winston. Reprint, Evanston: Illinois: Northwestern University Press, 1988.

Koren, Leonard. *Wabi-Sabi for Artists, Designers, Poets & Philosophers.* Point Reyes, CA: California Imperfect Publishing, 2005.

Laib, Jonathan. Foreword to *Ruth Asawa.* New York: David Zwirner Books, 2018.

Lanzillotto, Annie. "Healing through Colors," *Frames of Mind.* Podcast. The Metropolitan Museum of Art, March 2, 2022.

Lewis, Samella S. *The Art of Elizabeth Catlett.* Claremont, CA: Hancraft Studios, 1984.

Lewis, Samella S. *Elizabeth Catlett: Works on Paper, 1944–1992.* Hampton, Virginia: Hampton University Museum, 1993.

Lewis, Samella. "Interview with Samella Lewis on Elizabeth Catlett." Museum of the African Diaspora. November 27, 2018.

Linebaugh, Peter. *The Magna Carta Manifesto: Liberties and Commons for All.* Berkeley: University of California Press, 2008.

Linebaugh, Peter. *Stop Thief! The Commons, Enclosures, and Resistance.* Oakland: PM Press, 2014.

Lippard, Lucy R. *Mixed Blessings: New Art in Multicultural America.* New York: Pantheon, 1990.

Lorde, Audre. *Zami: A New Spelling of My Name.* Trumansburg, NY: The Crossing Press, 1982.

Louis-Dreyfus, William. "Address to the United States Commission on Fine Arts Regarding the Installation of L'Enfant and Washington at Georgetown Plaza," 1989.

Lucie-Smith, Edward, and Celestine Dars. *Work and Struggle: The Painter as Witness.* London: Paddington Press, 1977.

MacKinnon, Janice R., and Stephen R. MacKinnon. *Agnes Smedley: The Life and Times of an American Radical.* Berkeley: University of California Press, 1988.

Mantel, Hilary. *Giving Up the Ghost.* London: Harper Collins, 2003.

Marx, Karl. "Estranged Labour." Economic and Philosophical Manuscripts of 1844. https://www.marxists.org/archive/marx/works/1844/manuscripts/labour.htm.

Marx, Leo. "Does Improved Technology Mean Progress?" *Technology Review* (January 1987): 33–41.

Mason, Raymond. *At Work in Paris.* London: Thames & Hudson, 2003.

Mason, Raymond. "My Early Artistic Life in Birmingham." In *Raymond Mason: Sculptures and Drawings*, edited by Jane Farrington and Evelyn Silber. London: Lund Humphries in association with Birmingham City Museum and Art Gallery, 1989.

Mellow, David Allen. "'And Oh! The Stench': Spain, the Blitz, Abjection and the Shelter Drawings." In *Henry Moore,* edited by Chris Stephens, 52–63. New York: Skira Rizzoli, 2010.

Miracco, Renato, and Bianca de la Torre. *Federico Solmi.* New York: Charta Press, 2010.

Moleworth, Helen. *Leap Before You Look: Black Mountain College 1933–1957.* With Ruth Erickson. New Haven: Institute of Contemporary Art/Boston and Yale University Press, 2015.

Moss, Adam. *The Work of Art: How Something Comes from Nothing.* New York: Penguin, 2024.

Moss, Dorothy. *The Sweat of Their Face: Portraying American Workers.* Washington, DC: Smithsonian Institution, 2017.

Myerhoff, Barbara. *Number Our Days.* New York: Simon and Schuster, 1978.

Nadelman, Cynthia. "Introduction and Interview with Raymond Mason." In *Raymond Mason: Painted Sculptures and Bronzes 1952–1985.* Marlborough Gallery.

Neiman, Susan. *Left is Not Woke.* Hoboken, NJ: Polity, 2023.

Nickels, Heather. *Persevere and Resist: The Strong Black Women of Elizabeth Catlett.* Memphis: Memphis Brooks Museum of Art in association with Paul Holberton Publishing, 2021.
O'Connor, Aidan, and Juliet Kinchin. "Boy Meets Wall: Hanging Out with Jens S. Jensen." *Inside/Out,* July 11, 2012.
Olsen, Tillie. *Silences.* New York: Dell, 1978.
Olsen, Tillie. *Tell Me a Riddle.* New York: Dell, 1961.
Östlind, Niclas. *Jens S. Jensen: Samlat verk.* Bokförlaget Arena: Göteborgs Stadsmuseum, 2022.
Pileggi, Nicholas. "Portrait of the Artist as a Garage Attendant in the Bronx. *New York* 5, no. 44 (October 30, 1972), 37–45.
Powers, Joe, and Mark Rogovin. *Paul Robeson Rediscovered: An Annotated Listing of His Chicago History from 1921 to 1958.* Chicago: Columbia College Chicago, Paul Robeson 100th Birthday Committee, 2000.
Rey, Robert. *Honoré Daumier.* New York: Abrams, n.d.
"The Ritual of Elizabeth Catlett: A Conversation Celebrating the CMA Opening of *The Art of Elizabeth Catlett.*" From the collection of Samella Lewis. October 14, 2022.
Rogovin, Mark. *The Day Will Come: Honoring Our Working-Class Heroes: Stories of the Haymarket Martyrs.* Chicago: Illinois Labor History Society, 2011.
Rogovin, Mark, Holly Highfill, and Marie Burton. *Mural Manual: How to Paint Murals for the Classroom, Community Center, and Street Corner.* Boston: Beacon Press, 1972.
Rogovin, Mark, Rhoda Morrison, and Karen Peugh. *Silhouette Murals.* Illinois: Public Art Workshop, 1976.
Rogovin, Milton. *The Forgotten Ones.* Seattle: University of Washington Press, 1985.
Rogovin, Milton. *The Mining Photographs.* Los Angeles: Getty Publications, 2005.
Rogovin, Milton, and Michael Frisch. *Portraits in Steel.* Ithaca: Cornell University Press, 1993.
Rogovin, Milton, and W. E. B. Du Bois. "Storefront Churches: Photographs." *Aperture* 10, no.2 [38] (1962): 62–78.
Rogovin, Milton. *Triptychs.* New York: W. W. Norton, 1994.
Rukeyser, Muriel. "*Käthe Kollwitz.*" In Martha Kearns, *Käthe Kollwitz: Woman and Artist.* New York: The Feminist Press, 1976.
Said, Edward W. *The World, the Text, and the Critic.* Cambridge: Harvard University Press, 1983.
Scruggs, Dalila. "To that Degree and More." In *Elizabeth Catlett: A Black Revolutionary Artist and All that Implies*, edited by Dalila Scruggs. Chicago: University of Chicago Press, 2024.
Simon, Jean-Marie. *Guatemala: Eternal Spring, Eternal Tyranny.* New York: Norton, 1987.
Sims, Lowery Stokes. "Elizabeth Catlett: A Life in Art and Politics." In *Elizabeth Catlett Sculpture: A Fifty-Year Retrospective.* Purchase, State University of New York: Neuberger Museum of Art, 1998.
Small, Zachary. "Therapeutic Creative Expression." *New York Times,* June 16, 2020: C1, C5.
Smedley, Agnes. *Daughter of Earth,* 1929. Reprint, New York: The Feminist Press, 1975.
Smith, Ali. *Public Library and Other Stories.* UK: Hamish Hamilton, Penguin Random House, 2015.
Soelle, Dorothee. *To Work and To Love: A Theology of Creation.* With Shirley A. Cloyes. Philadelphia: Fortress Press, 1988.

Solnit, Rebecca. *A Paradise Built in Hell: The Extraordinary Communities That Arise in Disaster.* New York: Viking, 2009.
Szczelkun, Stefan. *The Conspiracy of Good Taste*. London: Working Press, 1993.
Terkel, Studs. *Working*. New York: Pantheon, 1972, 1974.
Thompson, E. P. *The Making of the English Working Class*. New York: Vintage, 1966.
Trachtenberg, Alan, Walter Rosenblum, Naomi Rosenblum, and Lewis Wickes Hine. America and Lewis Hine: Photographs 1904–1940. New York: Aperture, 1977.
Tremlett, Giles. *The International Brigades: Fascism, Freedom and the Spanish Civil War.* London: Bloomsbury, 2020.
Velie, Elaine. "Only 8% of UK Artists Come from Working-Class Background." *Hyperallergic*, December 14, 2022.
Von Blum, Paul. *The Art of Social Conscience*. New York: Universe Books, 1976.
Walljasper, Jay. *All That We Share: A Field Guide to the Commons*. New York: The New Press, 2010.
Watson, Mike. "Let's Talk about Class and Art." *ArtLeaks Gazette*, September 2017.
Watson, Patrick. *Fasanella's City*. New York: Ballantine Books, 1974.
Whitman, Walt. *Leaves of Grass and Selected Prose*. New York: The Modern Library, 1950.
Williams, Raymond. *Keywords: A Vocabulary of Culture and Society*. New York: Oxford University Press, 1983.
Williams, Raymond. *Marxism and Literature*. New York: Oxford University Press, 1977.
Williams, Raymond. *Resources of Hope*. New York: Verso, 1989.
Wilson, Sarah. "Raymond Mason—An Exalted Life." In *Raymond Mason: Sculptures and Drawings*, edited by Jane Farrington and Evelyn Silber. *London: Lund-Humphries, 1989,* 16–32.
Wright, Richard. *12 Million Black Voices*. 1941. Reprint, New York: Thunder's Mouth Press, 1988.
Yates, Pamela, and Newton Thomas Sigel, dirs. *When the Mountains Tremble. Brooklyn:* Skylight Pictures, 1983.
Yau, John. *Please Wait by the Coatroom: Reconsidering Race and Identity in American Art.* Boston: Black Sparrow Press, 2023.
Yoshino, Genzaburo. *How Do You Live?* 1937, 1982. Translated by Bruno Navasky. New York: Algonquin Young Readers, 2018.
Zandy, Janet. "Seeing Dirt, Seeing Beyond Dirt: Photographs by and about Workers." *exposure* 43, no. 2 (Fall 2010): 33–40.
Zandy, Janet. *Unfinished Stories: The Narrative Photography of Hansel Mieth and Marion Palfi*. Rochester, NY: RIT Press, 2013.
Zandy, Janet. "Mapping Working-Class Art." In *Routledge International Handbook of Working-Class Studies*, edited by Michele Fazio, Christie Launius, and Tim Strangleman. New York: Routledge: 2021, 343–58.
Zigrosser, Carl. *Prints and Drawings of Käthe Kollwitz*. New York: Dover, 1969.
Zorach, Rebecca. *Art for People's Sake: Artists and Community in Black Chicago, 1965–1975*. Durham: Duke University Press, 2019.
Zorach, Rebecca, and Daniel Tucker. *Never the Same—Archiving, Curating, Documenting, Teaching*. With Mark Rogovin. September 15, 2014. https://never-the-same.org.
Zweig, Michael. *Class, Race, and Gender: Challenging the Injuries and Divisions of Capitalism*. Oakland: PM Press, 2023.

Index

Page numbers in *italics* refer to illustrations.

JANET ZANDY is a visual artist and professor emerita of English at the Rochester Institute of Technology. Her books include *Unfinished Stories: The Narrative Photography of Hansel Mieth and Marion Palfi* and *Hands: Physical Labor, Class, and Cultural Work*.

The University of Illinois Press
is a founding member of the
Association of University Presses.

Designed by Jim Proefrock
Composed in 11.25/14 Gill Sans
with Gills Sans display
at the University of Illinois Press

University of Illinois Press
1325 South Oak Street
Champaign, IL 61820-6903
www.press.uillinois.edu